Issues in Germanic Syntax

Edited by

Werner Abraham
Wim Kosmeijer
Eric Reuland

Mouton de Gruyter
Berlin · New York 1991

Mouton de Gruyter (formerly Mouton, The Hague)
is a Division of Walter de Gruyter & Co., Berlin.

♾ Printed on acid-free paper which falls within the guidelines of the ANSI
to ensure permanence and durability.

Library of Congress Cataloging in Publication Data

Issues in Germanic syntax / edited by Werner Abraham, Wim
Kosmeijer, Eric Reuland.

      p.   cm. — (Trends in linguistics. Studies and mono-
graphs : 44)
Papers read at the Fifth Workshop on Comparative Germanic Syntax, held at Groningen, May 23 – 24, 1988.
   Includes bibliographical references
   ISBN 0-89925-611-2
   1. Germanic languages — Syntax — Congresses. I. Abraham, Werner. II. Reuland, Eric J. III. Workshop on Comparative Germanic Syntax (5th : 1988 : Groningen. Netherlands)
IV. Series.
PD361.I87   1990
430 – dc20
                                     89-28236
                                         CIP

Deutsche Bibliothek Cataloging in Publication Data

Issues in Germanic syntax / ed. by Werner Abraham. —
Berlin ; New York : Mouton de Gruyter, 1990
   (Trends in linguistics : Studies and monographs ; 44)
   ISBN 3-11-012205-7
NE: Abraham, Werner; Trends in linguistics / Studies and
· monographs

Printing: Gerike GmbH, Berlin. — Binding: Lüderitz & Bauer, Berlin.
Printed in Germany

Preface

The articles included in this volume originated as contributions to the Fifth Workshop on Comparative Germanic Syntax, which was held at Groningen University on May 23-24, 1988, and organized by the Department of Linguistics and the Department of German Language and Literature. At the conference it became clear that the issues discussed in the various contributions constituted a remarkably coherent set; virtually all of the contributions address core problems concerning the structure of Germanic, often on the basis of related data. Although particular solutions may differ, the various proposals have a high degree of mutual relevance due to the coherence in subject matter, and for most of the contributions, also in theoretical approach. A couple of rather unorthodox contributions may help one look afresh at seemingly well-established view-points. Because of this, the collection as a whole is more than just the sum of the individual contributions. Therefore, we felt that it was important to make the contributions to this meeting available as a book. We are very pleased that Mouton de Gruyter made it possible for these proceedings to be published.

As editors we are very much indebted to our fellow organizer, Jan Koster, who took the initiative to host this workshop in Groningen. We would also like to thank Hennie Zondervan en Liesbeth van der Velden for their invaluable help. The workshop, and therefore this book, would not have been possible without the financial support of the Faculty of Letters and the Executive Board of Groningen University. This support is hereby gratefully acknowledged.

Finally, we would like to express our gratitude to Ruurd van der Weij, who did the electronic typesetting of this manuscript; a time-consuming job which he carried out cheerfully, despite the fact that it turned out to be much more complicated than either he or we had anticipated.

Groningen, October 1990

Werner Abraham
Wim Kosmeijer
Eric Reuland

Contents

Part 3 Binding

Contributors

Werner Abraham, Department of German
University of Groningen

Johan van der Auwera, Department of Germanic Languages
University of Antwerp at Wilrijk

Hartmut Czepluch, Department of English
University of Hannover

Martin Everaert, Research Institute for Language and Speech
University of Utrecht

Gisbert Fanselow, Department of Linguistics
University of Passau

Elly van Gelderen, Department of English
University of Groningen

Giuliana Giusti, Department of Linguistics
University of Venice

Hubert Haider, Department of Linguistics
University of Stuttgart

Lars Hellan, Department of Linguistics
University of Trondheim

Eric Hoekstra, Department of Linguistics
University of Groningen

Anders Holmberg, Department of Linguistics
University of Uppsala

Wim Kosmeijer, Department of Linguistics
University of Groningen

Christer Platzack, Department of Scandinavian Languages
University of Lund

Eric Reuland, Department of Linguistics
University of Groningen

Ineke Schuurman, Eurotra
Catholic University of Leuven

Bonnie Schwartz, Department of Linguistics
University of Geneva

Rik Smits, Department of Linguistics
University of Leyden

Alessandra Tomaselli, Department of Germanic Languages
University of Pavia

Sten Vikner, Department of Linguistics
University of Stuttgart

Ron van Zonneveld, Department of Dutch
University of Groningen

Introduction

Werner Abraham and Eric Reuland

The articles in this volume reflect an interest in determining the nature of universal principles underlying natural language. The brief history of this kind of typological research in the Germanic languages shows traces of an emancipatory process. Initially, insights obtained from the study of English played a predominant role, molding, as it were, the analysis of the other languages as well.

Real progress could not be made until substantive theories of the major components of grammatical structure, such as phrase structure and transformational relations, were developed. The transition from a theory of transformations allowing detailed and language-specific structural descriptions to a theory allowing only general conditions on movement (Chomsky 1973; 1977) was crucial in this development (see Heny 1981 for an illuminating discussion). Equally important was the development of X'-theory expressing general constraints on phrase structure representations (Jackendoff 1977).

From 1974 on, a growing body of literature attempted to gain insight into the structure of continental Germanic languages on the basis of these new theoretical insights. For instance, Van Riemsdijk - Zwarts (1974) proposed an analysis of left-dislocation, Koster (1975) provided a detailed argument for the underlying SOV character of Dutch, which immediately carries over to German (Koster providing arguments which had not been used by Bierwisch (1963) and Bach (1962), who had also claimed underlying SOV for German), Evers (1975) presented his classical study of verb raising in Dutch and German, Den Besten (1977/1983) provided an analysis of so-called "verb second phenomena", which is still at the basis of all recent discussion of this issue, etc..

The emerging theories were strong enough to allow the detailed comparison of closely related languages such as Norwegian, Danish, Swedish and

Icelandic initiated by authors such as Maling, Taraldsen, Thráinsson, and others. Around the same time authors like for example Cinque, Kayne and Rizzi, started their work on the nature of the variation within the group of Romance languages. These investigations resulted in the insight that general principles of grammar determine the bounds within which variation takes place. Variation is possible where universal grammar contains an option, that is, an open parameter. Specific languages may differ in the values assigned to such parameters. Since grammatical principles interact in intricate ways, a difference in one parameter setting may have far-reaching consequences elsewhere in the grammar. A well-known example is the connection in Italian between its character as a null-subject language, and the fact that it does not obey an otherwise general restriction on subject extraction, a connection which was first noted by Perlmutter (1971) and eventually explained by Rizzi (1982).

Much of the recent discussion of Germanic languages focusses on a limited number of issues. For instance, the nature of the movement of the verb in verb-second sentences and its relation to the question of where Tense is realized (on Infl or on Comp) and matters of Case assignment have been studied by Den Besten (1977, 1981, 1985), Koopman (1984), Platzack (1983), and many others. Furthermore, matters involving the structure of the VP, including principles of Case assignment, free word order, verbal clusters, preposition stranding and extraposition in German, Dutch, and West-Frisian have been investigated by De Haan, Haider, Huybregts, Reuland, Van Riemsdijk, and others; witness the contributions in Abraham (1983, 1985), Toman (1985) and Haider - Prinzhorn (1986).

It is only quite recently that a point in the development of modern syntactic theory has been reached which allows one to properly evaluate grammatical analyses of traditional standing. It has become increasingly clear that those analyses often represent insights that are still relevant for our present concerns. This can be illustrated by the early analyses of the systematic changes in word order between root sentences and dependent clauses in the Scandinavian languages by Diderichsen (1946) and their re-evaluation in Platzack (1986), and by the reinterpretation in the generative framework in Scherpenisse (1986) of the German sentence typology developed by Drach (1937) and Boost (1955). Another traditional highlight reassessed at its full value not long ago is the work by the Danish linguist

Gunnar Bech (1955), who described types of infinitival and participial (supinal) constructions in German and their word order and government characteristics, anticipating movement and trace theory (see Von Stechow 1987; Grewendorf 1988; see also the earlier discussion in Evers 1975).

The parametric approach to comparative syntax represented by the work in this volume builds on the results of other typological investigations. There are differences in tradition, though, and hence in focus, of research and modes of explanation.

In nineteenth century historical grammar, variation between languages and their sharing of properties were primarily viewed in the light of issues concerning their ancestry; the mode of explanation was mostly evolutionary. In the European functionalist tradition, language is primarily viewed as a social product; an emphasis ensued on the study of language areas where the sharing of various grammatical charactistics was amenable to an explanation in terms of acculturation and interference between linguistic systems.

In the more recent Greenbergian tradition, (see Greenberg 1963, 1966, 1974), typological research strikes out on as wide a range of languages as possible, aiming at establishing an inventory of the existing diversities and patterns of variation in the various languages of the world. In certain respects this work seems most commensurable with the generative work on comparative grammar, though in a number of other respects it is not. It has seldom concentrated on groups of closely related languages such as just the Germanic, or just the Romance ones. Illustrative of this limitation is the recent survey on tense-aspect-word marking categories across the languages of the world in Bybee - Pagliuca - Perkins (in press), in which Danish is selected as the representative of the whole Germanic group. But, most importantly, this tradition is not easily characterized in terms of a commonly accepted mode of explanation. Therefore, it creates the superficial impression of primarily focussing on the most easily accessible linguistic facts, although such a characterization may not do justice to many individual authors.

Even so, this would not imply that its results can be ignored. Facts, patterns and correlations, however obtained, in principle have a theory-independent status. If valid, they must be accounted for by any theory, even if their significance is sometimes only indirect.

The results of the research in this tradition have been subject to extensive criticism. It has been argued that most of the universals claimed by Greenberg (1966), Hawkins (1983), Keenan (1978), Vennemann (1976, 1981) appear to possess just statistical value (see Hawkins [1983:40] on Greenberg, and also Abraham - Scherpenisse [1984], Fanselow [1987], Abraham [1989] and Haider [1988] for more discussion). Often the orders are defined on structures that are by no means sophisticated enough by present standards. Also, no clue is provided as to what to do with the phenomena unaccounted for (up to 30% of what should be covered by some of Greenberg's or Hawkins' universals). Yet, so far one cannot maintain that there is no factual basis in the generalizations made. Therefore, an explanation for both the standard and the deviations is still in order.

One attempt to account for such deviations is that of Vennemann (1981), who claimed that language change may lead to deviance from the norm expressed by the universal. However, such a course seems to beg the question, as it leaves open what principle would allow and cause a process of change to go against some universal. Rather, an answer requires a theory which not only represents the facts in terms of paradigmatic frequency, but also explains them on the basis of a notion of markedness against the background of a formal theory of grammar. Such issues are discussed by Hawkins (1983, 1990), who also develops a substantive proposal in this direction.

In the generative tradition the proper object of linguistics is considered to be the human language capacity; both the common and the distinguishing characteristics of specific languages are studied as shedding light on universal grammar. Universal grammar represents the cognitive structure underlying language as such and determines the format of individual grammars, providing the basis for language acquisition. Where universal grammar contains an option, variation between languages obtains. Some of these parameters may involve rather general properties, others may be quite specific. The set of possible grammars may be represented in a way that is somewhat reminiscent of the family tree marking the derivation of younger languages from ancestral ones in the spirit of the Neogrammarians. Closely related languages will differ in options that are far down in the hierarchy determined by the descriptive format, whereas language groups will branch off high up. However, as universal grammar constitutes a mosaic of independent modules, the result is not a univocal hierarchy among languages. Rather, languages may be close with respect to one module, and far apart with respect to another.

This concept of the structure of language is immediately linked to the distinction between marked and unmarked properties and that between core and periphery.

The former contrast is reflected in the theory of language acquisition. The fact that the child succeeds in constructing a correct grammar in the absence of negative evidence can only be explained if it starts out with a hypothesis space that is highly constrained. One may view this as a version of universal grammar in which the values of all parameters are preset. In the absence of evidence bearing on its setting, a parameter retains this unmarked value. Only specific evidence requiring a change may result in a different setting of some parameter, which will then represent a marked value.

The contrast between core and periphery can be (and has been) understood in two different ways. A phenomenon can be said to be peripheral, if it is peripheral to the linguistic system, or refers to extragrammatical principles, such as the "grammar" of newspaper headings, or the rules for proper address in English (but not in Japanese), etc. In much grammatical work, however, a phenomenon is called peripheral if it could have been different without notable consequences in other areas of the grammar. For instance, one might say that morphological Case is a peripheral phenomenon in English, but not in German. The possibility of null subjects is a central phenomenon in Italian, but much less so in Dutch. Both examples involve the setting of central parameters of the grammatical system. It is illustrative to add examples of verbs violating a general principle concerning the use of accusative Case (known as "Burzio's generalization"), such as subject-less verbs governing the accusative, non-agentive verbs with personal accusative objects ("psych-verbs"), or transitive three-place verbs governing two accusative objects (see Haider 1988).

Classifying a phenomenon as peripheral embodies an empirical claim, and should be supported by other facts of the language. In the cases cited there is such support. Verbs of the types mentioned are late in primary language acquisition, and early candidates for loss under traumatic impairment of the language faculty. The constructions they involve represent restricted paradigms and are unstable: there are no double accusatives in non-standard vernaculars in German, as little as there are "psych-verbs" governing the accusative; they appear to be first candidates for loss under diachronic change, or for literary obsoleteness. This suggests that deviations from the standard options have to be learned with extra effort and/or by appealing to non-linguistic cognitive mechanisms.

The effects of the theory that language learning involves the setting of parameters in a general grammar schema can also be observed in the creolization process of pidgin languagues. Bickerton (1981) observed that all creoles share a great number of grammatical properties many of which cannot be traced back to properties of the original pidgins since they were missing there in the first place. This fact can be most readily explained if these observed properties represent standard values of parameters in the underlying universal grammar, which are realized in the absence of data triggering a marked option.

We thus appear to be faced with the following goals for a typology of language (modelled on the criteria in Chomsky 1965):

a quantitative goal — a typology should cover as wide a range of languages as possible, and capture the existing diversities and patterns of variation in the various languages of the world

a qualitative goal — a typology should be based on detailed analyses of the languages involved, enabling one to go beyond mere statistical correlations, resulting in a precise theory of core and periphery

an explanatory goal — the results of typological study will find their justification by giving insight into processes of language acquisition and language change

The contributions in this volume are all, in a broad sense, representative of this approach. The volume contains important results based on the search for cross-linguistic evidence for the structure of universal grammar. Other contributions seek to understand newly discovered patterns of variations in the light of given assumption about the structure of universal grammar. One contribution shows how an appeal to the results of psycholinguistic research can help to decide between grammatical solutions that in other respects appear to be on a par with respect to descriptive and explanatory adequacy.

Together they present an excellent picture of the intriguing developments taking place in present day linguistics and of the fertility of detailed investigation of closely related languages.

References

Abraham, Werner (ed.)
1983   *On the formal syntax of the Westgermania* (Amsterdam: John Benjamins).
1985   *Erklärende Syntax des Deutschen* (Studien zur deutschen Grammatik 25) (Tübingen: Gunter Narr).
1989   "Language universals: The Chomskyan approach vs. Greenberg's typological approach", *Belgium Journal of Linguistics* 4: 9-25

Abraham, Werner - Wim Scherpenisse
1984   "Zur Brauchbarkeit von Wortstellungstypologien mit Universalanspruch", *Sprachwissenschaft* 8.3: 291-356

Bach, Emmon
1962   "The order of elements in a transformational grammar of German", *Language* 38:263-269

Bech, Gunnar
1955   *Studien über das deutsche Verbum finitum* 1 (Copenhagen: Det kongelige Danske Widenskabernes Selskab, Historisk-Filologiske Meddelelser; 2nd unaltered edition 1983, Tübingen: Niemeyer).

Bickerton, Dereck
1981   *Roots of Language* (Ann Arbor: Karoma Publishers).

Bierwisch, Manfred
1963   *Grammatik des Deutschen Verbs* (Berlin: Akademie Verlag 1966)

Boost, Karl
1955   Neue Untersuchungen zum Wesen und zur Struktur des deutschen Satzes (Berlin: Deutsche Akademie der Wissenschaften).

Bybee, John L. - William Pagliuca - Revere D. Perkins
in press "Back to the future", *Approaches to grammaticalization* vol. 1, edited by Elizabeth Traugott - B. Heine (Amsterdam: Benjamins).

Chomsky, Noam
1965   *Aspects of the theory of syntax* (Cambridge, Mass.: MIT Press).
1973   "Conditions on transformations", *A Festschrift for Morris Halle*, edited by Stephen R. Anderson - Paul Kiparsky (New York: Holt, Rinehart, Winston).

1977   "On Wh-movement", *Formal syntax*, edited by Peter Culicover - Tom Wasow
        - Adrian Akmajian (New York: Academic Press).
1980   " On cognitive structures and their development: A reply to Piaget", *Language
        and learning*, edited by Massimo Piatelli-Palmarini (London: Routledge &
        Kegan Paul).
1986   *Knowledge of language: Its nature, origin and use* (New York: Praeger).

Den Besten, Hans
1977   "On the interaction of root transformations and lexical deletive rules", published
        1983, *On the formal syntax of the Westgermania*, (Linguistik Aktuell 3.), edited
        by Werner Abraham (Amsterdam: Benjamins).
1981   "A case filter for passives", *Theory of markedness in generative grammar*,
        (Proceedings of the 1979 GLOW Conference), edited by Adriana Belletti -
        Luciani Brandi - Luigi Rizzi (Pisa: Scuola Normale Superiore di Pisa).
1985   "Some remarks on the ergative hypothesis", *Erklärende Syntax des Deutschen*
        (Studien zur deutschen Grammatik 25) (Tübingen: Gunter Narr).

Diderichsen, Paul
1946   *Elementær Dansk Grammatik* (Copenhagen: Gyldendal).

Drach, Erich
1937   *Grundgedanken der deutschen Satzlehre* (Darmstadt: Wissenschaftliche Buch-
        gesellschaft).

Evers, Arnold
1975   *The transformational cycle in Dutch and German*, doctoral dissertation (Ut-
        recht: University of Utrecht, distributed by the Indiana Linguistics Club).

Fanselow, Gisbert
1987   "Über Wortstellungstypologie anläßlich eines Buches von John Hawkins",
        Zeitschrift für Sprachwissenschaft 6.1: 114-133

Greenberg, Joseph H.
1963   "Some universals of grammar with particular reference to the order of meaning-
        ful elements.", *Universals of language* (Report of a conference held at Dobbs
        Ferry, New York, April 13-15, 1961, edited by Joseph H. Greenberg (Cam-
        bridge, Mass.: MIT Press).
1966   *Language universals* (Berlin: Mouton de Gruyter).
1974   *Language typology. A historical and analytic overview* (Berlin: Mouton de
        Gruyter).

Grewendorf, Günther
1988   *Aspekte der deutschen Syntax. Eine Rektions-Bindungsanalyse* (Studien zur
        deutschen Grammatik 33) (Tübingen: Gunter Narr).

Haider, Hubert
1983   "The case of German", *Groninger Arbeiten zur germanistischen Linguistik* 22:
        47-100

1986   *Deutsche Syntax generativ - Parameter der deutschen Syntax*, Habilitations-schrift (Vienna: University of Vienna).

1988   "'Markiertheit' in der generativen Grammatik" (Vienna/Stuttgart: unpublished manuscript universities of Vienna and Stuttgart).

Haider, Hubert - Martin Prinzhorn (eds.)
1986   *Verb second phenomena in Germanic languages* (Dordrecht: Foris).

Hawkins, John
1983   *Word order universals* (New York/London: Academic Press).
1990   "A parsing theory of word order universals", *Linguistic Inquiry* 21.2: 223-262

Heny, Frank
1981   "Introduction", *Binding and filtering*, edited by Frank Heny (London: Croom Helm).

Jackendoff, Ray
1977   *X'-syntax. A study of phrase structure* (Cambridge, Mass.: MIT Press).

Kayne, Richard
1975   *French syntax* (Cambridge, Mass.: MIT Press).

Keenan, Edward
1978   "Language variation and the logical structure of universal grammar.", *Language universals*. (Papers from the conference held at Gummersbach/Cologne, Germany, Oct. 3-8, 1976), edited by Hans Jakob Seiler (Tübingen: Gunter Narr).

Koopman, Hilda
1984   *Syntax of verbs* (Dordrecht: Foris).

Koster, Jan
1975   "Dutch as an SOV language", *Linguistic Analysis* 1: 111-136

Maling, Joan
1982   "Non-clause-bounded reflexives in Icelandic", *Papers from the Sixth Scandinavian Conference on Linguistics*, edited by Thorstein Fretheim - Lars Hellan (Trondheim: Tapir).

Perlmutter, David
1971   *Deep Structure and surface structure constraints in syntax* (New York: Holt, Rinehart, Winston).
1978   "Impersonal passives and the unaccusative hypothesis", *Proceedings of the Fourth Annual Meeting of the Berkeley Linguistic Society* (Berkeley, California: University of California).

Platzack, Christer
1983   "Germanic word order and the COMP/INFL-parameter", *Working Papers in Scandinavian Syntax* 2 (Trondheim: University of Trondheim).
1986   "Diderichsens positionsschema och generativ transformationsgrammatik", *Nydanske studier & almen kommunikationsteori* 17.17: 161-170

Rizzi, Luigi
1982   *Issues in Italian syntax* (Dordrecht: Foris).

Scherpenisse, Wim
1986   *The connection between base structure and linearization restrictions in German and Dutch* (Frankfurt/M.: Lang).

Taraldsen, Tarald
1981   "The theoretical interpretation of a class of marked extractions", *Theory of markedness in generative grammar*, (Proceedings of the 1979 GLOW Conference at Pisa, April 20-22 1979), edited by Adriana Belletti - Luciana Brandi - Luigi Rizzi (Pisa: Scuola Normale Superiore di Pisa).
1982   "The head of S in Romance and Germanic", *Papers from the Sixth Scandinavian Conference on Linguistics*, edited by Thorstein Fretheim - Lars Hellan (Trondheim: Tapir).

Thráinsson, Höskuldur
1979   *On complementation in Icelandic* (New York: Garland).

Toman, Jindřich (ed.)
1985   *Studies in German grammar* (Dordrecht: Foris).

Van Riemsdijk, Henk - Frans Zwarts
1974   "Left dislocation in Dutch" (Cambridge, Mass.: unpublished manuscript, MIT).

Vennemann, Theo
1976   "Categorial grammar and the order of meaningful elements", *Linguistic Studies offered to Joseph Greenberg on the occasion of his sixtieth birthday*, edited by Alphonse Juilland (Saratoga, California: Anma Libri).
1981   "Typology, universals, and change of language", *Historical syntax*, edited by Jacek Fisiak (Berlin: De Gruyter).

Von Stechow, Arnim
1984   "Gunnar Bech's government and binding theory", *Linguistics* 22: 225-241

Wexler, Ken - Peter Culicover (eds.)
1980   *Formal principles of language acquisition*, (Cambridge, Mass.: MIT Press).

Part 1
Phrase Structure

The position of Dutch complementizers[1]

Johan van der Auwera

1. Introduction

This paper focuses on the position of Dutch subordinating conjunctions or complementizers ("Comp").[2] The essential question is whether they take up the same structural position as subordinating wh-elements (pronouns and adverbs), which is a clause initial position. I will argue that Dutch Comps are in front of the "clause proper", that they thus precede subordinating wh-elements and do not share their structural position. Though the focus is on Dutch and on functional grammar (in the sense of Dik 1978), I hope that the hypothesis has both cross-linguistic and cross-theoretical relevance.

2. Functional Grammar and word order

Functional grammar allows five types of units in its syntax:

1) phrase or constituent structure categories, such as "Noun" and "Noun Phrase";
2) word order slots or structural positions, such as "P2" and "P1";
3) "semantic functions" such as "agent" and "source";
4) "subject" and "object"; these are called "syntactic functions";
5) "pragmatic functions" such as "topic", "focus" and "theme".

In the so-called "predication formation" component an underlying representation is built, which is a complete categorial and functional description of the sentence – "categorial" referring to phrase structure categories and "functional" to semantic, syntactic, and pragmatic functions (see [1], [3], [4], and [5] above). The underlying representation does not, however, describe phonology, morphology or word order. This is done in the second major component of the functional grammar model, the "expression component", in which expression rules relate the underlying representation to the actual surface form and word order.

What interests us here is only word order, and then again, only the word order of the clausal left periphery. The word order component in functional grammar operates on the as yet unordered constituents of the underlying predication and assigns them a position.[3] This assignment happens in accordance with a variety of factors, two of which are important for the problems addressed in this paper, viz. word order templates or "patterns" and "P-rules".

Word order patterns vary between languages both in detail and in number (a language may have more than one pattern). Typically, they specify linear order in terms of three kinds of entities: 1) structural positions, 2) categories, especially verb, and 3) functions–in the typical case, syntactic functions (i.e., subject and object). Thus Dik (1978:178,185; 1980:154-155) claims that Dutch has two word order patterns, viz. the verb-late pattern in (1) for embedded clauses (ECs), and the verb-second pattern in (2) for main clauses (MCs).

(1) P2 P1 Subj Obj V ...   [EC]
(2) P2 P1 Vf Subj Obj Vi ...   [MC]

[P stands for "Position", V for "Verb, finite and/or non-finite",
Vf and Vi for "finite verb" and "non-finite verb" respectively;
"..." means that I disregard the right periphery][4]

Before one can make sense of these patterns, I have to explain the P2 and P1 notions. By definition, P2 is the special position for left periphery wh-elements that precede the "clause proper". A typical P2 occupant is the left dislocation or, as it is called in functional grammar, the "theme".

(3) *Die man*, die heeft het begrepen
     that man that has it understood
     'That man, he has understood it'

P1, on the other hand, is a special clause-initial position. Thus for (3) it will be said that the *die* in front of *heeft* is in P1.

To claim that Dutch has patterns (1) and (2) simply means that Dutch allows material in front of the "clause proper" (P2) and that a Dutch "clause proper" must start off with some constituent in the special clause-initial position (P1), followed by either subject, object and verb or by finite verb, subject, object, and non-finite verb. Before we go on, it is useful to emphasize the similarities and the differences between P2 and P1. P2 and ·P1 are similar in that both characterize the left periphery of the clause. They are different in that P1 is in the "clause proper", while P2 precedes it. Thus P2 also precedes P1. Another difference is that P1 may attract constituents whose category or function would otherwise assign them a later position. Consider (4).

(4) Dat hoofdstuk heb   ik begrepen
    that chapter   have I   understood
    'That chapter I have understood'

Since (4) is a main clause, we should be able to check its acceptability with pattern (2). Pattern (2) requires the object to follow the subject. Yet in (4) the object precedes the subject, so the pattern seems to make the wrong prediction. It is here, however, that the notion of P1 comes in. Functional grammar claims that the object may indeed precede the subject, but only if the object is in P1. The object position in (2), which we now understand better as the position where the object goes unless it is in P1, is unfilled.

(5) Dat hoofdstuk - heb - ik   - ø - begrepen
    P1   - Vf - Subj - Obj -   Vi

In this view, the "clause proper" of (3) is analyzed as shown in (6).

(6) *Die* - heeft - ø - het - begrepen
    P1 - Vf - Subj - Obj- Vi

P2, in contrast, may attract subjects as well as objects, but this does not result in unfilled positions.

(7) a. *Die man*, - die - heeft - ø   - het - begrepen
       P2   - P1 - Vf   - Subj - Obj - Vi

b. *Dat hoofdstuk,* - ik - heb - ø - het - begrepen
   P2   - P1 - Vf - Subj - Obj - Vi

c. *Dat hoofdstuk,* - dat - heb - ik - ø - begrepen
   P2   - P1 - Vf - Subj - Obj - Vi

The second factor steering word order rules is the set of "P-rules". These capture the regularities as to what kind of entity can occupy the P slots. We have already illustrated a P2-rule when we claimed that themes go to P2. This particular P2-rule probably has universal validity. As an illustration of a language-specific P2-rule, consider the position of coordinating conjunctions. When in Dutch a main clause is coordinated, the ordinary main clause verb-second pattern of (1) is valid, which means that coordinating conjunctions are in P2 (cf. Basbøll 1986: 68). In (8a) and (8b) the earlier example sentences are preceded by *en* 'and'.[5]

(8) a. ... *en* - dat hoofdstuk - heb - ik - ø - begrepen
         P2 -   P1   - Vf - Subj - Obj - Vi

    b. .... *en* - die man - heeft - ø - het - begrepen
            P2 -   P1   - Vf - Subj - Obj - Vi

To see that coordinating conjunctions do not universally go to P2, consider Slovenian. Slovenian defines its P1 in terms of an obligatorily second position clitic group (CL).[6]

(9) P2, P1 CL ...

The Slovenian coordinating conjunction *in* 'and' tends to be in P2 when the conjoined clauses have a different subject, but in P1 when they share subjects.

(10) a. Jaž se   učim zemljepisja in moj brat   se   ženi
        I   REFL study geography   and my brother REFL marries
        'I am studying geography and my brother is getting married'

     b. ... *in* - *moj brat* - se - ženi
            P2 -   P1   - CL

(11) a. Poiskati   sem si   moral torej   drug   poklic   in
        have found am REFL had-to therefore another profession and

    em se   naučil pilotirati
    am REFL learned fly
    'I had to find myself another occupation, therefore, and I
    learned to fly'
  b. ... *in* - sem se - naučil pilotirati
      P1 - CL -

So much for P2-rules. As to P1-rules, about which more work has been done, the most important hypothesis says that there are three types, differing in the kinds of entities that are assigned to P1 and in the ordering of the rules (Dik 1980: 153).

(12) *P1-rules*
    Rule 1: P1 constituent $\rightarrow$ P1
    Rule 2: Topic, Focus $\rightarrow$ P1
    Rule 3: X $\rightarrow$ P1

Rule 1 stipulates that P1 accommodates obligatory clause-initial constituents, which are called "P1 constituents". If there are no such constituents in the clause, then we go to rule 2, through which P1 is filled by a constituent that has topic or focus function. Finally, if rule 2 does not apply either, then rule 3 makes provision for P1 fillers that are neither obligatorily P1, nor topic or focus. In their most general formulation, a P1-rule could apply more than once, thus giving rise to a multiply filled P1; yet, in the case of Germanic, the assumption is that such P1s are forbidden (Dik 1978: 180, 1981: 119; cf. also Scherpenisse 1986: 46).

    Rule 3 will not be of concern to us. Rule 2 concerns the optional P1 placement of topic and focus, which are respectively the constituent that the clause is about - in a preferred sense of "aboutness" - and the one that represents the most salient piece of new information.[7] Imagine (13a) as one of many assertions about someone identified earlier in the discourse and as having contrastive stress on *Jan* (represented by capitals). In the terminology of functional grammar, this means that (13a) has *hij* as topic and *JAN* as focus.

(13) a. Hij heeft JAN gezien
        he has   John seen
        'He has seen JOHN'

    b. Hij   - heeft - JAN - gezien
        Topic -   - Focus -

In (13) we thus get a topic in P1.

(13) c. Hij - heeft - ø   - JAN - gezien
        P1 - Vf - Subj - Obj - Vi

But note that the P1 placement of the topic is only optional: in (14) it is *JAN* which goes to P1.

(14) JAN - heeft - hij - ø - gezien
      P1   - Vf - Subj - Obj - Vi

    Rule 1, finally, takes care of those constituents that have to go to P1. The class is usually taken to have three kinds of members: 1) wh-questioned constituents, 2) relativized constituents, and 3) Comps. They are illustrated below:

(15) a. *Wie* heb je   gezien?
        who have you seen
        'Who have you seen?'
    b. Wie - heb - je   - ø - gezien
        P1   - Vf - Subj - Obj - Vi

(16) a. De man *die*   ik gezien heb ...
        the man whom I   seen   have
        'The man whom I have seen ...'
    b. De man - die - ik - ø - gezien heb
               - P1 - Subj - Obj -   V

(17) a. Ik geloof *dat* ik die man gezien heb
        I   believe that I that man seen   have
        'I believe that I have seen that man'
    b. Ik geloof - dat - ik   - die man - gezien heb
               - P1 - Subj -   Obj   -   V

    The above should suffice as a presentation of the functional grammar approach to word order. I should also point out that not all of the hypotheses presented above are uncontroversial (cf. De Schutter 1985a, 1985b).

3. The position of Comps: P2 or P1

We have just seen that functional grammar takes Comps to be P1 constituents. Positions analogous to the functional grammar view are found in the German Positional Fields tradition (Boost 1955; Höhle 1986) and corresponding work on Dutch (De Schutter 1967, De Schutter & Van Hauwermeiren 1983; ANS 1985), as well as in transformational grammar (Reis 1985; Scherpenisse 1986; Thráinsson 1986). In these theories, Comps are in the first position of the clause proper,[8] i.e. in what corresponds to an functional grammar P1. In some recent proposals within transformational grammar, however, in which the Comp is considered worthy of a specifier, the Comp is put in a second position, which I will call "post-P1" (e.g. Platzack 1986; Chomsky 1986). Except for these proposals in transformational grammar, all the theories stress the similarity of Comps to embedding wh-pronouns and -adverbs, henceforth "embedded clause whs", for both Comps and embedded clause whs end up in the first position of the clause - in the divergent views of transformational grammar, only embedded clause whs do.

A linguistic tradition that does not take the Comp to be part of the clause proper is that of the Danish linguist Diderichsen. In his view (cf. Diderichsen 1946: 185-186, 1966: 52-63, 364-386, 1986: 11), Comps precede the clause proper. If I translate Diderichsen's notion of *Forbinderfelt* as P2, then he ends up saying that Comps go to P2. Interestingly, Diderichsen stresses the similarity between Comps and embedded clause wh-expressions too: the latter are also put in P2.[9]

In this paper I will steer the middle course, going along with functional grammar, transformational grammar, German and Dutch structuralism and putting embedded clause whs in P1, but taking the Diderichsen view of assigning Comps to P2. The differences between the two linguistic traditions can be schematized as follows (here and in other examples EC stands for embedded clause):

(18)	EC wh	Comp
Diderichsen:	P2	P2
German and Dutch structuralism, functional grammar, some proposals in transformational grammar:	P1	P1
other proposals in transformational grammar:	P1	post-P1
new proposal:	P1	P2

My argumentative burden can thus be described as follows:

1) Diderichsen as well as German and Dutch structuralism, functional grammar, and some transformational grammar assign embedded clause whs and Comps to the same position (albeit P2 for Diderichsen and P1 for everybody else); I disagree and will have to argue for why I think Diderichsen is right for Comps and the others for embedded clause whs, but I agree that the similarity that the said proposals reflect is real and I will reflect it in a different way.

2) I agree with those transformational grammar proposals that put embedded clause whs and Comps in P1 and post-P1 respectively that embedded clause whs and Comps go to a different position, but I disagree as to which comes first.[10]

Before I come to these arguments, however, I will make a preliminary point. In the next section I will claim that if it is true that Comps go to P2 instead of P1, the P1-rules allow an interesting generalization.

4. A P1 generalization

As mentioned in section 2, the first of the ordered P1-rules concerns the obligatory P1 fillers or P1 constituents, which are standardly either wh-questioned constituents, relativized constituents, or Comps. The second P1-rule stipulates that topics and foci are optional P1 fillers.

(19) *P1-rules*

    Rule 1:   wh-questioned constituent, relativized constituent,

                Comp   → P1

    Rule 2   Topic, Focus   → P1

The suspicious feature of Rule 1 is that two of the three P1 constituents are specifiable by Rule 2. Under the standard functional grammar analysis, wh-questioned constituents are foci (Dik 1978: 149-150) and, under an analysis which is at least compatible with functional grammar – there is no "standard" functional grammar analysis here – relativized constituents are topics.[11] Comps, however, are never topic or focus. As this paper argues that Comps are not P1-fillers, we can subsume rule 1 under rule 2. This yields the generalization that P1 is a "landing site" for topics and foci. The fact that P1 attracts relativized and wh-questioned constituents is the consequence of the fact that the former are topics and the latter foci. It may be true that relativized and wh-questioned constituents are obligatory P1 fillers, while other topics and foci are only optional. If so, the unified rule should make this clear.

5. Embedded clauses have no V/2-P1

To support the hypothesis that Comps go to P2 rather than to P1, we will look at the types of P1s in Dutch declarative main clauses. First, there is the P1 that is followed by the finite verb, which we will call "V/2 P1". A second type of P1 is the one that contains a wh-constituent; we will call it "wh-P1". The former is illustrated in (20a), the latter in (20b), and (20c) shows how something can be both V/2-P1 and wh-P1.

(20) a. *Gisteren* heeft Jan het boek gelezen

             yesterday has   John the book read

             'Yesterday John read the book'

     b. *Waarom* zijn boek lezen?

          why   his book read

          'Why read his book?'

    c. *Wie* heeft het boek gelezen?
        who has the book read
        'Who has read the book?'

Starting from these notions, it is obvious that in Dutch Comp or wh-headed embedded clauses, only wh-P1s occur. (21a) shows that there is no way to keep the *gisteren* of (20a) in the P1 of an embedded clause. (21b) and (21c) are the embedded clause counterparts to (20b) and (20c), and (21d) illustrates a relative wh-P1.

(21) a. *Hij zei   dat *gisteren*   had Jan   het boek gelezen
          he   said that yesterday had John the book read
          'He said that yesterday John had read the book'
    b. Hij weet   niet *waar* naar toe te gaan
          he knows not where to   to go
          'He doesn't know where to go to'
    c. Ik weet niet *wie* het boek gelezen heeft
          I know not who the book read   has
          'I don't know who has read the book'
    d. Alles *wat*   ik heb, heb ik van   een ander
          all   what I have have I   from an   other
          'Everything I have is from someone else'

(22) illustrates the impossibility of a V/2-P1 with a Comp in P1.

(22) *Hij zei *dat* had Jan het boek gelezen

At this point, there are two possible ways to describe Dutch Comp headed embedded clauses: either one accepts a third type of P1, say a 'Comp P1' (standard functional grammar) or, under the proposal that Comps are in P2, one holds that Comp headed embedded clauses do not have a P1 at all.[12] Consider (23):

(23) Hij zei dat Jan het boek gelezen had

In standard functional grammar, (i) the embedded clause of (23) has *dat* in P1, (ii) it is a P1 that is neither of the V/2 nor of the wh-type, and (iii) the P2 position of the embedded clause is unfilled. Under the new proposal, (i) *dat* is in the embedded clause P2, and (ii) the embedded clause P1 is unfilled. Schematically:

(24)		P2	P1
standard functional grammar:	...	ø	*Dat* Jan ...
new proposal:	...	*Dat*	ø Jan ...

Note that the two proposals are equally successful in ruling out (21a). Under the standard analysis, (21a) would have a doubly filled P1, which is taken to be impossible in Germanic, and under the new analysis, (21a) would have an embedded clause P1, which is also impossible.

I retain the standard functional grammar analysis for wh embedded clauses. That is to say that Dutch wh embedded clauses have the wh-constituent in P1 and that their P2 is unfilled. The left periphery of a wh embedded clause is thus a kind of mirror image of the left periphery of a Comp embedded clause. Schematically:

(25)		P2	P1	
wh embedded clauses	...	ø	wh	...
Comp embedded clauses:	...	Comp	ø	...

The schema in (25) represents the difference between wh embedded clauses and Comp embedded clauses in a clear way, but it also represents the similarity. If I merely speak about a left P and leave it vague whether this left P is a P1 or a P2, then, of course, wh and Comp elements are most similar in that they both go to a left P, and prevent anything else from going there.

6. Similarities between wh-expressions and Comps in embedded clauses

There are a number of facts that demonstrate the similarity between Dutch Comps and embedded clause whs. These facts are used by the supporters of the claim that Comps and embedded clause whs go to the same structural position, which is P1 for standard functional grammar, German and Dutch structuralism, and some transformational grammar, but P2 for the Diderichsen tradition. In our proposal "same structural position" is interpreted as "left P", i.e., either P2 or P1.

(26)   same structural position
    standard functional grammar,
    German and Dutch structuralism,
    some transformational grammar: P1

    Diderichsen: P2

    new proposal: left P

I will discuss two similarities and argue that this new proposal is equally or more adequate.

6.1. The connection with finite verb-lateness

Embedded clauses starting with a wh or Comp generally have the finite verb in a late position (cf. examples [16], [17], [21], and [23]). The examples in (27) contain embedded clauses without wh or Comp, and with the finite verb in an early position.

(27) a. *Was ik in Parijs*, ik zou   naar de Marais gaan
        Were I in Paris   I should to   the Marais go
        'If I were in Paris, I would go to the Marais'
   b. Ik dacht,   *ik ga naar Parijs*
        I thought I go to   Paris
        'I thought I'd go to Paris'
   c. Als je   in Parijs bent en *je   ziet de Seine*, dan ...
        if   you in Paris   are and you see the Seine then
        'If you're in Paris and you see the Seine, then ...'

The superficial conclusion is that wh-expressions and Comps are taken to occupy the same position, whatever its name. If this position is filled, the finite verb goes to the end; if it is not filled, the finite verb must or can be in first or second position. This conclusion is wrong, however, for Comps differ from whs in that some Comps do not allow finite verb-lateness. This is the case for *als* 'as if' and *al* 'even if/though'.

(28) a. Als had hij het zelf gevonden ...
   as if had he it self found
   'As if he had found it himself ...'

   b. Al   zijn hier veel lui ...
   even if/though are here many people
   'Even if/though there are many people here ...'

Note that in an account that puts Comps in P2, the embedded clauses in (28) are verb first clauses, i.e. clauses that have the finite verb in P1, a claim which has independent support (Van Es 1949, 1951; König - Van der Auwera 1987). Wh-headed embedded clauses never have a verb first structure, the simple reason being that their P1 contains the wh-element. Thus I conclude that both Comps and embedded clause wh-expressions are in the embedded clause leftmost P, this P being a P2 for Comps and a P1 for embedded clause wh-expressions.

6.2. Clitic *-ie*

Both embedded clause whs and Comps can be followed by the clitic third person subject pronoun *-ie*.

(29) a. Ik vraag me af wat *-ie* gedaan heeft
   I   ask me   what-he done   has
   'I wonder what he has done'

   b. Ik zag wat *-ie* gedaan had
   I saw what-he done   had
   'I saw what he had done'

   c. Ik geloof dat *-ie* iets   gedaan heeft
   I believe that-he something done   has
   'I believe that he has done something'

If there was nothing more to be said, one could simply conclude that embedded clause wh-expressions and Comps take up the same structural position. There are however two complicating factors. Not every Comp can be followed by *-ie*; in particular, the Comps that are followed by verb first structures (28) do not allow *-ie*. Second, Comps and embedded clause wh-expressions are not the only categories that can be followed by *-ie*. The first other category is, at least in the spoken language, the coordinating conjunction.[13]

(30) Jan   liep weg   en *-ie* is nooit meer teruggekeerd
John ran   away and-he is never more returned
'John ran away and he never returned'

Since a coordinating conjunction goes to P2, (30) discredits the hypothesis that the possibility of being followed by *-ie* is an exclusive property of P1. The second category allowing *-ie* is a P1 or post-P1 finite verb.

(31) a. Heeft-*ie* het toch   gedaan?
has   -he it   anyway done
'Has he done it anyway?'

b. Gisteren heeft-*ie* het gedaan
yesterday has -he it   done
'Yesterday he did it'

Since Paardekooper (1955), the facts of (31) have been used to argue for a categorial or positional similarity between a finite verb and a Comp. But this is implausible, for then a finite verb would have to be declared equally similar to an embedded clause wh and a coordinating conjunction.

The account of *-ie* I propose is simply that *-ie* as a clitic follows the first available host.[14] In a main clause, the first available host is either a P2 conjunction, a P1 finite verb, or a post-P1 finite verb - a P1 filled by anything other than a finite verb does not qualify, for this type of P1 must be followed by the finite verb. In an embedded clause, the first available host is a P2 Comp, unless it has to be followed by a P1 finite verb, or a P1, whether filled by an embedded clause wh or finite verb. If this is correct, then we see that the *-ie* facts are perfectly compatible with assigning embedded clause wh-expressions and Comps to different left positions.

7. Embedded themes

It has been argued by Dik (1981) that embedded themes, typical of spoken Dutch, occur in two forms: either the Comp is repeated or the embedded clause has main clause order.

(32) a. Ik geloof *dat die man, dat die* ziek is
　　　　　I believe that that man that that sick is
　　　　　'I believe that that man, that he's sick'
　　b. Ik geloof *dat die man, die* is ziek
　　　　　'I believe that that man, he's sick'

Under the hypothesis that a Comp goes to P1, (32) represents an impossible P1 – P2 – P1 sequence.

(33) a. ... dat - die man, - dat - die ...
　　　　　　P1 -　　P2　　 - P1 - Subj
　　b　.... dat - die man, - die ...
　　　　　　P1 -　　P2　 - P1

Under the hypothesis that a Comp goes to P2, however, one obtains a multiply filled P2 sequence, a phenomenon for which there is independent evidence (cf. note 4).

(34) a. ... dat - die man, - dat - die ...
　　　　　$P2_3$ -　$P2_2$　 - $P2_1$ - Subj
　　b　.... dat - die man, - die ...
　　　　　$P2_2$ -　$P2_1$　　 - P1

Further evidence for the correctness of this analysis is that embedded themes are fully impossible after embedded clause wh-expressions.

(35) a. *De man die dat boek, dat gelezen heeft, is weggelopen
　　　　　the man who that book that read　　 has　 is run away
　　　　*'The man who that book, that has read, has run away'
　　b. *De man die dat boek, dat heeft gelezen, is weggelopen

The prediction that (35a) and (35b) are impossible follows from the ordinary claims that embedded clause wh-expressions are in P1 and themes in P2, for the clauses in (35) would then contain impossible P1 – P2 orders.

(36) a   .... - die_1 - dat boek, - dat_2 - $ø_1$ - $ø_2$ - gelezen heeft
            - P1 -   P2   - P1 - Subj - Obj -   V

    b.   .... - die_1 - dat boek, - dat_2 - heeft - $ø_1$ - $ø_2$ - gelezen
            - P1 -   P2   - P1 - finite verb - Subj - Obj - Vi

8. Conclusion

The basic claim of this paper is that the position of Dutch Comps is P2, rather than P1. This analysis allows one to express the similarity between Comps and coordinating conjunctions (both are "outside of the clause proper") and embedded clause wh-expressions (both are "on the left periphery"). The analysis allows a P1 generalization, stressing the essentially pragmatic (i.e., topic and focus oriented) nature of this position. By choosing functional grammar, I have attempted to show that functional grammar offers an interesting alternative to more widely-known frameworks. Simultaneously, I hope the proposal has some cross-linguistic and cross-theoretical appeal.

Notes

1.   This paper is a revision of parts of van der Auwera (1988). Thanks to all the commentators.
2.   The term "Comp" is confusing. In transformational grammar, "Comp" has been used as a name for the left peripheral position that is typically occupied by complementizers. In this paper, "Comp" is an abbreviation of "complementizer". The position categories will be "P", "P1" and "P2" (see below).

3.   Note that a functional grammar word order rule is not a movement rule. It does not change positions, but assigns them.

4.   In the original formulations P2 is separated from the rest by a comma. This comma is to represent an orthographic comma as well as a comma intonation. Later research has made it clear that this comma cannot be considered a necessary feature. Not even the "theme" or "left dislocation" construction, illustrated in (3) below, requires it, as has been shown for e.g., Dutch (Jansen 1981: 150-152) and English (Geluykens 1986).

5.   This is an appropriate place to point out that there is no a priori restriction on the number of constituents that can fill up a P slot. Thus the Dutch P2-rule should say that P2 can be filled by both a theme and a coordinating conjunction and that the order is necessarily conjunction - theme. We will use "$P2_2$" for the leftmost filler of a doubly filled P2, and "$P2_1$" for the rightmost one.

(a)... *en* - *die man,* - die - heeft - Ø   - het   - begrepen
       $P2_2$ - $P2_1$ - P1 - Vf - Subj - Obj - Vi

6.   Though Slovenian has not been studied from the point of view of functional grammar, closely related Serbo Croatian has (Dik 1980: 131). The point we are making in the text is based on Bennett (1986, 1987) and Browne (1986).

7.   For the purpose of this paper the definitions of topic and focus can be left vague. Cf. example (14) and section 4, as well as Dik et.al. (1981) and Hannay (1983, 1985).

8.   Within transformational grammar, the notion of "clause proper" is best understood as the maximal projection of S. It is not clear, however, whether this maximal S projection is S' (e.g. Chomsky 1986; Thráinsson 1986) or S" (e.g. Holmberg 1985), and it has furthermore been suggested that this is a language-specific decision.

9.   The theme, the most intensively studied P2-filler in functional grammar, goes to what Diderichsen calls *Ekstraposition*. So "P2" translates both *Forbinderfelt* and *Ekstraposition*. This still respects Diderichsen, for he explicitly says that both are outside the clause proper (cf. Diderichsen 1986: 11, 13; cf. also Basbøll 1986: 66). Diderichsen's term for "P1" is *Fundamentfelt*.

10.   Van der Auwera (1988) includes a discussion of Southern Dutch *die dat* "(rel) who that" and Northern Dutch *wie of* "(inter) who that" constructions, which are prima facie evidence for the claim that embedded clause wh-expressions precede Comps.

11.   More precisely, the claim is that the pronominal, adjectival, or adverbial relativizer represents the antecedent as the topic of the relative clause (Van der Auwera - Kucanda 1985).

12.   Here I follow Diderichsen (1946, 1966) again. In the Diderichsen framework, embedded clauses lack a *Fundamentfelt*.

13.   Maybe because the orthography does not normally reflect the cliticization of *-ie* to the coordinating conjunction, this fact has seldom been dicussed (cf. Schuurmans 1975: 12-14).
14.   I owe the essential idea to J. Lachlan Mackenzie.

References

1984   *ANS* [Algemene Nederlandse Spraakkunst] (Groningen: Wolters Noordhoff).

Basbøll, Hans
1986   "Diderichsen vs. Dik eller feltanalyse vs. funktionel grammatik.", *Nydanske studier & almen kommunikationsteori* 16/17: 56-76

Bennett, David C.
1986   "Towards an explanation of word order differences between Slovene and Serbo-Croat", *The Slavonic and East European Review* 64: 1-24
1987   "Word order change in progress: The case of Slovene and Serbo-Croat and its relevance for Germanic", *Journal of Linguistics* 23: 269-287

Bolkestein, Machteld
1981   *Predication and expression in functional grammar* (London/New York: Academic Press).

Bolkestein, Machteld - Casper de Groot - J. Lachlan Mackenzie (eds.)
1985a   *Syntax and pragmatics in functional grammar* (Dordrecht: Foris).
1985b   *Predicates and terms in functional grammar* (Dordrecht: Foris).

Boost, Karl
1955   *Neue Untersuchungen zum Wesen und zum Struktur des deutschen Satzes* (Berlin: Deutsche Akademie der Wissenschaften).

Browne, W.
1986   "Parameters in clitic placement: Serbo-Croatian and Slovenian", Paper presented at the 5th Balkan and South Slavic Conference, Bloomington, Indiana.

Chomsky, Noam
1986   *Barriers* (Cambridge, Mass.: MIT Press).

De Schutter, Gerrit
1967   "Principes van de woordvolgorde in de Nederlandse zin", *Handelingen van het XXVIe Vlaams filologencongres*: 47-55
1985a   "Pragmatic and syntactic aspects of word order in Dutch", *Syntax and pragmatics in functional grammar*, edited by Machteld Bolkestein - Casper de Groot - J. Lachlan Mackenzie (Dordrecht: Foris).

1985b   "Typological aspects of Dutch and German", *Antwerp studies in functional grammar*, edited by Jan Nuyts (Antwerp: Antwerp Papers in Linguistics 39).

De Schutter, Gerrit - P. van Hauwermeiren
1983   *De structuur van het Nederlands* (Malle: Sikkel).

Diderichsen, Paul
1946   *Elementær Dansk grammatik* (København: Gyldendal).
1966   *Helhed og struktur* (København: Gyldendal).
1986   [1945], "Dansk sætningsanalyse. Dens formål og metode", *Nydanske studier & almen kommunikationsteori* 16/17: 7-17

Dik, Simon C.
1978   *Functional grammar* (Amsterdam: North Holland Publishing Co.).
1980   *Studies in functional grammar* (London/New York: Academic Press).
1981   "Embedded themes in spoken Dutch: Two ways out", *Predication and expression in functional grammar*, edited by Machteld Bolkestein (London/New York: Academic Press).

Dik, Simon C. e.a.
1981   "On the typology of focus phenomena", *Perspectives on functional grammar*, edited by Teun Hoekstra - Harry van der Hulst - Michael Moortgat (Dordrecht: Foris).

Dik, Simon C. (ed.)
1983   *Advances in functional grammar* (Dordrecht.: Foris)

Geluykens, Ronald
1986   "Left-dislocation as a topic-introducing device in English conversational discourse", Paper at the 2nd annual Pacific linguistics conference, Eugene, Oregon.

Haider, Hubert - Martin Prinzhorn (eds.)
1986   *Verb second phenomena in Germanic languages* (Dordrecht: Foris).

Hannay, Mike
1983   "The Focus function in functional grammar: questions of contrast and context", *Advances in functional grammar*, edited by Simon Dik (Dordrecht: Foris).
1985   "Inferrability, discourse-boundness, and sub-topics", *Syntax and pragmatics in functional grammar*, edited by Machteld Bolkestein - Casper de Groot - J. Lachlan Mackenzie (Dordrecht: Foris).

Höhle, Tilman N.
1986   "Der Begriff 'Mittelfeld'", *Akten des VII. internationalen Germanisten-Kongresses*, Göttingen 1985. Band 3, edited by Walter Weiss - Herbert E. Wiegand - Marga Reis (Tübingen: Max Niemeyer).

Holmberg, Anders
1985   "Icelandic word order and binary branching", *Nordic Journal of Linguistics* 8: 161-195

Jansen, Frank
1981   *Syntaktische konstrukties in gesproken taal* (Amsterdam: Huis aan de drie grachten).

König, Ekkerhard - Johan van der Auwera
in press   "Clause integration in German and Dutch conditionals, concessive conditionals, and concessives", *Clause combining in grammar and discourse*, edited by John Haiman - Sandra Thompson (Amsterdam: John Benjamins).

Paardekooper, Piet
1955   *Syntaxis, spraakkunst en taalkunde* (Den Bosch: Malmberg).

Platzack, Christer
1986   "Diderichsens positionsschema och generativ transformationsgrammatik", *Nydanske studier & almen kommunikationsteori* 16/17: 161-170

Reis, Marga
1985   "Satzeinleitende Strukturen im Deutschen: Über COMP, Haupt-und Nebensätze, w-Bewegung und die Doppelkopfanalyse", *Erklärende Syntax des Deutschen*, edited by Werner Abraham (Tübingen: Gunter Narr).

Scherpenisse, Wim
1986   *The connection between base structure and linearization restrictions in German and Dutch* (Frankfurt/M: P. Lang).

Schuurmans, N.J.
1975   *Verbindingen met specifiek enclitische pronomina in het Westbrabants*, doctoral dissertation (Nijmegen: Catholic University Nijmegen).

Thráinsson, Höskuldur
1986   "V1, V2, V3 in Icelandic", *Verb second phenomena in Germanic languages*, edited by Hubert Haider - Martin Prinzhorn (Dordrecht: Foris).

Van der Auwera, Johan
1988   "On the position of Dutch complementizers", *Working Papers in Functional Grammar* 26

Van der Auwera, Johan - D. Kucanda
1985   "Pronoun or conjunction - the Serbo-Croatian invariant relativizer *sto*", *Linguistics* 23: 917-962

Van Es, Gustaaf
1949   "Oorsprong en functies van het voegwoord *al*", *It beaken* 12: 105-117
1951   "Syntaktische vormen van de concessieve modaliteit in het Nederlands", *Tijdschrift voor Nederlandse Taal-en Letterkunde* 68: 253-295

On the nature of proper government and syntactic barriers[1]

Gisbert Fanselow

1. Introduction

Since its original proposal in Koster (1978), the idea of a unification of the various local domains of syntactic theory has played a prominent role in generative research. Obviously, any program of this kind will face a number of both empirical and conceptual problems. On the empirical side, we have to account for the fact that, in spite of a certain degree of overlapping, the local domains of different principles never appear to be fully identical. While certainly a number of technical formulations might be found that would allow us to express these differences, this alone will not answer the more profound conceptual question of why these distributional differences should exist at all, and why a certain class of elements behaves just the way it does.

In this paper, I would like to sketch an answer to both of these questions. It will be argued that an account of locality in terms of a relativized concept of barriers by minimality is able to predict the differences that hold between various types of constructions. The central idea is that several principles of universal grammar can be unified if they are formulated in terms of a specification of syntactic features.

2. NP-traces and lexical anaphors

Let me begin with a rather straightforward observation. Chomsky (1986a) has demonstrated how locality restrictions on NP-traces can be derived from the empty category principle (ECP) if, on the one hand, proper government is restricted to antecedent government and if, on the other hand, elements that share indices enter into an extended chain, the links of which may also function as antecedent governors. Consider (1) for a brief illustration.

(1)   a. John$_i$ [$_{INFL}$ was$_j$] [$_{VP}$ t$_j$ invited$_j$ t$_i$]]
      b. *John$_i$ was$_j$ preferred$_j$ [for Bill$_k$ INFL$_k$ to [$_{VP}$ invite$_k$ t$_i$]]

Not being L-marked,[2] VP is a barrier[3] for a direct government relationship between *John* and its trace in both (1a) and (1b). The trace t$_i$ in (1a) is antecedent-governed by *invited*, however, since a verb generally is coindexed with the Infl position, which itself has to agree with the subject. In other words, the indices *i* and *j* are identical in (1a), *invited* is part of the extended chain *John, was, t$_j$, invited, t$_i$* is therefore able to antecedent govern the trace. In (1b), however, invite shares indices with the subject of the embedded clause only, but not with the subject position of the matrix clause that binds the trace t$_i$. Consequently, *i* is not identical with *k*, *invite* cannot be construed as an antecedent governor for t$_i$ and the structure will thus correctly be ruled out by the empty category principle.

While this seems to work quite nicely, this example also illustrates the two major problems mentioned above. Since lexical anaphors share an almost identical distribution with NP-traces, it is natural to assume that the binding of lexical anaphors will be restricted by the concept "barrier" and the empty category principle as well. This assumption, however, directly leads to the following questions: Why should a lexical anaphor be affected by a condition on empty categories such as the empty category principle? What could be the reason for distributional differences between overt and non-overt anaphors such as the one exemplified in (2)?

(2)   a. they$_i$ laughed at [each other$_i$'s friends]
      b. *they$_i$ have been laughed at [t$_i$'s friends]
      c. they$_i$ think that [each other$_i$'s photos] are for sale

d. *they_i were thought that [t_i's photos] are for sale

The mysterious fact that lexical expressions appear to behave as if they were subject to a condition like the empty category principle is not confined to overt anaphors, however, since there is also a near identity between the contexts of NP-movement and those licensed for pairs of expletives and arguments,[4] cf. (3), where the latter environment appears to be somewhat more restricted.

(3) a. there has arisen a problem
     b. there seems to be a unicorn in my garden
     c. *there seems that are unicorns in my garden
     d. there seem to be unicorns in my garden

In order to see what properties lexical anaphors, traces and expletives might have in common, it is helpful to turn to languages other than English. Generally, a category α can be coindexed with β only if α and β agree with respect to their specifications of person, number, and gender, i.e. φ-features. Inflectional endings prove *there* to be singular in (3b) and plural in (3d). Consequently, it is reasonable to assume that *there* does not bear φ-features inherently, but rather derives them from the (argument) position it is coindexed with.

German and Romance lexical anaphors seem to come quite close to the behaviour of *there* in this respect: there is no overt indication of φ-features, in contradistinction to pronominal elements:

(4) a. er / sie / es liebt   sich
        he she   it loves reflexive
        'he/she/it loves himself/herself/itself'
     b. die Männer lieben sich
        the men   love reflexive
        'the men love themselves'

(5) a. el hombre / la   mujer se   lava
        the man   the woman refl. washes
        'the man/the woman is washing himself/herself'
     b. los hombres / las mujeres se   lavan
        the men   the women refl. wash

'the men/ the women are washing themselves'

According to a survey of about 30 languages from different families carried out by one of my students, Ildiko Szakacs, the majority of the languages included in the sample behave like German and Romance in this respect. Consequently, it seems to be natural to assume that both expletives like *there* as well as lexical anaphors lack inherent specification of φ-features, which have to be derived from a coindexed category via some process of feature transmission. The differentiation in English between *himself, oneself, themselves*, etc. might then be considered to be a morphophonological spellout of features that have been assigned to these expressions in a syntactic process of such a feature transmission.

Massam (1985), however, has presented ample evidence for the assumption that assignment of syntactic features such as Case is indeed blocked by barriers. The distribution of expletives and lexical anaphors will thus be predicted to be confined by barriers if we require that every NP must bear a full specification of φ-features, i.e., if we extend the Case filter to a principle like (6):

(6) $*[_{NP} \, \alpha \,]$ if α has a phonetic matrix and lacks Case- or φ-features

To be concrete, let us briefly consider the data given in (7):

(7)   a. $he_i \, [_{VP} \, likes_j \, himself_i]$
      b. $*he_i \, thinks_j$ that $Mary_k \, likes_k \, himself_i$
      c. there has arisen a problem
      d. *there seems that a man has arisen

From the discussion in the preceding paragraphs, it follows that *himself* lacks inherent specification of φ-features. Due to the presence of the intervening VP-barrier, *himself* cannot derive these from *he* directly, but as in (1a), *he*, Infl and *likes* all share indices, therefore *himself* is able to derive φ-features from *likes* in (7a). On the other hand, (7b) is obviously parallel to (1b). *He, likes*, and *himself* cannot enter into a common extended chain, and consequently, successive feature transmission from *he* to *himself* as in (7a) will be correctly blocked for this example.[5] The explanation for (7c-d) will differ from the one just presented only with respect to the directionality of feature transmission: here, it is the lower category that provides the φ-features.[6]

This approach directly extends to traces of NP-movement, since, for obvious reasons, there can be no inherent lexical specification of φ-features for empty categories. Consequently, φ-features must be derived by some transmission process blocked by barriers. In other words, for each trace α there must be a category β not separated from α by a barrier from which α can derive its φ-features. Consequently, the need for an antecedent governor for traces, i.e., the empty category principle, will follow from (6) if reference to phonetic matrices is dropped.

(8) $*[NP\ \alpha\ ]$ if α lacks Case- or φ-features.

(8) appears to have certain advantages over the original formulation of the empty category principle. First, it subsumes three formerly independent principles of universal grammar, viz., the Case filter, the empty category principle and binding theory's principle A. Second, no analogue of the restriction of the empty category principle to traces has to be stipulated for (8). Rather, the fact that neither PRO nor *pro* need be antecedent-governed appears to follow from the (independently motivated) existence of two further means of feature assignment in universal grammar: a theory of control, and feature identification by agreement with a strong Infl-node. (8), thus, also subsumes condition (9) and the need of control for PRO. In other words, the differentiation between PRO, *pro*, and traces reduces to the existence of three feature determination processes in universal grammar, which have to be assumed in any variant of government binding-theory.

(9) *pro* must be identified by strong inflection.

The only problem that might derive from (8) seems to stem from the imposition of Case requirements on empty categories. However, this extension of the Case filter will have virtually no effect on *pro*: by (8), *pro* is subject to (9), and a governing strong Infl will always assign Case to the category it governs. Furthermore, the next two sections will show that the imposition of Case requirements on traces implies quite a number of welcome consequences. The only problematic case left to deal with is PRO. Data from Latin (10a) and Spanish (10b) suggest, however, that even non-finite Infl can also assign Case.[7] In general, it appears to be possible to maintain that PRO is Case marked by Infl. Distributional properties of these empty categories then must be shown to reduce to other factors, but for reasons of space, I cannot go into this issue any further here.[8]

(10) a. igitur   reges populi -que bellum temptare
        therefore kings people -and war   try-INF
        'therefore, kings and people tried with war'
     b. al haber-se   manifestado los estudiantes, el decano..
        at have- refl demonstrated the students,   the dean ..
        'the students having demonstrated, the dean ....'

3. Traces versus overt anaphors

In section 2, we have tried to account for similarities that can be observed in the behaviour of traces, expletives and lexical anaphors. Consequently, we now have to turn to distributional differences such as the ones exemplified in (2c) and (2d), repeated here as (11) for convenience.

(11) a. they$_i$ believe that [$_{NP}$ each other$_i$'s photos] are for sale
     b. *they$_i$ were believed that [$_{NP}$ t$_i$'s photos] are for sale

In (11), the closest category from which *each other* and the trace could derive φ-features is the verb *believe* coindexed and φ-feature marked by *they*. But since the specifier position in which both *each other* and the trace are embedded is not L-marked, the subject NP is a barrier. Furthermore, the dominating IP- and CP-projections of the complement clause will inherit barrierhood from the subject category. Consequently, both *each other* and the trace are separated from *believe* by three barriers, a fact that will block feature transmission as we argued above. While this is a correct result for (11b), the approach developed so far obviously makes incorrect predictions for (11a).

Under closer inspection, the problem turns out not to be restricted to lexical anaphors. Rather, specifiers appear to function as barriers for syntactic movement processes only. Thus, it has frequently been noted[9] that *everyone* can bind *him* in (12a). Since a quantifier α may bind a pronoun β only if α c-commands β at logical form, a representation such as (12b) must be the source of the interpretation for (12a). This indicates that specifiers cannot be barriers for movement at logical form.

(12) a. everyone's mother likes him
  b. every x_i: [$_{IP}$ [$_{NP}$ x_i's mother] likes x_i]

Spanish data such as (13) suggest identical conclusions:

(13) a. no quiero que ninguno venga
      not want-I that nobody comes
      'I don't want that nobody is coming'
  b. no quiero que venga ninguno
      'I don't want anybody to come'
  c. no quiero que las fotos de ninguno esten en la mesa
      not want-I that the photos of nobody are   on the table

(14) a. For no x: I want that x comes
  b. For no x: I want that the photographs of x are on the
      table

A negative quantifier in the specifier position of IP such as *ninguno* in (13a) does not allow for a wide scope reading, but this interpretation is available if the negative quantifier is inverted. I.e., a representation at logical form such as (14a) is available for (13b), but not for (13a), a fact that demonstrates - along the lines developed by Kayne (1981) and Rizzi (1982) - that the trace left by extraction at logical form of *ninguno* is subject to the empty category principle or, in the present approach, to principle (8).

On the other hand, there is a wide scope reading for *ninguno* in (13c), i.e., (14b) is a possible representation for this structure at logical form .[10] But since (14b) is related to (13c) by extracting *ninguno* from the subject position of the embedded clause, this specifier slot, again, cannot function as a barrier for extraction at logical form.

The same seems to hold for parasitic gaps. As (15) indicates, a parasitic gap is licensed in a position embedded within a clausal specifier as well.

(15) a. who do [close friends of e] admire t
  b. *who do [close friends of e] admire Bill

Consequently, it seems to be reasonable to assume that specifiers are not barriers in general, and that the ungrammaticality of (11b) and (15b) reduces to some other factor. Comparing (15a) and (15b) in this respect, the two occurences of *e* play a different role in these examples. In both cases, *e* has to derive φ-features from *who*, but only in (15b) does a Case relationship also have to be established between *who* and *e*, since in (15a), *who* can derive its Case feature from *t*, the real trace.

This difference with respect to Case characterizes the other constructions we have considered as well. Lexical anaphors do not share Case with their antecedent, and Case appears to be irrelevant at LF (in a sense to be made precise below). On the other hand, transmission of Case from the trace to the wh-word is mandatory with wh-movement. The situation with NP-traces is a bit more complex.

(16) a. John$_i$ was invited t$_i$
     b. *John$_i$ was believed that t$_i$'s pictures are for sale
     c. *John$_i$ was believed that pictures (of) t$_i$ are for sale

Due to passivization, t_i cannot be directly Case-marked in (16a), but the trace can be saved from violating condition (8) with respect to Case if - in accordance with standard assumption - the nominative Case assigned to *John* by Infl can be percolated down to the coindexed trace through the extended chain.[11] If, as our discussion has suggested so far, Case transfer is blocked by specifier projections, the traces will violate the Case part of principle (8). Consequently, the structures are predicted to be ungrammatical, as required.[12] To sum up, we may conclude that specifiers are barriers for the exchange of Case features, but do not block transmission of φ-features.

A similar differentiation can be observed in the behaviour of German PPs:

(17) a. *wen$_i$ hast du [an t$_i$] gedacht
        who   have you at   thought
        'who did you think of'
     b. daß Maria [an sich] denkt
        that Mary at refl. thinks
        'that Mary thinks of herself'

c. daß der Soldat eine Bombe hinter   jedem Haus   fand
   that the soldier a   bomb behind each   house found
   'that the soldier found a bomb behind each house'
c′ every x_i, x_i a house: there is an x_j, x_j a bomb: the soldier found x_j
   behind x_i

While PPs do not constitute barriers for reflexives (17b) and movement at logical form (i.e., [17c'] is a possible logical form for [17c]), they generally block syntactic extractions even if they are L-marked as in (17a).[13] This contrast appears to find a neat explanation in terms of the minimality condition, according to which the governor α closest to β will block any further government relationships for β.[14] But if we assume that the preposition *an* blocks a relationship of government between *wen* and its trace in (17a), the minimality effect has to be restricted to Case government since otherwise, we would incorrectly block φ-feature transfer in (17b) and (17c'). It is not difficult to see, however, why P should have blocking effects for Case only: in contradistinction to, e.g., Infl, P enters into government relationships for Case only, but not for φ-features. The data in (17) will thus be predicted by a relativized minimality condition:

(18)   α does not govern β for the feature f at level L
        in [...α...[$_Σ$...β...δ...]...]
        if Σ excludes α but includes β and δ and if δ governs β
        for f at L.

P governs its complement for Case, consequently, (18) will block the necessary Case relationship between *wen* and its trace in (17a). Case assignment takes place at S-structure, which implies that P will not bear any minimality effect for extractions at logical form by (18). Furthermore, there is no Case-relationship between anaphors and their antecedents that could be blocked by P.

Turning to English, (18) appears to be somewhat too restrictive since, as a marked property of the language, preposition stranding is licensed:

(19) a. who did you laugh at t
     b. who did you see a picture of t

Following suggestions made by Kayne (1979), the difference between English and German can be reduced to the fact that P and V govern Case in the same fashion[15] in the former language, but not in the latter. (19a) will be predicted to be grammatical if minimality barriers imposed by α can be extended to the next dominating category projected from δ when α and δ govern the relevant feature in the same way. (19b) will then fit into this approach as well, since *picture* does not assign Case at all, and will, consequently, be irrelevant for the computation of Case minimality.

These considerations, however, already suffice to predict the blocking effects of specifiers for syntactic extractions. In (20), there is no way of extending the Case minimality barrier imposed by *of*, since the next category assigning Case, Infl, does so in a fashion different from P. Consequently, PP is a barrier for Case transmission here, and this will leave the wh-phrases in (20a) and (20b) and the NP-traces in (20c) and (20d) without Case.[16]

(20) a. *which men did he think that photos [$_{PP}$ of t] are for sale
    b. *which men did he expect photos [$_{PP}$ of t] to be for sale
    c. *these men were thought that photos [$_{PP}$ of t] are for sale
    d. *these men were preferred for photos [$_{PP}$ of t] to be for sale

4. The behaviour of V and Infl

Section 3 has demonstrated how blocking effects exerted by specifiers on syntactic movement processes can be derived from a relativized concept of minimality. Obviously, this approach presupposes that a concept of general barrierhood can be identified that excludes specifiers. Furthermore, IP may not be considered to be a blocking category in general, since otherwise, inheritance of barrierhood from IP by CP would incorrectly block a transmission of φ-features in examples such as (11a). Consequently, intrinsic barrierhood appears to have to be restricted along the lines of (21):

(21) α is a barrier for β if α includes β and is an adjunct

This might appear to be quite a bold move, but closer scrutiny will reveal that the effects of barriers by L-marking on the original *Barriers* (LM-) account can be mirrored by the relativized minimality condition (RM-account) to the desired extent.

Let me begin with VP to illustrate this point in some detail. On both the LM- and the RM-account, VP will *ceteris paribus* constitute a barrier, and we have already seen how these effects can be overcome with NP-movement. VP-barriers are voided in the LM-account by adjunction to VP. In principle, the very same option is open in the RM-account as well, but for reasons that will become clear immediately, it seems to be preferable to follow a recent suggestion made by Staudacher (1988): in wh-movement structures like (22), the inflected verb moves to the Comp position.

(22) a. *wen hast du eingeladen* (= 22b)
     b. who have you invited

(23) who$_i$ have$_j$ [you t$_j$ [invited$_j$ t$_i$]]

Due to specifier-head agreement in CP, and verb-Infl agreement in IP/VP, (22b) is indexed as given in (23), with i = j. Since, as we shall argue directly, Infl is irrelevant in these cases, the extended chain wh,Comp,V,t will permit Case transfer, since no minimality barriers intervene.[17] Examples such as (24) without V-to-Comp-movement require a slight reformulation, however.

(24) I wonder what Bill might have said t

Comp and the wh-expression will automatically share indices, and V will bear the same index, and thus enter the extended chain if wh-movement passes through the specifier position of VP and triggers spec-head agreement there, i.e., if we assume that both the specifiers of CP and VP are A-bar-positions. In other words, this stipulation will replace the LM-stipulation, according to which adjunction is possible to VP in the context of wh-movement.

If this line of reasoning is correct, an interesting account of wh-island effects will follow. In (25), *what* cannot have passed through the specifier of CP, since it is occupied by *how*. Consequently, the lower V will not share indices with the Comp position, and no extended chain will emerge. The lower VP will therefore constitute a minimality barrier for Case transmission between *what* and its trace.

(25) ?*what$_i$ did you wonder how Bill [$_{VP}$ t$_i$[fixed t$_i$]]

If wh-island effects are thus reduced to Case minimality, the absence of similar effects for movement at logical form turns out to be a consequence of the approach developed here and does not have to be stipulated as in the LM-approach. Furthermore, in contradistinction to the examples we have discussed so far, the minimality condition will affect the intermediate trace t_i in (25) and not the root trace, if we allow Case assignment to apply any time between D- and S-structure. Thus, *fix* might Case-mark *what* directly after D-structure. *what* will then be moved to the specifier of VP, and can copy its Case features on the root trace, since no barrier intervenes. In the next step, *what* directly moves to the specifier of the upper VP, since *how* already occupies the CP-specifier, but now, Case transmission to the intermediate trace left behind is blocked for the reasons just discussed. The difference in acceptability between violations of the wh-island condition on the one hand, and extractions from PP-barriers or specifiers on the other, may consequently be reduced to the deletability of offending intermediate traces at logical form. It appears to be possible to subsume the entire subjacency condition under relativized minimality, but considerations of space again forbid me to go into details.[18]

Let me conclude with some remarks on the behaviour of Infl. Infl normally governs both Case and φ-features, so IP is predicted to be a barrier for φ-feature transmission in general. With regard to wh-movement, however, we have to account for the fact that (26a) is well-formed, whereas - *ceteris paribus* - (26b) is not:

(26) a. wh$_i$....[$_{CP}$...[$_{IP}$__VP V t$_i$]]]
      b. wh$_i$....[$_{CP}$...[$_{IP}$_$_i$ Infl VP]]

Following ideas developed by Aoun (1985) in a somewhat different framework, it is natural to assume that Infl is able to φ-govern just those positions with which it could be φ-coindexed. Infl cannot be φ-coindexed with a wh-trace in object position without giving rise to a violation of principle C of the binding theory.[19] Therefore Infl cannot φ-govern the trace in (26a). Consequently no φ-minimality effects will arise within IP, and

(26a) is predicted to be grammatical. On the other hand, nothing prevents a φ-coindexation of the subject with the governing Infl, so Infl will minimally φ-govern the subject in (26b), and IP functions as a φ-barrier.[20]

This integration of Aoun's account in an explanation for the contrast in (26) will not affect NP-traces and lexical anaphors, however, since the latter can be freely coindexed with Infl without a principle C violation. Aoun (1985), however, suggests that the i-within-i-condition will play a role in determining which categories can be coindexed with each other. This will predict that Infl cannot be coindexed with any category α embedded in the subject position, therefore, Infl will not trigger φ-minimality for α. This appears to be correct, since (27a) and (27b) as well as the representation for logical form (27d) for (27c) are well-formed, in which φ-features have to be transferred into the subject position.

(27) a. the men$_i$ think that each other$_i$'s photos are for sale
   b. who did [close friends of e] admire t
   c. everyone's mother likes him
   d. every x: [[x's mother] likes x]

If in a given language the i-within-i condition were irrelevant for φ-government relationships, the category IP should constitute a barrier even for the material in its specifier position. In other words, all the data in (27) for this language should be ungrammatical. Apparently, German is a language of this type:

(28) a. *die Männer denken, daß einanders   Fotos verkauft werden
        the men   think   that each other photos sold   are
   b. *wem haben nahe Freunde von geholfen
        who   have close friends   of helped
   c. *jedermanns$_i$ Mutter liebt ihn$_i$ (= 27c)

To sum up, the approach developed here makes two suggestions: first, several principles of universal grammar, viz. the Case filter, principle A of binding theory, subjacency, the empty category principle and the licensing condition of *pro*, should be reduced to a principle requiring full specification of Case and φ-features. Second, a relativized concept of barrierhood by minimality should play a more prominent role in universal grammar than it does in the approach developed in Chomsky (1986a).

Notes

1.   I would like to thank Sascha Felix and Peter Staudacher for helpful comments, and Susan Olsen for checking my English.

2.   α L-marks ß if a) α and ß are sisters, b) α is a lexical category, and c) α assigns a theta-role to ß.

3.   A maximal projection Σ is a *barrier* for α if
   a) Σ is a blocking category for α , Σ ≠ IP *or*
   b) Σ immediately dominates Φ, Φ a blocking category for α .
   A maximal projection Σ is a *blocking category* for α if
   Σ includes α and Σ is not L-marked.

4.   Cf. Chomsky (1986b), and Taraldsen (in press) for some discussion.

5.   Interpretive facts will follow if we make the natural assumption that an anaphor has to derive reference from the category it has derived its φ-features from.

6.   It would be more precise to say that extended chains are the result of free feature sharing between categories within the domains licensed by the relativized minimality condition developed below.

7.   Cf. also Reuland (1981), among others.

8.   Cf. Fanselow (in press) and Fanselow (in prep.) for an elaboration of this point.

9.   Cf., e.g., May (1977, 1985).

10.   Cf. Aoun (1981).

11.   I.e., if the Case-relationship between an NP-trace and its antecedent is identical to that found in pairs of expletives and arguments.

12. t_i might receive genitive Case *in situ* in (11b), and objective Case in (11c), however. The resulting A-chains of *John* and its trace would not be well-formed in this situation either, since it would both bear nominative (assigned to *John*) as well as genitive/objective. According to Chomsky (1986b), however, chains that are not uniquely marked for Case are not well-formed. Consequently, there is no way of saving (11b) and (11c) in the approach developed above.

13.   Preposition stranding appears to be possible with the elements *wo* "where", and *da* "there", however, (but see Oppenrieder [in press]) which are comparable to Dutch R-pronouns. See van Riemsdijk (1978), Koster (1987) for a discussion of these cases.

14.   We shall give a more precise formulation below.

15.   This notion will involve consideration of the type of Case that is assigned (dative vs. accusative, structural vs. lexical), and the directionality of Case assignment. This will relate the approach developed here to proposals of Kayne (1983) and Koster (1987).

16.   Recall that we assume non-finite Infl to be a Case assigning category as well.

17.   Cf. also Bouchard (1985) for a somewhat different account of wh-movement involving verb-trace-coindexation.

18.   Cf. Fanselow (in prep.) for an elaboration of this matter.
19.   Due to Infl subject coindexation.
20.   See Fanselow (in prep.) for an account of wh-extraction of subjects in construc-
       tions with exceptional Case marking

References

Aoun, Joseph
    1983   *The formal nature of anaphoric relations*, doctoral dissertation (Cambridge,
            Mass.: MIT).
    1985   *Generalized binding* (Dordrecht: Foris).

Belletti, Adriana - Luciana Brandi - Luigi Rizzi
    1981   *Theory of markedness in generative grammar* (Pisa: Scuola Normale Superiore
            di Pisa).

Bouchard, Dennis
    1985   *On the content of empty categories* (Dordrecht: Foris).

Chomsky, Noam
    1981   *Lectures on government and binding* (Foris: Dordrecht).
    1986a   *Barriers* (Cambridge, Mass.: MIT Press).
    1986b   *Knowledge of language: Its nature, origin and use* (New York: Praeger).

Fanselow, Gisbert
    in press "Barriers and the theory of binding", *Derivational and representational appro-
              aches to generative syntax*, edited by Hubert Haider - Klaus Netter (Dordrecht:
              Reidel).
    in prep   *Merkmale und Barrieren* (working title), habilitation thesis, Universität Passau

Grewendorf, Günther - Wolfgang Sternefeld (eds.)
    in press *Scrambling and barriers* (Amsterdam: Benjamins).

Haider, Hubert - Klaus Netter (eds.)
    in press *Derivational and representational approaches to generative syntax* (Dordrecht:
              Reidel).

Heny, Frank (ed.)
    1981   *Binding and filtering* (London: Croom Helm).

Kayne, Richard
    1979   "Case marking and LF" (Paris: unpublished manuscript Université de Paris
            VIII).

1981   "Two notes on the NIC", *Theory of markedness in generative grammar*, edited by Adriana Belletti - Luciana Brandi - Luigi Rizzi (Pisa: Scuola Normale Superiore di Pisa).

1983   "Connectedness", *Linguistic Inquiry* 14: 233-250

Koster, Jan
1978   *Locality principles in syntax* (Dordrecht: Foris).
1987   *Domains and dynasties* (Dordrecht: Foris).

Massam, Diana
1985   *Case theory and the projection problem*, doctoral dissertation (Cambridge, Mass.: MIT).

May, Robert
1977   *The grammar of quantification*, doctoral dissertation (Cambridge, Mass.: MIT-Press).
1985   *Logical form: Its structure and derivation* (Cambridge, Mass.: MIT-Press).

Oppenrieder, Wilhelm
in press   "Preposition stranding im Deutschen", Paper read at the 12th GGS-Conference, Passau, June 1988

Reuland, Eric
1981   "Empty subjects, Case and agreement and the grammar of Dutch", *Binding and filtering*, edited by Frank Heny (London: Croom Helm).

Rizzi, Luigi
1982   *Issues in Italian syntax* (Dordrecht: Foris).

Staudacher, Peter
1988   "Long movement from verb-second complements in German", *Scrambling and barriers*, edited by Günther Grewendorf - Wolfgang Sternefeld (Amsterdam: Benjamins).

Taraldsen, Tarald
in press   "NP-movement and expletive chains", *Derivational and representational approaches to generative syntax*, edited by Hubert Haider - Klaus Netter (Dordrecht: Reidel).

Van Riemsdijk, Henk
1978   *A Case study in syntactic markedness* (Dordrecht: Foris).

Null subjects and expletives in Romance and Germanic languages[1]

Hubert Haider

1. Introduction

The system of grammar seems to operate on the basis of a principle of "inertia": The processes are last resort operations, governed by a least effort maxime (cf. Chomsky 1988). The structures are subject to the principle of full interpretation (cf. Chomsky 1986a), which holds that representations should contain no superfluous elements.

Viewed from this perspective, expletives must be licensed. An expletive subject is not a legitimate element at the level of logical form, since it is uninterpretable, nor a legitimate D-structure element, given that D-structure is the pure thematic structure, since it cannot bear a thematic role. Hence it must be licensed at S-structure. Its licensing condition in a last resort scenario can be derived from the empty category principle. If there is an obligatory structural position for the subject, i.e. the specifier of IP, the empty category principle will be operative if the position is left empty and it will be empty if there is no thematic role assigned to it. The prototypical case is the passive of an intransitive verb in various languages:

(1) a. Swedish: Dansades *det* på skeppet?
         Was-danced there on the ship
     b. Dutch: Wordt *er*   gedanst?
         Is   there danced
     c. French: *Il* sera   parlé de   vous par tout le monde
         It will be talked about you by the whole world

There are, however, similar constructions in various other languages (cf. Platzack 1987) without overt subjects:

(2) a. Icelandic: Var — dansað?
               Was danced?
    b. Faroese: Var — dansað?
    c. German: Wurde — getanzt?

An account of this contrast requires a principled choice between two theoretically possible options: Either there is no obligatory subject position in these languages or the subject position is not empty in the relevant sense, i.e., the empty category principle is somehow satisfied. In the current literature the second option is chosen: It is assumed (cf. Koster 1986; Platzack 1985) that there is a null expletive, an expletive pro (cf. Chomsky 1986a:178). Languages with an expletive pro are said to be semi-pro-drop. In this contribution I will raise counterevidence and counterarguments in favor of the first option. First I shall argue that the assumption of an expletive pro is at variance with the facts of a pro-drop language like Italian. In section 3, I shall motivate the parameter responsible for the (non-)obligatoriness of the specifier position of IP, which allows one to differentiate between the languages in (1) and (2). Finally, it will be necessary to adress the exceptional status of pro and PRO, being empty categories not subject to the empty category principle. It will turn out that the lack of expletive pro in Italian has important theoretical consequence for the status of these pronominal empty categories.

2. Expletive pro in a pro-drop language

The common denominator for the empty subject in the examples in (3) is pro. It is questionable, however, whether (3c) should be analyzed in the same way as (3a) and (3b).

(3) a. e_i piove
        it rains
    b. e_i verrà
        he will see

    c. e_i verrà Gigi
        Gigi will see

If (3c) is analyzed as the result of adjoining the subject to VP, the empty category at the subject position is rather a trace than a resumptive expletive pronominal. Under the redefinition of command in Chomsky (1986), the postverbal subject will c-command the trace, because the postverbal subject is only covered but not dominated by the VP. Hence (3c) is a wellformed movement result.

There is also empirical evidence for separating the issue of post-verbal subjects from the pro-drop-syndrome. Languages like Occitan or Old French (cf. Adams 1987) are pro-drop languages which do not feature postverbal subjects.

If we take (3a) and (3b) as representative of the genuine pro-drop cases, we note that pro always represents an argument, i.e. that it bears a thematic role. This is a natural consequence of the theta-criterion. Since pro is a pronominal, i.e. equivalent to an NP, it must receive a thematic role. Hence it will not come as a surprise that constructions in which pro receives no thematic role are ungrammatical in Italian (cf. 4). This would be surprising, however, if pro could, according to widely held opinions, serve as an expletive.

(4)   a. *è   stato tossito
           has been coughed
    b. *non è da tossire
           not   is to cough
           (there has not to be coughed)
    c. non è da leggere
           (it) is not to (be) read

(4a) is an example of an intransitive passive and (4b) illustrates the auxiliary-plus-infinitive-construction, which yields a modal passive if the auxiliary is *essere*.

The absence of instances of constructions which require an expletive pro in Italian, the cardinal pro-drop language, casts doubt on analyses which make crucial use of this concept. If there are semi-pro-drop languages, their properties with respect to the distribution of pro must be a subset of the properties of pro-drop languages:

(5)   pro-drop > semi-pro-drop

This relation is acknowledged by Grewendorf (1986:160) in his analysis of German impersonal constructions, as well as by Koster (1986:24), by Platzack (1985:8), and by Rizzi (1986:541). None of them discusses the Italian cases in (4). In the framework of government and binding it is impossible, under the standard account of pro-drop, and without resort to ad hoc mechanisms, to deny a pro-drop language the semi-pro-drop properties. Rizzi (1982:143) characterizes the null subject phenomenology in the following way:

(6)   a.   Infl can be specified as [+pronoun]
      b. $\begin{bmatrix} +\text{pron} \\ F_i..F_n \end{bmatrix}$ can be referential

He explicitly excludes the possibility of finding a language without the property (6a) but with (6b), i.e. with referential pro only, but he does not discuss the constructions mentioned above. If we exclude the alleged expletive pro of the postverbal subjects, we end up with Italian as the language type that is excluded. This points to the conclusion that expletive pro might be a concept that has to be excluded from the theory of grammar.

3. Missing subjects versus missing subject positions

It is a controversial question whether Chomsky's (1982:10) extended projection principle, which postulates that every clause has a subject, holds universally. There is evidence (Haider 1987a) that this principle is characteristic for the type of configurational languages. In these language the subject occupies a distinguished position outside the maximal projection of V, i.e., outside of VP. In configurational languages this position is obligatorily present. The reason for that will be discussed below.

(7) $[_{IP}$ NP $[_{I'}$ I VP $]]$

If the subject position is empty, this empty position is subject to the empty category principle (Chomsky 1981:300ff.), which requires empty categories to be properly governed. *Properly governed* means either *lexically governed* or *locally coindexed*. Since in the finite clause the subject position is governed by Infl, which is a nonlexical category, the empty category principle can be satisfied only via coindexing. It is by means of coindexing that it is satisfied in a pro-drop-language. Infl is pronominal, hence it qualifies as an A-binder of the empty subject position. It is coindexed with this position due to specifier-head-agreement. Since a pronominal Infl requires a thematic role, a pro-drop configuration is ungrammatical if there is no thematic role for the subject. In this case Infl cannot be pronominal, since it would violate the theta-criterion. But a non-pronominal Infl does not antecedent-govern the subject position. Italian could have impersonal passives only if it had an overt expletive, like French.

(8) Il sera parlé de vous par tout le monde

Italian, however, does not have overt subject expletives. In general, it has to be predicted that pro-drop-languages with obligatory subject positions will lack impersonal constructions. Investigations in Slavic languages in this respect would be desirable. Having dismissed the possibility of an expletive pro, the Germanic data must be re-evaluated.

3.1 Missing subjects in Germanic languages

The basic facts are presented in Platzack's (1985,1987) pioneering studies of this matter. He emphasized a crucial difference among the Scandinavian languages. The mainland languages obligatorily require an expletive in presentational constructions, with weather verbs, in impersonal passives, and with extraposition. (9) presents the respective examples from Swedish:

(9) a. Idag har *(det) kommit många lingvister hit
         today have there arrived many linguists here
     b. Regnade *(det) i går?
         Rained there yesterday
     c. Dansades *(det) på skeppet?
         Was there danced on the ship

    d. Nu är *(det) uppenbart att John har slagit Maria
       Now is there clear that John has beaten Maria

The insular languages Icelandic and Faroese, however, do not need an expletive in these constructions. The respective examples of Icelandic are presented in (10):

(10) a. Í dag hafa — komið - margir málvísindamenn hingað
      b. Rigndi — í gær?
      c. Var — dansað?
      d. Nu er — augljóst að - Jón hefur barið Maríu

From the fact that a subject does not occur with weather verbs, i.e., verbs with non-referential quasi thematic roles, we might conclude that Icelandic is a restricted pro-drop language, i.e., a language where pronominal Infl cannot be referential. Rizzi (1982:143) refers to the dialect of Padua, where the null subject cannot have the interpretation of a definite pronoun:

(11) a. piove - rains (it rains)
      b. *(el) vien - *(he) comes

Icelandic differs from a pro-drop language, however, allowing subjectless passives (10c).

    The main differences between mainland and insular Scandinavian languages are the following two: The insular languages have a rich system of morphological Case marking. This property they share with German. Secondly, the mainland languages do not have subject-verb agreement. The basic verb object word order and the verb-second property is common for all Scandinavian languages. Platzack (1987) bases his account on the latter difference, assuming that subject-verb agreement is the crucial difference in terms of his expletive pro account. Having dismissed the theoretical concept of an expletive pro, I will present an analysis capitalizing on the difference in the Case systems, a system with morphologically differentiated Cases on the one hand and a non-morphological system on the other.

    In Haider (1987a, 1987c) I suggested that the so-called configurationality parameter should be deduced from a parametric option in instantiating the system of abstract Case.[2] Given that Case is the means for identifying the arguments for thematic role assignment, there are two different modes of implementing this identification system, a morphological mode and a structural one. In the first mode an argument turns out as uniquely identifiable in terms of morphological marking (e.g., Case affixes or particles), in the second mode an argument is identified in terms of its unique structural position. The structurally unique position for the external argument is the specifier position of IP and it is obligatory only in systems of the structural mode, since these systems require an A-position outside the verbal projection for identifying the external argument. In morphological systems, however, the external argument is identified by its specific Case, which is morphologically realized as nominative.

If this line of reasoning is on the right track, we do not expect an obligatory specifier positions of IP in languages with morphological Case systems. For our present concern this includes Icelandic, Faroese and German. In an object-verb language like German it is not so easy to demonstrate that there is no obligatorily filled subject position as it is in an verb-object language like Icelandic. Thráinsson (1986:173) states explicitly that the position preceding Infl is optional in Icelandic:

(12) Hann sagði að [*hefðu* þeir þá komið að stórum helli og ...]
      He said that [*had* they then come to a big cave and ...]
      'He said that they had then come to a big cave and ...'

In (12) the subject has not been fronted from its VP-internal position to the specifier position of IP. I assume, following Kitagawa (1986) and others that the D-structure subject position is VP-internal and that in configurational languages the subject raises to the specifier of IP. Moreover, this position is not reserved for nominative NPs. Interestingly, however, an NP in the specifier position of IP qualifies as a subject, irrespective of its Case (cf. Zaenen - Maling - Thráinsson 1985). This phenomenon is not observed in German, as they note. What might be the grammatical reason for this difference? In Icelandic, as in any verb-object language, raising to the specifier of IP, crossing Infl, is never string-vacuous; in German and Dutch, however, it is. Following the least-effort approach indicated above, we expect that there is no string vacuous movement (cf. also Chomsky 1986: ch.9). What we expect to find in this situation is a matching projection, an option described in detail in Haider (1987b): An empty projection is superimposed on a subjacent, homomorphous projection. In our case this results in an I-Projection superimposed on a V-projection, and consequently a specifier position of IP superimposed on the VP-internal subject position, i.e., the [NP,VP]-position. This property distinguishes Dutch from the mainland Scandinavian languages and German from Icelandic, respectively. German does not produce non-nominative subjects and Dutch does not require expletive elements to the extent required in Danish, Swedish or Norwegian:

(13) a. Vandaag zijn (er) veel linguisten aangekomen (cf. 9a)
  b. Wordt *(er) gedanst? (cf. 9c)
  c. Nu is (het) duidelijk dat Jan Maria geslagen heeft (cf. 9d)

In (13a) the VP-internal and the external subject position coincide, hence there is no empty category principle violation. In (13c), the subject position is both governed by V and antecedent-governed by the extraposed subject clause. It seems that both requirements have to be fullfilled, i.e., antecedent government presupposes lexical government (cf. Rizzi 1988 for independent arguments). The interesting case is (13b). Before entering into a theoretical argument on the status of impersonal passives, the data have to be clarified in more detail. Den Besten (1980:73) as well as Bennis (1987: 217) describe *er* as being obligatory in constructions like (13a). Den Besten presents the following set of data:

(14) a. Vanaf morgen wordt *(er) niet meer gewerkt
    From tomorrow is *(there) not anymore worked
  b. Toch werd *(er) gelachen
    Still was *(there) laughed
  c. In dit stadion wordt (?er) gevoetbald
    In this stadium is (?there played-soccer

Bennis (1987:217) notes that *er* can be replaced by a PP. If one checks the examples he and others (cf. Koster 1987; Hoekstra 1984) give, it is a locative PP.

(15) dat op het schip wordt gedanst
    that on the ship is danced

I think it is misleading to use examples like (15) as evidence for the claim that an expletive subject is optional in Dutch. Dutch is like English in this respect. The expletive element is a locative adverbial like the English *there* and, as in English, it can be replaced by a full locative PP (cf. 16a to 16c taken from Bolinger 1977):

(16) a. Across the street (there) is a grocery
      b. Down the mountain (?there) thundered a foaming stream
      c. In this cave (there) dwells a horrible monster
      d. Across my windowsill seemed to walk a whole army of ants
      e. *At the party was danced

(16d), an example noted by Bresnan, shows that PPs behave like *there* also under raising. What these examples show is that the function of *there* can be fulfilled by a full PP as well. Hence the absence of *there* should not be misinterpreted as a null-subject option. Therefore the crucial cases are (14a), (14b) and (16e). The difference between Dutch and English with respect to (17) follows from an independent difference, namely the verb-second property.

(17) a. dat er wordt gedanst
      b. *that there was danced

English has a weak Infl, which is reflected in the lack of V-to-I movement (cf. Chomsky 1988). Weak Infl needs an NP to be coindexed with in order to receive the relevant agreement features. Neither *there* nor a PP can provide the necessary nominal agreement features. Let us turn now to the question why the VP-internal subject position, on which the specifier position of IP is superimposed, cannot be left empty in structures like (13b). In the matching-projection structure, the specifier position of IP coincides with the VP-internal subject position. Hence, it is in the m-government range of V, and therefore structurally governed. Nevertheless, a gap leads to ungrammaticality. This indicates that the empty category principle operates on a stricter government requirement than structural government. What seems to be relevant is proper government in the sense of theta-government or antecedent government, as proposed by Chomsky (1986:88). In (16e), the subject gap is neither antecedent governed, nor theta-governed, because there is no theta-role to be assigned, and no sisterhood relation to a thematic role assigner. Having accounted for the obligatory status of the expletive in (16e) as a means of escaping the empty category principle, we have to explain how this condition is met in (13a) if there is no expletive present, or, in other words, why the expletive is optional. The expletive may occur because there is a structural position, the subject position, available. If this position is left empty, however, it is coindexed with the ergative subject for the following reason. First, there is obligatory specifier-head-agreement between Infl and the subject. Secondly, there is the agreement index shared by Infl and the nominative NP in the object position. Since this is the same kind of index as the index shared by specifier and head, the two indexations cannot be disjoint. Hence, by transitivity, the nominative NP ends up with the same index as the empty subject position. The nominative NP, however, m-commands this position, hence, m-governs it. Therefore, the nominative NP functions as the antecedent governor of the subject position.[3] This kind of antecedent government is possible only in matching projection structures. In a normal projection the VP-internal position cannot m-command the specifier position of IP.

To sum up: Dutch, as a language with a structural mode of thematic role assignment, has an obligatory subject position, on a par with the mainland Scandinavian languages. The differences, however, arise from the different directionality of government, i.e. object-verb vs. verb-object. Since object-verb patterns lead to string-vacuous movements, hence to matching projections, Dutch does not require expletives with extraposition (cf. 13c) or ergative subjects (cf. 13a).[4]

Expletive elements are licensed, however, since there is an obligatory structural subject position. This is the crucial difference between German and Dutch. For independent evidence I refer to Haider (1987c). For our present concern this difference is responsible for the ungrammaticality of a clause internal expletive subject in German (18d) to (18f) or in Icelandic (18g) to (18i) in the following examples:

(18) a. Er werd gisteren gedanst
 b. Gisteren werd *er* gedanst
 c. ??Gisteren werd gedanst
 d. Es wurde gestern getanzt
 e. *Gestern wurde *es* getanzt
 f. Gestern wurde getanzt
 g. þad var dansað í gaer

h. * Í gaer var það dansað
i. Í gaer var dansað   *(cf. Zaenen - Maling - Thráinsson 1985:445)*

The expletive may occur only in the Specifier of CP position, a structurally licensed topic position. It is a general property of German, which is left unaccounted for in recent investigations (cf. Grewendorf 1986), that clause internal expletive subjects are ungrammatical with passive and with presentative constructions, too:

(19) a. *Es* steht ein Mann vor der Tür
       there stands a man at the door
    b. *Vor der Tür steht *es* ein Mann
       at the door there stands a man
    c. Vor der Tür steht ein Mann

If there were an obligatory structural subject postion in German, the expletive should be licensed both in the specifier of CP, the topic-position and in the specifier of IP, the subject-position, according to the common analyses of German sentence structure.[5]

4. Towards an unrestricted empty category principle

After having raised empirical as well as theoretical issues against the concept of an expletive pronominal empty element, we have to ask now how to exclude this element from the system of universal grammar. Obviously, this element is consistent with the currently adopted system. Hence we have to seek a principled reason which excludes empty expletives, and show that this move is empirically well-supported. What I want to suggest is that the principled reason is embodied already in the system of universal grammmar, but camouflaged and blocked by a stipulative constraint. The principle is the empty category principle and the stipulative constraint is the restriction that the empty category principle should apply only to a subset of empty categories. Dropping this restriction will result in a maximally general wellformedness constraint on the distribution of empty categories on the one hand and a better empirical coverage on the other hand. Let us compare once more a wellformed pro-environment with an illformed one:

(20) a. *[*e* [è [stato ballato]]]
        has been danced
  b. [*e* [è [stato letto]]]
      (it) has been read

In both structures there is an empty specifier position of IP. Given that this position is subject to the empty category principle, we have to identify the crucial difference between (20a) and (20b), which turns (20b) into a wellformed structure with respect to the empty category principle. The difference is the thematic status of Infl. In (20b), Infl receives the thematic role of the passive subject - this is the pro-drop quality, i.e., the ability of Infl to act as the target of thematic role assignment - and is turned into a pronominal element. It seems a natural assumption that Infl is not pronominal per se but only if it actually represents a theta-bearing element. This follows from the theta-criterion. The pro-drop quality is the capacity of Infl to bear a thematic role and not a kind of absolute status of Infl as pronominal. If only an Infl that is assigned a thematic role thereby gains its pronominal status, it becomes evident why (20a) but not (20b) is ruled out by the empty category principle. A pronominal can act as antecedent for the empty subject position, hence as an antecedent governor that satisfies the empty category principle. Infl bears the thematic role for this position and it is coindexed with the specifier of IP due to specifier-head-agreement (cf. Chomsky 1986). This derivative coindexation relation plus thematic antecedenthood turns (20b) into a structure that would have arisen if a clitic subject had been cliticized to Infl, an intuition behind various treatments of the null-subject-property (cf. Rizzi 1982:130).

(21) [*e*$_i$ [è$_i$ [stato letto]]]

In (21), the structure of (20b), a pronominal Infl acts as an antecedent governor. (22a) is ill-formed, because Infl, not being pronominal, is neither a suitable antecedent governor nor, since it is not lexical, a proper structural governor for the empty subject position.

Having accounted for pro, we have to rethink the government status of PRO. Chomsky (1981) claims that PRO must be ungoverned in structural terms, an assumption challenged by Burzio (1987). What is crucial for our concerns, however, is antecedent government. In order to get a coherent account for empty categories, we have to show that the treatment of pro can be generalized in a way that covers PRO as well.[6] It is worth emphasizing that the pattern of pro-drop constructions exemplified by (20) holds for PRO-construction in general, i.e., not only in pro-drop languages:

(22) a. die Möglichkeit   [zu tanzen]
        the possibility   [to dance]
    b. *die Möglichkeit   [getanzt zu werden]
        the possibility   [to be danced]

In (22a), unlike (22b), there is a thematic role for PRO. This pattern is representative for any language with infinitival control clauses. The grammaticality patterns are the same for the corresponding pro-constructions, (23a) and (23b), respectively.

(23) a. balla
        (he/she) dances
    b. *è stato ballatto

A generalization would be missed, if there were no uniform account for the ungrammaticality of a non-theta-marked pronominal empty category. The generalization can be captured by extending the account suggested for pro, namely the requirement that the alleged pro is, rather, an empty subject position antecedent governed by a pronominal [+AGR]-Infl. Consequently, PRO must be an empty category which is antecedent governed by a pronominal [-AGR]-Infl. The unifiying concept is the retention of the subject thematic role by a pronominal Infl. The universal pronominal nature of [-AGR]-Infl should be seen as a consequence of the correlation between Case marking and thematic role assignment. If Case is the visibility criterion for thematic role assignment (cf. Chomsky 1981), the subject position of the infinitive will receive no thematic role if it does not receive Case; hence the thematic role will stay with Infl.[7] In the case of [+AGR]-Infl, the retention is subject to parametric variation, because the subject could receive Case.

There remains, however, a final problem for this account. It was claimed above that a language with a morphological system, e.g. German, does not have a subject-position unless there is a thematic role to license one. If our account for the difference in (22) rested only on an empty category principle requirement for the empty subject position, we would expect that (22b) would be on a par with (24), which is grammatical:

(24) die Möglichkeit [daß getanzt wird]
     the possibility   that danced is

This shows that the ungrammaticality of infinitival clauses without a thematic subject cannot depend primarily on the empty category principle. If there is no subject position in (24), there cannot be one in (23b) either. The ungrammaticality of infinitival clauses without a thematic role for the subject must have an independent reason. This reason is to be found in the feature-matrix represented by Infl. Under standard assumptions, Infl bears the tense and agreement features and, under appropriate parametrization, the theta-features of the subject. There is a natural assumption which accounts for the universal ungrammaticality of infinitival clauses with a non-thematic subject, namely a constraint against unspecified heads. (26) presents the four logically possible combinations of Infl-features:

(25) Specified head constraint: Heads are specified

(26)   AGR   T-related[8]
     a.   +   +   finite with subject or pro-drop
     b.   –   +   infinitival, i.e "PRO-drop"
     c.   +   –   finite without subject thematic role
     d.   –   –   * * *

The proposed constraint (25) against unspecified heads immediately rules out (26d). This constellation arises with infinitivals if there is no thematic role for the subject. Hence the ungrammaticality of this construction is independent of the presence or absence of a structural subject position.

If this line of reasoning is basically correct, a consequence crucial for the theory of empty categories arises: Any obligatory structural position is subject to the empty category principle, if it is empty. Furthermore there is no way to distinguish empty categories in terms of inherent properties. In other words, there is only one kind of emptiness. It is only the government status which determines the distribution of empty categories. Consider for

instance the distinction between PRO and an NP-trace in raising constructions. According to my proposal, there is nothing but an empty subject
position which is governed. If it is antecedent governed by Infl, we shall
call it PRO, and if not, we shall call it trace, because in this situation, in
order to be wellformed, there must be another governor and another
antecedent.

5. Summary

This paper tries to substantiate the claim that an analysis of missing subjects
in some Germanic languages based on the optional status of specifier of IP
in correlation with the system of Case marking is superior to an analysis in
terms of an expletive empty category. The latter analysis is at variance with
the facts of genuine pro-drop languages. In particular, I argued for the
following model:
1. There is no "expletive emptiness" (but cf. the claim to the opposite in
   Cardinaletti 1990: 141 ff.).
2. Empty categories do not have inherent properties.
3. The restriction on infinitival subjects is independent of a specifier
   position of IP.
4. Any empty category is subject to the empty category principle.

Notes

1   I am indebted to Werner Frey, Richard Kayne and Christer Platzack for helpful
        comments.
2.   A similar account is suggested by Kiss (1988).
3.   A similar constellation i.e., the antecedent lower in the tree than the gap, arises
        also in adjunction structures, e.g. with postverbal subjects in Italian.
4.   As for constructions with both subject and *er*, Bennis (1987:214) claims that
        there is a semantic difference:

a. dat een jongen werkt
that a boy works
b. dat er een jongen werkt

According to Bennis, the subject receives a generic interpretation in (a), but an indefinite one in (b). This alternation is remarkable in two respects. First it shows that even an unergative subject may stay inside the VP. That VP is no barrier for nominative Case assignment in Dutch is communis opinio. Clear cases are ergative contexts. Secondly, judging the alternation in (18) from the least effort perspective, we expect that the alternation is not arbitrary. The appearance of *er* should be a cost-factor.

5.   I, in contradistinction to others, assume that the C-projection and the I-projection are non-distinct in German: C hosts the I features.

6.   This is the explicit aim of Borer (1988).

7.   I assume, like Belletti - Rizzi (1986), that the thematic role for the subject is assigned by Infl, which receives it from the verb it is coindexed with.

8.   "T-related" covers both cases, namely the case that Infl is assigned the thematic role and the case that Infl is coindexed with an argument.

References

Adams, Marianne
   1987   "From Old French to the theory of pro-drop", *Natural Language and Linguistic Theory* 5: 1-32

Bennis, Hans
   1987   *Gaps and dummies* (Dordrecht: Foris).

Belletti, Adriana - Luigi Rizzi
   1986   "Psych-verbs and theta-theory", *Lexicon Project Working Papers* 13 (Cambridge, Mass.: MIT).

Bolinger, Dwight
   1977   *Meaning and form* (London: Longman).

Borer, Hagit
   1988   "Anaphoric AGR" (Irvine: unpublished manuscript UC at Irvine).

Burzio, Luigi
   1987   "The legacy of the PRO-theorem" (Cambridge, Mass.: unpublished manuscript Harvard University).

Cardinaletti, Anna
1990   "Es, pro and sentential arguments in German", *Linguistische Berichte* 126: 135-164

Chomsky, Noam
1981   *Lectures on government and binding* (Dordrecht: Foris).
1982   *Some concepts and consequences of the theory of government and binding* (Cambridge, Mass.: MIT-Press).
1986a   *Barriers* (Cambridge, Mass.: MIT-Press).
1986b   *Knowledge of language: Its nature, origin, and use* (London: Praeger).
1988   "Prospects for the study of language and mind" (Cambridge, Mass.: unpublished manuscript MIT).

Den Besten, Hans
1980   "A case filter for passives", *Theory of markedness in generative grammar*, edited by Adriana Belletti - Luciana Brandi - Luigi Rizzi (Pisa: Scuola Normale Superiore di Pisa).

Grewendorf, Günther
1986   "Ergativität im Deutschen" (Frankfurt/M: unpublished manuscript university of Frankfurt). See also: 1989, *Ergativity in German* (Dordrecht: Foris).

Haider, Hubert
1987a   "Theta-tracking systems - evidence from German", *Configurationality*, edited by Pieter Muysken - László Marácz (Dordrecht: Foris).
1987b   "Matching projections", *Constituent structure*, edited by Anna Cardinaletti - Guglielmo Cinque - Giuliana Giusti (Dordrecht: Foris).
1987c   *Deutsche Syntax, generativ - Parameter der deutschen Syntax* (Tübingen: Gunter Narr).

Hoekstra, Teun
1984   *Transitivity - Grammatical relations in government-binding theory* (Dordrecht: Foris).

Kiss, É. Katalin
1988   "Eliminating the configurationality parameter" (Budapest: unpublished manuscript Hungarian Academy of Sciences).

Kitagawa, Yoshihisa
1986   *Subject in Japanese and English*, doctoral dissertation (Amherst: University of Massachusetts).

Koster, Jan
1986   "The relation between pro-drop, scrambling and verb movement", *Groningen Papers in Theoretical and Applied Linguistics* 1
1987   *Domains and dynasties* (Dordrecht: Foris).

Platzack, Christer
  1985   "The Scandinavian languages and the null subject parameter", *Working Papers in Scandinavian Syntax* 20
  1987   "The Scandinavian languages and the null-subject parameter", *Natural Language and Linguistic Theory* 5: 377-401

Rizzi, Luigi
  1982   *Issues in Italian syntax* (Dordrecht: Foris).
  1986   "Null objects in Italian and the theory of pro", *Linguistic Inquiry* 17: 501-557
  1988   "Relativized minimality" (Geneva: unpublished manuscript university of Geneva).

Thráinsson, Höskuldur
  1986   "V1, V2, V3 in Icelandic", *Verb second phenomena in Germanic languages*, edited by Hubert Haider - Martin Prinzhorn (Dordrecht: Foris).

Zaenen, Annie - Joan Maling - Höskuldur Thráinsson
  1985   "Case and grammatical functions: the Icelandic passive", *Natural Language and Linguistic Theory* 3: 441 - 483

The phrasal nature of double object clusters[1]

Lars Hellan

By a double object construction we understand a sequence like *give Mary a book*, where *Mary* is the indirect object (IO), *a book* the direct object (DO), and the sub-sequence *Mary a book* a double object cluster. We will argue that in Norwegian, and generalizing to the other Scandinavian languages and English, indirect object and direct object together form a phrasal constituent, with the direct object as its head.

Analyses of double object constructions classically relate to at least the following theoretical parameters: 1) Whether the construction is derived or not, the underlying structure in question being usually the sequence "NP PP", where NP corresponds to the direct object and the PP to the indirect object (as in *John gave a book to Mary*) (but for a more complex derivational history, see Larson 1988). Our analysis is strictly non-derivational. 2) Constituency of the construction (whether it results from a derivation or not). The main possibilities can be classified roughly as a flat structure, as shown in (1a) (the default analysis, given that VP is a well motivated constituent), a left-branching structure, as shown in (1b) (proposed in Stowell 1981), and a right-branching structure. Our analysis falls within the latter group; here also belongs a proposal, distinct from ours, by Kayne (1984: Introduction), shown in (1c):

(1) a.

b.

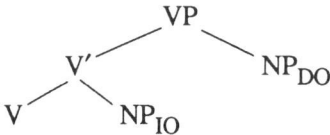

c.

```
                   _____ VP _____
              ____/       |       \_____
           V            PP              NP_DO
                    ____/  \____
                 [e]_P          NP
```

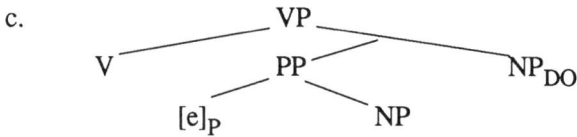

The empty preposition in (c) assigns Case and a thematic role to the first NP; the category of the node dominating PP and NP_{DO} is left partly open.[2] The main motivation for this structure is to provide an unambiguous path for government from the V to the direct object. As will be seen in section 2, a similar concern forms part of the motivation for the present analysis.

Our analysis can be displayed as in (2a), with the subpart (2b) being the phrasal representation of the double object cluster:

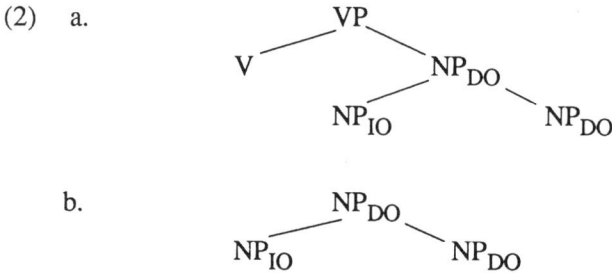

(2)   a.

```
              _____ VP _____
           __/              \__ NP_DO
        V     __/            \__
           NP_IO               NP_DO
```

b.

```
              _____ NP_DO _____
           __/                  \__
        NP_IO                     NP_DO
```

Throughout the whole paper, when we refer to a constituent as "direct object", it is always the daughter NP_{DO} in (2b) we have in mind.

The analysis of an NP with an NP as head may superficially resemble the possible analysis "[NP S]$_{NP}$" of relative clause constructions; contrary to that case, however, the constituents of a double object cluster have distinct argument functions, since they carry distinct thematic roles relative to the same verb. With regard to this property, we call the configuration (2b) a group: this is a phrase whose constituent parts have independent argument functions within the same argument complex.

The constellation [YP XP]$_{XP}$ is otherwise one which may arise via adjunction processes tied to movement (although X=N in this case is not the typical instantiation, and definitely not when the NP is an argument; cf. Chomsky 1986), but the constellation (2) is base generated. The analysis thus lacks clear precedents; what comes closest is presumably the "small clause" analysis of constructions like *make Mary sick*, according to which

Mary sick forms a constituent; we comment on the relation between these constructions in section 6.

There are two types of circumstances which motivate the structure in (2). The first type resides in a typical attribute-like behavior of the indirect object vis à vis the direct object, as one finds it in standard endocentric constructions. The second resides in the circumstance that for various processes, the direct object acts as if it is the only NP in the double object sequence which is grammatically "visible" to the processes; this resembles the way in which the head of a standard phrase determines the behavior of the phrase with regard to the environment. We will treat these types in turn throughout sections 1 to 3, with additional evidence in section 4. Assumptions concerning such notions as "govern" and "license" are also spelled out in these sections. Section 5 presents speculations of parametric and typological nature arising from the analysis, and section 6 considers the relation between double object groups and small clauses. On the whole, the background theory of the analysis is a rather functionally and thematically geared version of government binding theory, along the lines of Hellan 1988; nevertheless, the proposal of this paper defines an entity of a highly structural nature.

1. Attribute-like behavior of the indirect object

In a double object construction one can typically remove the indirect object without removing the direct object, but not conversely (this holds also in English):[3]

(3) a. Vi ga   Peter en bok
         we gave Peter a book
     b. Vi ga   en bok
         we gave   a book
     c. *Vi ga   Peter
         we gave Peter
     d. Vi ga   (av fullt hjerte)
         we gave (of full heart)

(In [c], *Peter* is to be interpreted as the benefactive of the act, not as the theme.)

This situation is what one typically finds in endocentric structures, the paradigm case of phrases, where the head is the thing which cannot be removed alone (cf. the impossibility of omitting *big* from *very big*). This regularity may be formulated in the principle (4):

(4)   The head of a projection cannot be omitted.

In "omit", we do not include movement, or deletion under identity, or any other type of recoverable absence.

Given (4), the structure (2) yields the right predictions for the typical paradigm in (3). In contrast, none of the structures in (1) seem capable of contributing to an explanation. For (1c), a possibility might be seen to reside in the status of the indirect object as a PP, which is often an optional category; a similar possibility might be seen in the derivational approach, given a base structure where, as is often the case, the direct object corresponds to an obligatory NP and the indirect object to an optional PP. However, in this type of structure, a possibility is still to omit the direct object in certain cases but retain the PP; thus, (5a) is possible, just as (3d) is. The question is then how to prevent (5b) - it cannot be done by resort to the general optionality of the PP.

(5)   a. Vi ga   til de fattige
          we gave to the poor
      b. *Vi ga   de fattige
          we gave the poor

A similar point applies to (1c). Conceivably one might propose that the "promotion" of the PP to indirect object cannot take place unless a direct object is present. But this would be a sheer stipulation, prompting anew the question why the direct object has such a special status, and (2) then offers itself once more as a possible solution. Thus, at least within the range of alternatives surveyed here, the analysis involving (2) seems clearly preferable.

2. Government of the direct object

2.1. The direct object as the unique governee of the verb

We assume that in the double object cluster, only the direct object is governed by the verb. One part of this assumption, that the direct object is governed, comes from a cross-linguistic consideration. In languages with morphological Case, the common view, which we adopt, is that accusative is the default Case of a verb governee, and by this criterion, the direct object emerges as a verb governee in these languages. Norwegian and English having no morphological distinction between accusative and oblique Cases, in deciding which NP is the governee in these languages we extrapolate from Case languages such as German and Icelandic, and thus obtain the result that the direct object is a verb governee also in Norwegian and English.

The second part of the assumption is that only one NP is a governee. This we base on a theoretical consideration. Government, we assume, is functionally a tool in the service of theta-role assignment. It is important that thematic roles be assigned in a non-ambiguous way. To some extent, it is possible to associate particular grammatical markers (like Case, preposition and position) with particular roles, but in many instances the best way of indicating which role is in question is by simply pointing to the verb of whose content the role is a part. The status as governee signals that the role of an NP is to be inferred by "looking at the verb". Clearly, for such a procedure to be functionally viable, there cannot be many NPs whose role is identified in that way. At most there could, presumably, be two, if there is a clear-cut way for the two to share the candidate roles between them. It may be assumed that in many languages, Norwegian and English included, there are in effect two such NPs (see 5.3. for languages where there is possibly only one), the external argument (subject) and the governee, the theta-role associated with the former being systematically higher on a theta-role hierarchy than the role associated with the latter. But in such a situation, there is clearly no room for both indirect object and direct object to serve as governees. Consequently, only the direct object can be assumed to have governee status.

This position may seem to conflict with another common assumption concerning government, namely that governor and governee be adjacent: V and direct object certainly are not adjacent when an indirect object intervenes. However, if the adjacency restriction were to be given up, the question is how the verb goes about determining exactly which NP it governs.

However, according to the present analysis, V simply governs indiscriminately the first NP to its right, and thus in accordance with the adjacency requirement. When the verb has a double object cluster to its right, this cluster is perceived as a single NP, namely the dominating NP in (2). It is then the head status of the direct object within this cluster which accounts for why the direct object is the NP which comes to carry the status as governee, through head projection percolation of properties.

This answer presupposes that the verb by necessity relates only to the dominating NP in (2) in its search for a governee. This means that we are presupposing the effect of the "A-over-A-principle" of Chomsky (1964). As was shown among others by Ross (1967), this is far from being an exceptionless principle, and we return in 3.2. to one of the delimitations which must be imposed on its application.

By this analysis, no specific instructions concerning the "routing" of government from a verb are necessary to guarantee that only the direct object is governed: this is obtained through the adjacency requirement on government, whereby a verb picks the unique closest NP as governee, in conjunction with the general structural configuration (2), and A-over-A.

2.2. The status of the indirect object and conditions on licensing

A question may now be raised concerning the status of the indirect object: if one assumes, in accordance with the standard government binding view, that an NP must have abstract Case in order to count as legitimate, and Case is assigned only via government, how then are occurrences of indirect objects in general to be licensed? Our answer is to reject these assumptions: it is necessary that an NP be licensed, but since abstract Case is essentially just a marking of licensedhood, we prefer to omit the notion of abstract Case and talk in terms of licensing directly. Licensing of an NP, now, essentially resides in the circumstance that the NP is assigned a theta-role in an unambiguous way. We have already said that government is one way of implementing this, hence government serves as licensing; but other devices of unambiguous theta-marking serve as well. The indirect object is a case in point: by its specific position (the one in [2]) in languages like Norwegian and English, it encodes a particular theta-role, viz. that of benefactive (or malefactive), and it is by thus serving as a grammatical mark of a specific theta-role that an indirect object gets licensed. The licensing of the indirect object in (2) is thereby ensured. (A similar role is played by dative Case in a language like German.)

2.3. Comparison with other approaches

First consider the analysis proposed by Kayne 1984, represented by (1c). Although it too has government going from the verb to the direct object along an unambiguous path, independently of actual adjacency between verb and direct object, the difference from the present analysis is still clear: the present analysis in principle requires linear adjacency for government, contrary to Kayne's analysis, and the "path"-like transmittance route of government in the double object construction in our analysis is due only to the phrasal nature of the double object cluster, whereas in Kayne's approach, such transmittance is less tightly restricted.[4]

The use of an empty preposition governing the indirect object in (1c) otherwise does much of the work done by structure on the account just given, but we regard it as preferable to avoid empty prepositions as long as they are not bound. (1a) definitely cannot yield results like the present analysis.

On (1b), the "left branching" analysis, the governing force of the verb could conceivably be "withheld" until V'-level, and the government relation would then obtain under adjacency. With the constellation in (1b), it might be technically possible to hold that both indirect object and direct object are governed here, the indirect object by V and the direct object by V', both relations observing adjacency and both being unique with regard to the governor. This might seem desirable insofar as the indirect object would now get Case, in a theory requiring that it does. What technically looks like obedience of the uniqueness condition on government in this analysis, however, is illusory in our view, since there is still only one verb, and so, by the functional rationale for why government should be unique, there should be just one governee altogether, and just one governor. Preferably the latter should be V, of course, rather than V', so the analysis (1b) does not seem very desirable either.

Looking at the endocentricity phenomenon and government together, what favors our analysis is that exactly the same mechanism serves in the accounts of both of them; this contrasts with the approaches represented under (1).

At this point, mention should also be made of the analysis proposed in Larson (1988). At the final derivational stage according to this analysis, the direct object is represented as an adjunct, somewhat analogous to a demoted agent-NP in passives, and the indirect object is the governee of the verb. This conflicts with some expectations concerning adjuncts in Norwegian: they generally do not become passive subjects, whereas direct objects do, even in the presence of an indirect object (cf. [8b] below), and they do not allow *hva for*-extraction, as direct objects do (cf. 4.1. below); it is also uncertain how the direct object-properties mentioned in 3.1. and 3.2. below can be made to follow if direct objects are analyzed as adjunct-like. Larson's analysis, if transferred to Norwegian, also falsely predicts (8b) below to be impossible, for reasons related to the adjunct status of direct objects. How critical these points are to Larson's full analysis, though, is a matter it would lead too far to discuss here.

3. Processes applying to direct objects

3.1. The indefiniteness requirement

In presentational constructions in Norwegian there is a requirement on the NP in direct object position (if there is one) that it be indefinite; for an NP in indirect object position, there is no such condition. (6) illustrates this:

(6) a. Det ventet   Jon en overraskelse /*overraskelsen
        there awaited   Jon a surprise   / the surprise
     b. Det ble gitt Jon et stort ansvar   /*ansvaret
        there was given Jon a   great responsibility /the responsibility

The question concerning us here is why it is the direct object rather than the indirect object which becomes subject to the indefiniteness requirement (the question why there is such a requirement at all remaining open). With the analysis developed above, it is possible to give a simple answer to this question, namely that the requirement applies to the immediately adjacent NP-node. The latter being the dominating NP-node in (2), the indefiniteness property percolates down to the head of the cluster, the direct object. Thus, the required indefiniteness and the governee status end up on the same NP in virtue of the configuration (2), and no extra procedure is needed for differentiating between indirect object and direct object. (The rule in question might alternatively refer to the "maximal" governee of the verb, with equivalent result.)

3.2. "Ergative" promotion

In Norwegian, if an active presentational construction has an NP in the direct object position, there is usually an alternative construction with exactly the same meaning where this NP occurs as subject; when the NP is non-agentive, this construction falls within the class of what is commonly called "ergative" constructions (cf. Burzio 1986). An interesting restriction on this alternation is that when the verb has both an indirect object and a direct object, it is only the direct object which can be "promoted" in this meaning-preserving way. Thus, from (6a), we can only form (7a) with the same meaning:

(7) a. En overraskelse ventet   Jon
        a   surprise   awaited Jon
     b. Jon vented   en overraskelse
        Jon expected a   surprise

Leaving most aspects of the "ergativity" phenomenon open, it seems clear that to account for this restriction, the configuration (2) can be invoked again, once we take the presentational form as basic. Given a rule to the effect that the promovee status is assigned to the NP adjacent to the verb (or to the "maximal" governee), by a reasoning parallel to that which was presented in the preceding section, the choice of promovee then falls on the direct object, without any specific instruction needed to pick out this NP rather than the indirect object.

Two comments are in order here. The first concerns the relation between this promotion and the kind of promotion found in passive constructions. In the latter, not only direct objects, but also indirect objects and NPs governed by a preposition can become subjects, as illustrated in (8) (in [a] with an indirect object, in [b] with a direct object, and in [c] with the governee of *om* promoted):[5]

(8) a. Jon ble gitt   en bok
       Jon was given a   book
    b. En bok ble gitt   Jon
       a   book was given Jon
    c. Jon ble snakket om
       Jon was talked   about

Clearly, the promovee in the passive construction is identified by different properties than the "ergative" promovee, the requirements for an NP to be passivized being (roughly) that it either have what may be called a central theta-role relative to the verb, or that it be governed by the verb (or both). The former requirement is fulfilled by all of (8), the latter by (8b) and constructions like *Jon ble sett gå* ("Jon was seen walk[ing]"). It is interesting that the two promotion processes, at least in Norwegian, must be kept distinct, and various questions pertain to how this should be done in the formal account; for our purposes, however, the important point to notice is that ergative promotion is a process distinct from passive movement, and that in ergative promotion the direct object has the privileged status.

3.3. Limitations on "A-over-A"

The second comment is as follows. In discussing the verb's choice of governee, we noted that this process must respect the A-over-A principle. In the account of why ergative promotion from a structure corresponding to (6a) can only produce (7a) and not (7b), on the other hand, it is essential that selection of the NP to be moved does not obey A-over-A - (9) is completely out:

(9)   *Jon en overraskelse ventet
      Jon a   surprise   awaited

This point applies in general: no rule can move a double object cluster as one constituent. Even topicalization, which moves almost any type of phrasal constituent in Norwegian, is blocked for the double object cluster:

(10) *Peter en gave vil vi ikke gi
     Peter a gift will we not give
     (we will not give Peter a gift)

One may conceive of various reasons why a construction like (10) is illformed. Our proposal is that a clausal construction necessarily expresses a predication, and that a predication requires a unique subject. (As predicational constructions we here count both "NP VP" and "XP C' "). Given that *Peter* and *en gave* are distinct referential expressions both occurring in the position of subject of the predication, the uniqueness condition is not met. The same explanation holds for (9). This, then, gives a possible account for why A-over-A is inoperative when it comes to selection of movable constituents: the uniqueness requirement on predication-subjects overrides A-over-A.

There are other respects in which access must be had to indirect object and direct object separately, rather than to the whole group. The main one is the association of theta-roles with NPs. A theta-role, like the status as subject of a predication, requires a unique referential function, hence a verb assigns theta-roles to indirect object and direct object separately.[6] Connected with this is the parameter of "obligatoriness" of the double object group, residing in the following three possibilities: that both the double object construction and the option with "NP PP" are available (as with verbs like *give*); that only the first option is available (as with *deny*); and that only the second option is available (as with *distribute*). The determining factors seem to reside largely in the role potential of the verb and the prepositions in question (see, e.g., Larson 1988 for proposals as to how these interact), so again, although the mechanisms needed for these phenomena may formally have to conflict with A-over-A, this has a principled basis: functional factors like those now mentioned take precedence over A-over-A.

4. Corroborating evidence

Having presented the main motivation for the group analysis, we now turn to phenomena which support aspects of the approach we are following, even though not all of the phenomena are fully understood.

4.1. *Hva for*-extraction

The phenomenon of *hva for* (German: *was für*)-extraction removes the word *hva* from a phrase of the form "[hva for NP]", leaving the rest of the phrase behind. It is commonly assumed that such extraction is possible only when the "host" phrase receives some specific type of government (such as proper government), even if it is not obvious why this kind of restriction should hold. Interestingly now, *hva for*-extraction can apply to a direct object, but not to an indirect object:[7]

(11) a. Hva ga du barna   for noe?
         what gave you the children for something
         (= what did you give the children?)
     b. *Hva ga du for noe   mat?
         who gave you for something food
         (= what (IO)did you give food?)

In both (a) and (b) there is extraction from the NP *hva for noe*. If we assume that the host of a *hva for*-extraction requires government, the contrast in (11) follows straightforwardly from our analysis.

4.2. Wh-extraction in English

It is well known that English shows a contrast in ordinary wh-movement which exactly parallels the one in (11):

(12) a. What did you give Peter?
    b. *Whom did you give a book?

If the group-analysis is carried over to English, as we are assuming, and we require of a wh-trace that it be governed, then the contrast in (12) follows. A possible catch to this reasoning is that in Norwegian the counterparts of (12) are both wellformed:

(13) a. Hva ga   du Peter?
      what gave you Peter
    b. Hvem ga   du pengene?
      whom gave you the money

This, however, fits into a picture suggesting that, in general, Norwegian is milder in its enforcement of an empty category principle type restriction than English is. Thus, there seems to be no "that-trace" prohibition in Norwegian, as opposed to English; cf. (14):

(14) Hvem sa du at liker tran?
    who said you that likes cod liver oil
    (= who did you say that likes cod liver oil?)

Our conjecture is thus that the contrast from (12) is absent in (13) simply because Norwegian does not require a wh-trace to be governed. English does, and (12) therefore bears out the contrast predicted by our analysis.

    In order to have our analysis of (11) fit with this conjecture, we will have to distinguish between an NP-position which consists exclusively of a trace, and one which contains a trace bound from outside, as far as governmental requirements are concerned: in Norwegian, only the latter has to be governed.

4.3. Anaphors

Various authors, such as Barss and Lasnik (1986), Kiss (1987) and Larson (1988), have noticed that the indirect object has enough of a superiority status vis à vis the direct object to serve as a binder when the direct object is or contains an anaphor; examples are (15), generalizing also to Norwegian reciprocals and anaphors with *selv*:

(15) a. The therapist gave Mary herself.
　　 b. I gave them each other's books.

If we assume that such binding requires a c-command relation (in the first branching node-sense) between binder and bindee, then configurations like (1b) and (1c) are unable to account for these binding relationships. (As is well known, there are cases of anaphoric binding where the binder is located inside a PP, as in *I talked to Mary about herself*, but in such cases, the anaphor is also contained in a PP, so these cases do not comply with [1b] or [1c] either). Hence, among the constellations in (1), only (1a) is compatible with the facts in (15); but so is our analysis (2). Given the way (1a) fails in many of the other respects mentioned above, (15) then provides extra support for (2) vis à vis the other analyses.

We argue in Hellan (1988: chapter 3), that the structural relation c-command is only one of the licensing conditions on anaphora binding, role-command (the theta-role of the binder being higher than the role of the bindee or the NP containing it, on a theta-role hierarchy, given that these NPs belong to the same argument complex) being another condition (the same position is developed in Kiss 1987). If correct, this circumstance still does not make the above point irrelevant, since c-command (modulo the possibility of binding out of certain PPs) remains a necessary condition on anaphora binding.

5. Some parametric perspectives

5.1. Double object clusters in SOV languages

It might be speculated that a reason why languages like Norwegian and English have the double object group (i.e., the configuration [2]), is in order to obtain adjacency between V and the direct object in the presence of an indirect object. In SOV languages like German and Dutch, the direct object is always adjacent to V, and so, according to this speculation, one would expect the group to be absent in these languages[8]. Space prevents us from investigating this prediction, but it is among the more obvious points to follow up.

5.2. A parameter concerning "left attributes"

French and other Romance languages exhibit the following cluster of properties, all contrasting with Norwegian and other Germanic languages: French has no double object construction; it has postnominal attributes, and postnominal genitives (with a preposition). Under the group analysis, the idea suggests itself that all of the constituent types of indirect object, attributive adjectival phrase, and prenominal genitive, can be classified together under the notion "left attribute", and that the distinguishing parameter at work is whether the language in question takes left attributes or not.

How the notion "left attribute" should be more properly defined and incorporated into the formal theory is a question we will not pursue here, nor do we consider how clear-cut this clustering of properties is on a more general basis. The success of a parametric account in terms of "left attribute" will clearly in part have to be measured against proposals such as the one by Kayne (1984: chapter 9), a task we do not undertake here.[9]

5.3. An ergativity parameter

The constellation we have been considering is (16), with the typical associated Case and theta-roles marked (what we said about government signalling verb-dependent role status notwithstanding, we enter "theme" as the typical direct object-role, partly because this in itself is the least precise of the role-notions, partly since in a majority of cases, direct objects are classified under this notion):

(16)

```
                        VP
        V  _____/\
                        / \  NP_DO _
                      /           \
            NP_IO                   NP_DO
            dative                  accusative
            benefactive             theme
```

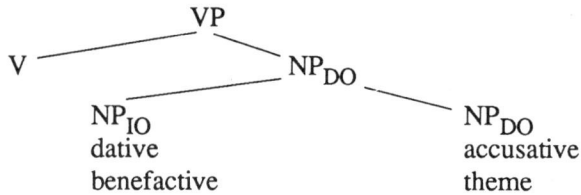

An important assumption in our analysis is that indirect object-status, either signalled by position or Case, expresses the benefactive/malefactive role. Now suppose that, instead, the NP called indirect object in (16) had the theta-role agent, and a Case specifically expressing agenthood, while otherwise the same government relations held as before. This would be exactly the constellation typically associated with ergative languages, with absolutive being the Case of the verb governee and ergative being the agentive Case:

(17)

```
                        VP
        V  _____/\
                        / \  NP_DO _
                      /           \
            NP_SU                   NP_DO
            ergative                absolutive
            agent                   theme
```

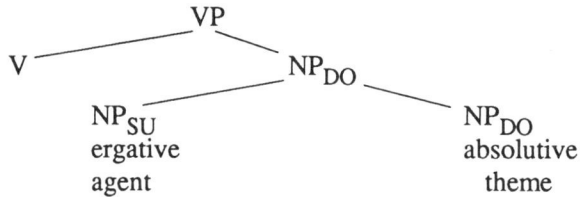

A usual conception of the standard ergative pattern is that the verb has two directly mediated arguments, an external argument and a governee, just like the nominative-accusative languages, the only difference being that when there is only one argument, in the ergative language this argument somehow selects the governee properties, whereas in the nominative-accusative Case it behaves as an external argument. The idea suggested here is that in ergative languages, there simply is no external argument. A typical way for an agent to be expressed is by serving as attribute in a group headed by the governee of the verb. The governee always having absolutive Case, this explains why this is the Case which prevails when there is only one NP.

Lack of external argument is in itself independent of the group constellation, but if the agent, in the lack of an external argument position, appears between V and its governee, then, by the reasoning in 5.1., the group may naturally be resorted to in order to obtain V-governee adjacency. Hence, on the idea that ergative languages lack an external argument, (17) is a configuration one expects to find. Another expected configuration will be an SOV pattern, where S is not an external argument, but acts analogously to a dative NP in a language like German, again with the ergative Case signalling agenthood. In accordance with the ideas from 5.1., no group properties need be manifest here. What we will not expect is an SVO order, since this is what presupposes most independence on the part of the subject, the kind which goes together with the status as external argument.

From a typological survey like that of Mallinson and Blake (1981: 144ff), it seems that these predictions may well turn out to be right. Among the languages listed as ergative, none are SVO; some are SOV (Avar and Abkhas of Northern Caucasian, Basque, Tibetan, Gurung, the Papuan language Enga, and Central Arctic Eskimo, to mention some), others VSO (all Polynesian languages, Jacaltec, Quiche, Squamish, to mention some). As for the "reducibility" of VSO pattern to SVO, as is rather commonly assumed for nominative-acccusative languages, this is clearly a rather theory-internal matter; but at least in the Polynesian languages, the verb is accompanied by a large cluster of elements for which movement from sentence-internal position seems very unlikely (cf. Chung 1978; Seiter 1980). Of course, whether group characteristics will also turn up in the way predicted is another question; see Wennevold (in press) for explorations.[10]

6. Double object groups and small clauses

Various authors have noted the apparent similarity between double object groups and small clause constructions, exemplified by *Mary sick* in *John made Mary sick*. We here address two possible hypotheses concerning the relationship between them.

6.1. Are double object clusters small clauses?

The idea has been suggested in Kayne (1984: chapter 7), and Herslund (1986) that double object clusters in some respect "are" small clauses. Structurally there is a similarity between the constructions in the shared superficial pattern "V NP XP", and semantically both may seem to express a predication with the NP as subject and the XP as an essential part of the predicate. More precisely, in small clauses the understood predicate is paraphrasable as "be XP", in double object constructions as "have XP".

There are various ways of formally construing this putative parallellism. One possibility is that syntactically the small clause is represented with an explicit marking of the predication relation, the same marking being present in the double object construction. Another possibility is that the predicational resemblance is explicitly represented only at an interpretive level. Facts about the Scandinavian *seg/sin*-reflexive suggest that the latter may be the most plausible route to take on this approach. Consider the contrast in (18), mentioned by Herslund:

(18) a. *Vi fortalte Peter om pengene sine
     we told Peter about money his (refl)
     (we told Peter about his money)
  b. ??Vi ga Peter pengene sine
     we gave Peter money his (refl)
     (we gave Peter his money)

One of the conditions on the use of *seg/sin* is that it be predication-commanded by its binder, that is, contained in a constituent which is predicated of the binder (cf. Hellan 1988). In (18a), no predication-command obtains between *Peter* and *sin*, so the construction is excluded, despite the c-command. In the superficially similar (18b), the reflexive is marginally possible, and Herslund suggests that this be attributed to the predication relation expressed in this construction.

It seems clear that the predication relation is more explicit in the small clause construction than in the double object cluster, as no verb "have" has to be interpolated to render the meaning.[11] At the outset, let us suppose that a formal representation of predication is included in the syntactic representation of small clauses. On Herslund's approach, the question is whether, on the basis of (18b), a formal representation of predication should be present also in the syntactic analysis of double object clusters. The contrast between (18b) and (19) suggests that the answer is no: this contrast could be accounted for by saying that the predication-command condition ideally be fulfilled in a structure where predication-command is syntactically represented; only in such cases are predication-governed phenomena fully acceptable. This is the case in (19), and the predication representation in (18b) being only at a semantic level, the contrast is then accounted for.

(19) Vi gjorde Peter glad i   pengene sine
     we made Peter fond of his money

This position is consistent with Herslund's analysis.[12]

The contrast between (18b) and (19) invites a different analysis, however, which rejects even the semantic parallellism view of small clauses and double object clusters. An interpretation of the marginality of (18b) is that, on the one hand, the predication-command condition is not met at all, neither at a syntactic nor at a semantic level, whereas on the other hand, a condition which is fulfilled is the role-command condition mentioned in 4.3. The latter is met since the benefactive role associated with the indirect object ranges higher on the theta-role hierarchy than the theme-role associated with the direct object.

We will opt for the latter analysis, thus denying that the predication relation plays a role in the double object construction, even from a semantic level. This conclusion we generalize to the whole issue of whether double object clusters can be regarded as small clauses, since these contrasting reflexive patterns seem to be the sharpest probes available. To the question heading this subsection, we therefore propose that the answer is no.

6.2. Are small clauses groups?

The possibility remains that double object clusters and small clauses share the group structure, that is, the structure "[NP XP]$_{XP}$", where the NP and the internal XP have distinct argument functions. In the first place, it is clear that small clauses do not fulfill the usual phrase criterion of being movable in one piece - (20) is as bad as (10) is:

(20) *Marit syk må du ikke gjøre
    Marit sick must you not make

The only type of phrase that small clauses could exemplify is thereby the group. The illformedness of (20) parallels that of (10) in being attributable to a violation of a uniqueness restriction: in (10), the restriction is that a predicate have a unique subject; here it is the other way round, since in (20) there are two predicates with only one overtly marked subject. This common behavior of small clauses and double object clusters is reflected in the notion "group" as applied to both, once we count subject and predicate as both having argument function.

In evaluating whether small clauses are groups, consider first the predication relation expressed in small clauses. We argued in the preceding subsection that this relation may well be represented in the syntactic analysis of small clauses, and if this representation takes the form of a binary branching structure, then this is one step towards the group configuration. Now, among the proposals for such a representation, "V [NP XP]$_S$" is a fairly traditional one, with binary branching.[13] However, it is not the only analysis available: explicit marking of predication as a relation is another possibility (cf. Hellan 1988), and coindexation a third (cf. Williams 1980, 1983), both devices being in principle combinable with a flat structure. Since the binary branching constellation has no obvious advantages over the latter two as a representation of predication, the predicational property of small clauses cannot be used as a cue to assessing whether they should receive a group analysis. We have to focus rather on the type of factors motivating the group analysis of double object clusters.

The first factor, the endocentricity effect, is absent for obvious reasons: XP being a predicate, the NP is required as its subject. The other factor is government. There is clearly a connection between V and XP, in that various V select different heads of XP (at least with XP=AP), and that the head of XP often can be incorporated into V (in Norwegian this happens to a considerable extent). Suppose that we call this a governmental relation. Its functional basis is clearly not that of signalling choice of theta-role, so that the exclusiveness tied to government of NPs will not exclude the V-AP government from coexisting with the government of an NP. This is important, since in a construction like *make Mary sick*, *Mary* is governed by *make*.

Suppose that we label the two types of government "np-government" and "xp-government"; the analysis under consideration for *make Mary sick* can then be illustrated as in (21):

(21)

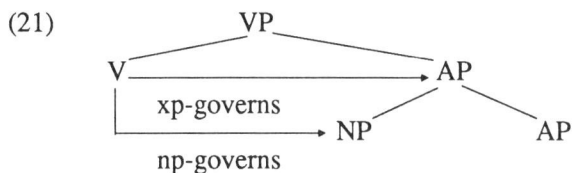

Presumably, as long as the types of government are different, there should be no difficulty in having one governmental relation going into the domain of another, as in (21).

The question is now whether we can assume a requirement of adjacency between xp-governor and governee in a similar way as we did for np-government, serving in a similar way as motivation for a group analysis. A possible problem is that if incorporability and selection are the main criteria of xp-government, then constructions like (22) may necessitate, as a matter of brute fact, that xp-government be allowed without adjacency:

(22) Peter talte   til   folket om   usynlige verdier
     Peter talked to the people about invisible values

Both *omtale* "talk about" and *tiltale* "talk to" are possible verbs in Norwegian, and the selected character of the prepositions is equally strong in (22) as when one of these PP-types occurs alone. Hence it seems that both PPs must count as being xp-governed, and, if so, either the last PP is xp-governed without adjacency, or the last PP heads a group consisting of the two PPs. In the last case we get xp-government into the domain of another xp-government relation, which may be problematic according to standard assumptions. If (22) displays a case of xp-government without adjacency of the last PP, a possibility might still be not to take adjacency as an absolute requirement in the case of xp-government, but only to require that adjacency be maximized, and therefore obtain whenever formally possible. Such a principle would then still dictate (21) as the analysis of small clause constructions, whereas in (22) both PPs would be xp-governed, with only the former obeying adjacency.

Modulo these considerations, there clearly is a possibility that small clauses can be analyzed as groups (rather than syntactically flat structures). Our answer to the question heading the present subsection is therefore "possibly, but with provisos".

7. Conclusion

The phrasal analysis of double object constructions has proved successful for a large range of phenomena in Norwegian, including the attribute-like properties of indirect objects, the distribution of government to direct objects, the fact that direct objects are subject to the indefiniteness requirement in presentational constructions, the eligibility of direct objects for "ergative" promotion, the eligibility of direct objects for *hva for*-extraction, and the superiority of indirect objects over direct objects with regard to anaphora binding. In most respects it generalizes to English, and it also opens perspectives in the typological area, concerning the ergativity parameter, the VSO-SVO-SOV-parameter and the placement of attributes in relation to nominal heads. The type of phrase which we call group, which is what the double object clusters exemplify, has been found to possibly cover small clause constructions as well, without small clauses and double object clusters thereby being in any way identical.

In comparison with other theories, the present theory has most in common with that of Kayne (1984), in positing a right-branching analysis of the double object cluster. Whereas his structure conforms to his general theory of paths, however, and neither adjacency as a condition for government nor a phrasal structure of the double object cluster play any role, the latter factors are the crucial building blocks of the present analysis. A further difference is that Kayne to some extent assimilates double object clusters and small clauses, contrary to the present theory.

From the totality of considerations made here, the present analysis seems preferable to the other approaches mentioned. The issue has many ramifications, though, and the present note obviously makes just a little step towards obtaining a full understanding of the phenomena involved.

Notes

1. Versions of this paper were presented at the University of Tilburg in 1985, at the MONS conference at the University of Trondheim, 1987, at the "Grammatik i Fokus" conference at the University of Lund, 1988, and at the Comparative Germanic Workshop at the University of Groningen, 1988. I am grateful to participants and audiences in these fora for valuable comments and discussion. Particular thanks to Tor Åfarli, Anders Holmberg, Hans Peter Kolb and Eric Hoekstra.
2. In chapter 7 of Kayne (1984), this node is labelled S, an analysis which is dropped in the Introduction to the same work. (See also note 3 below.)
3. As we remark in 3.3., there are cases - with verbs like *deny* - where neither direct object nor indirect object can be omitted. Such cases are compatible with the proposal to be made here, since the obligatoriness of an indirect object can be seen as a property of the verb, superimposed on the endocentric status of the direct object-group. As predicted on this construal, one never has an obligatory indirect object and an optional direct object.
4. If the unlabelled node in (1c) were treated as a projection of the direct object, these differences might be eliminated. From a remark in Kayne (1984: XIV n. 5) and Kayne's analysis of double object clusters as small clauses in Kayne (1984, chapter 7), it would follow that this is at least a possibility within his approach.
5. Once the indirect object is denied status as a governee, (8a) (and its English counterpart) may appear formally as violations of the empty category principle, despite their wellformedness. We assume that the way the indirect object is licensed, in our account, is sufficient to provide the trace with the necessary "visibility".
    In view of the discussion in 4.1. and 4.2. below, the same cannot be said about a wh-bound empty indirect objects in English - here government appears to be necessary, as opposed to Norwegian. It is an interesting question whether this difference can be related to another difference between these languages, residing in the fact that (8b) is not possible in English; we have no proposal to offer at this point.
6. The account of the indirect object as a configurational encoding of specific thematic roles (cf. 2.2.) is compatible with saying that the verb "assigns" the role in question, since the encoding can only take place if the role is among the central or marginal roles associated with the verb.
7. For discussion of this type of extraction, see, e.g., den Besten (1982) and Lie (1982). (I am grateful to Anders Holmberg for pointing out its relevance in the present connection.)

8.   I am grateful to Eric Reuland for bringing this point up. It may be mentioned immediately that Dutch and German do not seem to behave quite uniformly with regard to the group-criteria: from indirect objects in Dutch, *wat voor (hva for)*-extraction seems possible, but not from indirect objects in German; cf. (i) versus (ii):

       (i)   Wat heb jij [voor mensen]een boek gegeven?

           what have you for people a book given

           ("which people have you given a book?")

       (ii)   *Was hast du [für einer Person] diese Geschichte erzählt?

           what have you for a person this story told

           ("what person have you told this story?")

9.   For discussion of this type of parameter, see also Herslund (in press).

10.   I am grateful to Elisabeth Wennevold for information and discussion concerning the ergativity parameter.

11.   Even though, as Kayne (1984) notices, verbless constructions with "have" interpretation exist in languages like Russian and French, alongside the more common verbless constructions with "be"-interpretation.

12.   Kayne may be seen as opting for a representation of predication both syntactically and semantically, with "V [NP XP]$_S$" as the syntactic structure, later modified to "[NP XP]$_{XP}$" (Kayne 1984: introduction and chapter 7) and an abstract verb perhaps in the semantic analysis (1984: 135). He does not address the reflexive data used here.

13.   Even "[NP XP]$_{XP}$" has been suggested, cf. Kayne (1984: XIV, n.5), which is hardly revealing as a representation of predication, but perhaps anticipates the present discussion.

References

Barss, Andrew - Howard Lasnik

    1986   "A note on anaphora and double objects", *Linguistic Inquiry* 17: 347-354

Burzio, Luigi

    1986   *Italian syntax* (Dordrecht: Reidel).

Chomsky, Noam

    1964   *Current issues in linguistic theory* (The Hague: Mouton).

    1986   *Barriers* (Cambridge, Mass.: MIT Press).

Chung, Sandra
1978   *Case marking and grammatical relations in Polynesian* (Austin: University of Texas Press).

Den Besten, Hans
1982   "Some remarks on the ergative hypothesis", *Groningen Arbeiten zur germanistischen Linguistik* 21: 61-82

Hellan, Lars
1988   *Anaphora in Norwegian and the theory of grammar* (Dordrecht: Foris).

Herslund, Michael
1986   "The double object construction in Danish", *Topics in Scandinavian syntax*, edited by Lars Hellan - Kirsti K. Christensen (Dordrecht: Reidel).
in press *Le Datif. Étude sémantico-syntaxique des structures á N en francais* (Louvain: Bibliotèque de l'information grammaticale, Peeters).

Kayne, Richard
1984   *Connectedness and binary branching* (Dordrecht: Foris).

Kiss, É. Katalin
1987   "More on anaphora and double objects" (Budapest: unpublished manuscript Hungarian Academy of Sciences).

Larson, Richard K.
1988   "On the double object construction", *Linguistic Inquiry* 19: 335-392

Lie, Svein
1982   "Discontinuous questions and subjacency in Norwegian", *Readings on unbounded dependencies in Scandinavian languages*, edited by Elisabet Engdahl - Eva Ejerhed (Umeå: Acta Universitatis Umensis, Almqvist & Wiksell).

Mallinson, Graham - Barry J. Blake
1981   *Language typology* (Amsterdam: North Holland).

Ross, John R.
1967   *Constraints on variables in syntax*, doctoral dissertation (Cambridge, Mass.: MIT).

Seiter, William J.
1980   *Studies in Niuean syntax* (New York: Garland).

Stowell, Tim
1981   *The origin of phrase structure*, doctoral dissertation (Cambridge, Mass.: MIT).

Wennevold, Elisabeth
in press *Ergativity and word order: a configurational analysis*, hovedoppgave (Trondheim: University of Trondheim).

Williams, Edwin
    1980   "Predication", *Linguistic Inquiry* 11: 203-238
    1983   "Against small clauses", *Linguistic Inquiry* 14: 287-309

On the role of inflection in Scandinavian syntax

Anders Holmberg and Christer Platzack

1. Introduction

In this contribution[1], we want to show how the presence versus absence of morphological inflection, both Case and agreement inflection, split the Scandinavian languages into two groups:

Group 1 All old Scandinavian languages (roughly the medieval variants), Modern Icelandic and Modern Faroese, some Swedish and Norwegian dialects.

Group 2 The modern mainland Scandinavian languages (Danish, Norwegian and Swedish).

We will refer to the languages of the first group as Insular Scandinavian (ISc.), to the languages of the second group as Mainland Scandinavian (MSc.).

    The Insular Scandinavian. languages are typical representatives of what is often called "synthetic languages": they have both morphological Case and subject-verb agreement. The languages of the second group are typical "analytic languages": disregarding the genitive, they have no Case morphology, except on pronouns, and no subject-verb agreement. These characteristics are illustrated in (1) and (2):

(1) a. Við elskum Ólaf,   en   Ólafur   elskar   ekki oss. (Ice.)
    b. Vi älskum Olaf,   män Olafer`   älskar   ikke os. (OSw.)
    we love-1pl. Olaf-acc, but   Olaf-nom love-3sg not us

(2) a. Vi elsker Olof, men Olof elsker ikke os.   (Da.)
    b. Vi älskar Olof, men Olof älskar inte oss.   (Sw.)
    we love Olof, but Olof loves not us

In Insular Scandinavian, the verb agrees with the subject in person and number, and the NPs have different forms for nominative, genitive, dative and accusative Case. Some examples of verbal inflection and Case inflection in Icelandic are given in (3) and (4):

(3) Verbal inflection in Icelandic

	Present indicative		Present subjunctive		Past indicative		Past subjunctive	
Sing.								
1.	tek	segi	taki	segi	tók	sagði	tæki	segði
2.	tekur	segir	takir	segir	tókst	sagðir	tækir	segðir
3.	tekur	segir	taki	segi	tók	sagði	tæki	segði
Pl.								
1.	tökum	segjum	tökum	segjum	tókum	sögðum	tækjum	segðum
2.	takið	segið	takið	segið	tókuð	sögðuð	tækjuð	segðuð
3.	taka	segja	taki	segi	tóku	sögðu	tækju	segðu
	take	say						

(4) Case inflection in Icelandic (indefinite, strong declension)

	Masc.		Fem.		Neutr.	
	sg.	pl.	sg.	pl.	sg.	pl.
nom.	hest-ur	hest-ar	nál	nál-ar	borð	borð
acc.	hest	hest-a	nál	nál-ar	borð	borð
dat.	hest-i	hest-um	nál	nál-um	borð-i	borð-um
gen.	hest-s	hest-a	nál-ar	nál-a	borð-s	borð-a
	horse		needle		table	

In Mainland Scandinavian, the verb has an invariant form (it is only inflected for tense), and full NPs have only two forms, a basic form and a genitive form, as in modern English. Only the pronouns have distinct forms depending on their grammatical function.

As we will show, there are several syntactic differences between the two groups of Scandinavian languages which depend on their different inflectional systems. A non-exhaustive list of these differences is given in (5): consider also the appendix, in which we give examples which illustrate the list in (5).

(5)			Insular Scandinavian	Mainland Scandinavian
	a.	Null expletives	+	-
	b.	Heavy subject postposing	+	-
	c.	Indirect subject questions without resumptive element	+	-
	d.	That-trace violation	+	±
	e	Oblique subjects	+	-
	f.	Verb second in embedded clauses	+	-
	g.	Verb first declaratives	+	-
	h.	VP topicalization	-	+
	i	Stylistic fronting	+	-
	j.	Have/Be variation	+	-
	k.	Inverted accusative with infinitive	+	-
	l.	Adverbial between C and Spec-IP	-	+
	m.	Pseudopassives	-	+
	n.	Object shift of non-pronominal NPs	+	-
	o.	Inverted double object construction	+	-
	p.	Prenominal genitive of full NPs	-	+

Despite differences like the ones listed in (5), what is striking when you look at two Scandinavian languages, even if they belong to different groups, is their overall similarity. Consider (1) and (2) again: apart from inflection and spelling (pronounciation), the sentences are basically identical. Against the background of traditional views of the relation between inflection and word order (the idea that rich inflection correlates with free word order, and poor inflection with rigid word order) it may seem surprising that the two types of Scandinavian do not differ more. In fact, it is not obvious that Insular Scandinavian word order is freer than Mainland Scandinavian word order. Insular Scandinavian word order is fairly rigid, in spite of all the inflectional morphology in these languages, while Mainland Scandinavian word order may be considered surprisingly free, given that the Mainland Scandinavian languages have almost no inflection morphology[2]. Consider e.g., the discussion in Holmberg (1986:1 ff.).

Careful investigation of syntactic variation between the two types of Scandinavian languages is interesting because it can tell us a number of things about the role of inflection in syntax, both about what inflection can do, but also what inflection cannot do, in other words, about the limitations of inflection. What makes the Scandinavian languages a particularly good object of study in this respect is that they are so similar, other than with regard to inflectional morphology. In terms of a principles-and-parameters model of universal grammar (UG), cf. Chomsky (1986), there does not seem to be any other major parameter where the Scandinavian languages would differ from each other. Hence, the Scandinavian languages offer an almost ideal experimental situation for studying the effects of inflection.

In this paper, we will discuss seven of the sixteen differences listed in (5) above, viz. null expletives (5a), oblique subjects (5e), verb second in embedded clauses (5f), VP topicalization (5h), stylistic fronting (5i), adverbial between C and Spec-IP (5l), and pseudopassives (5m).We will mainly restrict ourselves to comparing modern Icelandic and modern Swedish. Since Swedish (like Danish and Norwegian) has changed from being an Insular Scandinavian language to a Mainland Scandinavian language, we will also now and then compare old and modern Swedish, showing the syntactic consequences of the loss of morphological Case and subject-verb agreement.

2. Basic sentence structure

We assume that all Scandinavian languages share the basic sentence structure in (6) below. The examples in (7a) to (7d) illustrate the word order properties of main clauses and subordinate clauses in Swedish and Icelandic.

The only difference with respect to word order is found in subordinate clauses, (7c) and (7d): in Swedish, the finite verb follows the negation and other sentence adverbials, as illustrated in (7c); in Icelandic, the finite verb precedes the negation, etc., as shown in (7d). As indicated by the examples, we take this difference to be the result of a movement of V to I in Icelandic subordinate clauses, and the absence of such a movement in Swedish. To the best of our knowledge, this way of accounting for the different word orders of subordinate clauses in Swedish and Icelandic was first proposed by Wim Kosmeijer in his speech at the Third Workshop on Comparative

Germanic Syntax at Turku 1986. Consider Kosmeijer (1986); compare also
Holmberg (1988), Platzack (1988) and Sigurðsson (1989):

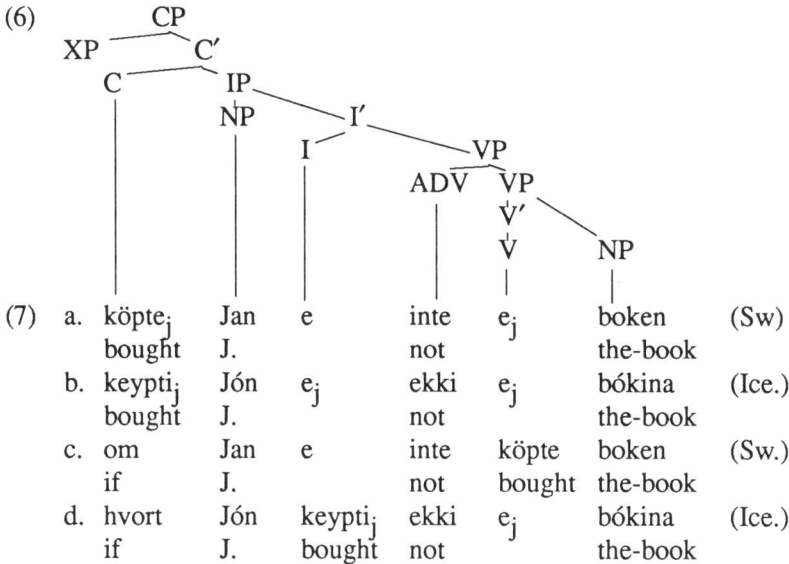

(6)

```
            CP
    XP ‾‾‾‾‾‾ C′
      C ‾‾‾‾‾ IP
               NP ‾‾‾‾ I′
                  I ‾          ‾‾‾ VP
                              ADV   VP
                                    V′
                                    V ‾‾‾ NP
```

(7)								
	a.	köpte$_j$	Jan	e	inte	e$_j$	boken	(Sw)
		bought	J.		not		the-book	
	b.	keypti$_j$	Jón	e$_j$	ekki	e$_j$	bókina	(Ice.)
		bought	J.		not		the-book	
	c.	om	Jan	e	inte	köpte	boken	(Sw.)
		if	J.		not	bought	the-book	
	d.	hvort	Jón	keypti$_j$	ekki	e$_j$	bókina	(Ice.)
		if	J.	bought	not		the-book	

In main clauses, the finite verb moves to C through I in Icelandic, directly
from VP to C in Swedish. As we will show below, this movement is possible
since there is no subject-verb agreement in Swedish.

3. V-movements in Icelandic and Swedish

3.1. The operator [+finite] tense, AGR, and the Case theory

To be able to answer the question why the verb has to move to INFL in
subordinate clauses in Icelandic but not in Swedish, we have to discuss the
movement of V in general. Following Pollock (1989), we assume that
movement of V is triggered by an operator [+finite] tense, [+F] for short.
This operator is situated in C, presumably in all verb second-languages.

When lexicalized, [+F] governs (and must govern) nominative Case, as expressed in (8):

(8)   Lexicalized [+F] has to govern nominative Case.

Presumably, (8) is an instance of a general mutual dependency relation between heads and Cases: just as every Case must be licensed, every Case-licensing head must have a Case to license.

There are two ways for the operator [+F] to be lexicalized: it may be realized as a subordinate complementizer, or it may fuse with the finite verb. Hence verb movement to C (i.e., the verb second-phenomenon) makes C a governor of nominative Case in languages where [+F] is in C.

As noticed in the introduction, Icelandic and Swedish differ with respect to subject-verb agreement: there is such agreement in Icelandic, but not in Swedish. We take the presence of subject-verb agreement to be a visible reflection of an element AGR in Infl. We claim that AGR in Insular Scandinavian is [+N] and inherently nominative. As such it must be licensed according to the same rules as other nominal elements.

Icelandic and Swedish also differ with respect to morphological Case (m-Case): there is m-Case in Icelandic but not in Swedish. Concerning the relation between m-Case and abstract Case in the sense of the Case filter, we will say that m-Case provides NP with Case, but that the m-Case must be licensed by government, either by a lexical subcategorization feature (the so-called lexical Cases), or by a structural Case assigner, i.e. a certain type of head feature.

The following are the licensing conditions on the various Cases in Insular Scandinavian:

(9)   Structural Cases:
      Nom is licit if it is governed by [+F]
      Acc is licit if and only if governed by transitive V,
      Gen is licit if and only if governed by N.

(10) Lexical Idiosyncratic Cases[3]:
      Acc is licit if governed by a head subcategorized [__Acc]
      Dat is licit if governed by a head subcategorized [__Dat]
      Gen is licit if governed by a head subcategorized [__Gen]

The licensing conditions of (9) apply at S-structure, the licensing conditions of (10) at D-structure. We formulate them as licensing conditions rather than as assignment rules in line with the assumption that the Case-morphemes, including the structural Case affixes, are drawn from the lexicon and inserted in D- or S-structure. We also assume a one-to-one relation between head-feature and Case: a head may license one and only one structural Case, and one and only one lexical Case. In some cases a head may license a structural Case (by virtue of its category) and a lexical Case (by virtue of its subcategorization).

If a sentence contains a nominative NP, the finite verb regularly agrees with this NP. If there is no nominative NP there is no agreement: the verb bears a neutral third person singular form. That is to say, (a) AGR can only be coindexed with a nominative NP, and (b) must be, if there is a nominative NP broadly speaking in the domain of AGR. (a) is a consequence of AGR being itself nominative: coindexing of AGR and an NP bearing any other Case than nominative will result in a Case conflict. In the cases we shall consider here, (b) is simply a consequence of free coindexing: if AGR is not coindexed with a nominative NP, its Case will not be licensed (cf. below). In the cases mentioned in footnote 3, we may need some additional mechanism to ensure coindexing of AGR and a nominative NP.

Now consider the formal relation between [+F], AGR, and nominative: from its position in C [+F] governs IP, and (according to the definition of government in Chomsky (1986a) the specifier position of IP and AGR. It may license an NP marked Nom in the specifier position of IP. This NP will be coindexed with AGR, thus forming a chain with the NP in the specifier position of IP as the head and AGR as the coda (this implies that AGR has essentially the status of a resumptive element, a hypothesis that will be important later on). Thereby the Nom feature of AGR is licensed.

Alternatively [+F] may license the Nom of AGR directly. In this case the specifier position of IP may be empty, or filled (through movement) by an NP bearing a lexical Case: since (8) is satisfied by AGR the presence of a lexical nominative NP in the specifier position of IP is not required.

This theory of Case and agreement makes the strong prediction that a language which does not have AGR marked [+N] cannot have empty subjects. Swedish is a language of this kind. We assume Swedish and the other Mainland Scandinavian languages have structural Case rules essentially like the ones in (9) (with certain differences concerning accusative and gentive which we may disregard here), except that in the case of nominative and accusative the Case features are abstract, not born by Case morphology. As mentioned, Swedish has no AGR of any kind. Now, since [+F] must govern Nom, there must be an NP bearing the feature Nom in the governing domain of [+F]. This NP must be in the specifier position of IP. In languages like Icelandic there is always AGR marked [+N] available to satisfy (8); hence, the theory does not predict anything about the specifier position of IP in such a case.

Our theory also predicts that a language which does not have AGR marked [+N] cannot have NPs marked with any other Case than nominative in the specifier position of IP, while this is possible in a language with AGR marked [+N], such as Icelandic. Consequently we find so-called oblique (or "quirky Case") subjects in Insular Scandinavian, but not in Mainland Scandinavian (cf. 5e). Examples of this phenomenon are given in (12a) to (12c), whereas (11) illustrates the case with a nominative subject:

(11) a. Ólafur hvatti Maríu til þátttöku.
       Olaf (nom.) encouraged Mary (acc.) to participation (gen.)

(12) a. Ólaf   vantar skó.
       Olaf (acc.) needs shoes (acc.)
    b. Ólafi   batnaði   veikin.
       Olaf (dat.) recovered-from the-disease (nom.)
    c. Ólafi   var bjargað.
       Olaf (dat.) was saved.

There are several tests which show that the first NP in examples like (12a) to (12c) is the structural subject, and not a topicalized object. For such tests, and on the existence in Icelandic of oblique subjects in general, cf. Andrews (1976), Thráinsson (1979: 462 ff.), Maling–Zaenen–Thráinsson (1985), Platzack (1987), and Sigurðsson (1989). Notice also that our description explains why oblique subjects are not found in Swedish: since there is no AGR in Swedish, the lexicalized operator [+F] must govern an NP marked Nom in the specifier position of IP. Thus, a non-nominative NP in this position would create a Case conflict.[4]

3.2. Verb movements

We are now in a position to explain the different kinds of V-movement in Icelandic and Swedish. Consider the assumption mentioned above that [+F] is an operator. Being an operator, [+F] must bind an empty category (or a resumptive element) to be licensed. Furthermore, [+F] must be lexicalized to license Nom in AGR (in Icelandic) or the specifier position of IP (in Swedish).

In main clauses, the lexicalization of [+F] is effected by movement of V to C in both Swedish and Icelandic, as mentioned above. V-movement is an instance of head movement. According to the head movement constraint (Travis 1984; Chomsky 1986a), a head may not move across the closest governing head. In both Swedish and Icelandic, C is the closest head governing V, cf. the definition of head government in (21) below. In Icelandic, V must move to I to pick up the agreement features before moving on to C;[5] there is no need for such a movement in Swedish, and as we will see in 3.3., there are facts indicating that V moves directly from VP to C in Swedish. The difference between Swedish and Icelandic is outlined in (13):

(13) a. $[_{CP} [_C$ finite verb$_i][_{IP}$ NP $[_I$ e$_i]$ $[_{VP}$ ...e$_i$..]]]   (Ice.)
     b. $[_{CP} [_C$ finite verb$_i][_{IP}$ NP $[_I$ e] $[_{VP}$ ...e$_i$..]]]   (Sw.)

Notice that the empty category in I is licit whether or not there is a trace of V in I: following Haider (this volume), we assume C-I coindexation in all verb second languages. Hence, the empty category in I is head governed and antecedent governed by [+F] in C. Consider the definitions given below in section 4.2.

In subordinate clauses, V-movement to C is blocked by the presence of a complementizer in C. As in main clauses, V must move to I in Icelandic to pick up AGR. Assuming AGR to function as a resumptive pronoun bound by [+F], the operator is licensed. In Swedish, on the other hand, movement of V to I is blocked, since I must be empty to license the operator (there is no resumptive AGR in Swedish). This accounts for the different word order of Swedish and Icelandic subordinate clauses, discussed above.[6,7,8]

3.3. Adverbials between C and the specifier position of IP

The difference noticed in (51) with respect to the possibility of inserting adverbials between C and the specifier position of IP provides an interesting support for the assumption that V moves to C through I in Icelandic main clauses, but directly from VP to C in Swedish. Consider the relevant data given in (14):

(14) a *að aldrei Jón getur komið /Getur aldrei Jón   komið? (Ice.)
     b. att aldrig Johan kan komma /Kan aldrig Johan komma? (Sw.)
         that never J. can come / can never J. come

As indicated by these examples, both Swedish and Icelandic allow the occurrence of a negation or sentence adverbial between the finite verb in C and the specifier position of IP; however, when C is filled by a complementizer, this option is found only in Swedish.

Assuming with Platzack (1986) that adverbials of the discussed type are clitics, we expect them to behave like other clitic elements: they should adjoin to the closest (lexicalized) governing head (Kayne 1987). In Swedish, the governor of VP is C. Thus, we expect the adverbial to adjoin to C in Swedish in both main clauses and subordinate clauses, deriving the data in (14b).

In Icelandic, movement of V to I makes I a governor of VP. Hence, the adverbial must cliticize to the verb moved to I. In subordinate clauses, where there is no further movement of V, the adverbial thus ends up in I. In main clauses it will follow the finite verb from I to C. As a result, we find an adverbial between C and the specifier position of IP only in main clauses in Icelandic, as in (14a). The same idea is outlined in Sigurðsson (1989).

3.4. VP topicalization

A final argument for the presence of AGR in I in Icelandic and its absence in Swedish is provided by VP topicalization. All Scandinavian languages accept the fronting of VP governed by an auxiliary, as shown in (15a) and (15b), whereas Insular Scandinavian differs from Mainland Scandinavian in not accepting the equivalent of English VP-fronting with do-insertion (cf. [15c] and [15d]); the examples are taken from Zaenen (1985: 24):

(15) a. Kaupa bíl mun hún.   (Ice.)
    b. Købe bil vil hun.   (Da.)
       buy   car will she
    c. *Kaupa bíl gerði hún.   (Ice.)
    d Købe   bil gjorde hun. (Da.)
       buy   car did   she

The difference between Insular Scandinavian and Mainland Scandinavian noticed in (15) may be taken as a reflection of the presence of AGR in Insular Scandinavian, its absence in Mainland Scandinavian. In Mainland Scandinavian, the realization of the operator [+finite] in C by the dummy *gøre* "do" is possible, since the empty I provides this operator with a licensing variable. In Insular Scandinavian, on the other hand, there is AGR in Infl: hence, realizing the operator by *gera* "do" in Icelandic would leave AGR dangling, without proper lexical support. As a consequence the equivalent of *do*-insertion is possible in Mainland Scandinavian, but not in Insular Scandinavian

4. Empty expletive subjects

4.1. Introduction

As indicated by (5a), Icelandic but not Swedish may have empty expletive subjects. See Sigurðsson (1989: chapter 5) for an overview. In this section, we will show that this difference follows from the presence of AGR in I in Icelandic and the absence of AGR in Swedish. This is partly due to Case theory: as noticed in the previous section, there must be an NP in the specifier position of IP in Swedish to pick up nominative Case; in Icelandic, nominative Case is assigned to AGR, meaning that Case theory does not force the specifier position of IP to be filled in Icelandic.

    There are four types of structures where Icelandic can have a null subject which corresponds to an expletive pronominal subject in Swedish: cases with a "quasi"-argument (corresponding to *it* in English *it is raining*), cases with an extraposed clause (corresponding to *it* in English *it is nice that ...*), cases with an existential reading (corresponding to *there* in English *there are some papers on the table*), and cases with impersonal passives, which lack correspondence in English. These four types are illustrated in (16) to (19):[9]

(16) a. Rigndi (*það)   í gær?   (Ice.)
     b. Regnade *(det) igår?   (Sw.)
        rained it   yesterday

(17) a. Er (*það) líklegt að   María er saklaus?   (Ice.)
     b. Är *(det) troligt att   Maria är oskyldig?   (Sw.)
        is it   likely that Mary   is innocent

(18) a. Í dag hafa (*það) komið margir málvísindamenn hingað. (Ice.)
     b. Idag har *(det)   kommit många lingvister   hit.   (Sw.)
        today have there come   many   linguists   here

(19) a. Í gær   var (*það) dansað á skipinu.   (Ice.)
        yesterday was it   danced on the-ship
     b. Igår   dansades   *(det) på skeppet.   (Sw.)
        yesterday was-danced it   on the-ship

As we will show below, these differences between Icelandic and Swedish follow from Case theory and the empty category principle, given that AGR is present in Icelandic and absent in Swedish. To demonstrate this, we must first give our definition of the empty category principle.

4.2. Definitions

Following Rizzi (1987), we adopt the version of the empty category principle given in (20):[10,11]

(20) Empty category principle
     An empty category is
     (i)   head governed, and
     (ii)   antecedent governed or theta-governed

Head government, antecedent government and theta-government are defined in the following ways:

(21) Head government:
   X head governs Y if and only if
   (i)   X ∈ {A, N, P, V, [+F]}
   (ii)   X m-commands Y
   (iii) No barrier intervenes between X and Y
   (iv)   Relativized minimality is respected

(22) Antecedent government (Rizzi 1987):
   X antecedent governs Y if and only if
   (i)   X and Y are coindexed
   (ii)   X c-commands Y
   (iii) No barrier intervenes between X and Y
   (iv)   Relativized minimality is respected

(23) Theta-government (Chomsky 1986a: 15):
   X theta-governs Y if and only if X is a zero-level category that theta-marks Y, and X and Y are sisters.

The definition of head government is close to the definition given in Rizzi (1987); however, Rizzi includes AGR instead of [+F] among the relevant heads. Since Rizzi also allows for the possibility that certain complementizers might function as head governors, there is a certain redundancy in his definition, which we try to avoid by suggesting that the operator [+F], rather than AGR, is a head governor.

The concept "relativized minimality" is developed in Rizzi (1987). In short, relativized minimality says that if X potentially head governs Y, an intervening potential head governor would block head government of Y by X, and if X potentially antecedent governs Y, an intervening potential antecedent governor would block antecedent government of Y by X. On the other hand, a potential head governor between X and Y does not block antecedent government of Y by X, and a potential antecedent governor between X and Y does not block head government of Y by X.

As far as we can tell, the definitions given in (20) to (23) account for the set of cases handled by Rizzi's formulation of the empty category principle. The changes we are arguing for do not seem to have the disadvantage of erraneously licensing empty categories not licensed by Rizzi's empty category principle.

4.3. Description

The relevant parts of the S-structures of (19) are outlined in (24):

(24) a. $[_{CP}$ Í gær $[_C$ var$_j$ $[_{IP}$ e e$_j$ $[_{VP}$ e$_j$ dansað á skipinu]]]]
   b. $[_{CP}$ I går $[_C$ dansades$_j$ $[_{IP}$ det e $[_{VP}$ e$_j$ på skeppet]]]]

As mentioned in 3.1., Case theory blocks the occurrence of an empty subject in languages like Swedish, where there is no AGR marked [+N]. This description correctly predicts that Swedish should lose expletive empty subjects when AGR is lost around 1700. Cf. Platzack (1985, 1987).[12]

To account for the Icelandic examples in (16) to (19), it is not enough to show that Case theory does not block the occurrence of an empty subject: we must also show that an empty category in the specifier position of IP is licensed in these cases. Consider (24a). Due to spec-head agreement (Chomsky 1986a: 24), the empty category in the specifier position of IP is coindexed with AGR in Infl. Since AGR is fused with the finite verb, this means that the specifier position of IP is coindexed with the finite verb in cases like this. Hence, in a structure like (24a), where the finite verb is in C, the empty category in the specifier position of IP is head governed by [+F] and coindexed with the finite verb in C, i.e., it is antecedent governed. Being both antecedent governed and head governed, this empty category is licensed by empty category principle, according to the formulation in (20).

It is to be noticed that this way of licensing an empty category in the specifier position of IP is possible only in verb second languages, where V may be moved to C. In a language like Italian, e.g., empty expletive categories of the type illustrated in (24a) do not exist, as mentioned by Haider (this volume). Since there is no V-to-C in Italian,[12] (the operator [+F] is presumably located in Infl), there will be no antecedent governor of an empty category in the specifier position of IP in a case corresponding to (24a). On the other hand, Italian accepts empty non-expletive subjects, as in *credo* "I believe", a kind of empty subject which is not found in Icelandic. We will assume that the specifier position of IP in cases like this is theta-governed, meaning that AGR in some way may function as a theta-role assigner in Italian, but not in Icelandic.[14]

The account of expletive empty subjects in Icelandic outlined above predicts that expletive empty subjects are found only in main clauses, i.e., clauses where the finite verb is moved to C: otherwise, there will be no antecedent governor of the empty category. This prediction is supported by the fact that Icelandic very reluctantly accepts subordinate clauses with an empty specifier position of IP, unless the empty category is a variable. Consider Sigurðsson (1985), and the examples in (25). In most subordinate clauses with an empty subject, Icelandic moves some other element of the clause to the position in front of the finite verb (Stylistic Fronting (SF)), (cf. Maling 1980; Platzack 1987). As Maling has shown, stylistic fronting is possible only if the subject position is empty; hence, in cases like (25b) and (26b) below, we may assume that the fronted element actually is in the specifier position of IP. As a consequence, there is no empty category in the specifier position of IP to be licensed.

(25) a. ??...að hefur aldrei rignt á Ítalíu
             that has   never rained in Italy
     b. ...að aldrei hefur rignt á Ítalíu   (stylistic fronting of
             that never has   rained in Italy   aldrei "never")

(26) a. ??Hann vissi   að   var dansað á skipinu   í gær.
           he   knew   that was danced on the-ship yesterday
     b. Hann vissi að í gær   var dansað á skipinu   (stylistic
           he   knew that yesterday was dansed on the-ship   fronting of
                                                                    í gær
                                                                 "yesterday")

It is to be noticed that examples with stylistic fronting are possible in Icelandic for the same reason as examples with oblique subjects. In Icelandic, nominative Case is assigned to AGR. In Swedish, where there is no AGR, nominative Case must be assigned to a nominal element in the specifier position of IP; hence, the specifier position of IP cannot be occupied by a fronted element. From a historical point of view, this should mean that Swedish loses stylistic fronting when AGR is lost, i.e., around 1700. This is a correct prediction, as shown in Platzack (1985, 1987).

5. Pseudopassives

As discussed by Maling - Zaenen (1985), Icelandic does not allow P-stranding by NP-movement, although it allows P-stranding by wh-movement. In other words, Icelandic does not have pseudopassives (prepositional passives). This is true of Insular Scandinavian in general. As shown in (27), the pseudopassive is ill-formed in Icelandic when the subject bears nominative Case as well as when it bears the lexical Case required by the preposition, i.e., an oblique subject construction. Mainland Scandinavian, on the other hand, allows pseudopassives, as shown in (28):[15]

(27) a. *Ólafur var alltaf talaður vel um.　(Ice.)
　　　O. (nom.) was always spoken well of
　　b. *Ólaf var alltaf talað vel um.[16]　(Ice.)
　　　O (acc.) was always spoken well of

(28) Babyn har inte blivit bytt blöjor på.　(Sw.)
　　the-baby has not been changed nappies on

We claim that the difference between Insular Scandinavian and Mainland Scandinavian with respect to pseudopassives is due to the presence versus absence of m-Case in the two types of Scandinavian. This would then be a case where lack of m-Case entails increased freedom of word order, providing a neat counterexample to the traditional generalization that lack of m-Case entails more rigid word order.[17]

Essentially following Hornstein - Weinberg (1981), we assume that pseudopassive presupposes a reanalysis of V and P as a complex verb, as shown schematically in (29):[18]

(29) $[_{V'} [_{V'} V X] [_{PP} P NP]] \rightarrow [_{V'} [_V V X P] NP]]$

As discussed by Hornstein - Weinberg there are strict conditions on X in this rule: for instance, if it is an NP as in (28) it must be indefinite, and in general be "low in referentiality". The structure of the relevant part of (28) after reanalysis is given in (30):

(30) $Babyn_i$ har inte blivit $[_{VP} [_{V'} [_V$ bytt blöjor på $] e_i]]$

Reanalysis applies between D- and S-structure. We know it applies after D-structure because thematic relations are not affected in any way, which we would expect them to be if reanalysis were a lexical (pre D-structure) matter.[19] We know reanalysis applies before S-structure because after reanalysis P does not license structural Case on the object NP. If it did, the chain in (30), whose head is the subject and whose coda is the empty category, would have two conflicting Cases: nominative since it is governed by [+F], and objective since it is governed by a preposition. At S-structure P is embedded inside a participial verb, its Case being presumably absorbed by the passive morphology, just as in the case of participles of transitive verbs (cf. Jaeggli [1986: note 10] for a partly different proposal).

Now consider Insular Scandinavian. The crucial difference between Insular Scandinavian and Mainland Scandinavian is that all prepositions in Insular Scandinavian are subcategorized for a particular lexical idiosyncratic Case. For instance *um* (cf. [27]) is subcategorized for a complement with accusative m-Case. There is a mutual dependency relation between a lexical Case and the subcategorization feature, expressed in the two following conditions (on the notion "chain", cf. Chomsky (1981: 332 ff.)):

(31) a. A chain marked for lexical Case ¢ must be governed by a
category subcategorized [__ ¢].
(cf. the licensing conditions in (10) above)
b. The category subcategorized [__ ¢] must govern a chain marked
for lexical Case ¢.

Given the projection principle (Chomsky 1981: 29), (31a) and (31b) must hold at S-structure as well as at D-structure. In this way, we derive from the projection principle the familiar condition that lexical Case must not be changed in the course of a derivation. The conditions in (31) are met in well-formed instances of the oblique subject construction, e.g. (12c), the structure of which is given in (32):

(32) $[_{IP}$ Ólafi$_i$ ...$[_{V'}$ bjargað e$_i$]]
          [__Dat]

Here *bjargað* which is subcategorized for [__DAT] governs the object position at S-structure as well as at D-structure. Hence the chain (Ólafi, e), marked dative by virtue of having a head marked dative, is governed by

[__DAT] at S-structure, satisfying the conditions in (31) as well as the projection principle.

Now consider (27a) and (27b): the relevant parts of the structure after reanalysis will be (33):

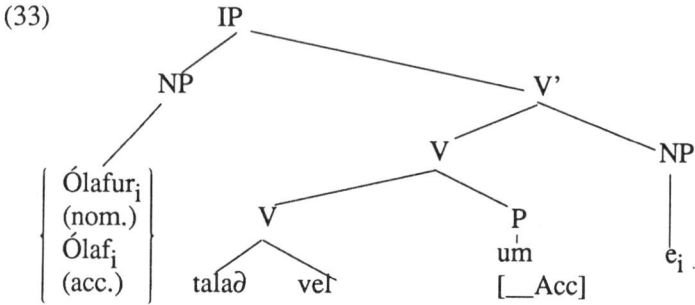

(33)

```
                    IP
          _____/  _____
        NP                    V'
       /              _____/  _____
   | Ólafur_i |      V               NP
   | (nom.)   |    __/ \__            |
   | Ólaf_i   |   V      P           e_i
   | (acc.)   | talað veł  um
                         [__Acc]
```

Since P is embedded inside a verb, its subcategorization feature does not govern the object position. Hence, (31b) is not met at S-structure, leading to a violation of the projection principle.[20] If the subject in (33) is accusative, we have a violation of (31a) as well, hence a double violation of the projection principle.[21]

6. Summary

Summarizing, we have shown how the presence of overt subject-verb agreement and m-Case in Icelandic and the absence of such inflection in Swedish accounts for several syntactic differences between these two Scandinavian languages. As we have seen, it is the interaction of morphological Case and the presence vs. absence of AGR marked [+N] with Case theory, the empty category principle, and verb second that explains the different behavior of Icelandic and Swedish with respect to empty expletive subjects, oblique subjects, pseudopassives, topicalizing of VP, stylistic fronting, subordinate clause word order and the possibility of inserting an adverbial between C and the specifier position of IP.

Appendix

Examples illustrating the list in (5):

(5a)   Null expletives: (16)-(19)

(5b)   Heavy subject postposing:

 (Ice.) það munu kaupa þessa bók margir stúdentar.

 (Sw.) *Det ska köpa den här boken många studenter.

   it/there will buy this book many students

(5c)   Indirect subject questions without resumptive element:

 (Ice.) Finnur spyr, hvað sé í pokanum.

 (Sw.) Finn frågar vad *(som) är i påsen.

  F. asks what (that) is in the-bag

(5d)   *That*-trace violation:

 (Ice.) Hver heldur þú að hafi framið glæpinn?

 (Sw.) *Vem tror du att har begått brottet?

   who believe you that has committed the-crime

(5e)   Oblique subjects: (12)

(5f)   Verb second in embedded clauses: (7c,d)

(5g)   Verb first declaratives:

 (Ice.) Hittu hann þá einhverja útlendinga

 (Sw.) Träffade han då några utlänningar?

  met he then some foreigners

   a. Did he then meet some foreigners? (Ice., Sw.)

   b. He then met some foreigners. (Ice.)

(5h)   VP topicalization: (15)

(5i)   Stylistic fronting: (25b, 26b)

(5j)   Have/Be variation:

 (Ice.) Hann er kominn. / Hann hefur komið.

 (Sw.) *Han är kommen. / Han har kommit

  he is come   he has come

(5k)   Inverted accusative with infinitive:

 (Ice.) Jón telur vera mýs í baðkerinu.

 (Sw.) *John tror vara möss i badkaret.

  J. believes to-be mice in the-bathtub

(5l) Adverbial between C and the specifier position of IP: (14)

(5m) Prepositional passive: (27), (28)

(5n) Object shift of non-pronominal NPs:

  (Ice.)Jón keypti ekki bókina. / Jón keypti bókina ekki.

  (Sw.) John köpte inte boken. / *John köpte boken inte.

  J. bought not the-book / J. bought the-book not

(5o) Inverted double object construction:

  (Ice.) Hún gaf bókina JÓNI (en ekki mér).

  (Sw.) *Hon gav boken JOHN (men inte mig).

  she gave the-book John (dat.) but not to-me

(5p) Prenominal genitive of full NPs:

  (Ice.) hús Jóns / *Jóns hús

  (Sw.) *hus Johns / Johns hus

  house John's / John's house

Notes

1.   Thanks to Richard Kayne and Halldór Sigurðsson for valuable comments. The authors are responsible for any errors.

2.   Notice, however, that NP in all Scandinavian languages is inflected for number and gender. Mainland Scandinavian also has an inflected form for the passive voice.

3.   In addition, Insular Scandinavian has a semantically predictable lexical Case typically born by the indirect object of many di-transitive verbs. Its licensing condition is given in (i):

  (i) Dat is licit on an argument assigned Recipient role.

  Furthermore, Nom is the default m-Case, carried by NPs in isolation. This implies that the morphological nominative can help an NP pass the Case filter, even in the absence of a licensing governor. This, we believe, is what makes it possible to have a nominative NP in object position in certain constructions, and in subject position in certain infinitival constructions (cf. Yip - Maling - Jackendoff [1988], Sigurðsson [1989] and Holmberg - Platzack [in prep.]).

4.   Subject-verb agreement is lost in Swedish around 1700. Thus, we expect all differences between Old Swedish and Modern Swedish which depend on AGR to be lost at about this time. This is also the case, as shown e.g.

in Platzack (1985, 1987). With respect to oblique subjects, we notice that Swedish loses its oblique subjects around 1700.

5. Notice that Affix Hopping is ruled out: being a nominal element, AGR must bear Case, and this Case must be governed by [+F], as mentioned above.

6. Not surprisingly, Old Swedish was like Icelandic in having the finite verb in front of sentence adverbials in subordinate clauses. As expected, this word order is lost around 1700, when AGR is lost, as shown in Platzack (1988).

7. Some Scandinavian dialects are Mainland Scandinavian with respect to word order and null-subjects, despite the fact that they have subject-verb agreement. Cf. Trosterud (in press). We assume that these dialects have non-nominal AGR. When AGR is not nominal, it cannot function as a resumptive element. Hence, V-movement to Infl in subordinate clauses is blocked (Infl must be empty to license the operator [+F] in C). Furthermore these dialects must have overt subjects: since there is no nominal AGR, [+F] in C must govern an NP marked Nom in the specifier position of IP.

8. Scandinavian infinitives raise difficult problems which are beyond the scope of the present paper. Thus, e.g., Icelandic has obligatory V-to-I in control infinitives, as demonstrated by Thráinsson (1986); consider also the discussion in Sigurðsson (1989: chapter 3), from which the Icelandic examples below are taken. As shown by the corresponding Swedish examples, there is no V-to-I in Swedish control infinitives:

(i) a. María lofaði   [að lesa$_i$ ekki [e$_i$ bókina]] (Ice.)
    b. *Maria lovade [att läsa$_i$ inte [e$_i$ boken]] (Sw.)
       M.   promised to read not   the-book
(ii) a. *María lofaði   [að ekki [lesa bókina]] (Ice)
     b. Maria lofade   [att inte [läsa boken]] (Sw.)
        M.   promised to not read the-book

It is interesting to notice that Italian exhibits a similar likeness between finite clauses and infinitives. Since Italian, like Icelandic, is a null-subject language, it is tempting to assume that the null-subject parameter is involved. Cf. Pollock (1989) for a suggestion.

9. All Scandinavian languages accept contextually determined subjectless clauses of a kind which can be analyzed as German pronoun zap (Ross 1982; Huang 1984: 546 ff.), i.e., the element is dropped from the specifier position of CP, as indicated by the fact that also objects may be deleted in this way (cf. [ii]); as for German, this kind of topic-drop is typical of diaries, letters etc.:

(i) a. Ligger på stranden   och skriver detta brev. (Sw.)
       lie   on the beach and write   this letter
       I am lying on the beach, writing this letter'

  b. Vaknaði snemma í morgun. Rakaði mig, ...(Ice)
  woke-up early   in mornig shaved myself
  'I woke up early this morning, shaved myself...'
  c. $[_{CP}$ e$_i[_C$ ligger]$[_{IP}$ e$_i$I $[_{VP}$ e på stranden]]]
(ii) a. Tror   jag inte.(Sw.)
  b. Held   ég ekki.(Ice)
  believe I not
With respect to the occurrence of such examples in Icelandic, cf. Sigu-rðsson (1989).

10. Rizzi (1987) states that (20) only holds for non-pronominal empty categories. Since it is not obvious to us why *pro* should be different from other non-controlled empty categories, we assume (20) to hold for all types of empty categories, except PRO.

11. According to Rizzi, (20i) should refer to canonical head government. A head governs canonically if it governs in the direction that is canonical for the language in question. In Scandinavian, canonical government is government from left to right. The only arguments given for this limitation of head government by Rizzi are provided by examples like (ia,b), which suggest that Infl can license an empty category to the right, but not to the left:

  (i) a. I asked John to go home, and [go home] I think [t' that[he did t]]
  b. *Who do you think [t' that [t left]]

It is not clear to us that the existence of these examples in standard English justifies the introduction of the concept "canonical" in the definition of the empty category principle. Taking Icelandic as the point of departure, where government canonically is to the right, as in English, you could just as well end up with the opposite assumption, since Icelandic does not accept examples corresponding to (ia), whereas examples corresponding to (ib) are well formed.

12. Falk (1987) notices the presence of a certain type of subjectless clause in present-day Swedish, illustrated in (i):

  (i) a. På det här hotellet har [e] bott   många kungligheter.
  at this   hotel   have lived many royal-persons
  b. På hotellrummet   är [e] smutsigt.
  'in the-hotel-room is   dirty
  c. Här blåser [e] förskräckligt.
  here blows   terribly

According to Falk, the empty category in the specifier position of IP in these constructions, indicated by [e] in the examples in (i), is both a trace of the fronted adverbial and a position Case marked by the finite element in C. Being both antecedent governed and head governed, it meets the requirements on empty categories in (20).

13. Except in some uninflected clauses where the auxiliary element is optionally moved to C (cf. Rizzi 1982: 77 ff.). Interestingly, according to Rizzi (1982: 128), these constructions can take a null-subject only if it is interpreted as a dummy.

14. It is interesting to notice that this difference between Italian and Icelandic does not seem to have anything to do with the "strength" of AGR: in both languages there is extensive subject-verb agreement. Notice also that Old Icelandic accepted non-expletive null subjects, as shown by Hjartardóttir (1987). According to her investigation, this possibility was lost during the eighteenth century. Morphologically, nothing happens to subject-verb agreement at this time. Our description predicts, though, that AGR should lose the property of being a theta-assigner during the eighteenth century.

As noticed by Sigurðsson (1989), modern Icelandic may have arbitrary empty subjects, corresponding in meaning to *one* in English:
   (i)   Má e skila bókinni   seinna?
         may deliver the-book later
         'May one deliver the book later?'

15. There are differences within Mainland Scandinavian, though. Norwegian seems to be most liberal, whereas many Danes do not accept pseudopassives at all (Herslund 1984). Swedish lies somewhere in between; cf. Körner (1984).

16. Notice that *Olaf* is in the specifier position of IP in the pseudopassive reading of this example. (27b) is well-formed as an impersonal passive where *Olaf* is topicalized, and the specifier position of IP is empty. As shown by Maling - Zaenen (1985), the two readings have quite distinct syntactic properties.

17. The first attested case of pseudopassive in Swedish is from the middle of the seventeenth century (as reported in Berg 1910). At this time, m-Case was lost in standard Swedish. The same observation is made for English by van Kemenade (1987: 217), who notices that pseudo-passives do not appear until oblique Case is lost.

18. Contrary to Hornstein - Weinberg (1981), we do not believe that P-stranding by wh-movement also presupposes reanalysis. As pointed out by van Riemsdijk (1978), stranding by passivization seems to be subject to severer lexical restrictions than stranding by wh-movement. Consider also Herslund (1984).

19. This is apparent when we compare (28) with a construction where reanalysis cannot apply, due to an intervening adverbial:
   (i)   a.   Du har inte bytt   blöjor   idag på babyn.
              you have not changed nappies today on the-baby
         b.   *Babyn har inte blivit bytt blöjor idag på.
   (ib) shows that reanalysis cannot apply when there is an intervening

adverbial. However, the thematic relations in (1) are the same as in (28), where reanalysis does apply.

20. Lexical Case cannot be absorbed by passive morphology (cf. Haider 1985 and 12c above); hence, the subcategorization feature cannot be satisfied by the passive morphology in (33). Consider also Sigurðsson (1989).

21. It could be argued that even if prepositions are not subcategorized for a lexical Case in Mainland Scandinavian, they are subcategorized [_ NP]. This feature falls under condition (31b), and thus reanalysis should entail a violation of the projection principle in Mainland Scandinavian as well. However, basically following Stowell (1981), we assume there is no subcategorization feature [_ NP]: prepositions are lexically marked as assigning a theta-role and, in Mainland Scandinavian, structural Case. This entails that they must govern a nominal complement: the subcategorization feature [_ NP] is redundant. The feature [_ ACC/DAT/GEN] in the case of Insular Scandinavian prepositions is not redundant: it expresses a basically idiosyncratic property of P, not predictable (other than partially, in certain cases) from the thematic properties of the preposition. Hence it cannot be unified with theta-role assignment.

References

Andrews, Avery
   1976   "The VP complement analysis in modern Icelandic", *NELS* 6: 1-21
Berg, Rudolf G:son
   1910   "Konstruktionen *hon skrattas åt*", *Språk och stil* 10: 143-144
Chomsky, Noam
   1981   *Lectures on government and binding* (Dordrecht: Foris).
   1986   *Knowledge of language: Its nature, origin, and use* (New York: Praeger).
   1986a   *Barriers* (Cambridge, Mass.: MIT Press).
Falk, Cecilia
   1987   "Subjectless clauses in Swedish", *Working Papers in Scandinavian Syntax* 32
Haider, Hubert
   1985   "The Case of German", *Studies in German grammar*, edited by Jindřich Toman
           (Dordrecht: Foris).
Herslund, Michael
   1984   "Particles, prefixes and preposition stranding", *Topics in Danish syntax*, [Ny-

danske Studier & Almen Kommunikationsteori 14: 34-71] (København: Akademisk Forlag).

Hjartardóttir, Þóra Björk
1987 *Geti í Eyurnar. Um eyur fyrir frumlög og andlög í eldri íslensku,* master's thesis (Reykjavík: Department of Linguistics, university of Reykjavík).

Holmberg, Anders
1986 *Word order and syntactic features in the Scandinavian languages and English,* doctoral dissertation (Stockholm: Department of General Linguistics, university of Stockholm).
1988 "The head of S in Scandinavian and English", *McGill Working Papers in Linguistics*: 123-155

Holmberg, Anders - Christer Platzack
in prep "The role of inflection in Scandinavian syntax."

Hornstein, Norbert - Amy Weinberg
1981 "Case theory and preposition stranding", *Linguistic Inquiry* 12: 55-92

Huang, James
1984 "On the distribution and reference of empty pronouns", *Linguistic Inquiry* 15: 531-574

Jaeggli, Osvaldo
1986 "Passive", *Linguistic Inquiry* 17: 587-622

Kayne, Richard
1987 "Null subjects and clitic climbing" (Cambridge, Mass.: unpublished manuscript MIT).

Körner, Rudolf
1948 *Studier över syntaktisk nybildning i svenskan* (Lund: Cleerups).

Kosmeijer, Wim
1986 "The status of the finite inflection in Icelandic and Swedish", *Working Papers in Scandinavian Syntax* 26 (Trondheim: University of Trondheim).

Maling, Joan
1980 "Inversion in embedded clauses in modern Icelandic", *Íslenskt Mál* 2: 175-193

Maling, Joan - Annie Zaenen
1985 "Preposition-stranding and passive", *Nordic Journal of Linguistics* 8: 197-209

Platzack, Christer
1985 "Syntaktiska förändringar i svenskan under 1600-talet", *Svenskans beskrivning* 15, edited by S. Allén et al. (Göteborg: University of Göteborg).
1986 "The position of the finite verb in Swedish", *Verb second phenomena in Germanic languages,* edited by Hubert Haider - Martin Prinzhorn (Dordrecht: Foris).
1987 "The Scandinavian languages and the null subject parameter", *Natural Language & Linguistic Theory* 5: 377-401

1988   "The emergence of a word order difference in Scandinavian subordinate clauses", *McGill Working Papers in Linguistics* May 1988: 215-238

Pollock, Jean-Yves
1989   "Verb movement, universal grammar, and the structure of IP", *Linguistic Inquiry* 20: 365-424

Rizzi, Luigi
1982   *Issues in Italian syntax* (Dordrecht: Foris).
1987   "Relativized minimality" (Geneva: unpublished manuscript university of Geneva).

Ross, John
1982   "Pronoun deleting processes in German", Paper presented at the annual meeting of the LSA, San Diego, California.

Sigurðsson, Halldór
1985   "Subordinate V/1 in Icelandic. How to explain a root phenomenon", *Working Papers in Scandinavian Syntax* 18 (Trondheim: University of Trondheim).
1988   *Verbal syntax and Case in Icelandic Within a comparative GB approach*, doctoral dissertation (Lund: Department of Scandinavian Languages, university of Lund).

Thráinsson, Höskuldur
1979   *On complementation in Icelandic* (New York: Garland).

Travis, Lisa
1984   *Parameters and effects of word order variation*, doctoral dissertation (Cambridge, Mass.: MIT).

Trosterud, Trond
in press   "The null subject parameter and the new Mainland Scandinavian word order: A possible counterexample from a Norwegian dialect", *Proceedings of the Eleventh Scandinavian Conference of Linguistics*, Joensuu 1988.

Van Kemenade, Ans
1987   *Syntactic Case and morphological Case in the history of English* (Dordrecht: Foris).

Van Riemsdijk, Henk
1978   *A case study in syntactic markedness: The binding nature of prepositional phrases* (Dordrecht: Foris).

Yip, Moira - Joan Maling - Ray Jackendoff
1987   "Case in tiers", *Language* 63: 217-250

Zaenen, Annie
1985   *Extraction rules in Icelandic* (New York: Garland).

Zaenen, Annie - Joan Maling - Höskuldur Thráinsson
1985   "Case and grammatical functions: The Icelandic passive", *Natural Language & Linguistic Theory* 3: 441-483

On the division of labour between the grammar and the parser: Some evidence from matching phenomena

Rik Smits

1. Grammars and parsers

Over the past decades, generative linguistics has been busy trying to find out the general characteristics of the grammar that is embodied in each human being. Although most of the way is of course still before us, one might well feel safe in claiming that, so far, the quest has by no means been ineffectual.

In the process, ideas about the contents of the notion "grammar" changed. In the beginning, the search was for a body of rules that would generate all and only the sentences of a language, a period best characterized by work such as *Aspects of the theory of syntax* (Chomsky 1965). In the years that followed, grammar changed more and more from a body of specific rules into a set of principles and wellformedness conditions. The construction-specific transformations, that were so characteristic of the earlier years, all but vanished, giving way to yet another principle, "move alpha", which is perhaps not unfairly paraphrased by "anything goes, put it wherever you want it". The apparent chaos thus created is kept at bay by fellow principles and conditions, such as constitute, for instance, X-bar theory, or the binding theory, in conspiracy with a much strengthened lexicon.

The outward appearance of the earlier, transformational models, with their lists of phrase structure rules and transformations was responsible for a very persistent mistake about the nature of the model. It looks, very much, like a productive machine, as, unfortunately, the name too suggested, actually generating sentences out of something mysterious buried deep inside the psyche - let us call it "thoughts". The transformations were processes, or at least they were formulated as such, that did things to structures. The effect was strengthened by the strict cycle condition, and other ordering principles, which introduced a time dimension into the structures of sentences. The metaphors of movement, and of deep structure changing, ultimately, into surface structure, took over, and in many cases they still do.

With the change from transformational grammar to the present-day models of principles and wellformedness conditions, the possibilities for taking the grammar as a productive system diminished, although this is certainly not realized ubiquitously, perhaps due, to a large extent, to the persistence of the movement metaphor. Nevertheless, principles and conditions are not processes in any way. They are data.

Consequently, our present-day models of the grammar(s) of human language(s) are nothing but sets of data, describing, ultimately, all grammatical configurations of nodes, and only those. Every actual structure that happens to match such a set in all respect is grammatical.

Since the grammar itself, therefore, is essentially inert, it must be complemented by something that does the actual matching, and functions as the interface between strings,[1] i.e., sentences as we hear, see, speak or write them, and the grammar proper. It is this process that I shall call "the parser".

The question is, then, whether the role of the parser is trivial or not. That is: does it, or does it not, of its own accord contribute to the interpretation or interpretability of sentences? And, conversely, does it put its own limits on productive generability, or can it realise effortlessy every possible structure that conforms to the grammar? My contention is that its role is, in fact, far from trivial, and that, therefore, a complete and correct description of the grammar cannot be arrived at without investigating the role of the parser as well.

There are two main reasons for this contention. The first one lies in the different types of judgments that people have about sentences.

Suppose that the grammar proper is decidable in every respect. That is, for each principle and for each parameter value, there is a set of structures that conforms to it, and a complementary set that does not, but there are no pertinent structures that neither comform to it nor violate it. Then, the world of sentential structures should ultimately be clearly and unequivocally divided into grammatical and ungrammatical sentences, even though judgments may, of course, sometimes be subtle. Moreover, ungrammatical sentences ought to be uninterpretable as well, since no sensible structure can be assigned to them. This, however, is not at all what we actually find. There are many cases which are commonly classed as acceptable, meaning that they are grammatically doubtful, but nevertheless quite interpretable. Without sacrificing decidablity, this leniency cannot reside in the grammar itself. Also, acceptable sentences are qualitatively of a different order than mere ungrammatical or incomplete sentences that can be, to some extent, reconstructed by using the redundancy present in the linguistic and extra-linguistic environment, such as headlines, or speech in a bad telephone connection. What is left, is the parser.

Conversely, I would claim that there are numerous sentences that are completely, provably, grammatical, but nevertheless unacceptable, or even completely uninterpretable. Center-embeddings are a case that immediately springs to mind, of course, but also sentences with manyfold quantification are a case in point: nobody without pen and paper and a thorough training in logic will pick out more than two or perhaps three interpretations from an actually 64 times ambiguous sentence, such as the one about senators attending election rallies that figures in many places in the linguistic literature of the seventies.

In fact, far from a clear cut division of the world of sentences into grammatical and ungrammatical, coextensive with a division between interpretable and uninterpretable, what we seem to have is a partitioning as in (1).

(1)

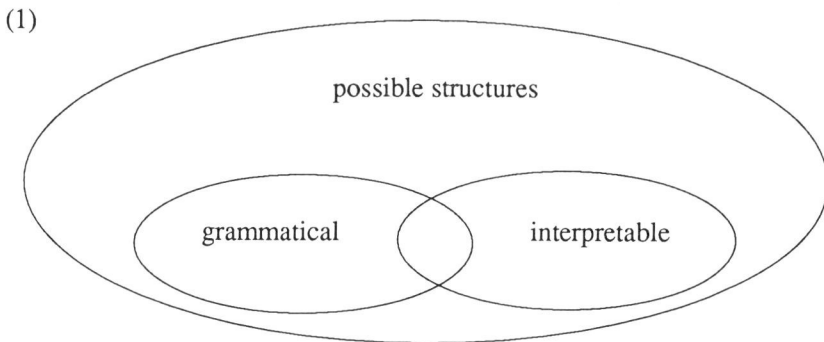

possible structures

grammatical interpretable

In (1), the product of the set of grammatical sentences and that of interpretable sentences is what we usually call grammatical sentences. The interpretable but not grammatical ones are the acceptable sentences, and, e.g. center-embeddings are grammatical but not interpretable.

The second reason lies in the existence of matching phenomena.

2. Matching phenomena: an inventory of characteristics

The best known, and best investigated, matching phenomena are those involved in free relatives.

Free relatives are structured as in (2).

(2) Free relative

  $[_{XP}$ ∅ $[_{Rel.clause}$ Rel.phrase$_i$ ... e$_i$ ...]]

Thus, a free relative is a relative construction lacking an expressed antecedent. The relative phrase in Comp of the relative clause in the free relative is or contains a relative pronoun.

Matching in free relatives means that the relative phrase in Comp must conform to demands set both to the gap in the relative clause itself, and to the free relative as a whole, by their respective structural environments, i.e., the demands p and q in (3).

(3)

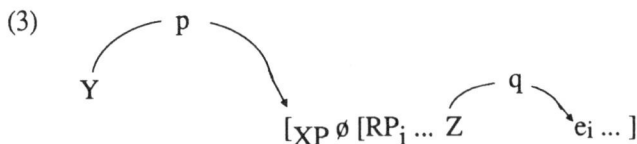

First and foremost, the demands in question include Case properties. As the German examples in (4) show, the relative phrase of a free relative must conform to both the Case assigned to the associated gap and the Case assigned to the whole free relative. Notice that syncretism saves (4c).

(4) a. ich nehme, [*wen* du mir e$_{acc}$ empfiehlst]$_{acc}$.

  I take whom you me recommand.

    b. *ich nehme, [*wem* du e$_{dat}$ vertraust]$_{acc}$.
        I take who you trust.

    c. ich habe [*was* e$_{nom}$ noch übrig war]$_{acc}$ weggeschmissen.
        I have what yet left was away thrown.

Apart from exceptions created by ill-understood relabelling strategies that seem to reflect certain Case-hierarchies (see, e.g., McCreight 1987; Harbert 1983, and references cited there), Case matching seems to be a universal requirement among languages that show overt Case, and syncretism is an equally universal neutralising factor. Thus, both Polish and Russian require Case matching accross the board, but allow a Case conflict in (5) and (6), respectively, because the relative phrase is syncretic between nominative and accusative.

(5) kupiłam [ø [*co* e$_{nom}$ było w sklepie]]$_{acc}$.
     I bought what was in the shop.

(6) kupila [ø [*čto* e$_{nom}$ bylo v magazine]]$_{acc}$.
     I bought what was in the shop.

Next to Case properties, categorial properties must usually be satisfied in a similar fashion. Thus, generally speaking, if there is a pied piped PP in Comp of the free relative, then the whole free relative cannot be in a position that allows NPs only, as (7) and (8) exemplify.

(7) a. Jane loves [*whom*$_i$ you despise e$_i$].
     b. *Jane loves [[with *whom*]$_i$ you were talking e$_i$].
     c. *Jane loves [*whom*$_i$ you were talking e$_i$].

(8) a. Jane fights for [*what*$_i$ she considers e$_i$ important].
     b. Jane fights for [*what*$_i$ she believes in e$_i$].
     c. *Jane fights for [[in *which*]$_i$ she believes e$_i$].

The latter phenomenon has inspired the thought that, in a way, the whole free relative takes on the categorial guise of its relative phrase. A view that was most radically formulated in the so-called head-hypothesis, according to which the relative phrase is supposed to actually move to the empty antecedent position, thus forcing its categorial properties on the whole free relative. But does any change in categorial properties actually come about?

In other words, what is the categorial status of XP in (1), and does it ever change?

As an obviously restrictive relative construction, the unmarked value of XP in (1) would be NP. Since pied piping in free relatives is very limited, restricted to PPs and/or possessive NPs only, the whole question of categorial matching boils down to whether a free relative ever acquires PP-hood. If this were indeed the case, we would expect free relatives with a prepositional relative phrase to occur in positions that do accommodate PPs, but not NPs. Many adjunct positions - where no Cases are assigned - are such positions, as are the object positions of verbs that only take prepositional objects.

The examples in (9) and (10) clearly show that there is no question of categorial status of free relatives changing. Whether or not there is a PP in Comp makes no difference: positions that exclude NPs consistently exclude free relatives as well. As a consequence, we are forced to conclude that the categorial value of a free relative is always NP.[2]

(9) a. John ate a sausage [in the kitchen].
     b. *John ate a sausage [the kitchen].
     c. *John ate a sausage [in which he was preparing dinner].
     d. *John ate a sausage [which/what he was preparing dinner in].
     e. he did that [for a simple reason].
     f. *he did that [a simple reason].
     g. *he did that [for which he drank his milk there too].
     h. *he did that [what he drank his milk there too for]

(10) a. John never talked *to his wife*.
     b. *John never talked *his wife*.
     c. *John never talked [*to whom*$_i$ I spoke e$_i$].
     d. *John never talked [*who*$_i$ I spoke to e$_i$].

Rather surprisingly, the categorial matching requirement is somewhat relaxed in certain languages for free relatives in subject position, but never in other positions. Within the Germanic and Romance languages, it is the Romance group minus French which may, albeit at times only grudgingly, allow matching violations. The examples (11) are illustrative cases from Catalan, Spanish, Romanian, French, English and Dutch, respectively.

(11) a. [[al *que*] s'enganya] pren cautela   i   s'apanya.
       (to) whom one cheats   takes precautions and manages

     b. [[con *quien*] me quiero casar R] vive a   la vuelta.
       with whom I   want   to marry lives around the corner

     c. [[la *ce*] se uità Maria R]   costà muli bani.
       at what   M. is looking costs much money

     d. *[[à *qui*] tu as parlé R hier]   m'aime pas.
       to whom you talked   yesterday doesn't love me

     e. *[[with *whom*] I danced yesterday] is sitting at that table
       in the corner.

     f. *[[over *wie*] Marja het gisteren had R] is vandaag tegen
       een boom gereden.
       about whom M. was talking yesterday has driven into
       a tree today

Clearly, therefore, the divide runs along the pro-drop parameter. Case and categorial matching phenomena are not restricted to free relatives alone. As we saw in the examples above, adjunct positions do not accept NPs in general, including free relatives. Similarly, we find both Case and categorial matching effects in left dislocations.

Left dislocation basically occurs in two varieties, which go by the names of hanging topic left dislocation (HTLD) and contrastive left dislocation (or: clitic left dislocation) respectively.[3] Contrastive left dislocation features a moved and/or special pronoun (e.g. a clitic), resuming the function of the left dislocated phrase. Hanging topic left dislocation lacks such a special pronoun. Here, the pronoun that refers to the left dislocated constituent is an ordinary personal pronoun in its basic position. These types are illustrated from Dutch and Icelandic in (12) and (13).

(12) Hanging topic left dislocation: ordinary pronoun,
     in normal base position.

     a. *de prinses*,   ik ken haar nauwelijks.
       the princess, I hardly know her

     b. **in zijn nopjes*, hij is het niet.
       in good spirits, he is not it

     c. *þessi hringur*$_{nom}$, Ólafur hefur lofað Maríu honum$_{dat}$.
       this   ring,   O.   has   promised it to M.

(13) Contrastive left dislocation: special pronoun, clitic,
   or moved pronoun.
   a. *de prinses,*   die$_i$ ken ik e$_i$ nauwelijks.
      the princess, that-one I hardly know
   b. *In Siberie,* daar$_i$ ben ik nooit e$_i$ geweest.
      in S.,   there I've never been
   c. *þessum hring*$_{dat}$, honum$_{dat}$ hefur Ólafur lofað   Maríu e.
      this   ring,   it   has   O.   promised to M.

These examples show clearly the different properties of hanging topic
left dislocation and contrastive left dislocation, respectively. Hanging topic
left dislocation allows no PPs in left dislocated position, only NPs, whereas
contrastive left dislocation allows both, on provision that the category of
the left dislocated constituent matches that of the gap or special pronoun
connected to it. Contrastive left dislocation, on the other hand, requires Case
matching between the left dislocated constituent (13c) and the pronoun
connected with it, in contrast with hanging topic left dislocation, which
yields a default nominative (12c). Left dislocated free relatives confirm this
once more, as shown from Dutch in (14) and (15) for the categorial aspect.

(14)   Hanging topic left dislocation
   a. *wat je ze ook beloofd hebt*, je moet het ook echt doen.
      whatever you promised them, you must really do it too
   b. **over wie jij net sprak*, ik draai *hem* zijn nek om!
      about whom you were talking just now, I'll wring his neck

(15)   Contrastive left dislocation
   a. *bij wie je goed eet, daar* moet je een paar dagen blijven.
      at whose (house) you eat well, there you must stay for a few days
   c. ?**wat zij een goed hotel noemen, daar* is niet eens een wc.
      what they call a good hotel, there is not even a toilet

The fact that hanging topic left dislocation, where there is no obvious
syntactic connection, no chain in any syntactic sense of the word, between
the left dislocated constituent and the rest of the sentence, can accommodate
NPs, entails that the left dislocated position is a position to which Case is
assigned independently. Although the mechanism responsible for doing so
is far from clear, this seems like a safe assumption, all the more since, as

the Icelandic example shows, it is the nominative, which seems to have default properties anyway, that is assigned here. In contrastive left disloca-tion, then, assuming that both types of left dislocation employ the same structural position, this default Case assignment gives way to Case inher-itance along a chain, connecting the left dislocated phrase to the special pronoun.[4]

The structural position of the left dislocated phrase is a very weak one. In fact, it is outside the structure of the sentence proper, as the Dutch example (16) shows. In Dutch main clauses, the verb moves to the Comp position, and one constituent, never more, moves to the left thereof: to the specifier position of the CP. This position is the landing site for all wh-mo-vement: fronting in main clauses as well as questioning and topicalisation. That is: all of these are mutually exclusive. The left dislocated position, however, is still farther out, although there does not seem to be a structural position available there.

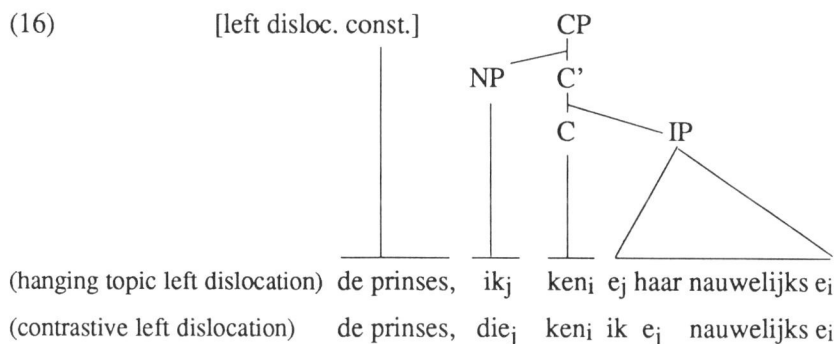

(16)   [left disloc. const.]   CP
                                          NP   C'
                                                 C   IP

(hanging topic left dislocation) de prinses, ik_j ken_i e_j haar nauwelijks e_i

(contrastive left dislocation)   de prinses, die_j ken_i ik e_j nauwelijks e_i

To be interpretable, the left dislocated constituent must be connected to the rest somehow, and there seem to be only two ways of doing that: either by the kind of connectedness introduced by contrastive left dislocation, or through default nominative Case assignment.

But hanging topic left dislocation does not only allow NPs, it disallows PPs as well. This suggests that default Case assignment in this position is simply obligatory, since there are no other factors involved that might exclude PPs.

Now, finally, the contours of a coherent picture of matching phenomena are emerging. As it turns out, all the cases of categorial matching have some to do with Case assignment: NPs in adjunct positions are, not surprisingly, excluded for lack of Case (9); free relatives with a prepositional relative phrase are allowed in subject position only in pro-drop languages (11); PPs in hanging topic left dislocation are excluded because of the obligatory nominative Case assignment (14). More or less the same holds for free relatives in object positions. If the object position is suitable for a NP, free relatives are in principle allowed, but not with a prepositional relative phrase (7,8). If the object position is not suitable for a NP, then free relatives are impossible altogether (10). Chances are, therefore, that categorial matching is nothing but an epiphenomenon of Case matching, and that a solution for the latter phenomenon should cover categorial matching as well.

3. The status of matching phenomena

The most striking aspect of Case matching is its sensitivity to syncretism. On the positive side, this sensitivity explains why we seem to find Case matching effects only in languages that show overt Case marking. Languages that have no overt Case marking are simply languages with syncretism across the board. Thus, we may conclude, Case matching is ubiquitously present.

On the other hand, however, the status of Case matching with respect to the grammar becomes quite problematic. The syncretism sensitivity suggests that, at best, Case matching is linked to the morphology. However, morphological rules are confined to the word domain, and the effects of Case matching are, if anything, strictly syntactic, and by no means morphological. Our conclusion must be, then, that Case matching has to do with the terminal string, which is the only linguistic level surpassing word boundaries where syncretism is visible, rather than with the actual grammatical structure, the tree, where abstract Case is visible.

Moreover, categorial matching, which is probably linked to Case matching, introduces the problem of the mix-up of the relative phrase with the (absent) antecedent. That is, the actual structure (17a) behaves as if it were (17b).

(17) a. $[_{NP}$ ø $[$ XP ... $]]$
    b. $[_{XP}$ ... $]$

The only perspective from which (17a) and (17b) can be perceived as equal is, once more, that of the terminal string. For only XP will be present there, no bracketing, no labels, no empty nodes.

So, both Case matching and categorial matching turn out to have to do with appearance rather than structure, with the terminal string rather than the tree. In short: matching must be an effect of the interface between strings and structures, i.e., of the parser as defined before, and not of the grammar proper.

4. Prolegomena towards a human parser

What should a feasible human parser look like in general, and what properties will it need to yield matching effects? The basic properties in (18) seem to be no more than reasonable, and have already, either implicitly or explicitly, been proposed in several places.

(18) Basic properties of a human parser
    1. smallest structure seeking.
    2. left to right.
    3. backtracking.

All three properties are easily defendable.

Firstly, a parser should, as its basic strategy, always strive towards completing a structure as quickly and simply as possible, it must be an algorithm. If not, it would at some point just go on generating empty and senseless hypothetical structure for ever, and one might never finish interpreting the sentence. Secondly, suppose that a parser did not operate from left to right. At least two very common things would never occur then: false starts[5] (for a sentence should be completely ready before even beginning to utter it: something might move up front at the last moment), and take-overs, the situation where a speaker is in the middle of a sentence and the hearer already knows what he is going to say, and finishes the sentence for him. Thirdly, backtracking is certainly a characteristic of the human parser since we do have the capacity to interpret garden path constructions correctly, with reasonable success.

A fourth property of the parser will account for matching phenomena: the parser will act on available information only. That is, it may use information from the parts of a structure already parsed, and draw from the rules that the grammar implies, but nothing else. Specifically, it will, on encountering some item in the string, create a continuation of the structure only in accordance with this available information.

(19) Available information principle
Every next state follows directly from the intersection of properties of the previous state with the grammar.

Let us consider how this affects a case of Case matching.
Suppose we have a partial structure like (20a).[6] The parser has found a transitive preposition at word w^i, and set up a PP projection. It has also checked in the lexicon that this preposition assigns dative Case.

(20) a.

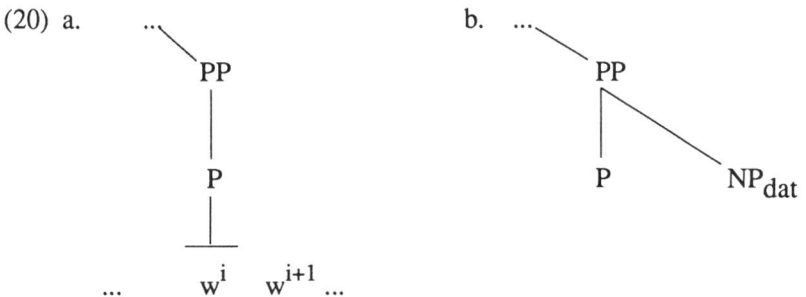

The information available from the present state is: there is a dative Case to be assigned within the open maximal projection. The grammar will yield only one rule for expanding this partial construction: PP — P - NP. This yields the next state: (20b). So the information that a NP must follow is also available. Now suppose that the complement of this preposition is a free relative without pied piping. Then, the next word encountered is a Case marked pronoun. Suppose that this pronoun is overtly marked accusative, as distinct from dative. It will not fit as complement NP. So all the parser can do is check the available rules for expanding NP, to find one that starts with an accusative NP. There is no such rule and, since no rule applies, the parser gives up the parse as nonterminable.

Notice that backtracking will not help: there is no point at which an alternative choice could have been made within the limits allowed, either for better or for worse.

Now suppose that the pronoun is either marked dative, or syncretic with dative marking. The parser will happily, although wrongly, take the pronoun to be the sought NP in (20b), and close the PP projection. Upon parsing on, however, it will discover that its choice was incorrect, and that it should probably be building up a clause. And now backtracking will help: the available information upon coming back to state (20b) now also includes the fact that probably a wh-clause follows. So now the grammar can be checked for rules that unify NPs and clauses. Such a rule is indeed present: the relative rule that says something like NP → N - CP. Only at this point, (20b) can be expanded into (21), on the right track.

(21)

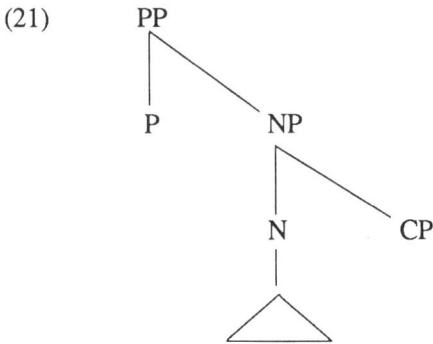

Suppose there was a prepositional relative phrase in the free relative of (20). Then the first thing that the parser would have encountered trying to expand (20b) would have been a preposition. That can mean only one thing:

the start of a PP, instead of the expected NP. The only way out would be a rule of the type NP → PP ..., but no such rule falls out from the grammar. Thus, precisely the same will happen as with incompatibly Case-marked relative pronouns: the parser will give up, unable either to find an expansion or to close the current CP grammatically.

Similar strategies will explain the distribution of matching violations in subject position. In a non-pro-drop language, there must be an identifiable subject carrying the nominative Case. A non-matching free relative will therefore be unequivocally classed as "cannot be the subject". In the end, a subject will fail to appear altogether, to the parser, at least, and rejection ensues. In a pro-drop language, however, nominative may be carried by Infl. This is why no overt subject is syntactically needed there. Conversely, however, pro-drop opens the way for non-matching subjects: at first, they will, again, be parsed as "not the subject", but on backtracking they may be reclassified as subjects even though they are stringwise incompatible with nominative Case: for by then the parser has already decided that nominative has been expressed on Infl, so it will not bother about Case assignment at all.

Also, we can explain why default Case assignment in hanging topic left dislocation is obligatory, a property we would like to avoid in the grammar. Suppose the parser encounters a PP in hanging topic left dislocation position. It will correctly parse it for what it is, but never see the default Case marking which would identify it as a hanging topic left dislocation phrase. Instead, it will just take it to be some sentence adverbial, thus arriving ultimately at an incoherent (or simply different) interpretation.

Of course, this has been no more than a very impressionistic first sketch of what a human parser could perhaps look like. Nevertheless, I feel that the evidence I have presented from matching effects makes it quite clear that further serious investigation into the nature and workings of the parser, as complementing the grammar, is in order if we want to come closer to our ultimate goal: a correct description of human language.

Notes

1.   Or other appropriate "structures", such as we find in sign language, where simultaneity seems to occur, and where linguistic space, other than with ordinary spoken or written utterances, is certainly not one-dimensional.

2.   On free relatives in *where* and *when*, etc., see Smits (in press).

3.   See v. Haeften - Smits - Vat (1983); Cinque (1977).

4.   Possibly the link from pronoun to left-dislocated phrase is of the same or similar make as that between relative pronouns and their antecedent, although much is still unclear here. In van Haeften - Smits - Vat (1983), a contrastive left dislocation analysis is proposed which employs the "promotion analysis" that was proposed for relatives in Vergnaud (1974). Unfortunately, that promotion analysis is not unproblematic in relatives, and these problems carry over, for the most part, to contrastive left dislocation. To my knowledge, there are no really satisfying alternatives for left dislocation available. For a discussion of the promotion analysis see Smits (in press).

5.   For lack of space I cannot here go into the question of how the parser plays a crucial role in generation, except by saying that feedback is one of the factors involved. See Smits (in prep.).

6.   Only the absolutely essential aspects are represented here.

References

Chomsky, Noam
 1965   *Aspects of the theory of syntax* (Cambridge, Mass.: MIT Press).

Cinque, Guglielmo
 1977   "The movement nature of left dislocation", *Linguistic Inquiry* 8.2: 397-412

McCreight, K.
 1987   "Case hierarchies: the evidence from free relatives", *CLS* 23

Groos, Anneke - Henk van Riemsdijk
 1981   "Matching effects in free relatives", *Theory of markedness in generative grammar*, edited by Adriana Belletti - Luciana Brandi - Luigi Rizzi (Pisa: Scuola Normale Superiore di Pisa).

Harbert, Wayne
 1983   "On the nature of the matching parameter", *The Linguistic Review* 2.3: 237-284

Smits, Rik
  in press *The Grammar of relative and cleft constructions in the Germanic and Romance languages* (Dordrecht: Foris).
  in prep. "On the human parser"

Van Haaften, Ton - Rik Smits - Jan Vat
  1983 "Left dislocation, connectedness, and reconstruction", *On the formal syntax of the Westgermania*, edited by Werner Abraham (Amsterdam: John Benjamins).

Vergnaud, Jean R.
  1974 *French relative clauses*, doctoral dissertation (Cambridge, Mass.: MIT).

Syntactic nominalization:
A study in Dutch X-bar syntax and semantics[1]

Ron van Zonneveld

1. Background

Nominalization is a hydra-headed linguistic object, showing up in different components of the grammar as a different phenomenon. In semantics, it is an operation for making terms (Noun Phrases) out of predicates (Verb Phrases), or, more generally, any process enabling reference to abstract entities. In morphology, it is a lexical operation for deriving abstract nominals, such as Dutch *oprechtheid* and English *sincerity*, based on the adjectives *oprecht* and *sincere*. In syntax, this process view on nominalization seems the predominant one. The nominal use of the non-finite verb in Dutch or the English *-ing*-gerunds, then, is seen as a syntactic operation, a transformation in the original sense of the word, or a deverbalization rule in terms of X-bar syntax. The following example may help to illustrate this point: Groningen University makes use of the advertising slogan (1), in which two infinitives function as nouns, so to speak. The phrase is an NP, and *werken* is the head of the phrase.

(1) Rijksuniversiteit Groningen: *werken* aan de grenzen van het *weten*
    University of Groningen: working at the limits of the knowing
                             'working at the limits of knowledge'

If we add the predicate *is bijzonder aantrekkelijk* 'is very attractive', then phrase (1) may serve as an instantiation of the notion "syntactic nominalization", provisorily defined as in (2).

(2) Syntactic nominalization (SN):
    Syntactic nominalization involves a construction with external nominal and internal verbal properties.

Definition (2) can be pictured as in (3), where the syntactic nominalization phrase is the subject of the sentence.

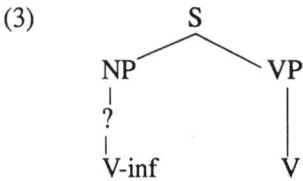

(3)

```
                S
          ╱         ╲
       NP             VP
        |              |
        ?              |
        |              |
      V-inf            V
```

The present article is about the dotted line in (3), hence the presence of a question mark. In the spirit of Jackendoff (1977), X-bar syntax deals with syntactic nominalization in terms of deverbalization (cf. Hoekstra - Wehrmann 1985, Van Haaften et al. 1985, Hoekstra 1986, Stuurman 1987), and (4) demonstrates how this would work for (1), assuming a maximal two level projection.

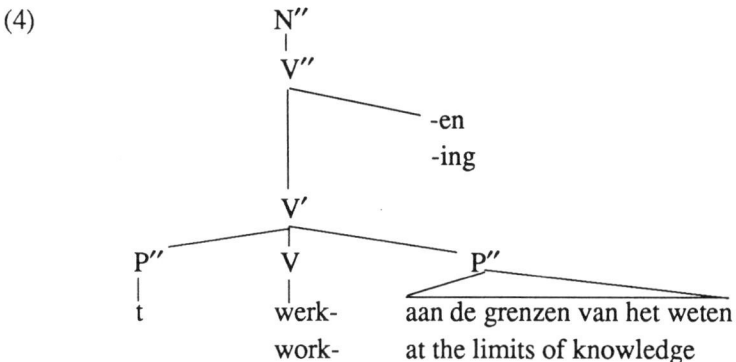

(4)

```
                    N″
                    |
                    V″
                    |    ╲
                    |     ╲ -en
                    |       -ing
                    |
                    V′
            ╱       |        ╲
         P″         V          P″
          |         |         ╱  ╲
          t       werk-      aan de grenzen van het weten
                  work-      at the limits of knowledge
```

A striking feature of this representation is the phrasal scope of the infinitival affix, intending to express the idea that the deverbalization process starts at the V′-level. Since Dutch is assumed to be an SOV-language, the verbal P-complement must have been extraposed from pre-verbal to post-verbal position, leaving behind a trace t.[2] As an alternative, the infinitive could be taken to be a noun, the P-complement being interpreted as an instance of argument-inheritance. Of course, there are other alternatives accounting for the mixed noun-verb nature of syntactic nominalizations, and here Reuland (1986) and Reuland - Kosmeijer (1989) deserve special mention, although we will not make use of their null-head analysis of this construction. First, because of the restricted domain of application: null-heads are supposed to be licensed by the determiner and so this theory is not appropriate for determiner-less kinds of syntactic nominalizations, such as in (1). Second, because of the incorporation of Infl in these structures, which makes this analysis incompatible with the one to be developed here. Reuland's analysis of syntactic nominalizations with a determiner and a variable representing the null head, looks as (5). The dots stand for the complementation possibilities at the different levels, as utilized in the example.

(5) $[_{X''}$ Det $[_{X'}$ .... $[_{I''}$ .... V-inf] (x) ....]]   (X = N)
  dat afschuwelijke dieren   pesten   van Karel (is een schandaal)
  that terrible   animals harassing of Karel (is a   scandal)
  'that terrible harassing of animals by Karel is a scandal'

The analysis of syntactic nominalization that we prefer will neither give rise to zero heads or deverbalization processes, nor to an Infl-structure within the SN-projection. Rather, the absence of Infl, conceived as a kind of sentential operator marking the subject-predicate agreement and providing the tense features, will be taken to be one of the essential properties of syntactic nominalizations, with or without a specifier.

Since we concentrate on syntactic nominalization, other types of nominalization, such as the ones exemplified in (6), as adapted from Chierchia (1985), remain outside the scope of our interest.

(6) a. Wijsheid is nauwelijks te vinden
     wisdom is hard   to find
  b. De eigenschap wijs te zijn is nauwelijks te vinden
     the property   wise to be is hard   to find
     'the property of being wise is hard to find'
  c. ?Wijs te zijn is gek
     wise to be is crazy
     'to be wise is crazy'

The nominalization type (6a) and (6b) belongs to morphology or lexicology as it is subject to several kinds of lexical restrictions. In this respect,

Dutch is not very different from languages such as English or German (cf. Ten Cate 1985, Lachlan Mackenzie 1986, Ok Oh 1988, and many others).

Of particular interest is (6c), since according to our intuitions the Dutch infinitive marker *te* is not equally acceptable in syntactic nominalizations as the English *to*. Both 'to be wise' and 'being wise' correspond to the Dutch phrase 'wijs zijn'. This distributional observation points in the direction of an analysis for *te*-infinitive phrases as oblique tenseless clauses, i.e., clauses that cannot function as external arguments (subjects). Some support for this point of view can be found in the observation that extraposition of the *te*-phrase in (6c), followed by the substitution of the empty subject by the pronoun *het* 'it', results in the perfect sentence (7a). However, we would not count (7a) as a straightforward instance of syntactic nominalization, but rather as a case of sentential complementation, just like (7b) and (7c).

(7) a. Het is gek   om wijs te zijn
       it is crazy for wise to be
       'it is crazy to be wise'
    b   Het is fijn om thuis te komen
        it is nice for home to come
        'it is nice to come home'
    c. Het is moeilijk om een baan te vinden
       it is hard   for a   job to find
       'it is hard to find a job'

Recent literature dealing with syntactic nominalization in terms of X-bar theory apparently gives preference to descriptions in terms of juggling with categorial features, percolation conventions, zero heads and moving affixes. But in spite of some descriptive succes, we think that the phenomenon of syntactic nominalization by itself still remains a mystery. For instance, syntactic categorial features are by no means self-explanatory and so a description of the syntactic nominalization along these lines must be based on the assumption that Dutch has two homonymous infinitives, the one carrying nominal features and the other verbal ones. But this solution simply begs the question and hence no new insight is gained. Likewise, the deverbalization analysis and the affix-movement strategy come down to a restatement of the problem of syntactic nominalization, even adding new questions like why there would be deverbalization and not also denominalization, for instance, or why bound morphemes would be free only in underlying structures, and so on.

What we want to do is to try to establish a link to X-bar theory, flirting with formal semantics, with the old structural tradition and base this connection on the Bloomfieldian notions of endocentricity and exocentricity, or equivalently, the Jespersonian notions of junction and nexus. The reader might be well aware of the fact that this old phrasal distinction is somehow suppressed or disguised in X-bar theory, since within this theory the phrasal categories are developed as projections of lexical and non-lexical head categories and hence they all look like endocentric categories. However, projections headed by Infl or Comp represent the traditional exocentric phrases, typically subject-predicate connections such as 'John ran', where the resultant phrase, i.e. the combination of *John* and *ran*, belongs to the form-class of no immediate constituent (Bloomfield 1933: 194). We suggest that this distinction in phrasal categories should be exploited for the analysis of syntactic nominalization, the outstanding representatives of endocentricity and exocentricity being a Noun Phrase and a sentence, respectively. A picture of this idea is presented in (8), along with the corresponding semantic types. Here the Montagovian point of view is adopted, in the sense that all syntactic categories but for the maximal S-projection (S' or S'') are interpreted as functions of greater or lesser complexity: N and S are property or set-expressions, i.e., functions from entities to truth-values and full NPs are interpreted as properties of properties. With this presentation of the semantics, of course, we disregard the actual vivid discussion on NP-interpretation and type-shifting principles.[3]

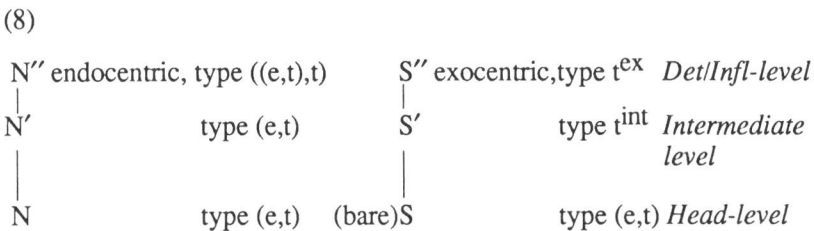

(8)

N″ endocentric, type ((e,t),t)		S″ exocentric, type t^{ex}	*Det/Infl-level*
N′	type (e,t)	S′	type t^{int} *Intermediate level*
N	type (e,t) (bare)S		type (e,t) *Head-level*

The semantic types of the different sentential levels S' and S'' are given here as intensions and extensions, without using the proper categories (s,t) and t. This is done for reasons of simplicity, since we do not want to add intensions to the type-categories. Perhaps any phrase might be interpreted intensionally, then leaving the extensional connection with the universe of discourse to Infl. We can safely get around this issue, for it does not touch on our analysis.

The central move in this analysis is pictured in (9), where the head-level categories N and S are identified as possible starting-points for a noun phrase projection. This identification is justified by the semantics, for both N and S are set or property denoting expressions. Moreover, this move is also covered by syntactic considerations, since N and S have an overlapping distribution, in the sense that S may project just like N as a maximal NP.

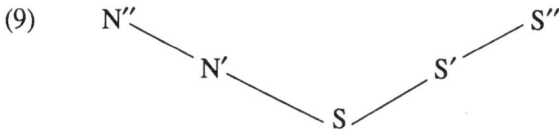

(9)
$$N'' \diagdown \qquad \diagup S''$$
$$\diagdown N' \diagdown \qquad \diagup S' \diagup$$
$$\diagdown S \diagup$$

According to this picture, syntactic nominalization is not a process or a transformation, but rather a choice for a projection direction. In the next sections, we will discuss some distributional evidence in support of this claim. First, we will examine the factual range of options for the bare S head and suggest that this S may also function as the head of an adjectival phrase, where the choices are triggered by the inflectional properties of the verb. This will be the topic of section 2. In section 3 the phrase-internal properties of syntactic nominalizations are put on the stage. There the basic distinction of infinitives within the domain of a determiner on the one hand and determinerless infinitives on the other, as established in Dik (1985), Hoekstra - Wehrmann (1985), Van Haaften et al. (1985) and Reuland (1986), is incorporated in our bare S-based analysis.

2. The many faces of bare S

To start with, let us assume that bare S is a maximal V-projection including an empty subject position. This assumption is in harmony with the extended projection principle (Chomsky 1981), to the extent that at least a variable standing for the external argument is projected within the lexically determined V-projection structure, but it deviates in the sense that the overt external argument is excluded from this projection. The effects of this move are of two kinds. On the one hand, we express the idea that a VP is an incomplete or unsatisfied category, in need of satisfaction by a subject NP, whether or not this subject is lexically expressed. So we arrive at a complete picture of a maximal V-projection, to be identified with bare S, if both internal and external V-argument positions are represented. Semantically, this means that a regular first-order VP is not interpreted as a set-expression, but as a function from entities to sets (or properties), whereas the result of combining an empty subject *e* with a VP is indeed a set-expression. The canonical form of bare S, then, is taken to be as in (10), representing an SOV-language such as Dutch or German, and neglecting VP-internal semantics. This VP equals the category IV in Montague-grammar, and its incompleteness is nicely expressed by the one bar level.

(10)

$$S\,(e,t)$$

$$N''\,e \qquad V'(e,(e,t))$$

$$X'' \qquad V$$

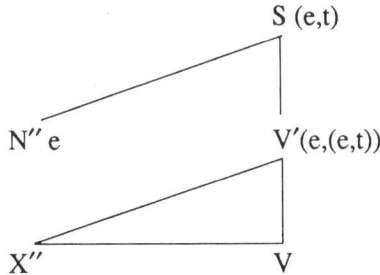

Now, on the other hand, this make-up of bare S puts us in a position to relate syntax and semantics in yet another respect, for if we bind the subject variable with an overt external argument, we are doing something like closing an open sentence. We might as well say that a bare S is an open sentence and that the subject variable is a PRO-subject. Normally, its denotation is taken to be *e*, standing for whatever individual entities in the world, although this arbitrariness might be governed by semantic properties of the VP or by general contextual features. In special cases, the subject variable is of a higher order (cf. section 3). The generic flavour of the empty subject interpretation is nicely demonstrated by the choice of the generic reflexive pronoun *jezelf*, as in the first example of (11), where other reflexives without a binding antecedent are excluded. For the sake of concreteness, in (11) some instantiations are presented of the general bare S projection (10), where X'' stands for any maximal category.

(11) $[_S N''$ X'' V-inf]

	X''	V-inf	
x	jezelf	tatoeëren	
	oneself	tattooing	'tattooing oneself'
	elkaar	helpen	
	each other	helping	'helping each other'
	dieren	pesten	
	animals	harassing	'harassing animals'
	naar de maan	vliegen	
	to the moon	flying	'flying to the moon'
	een boek lezen	proberen	'proberen een boek te lezen' =
	a book to read	trying	'trying to read a book'

As is pictured in (9), the crucial point in our analysis is that bare S projects either exocentrically or endocentrically. Before sticking to the endocentric construction, let us first see what an exocentric S-projection would look like. We suggest that the external argument is a sister of bare S and that this position receives nominative Case, because it is outside the domain of any lexical Case-assigning category.[4] The result of combining bare S with an external argument is the intermediate S' level, under the assumption that the maximal sentential level is reached by applying agreement morphology on the subject-predicate-combination S'. The semantic function of the agreement features might be seen as expressing the connection between the closed sentence S' with the time-place coordinates of an interpretation model. As we will see below, aspectual inflection, such as encoded in present and perfect participles, must already be available at the head-level of the projection. Consequently, the visible effect of Infl is limited to the choice of the finite verb in combination with the gender, person and number features of the external argument. Next, complementizers are not incorporated in the maximal S-projection, since it is a categorial property of complementizers that they combine with maximal sentences, resulting in syntactically dependent or subordinate clauses. So, in a theory of movement, the landing-site for topicalized constituents could not easily be the complementizer position, for the only empty position meeting the c-command requirement for antecedent-anaphor binding would be Infl. We cannot pursue the matter further, but the absence of complementizers within an S″ projection serves the semantics as well, in that the denotation of a full sentence is taken to be a truth-value. Evidently, the combination of a complementizer and a sentence does not denote a truth-value, but a function of some sort. The picture that arises from these speculations is presented in (12).

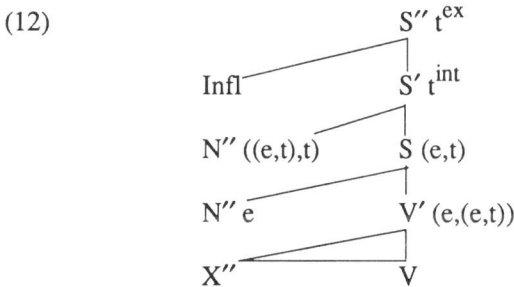

(12)

$$S''\ t^{ex}$$
$$\text{Infl}\qquad S'\ t^{int}$$
$$N''\ ((e,t),t)\qquad S\ (e,t)$$
$$N''\ e\qquad V'\ (e,(e,t))$$
$$X''\qquad V$$

Some verb features that are usually taken to reflect the working of Infl have to be available within the level of bare S. For example, in syntactic nominalizations the verb, which is not necessarily the main verb, appears in its infinitival form. So within these constructions we come across verbal complexes as exemplified in (13).

(13) a. Iemand   ontslaan aan de Groningse universiteit (is moeilijk)
         somebody firing   at the Groningen university (is difficult)
         'firing somebody at the Groningen university is difficult'
      b. Iemand   ontslagen hebben (kan opluchting geven)
         somebody fired   having (may relief   give)
         'having fired somebody may relieve'

    c. Ontslagen worden (is geen schande)
        fired   being (is no disgrace)
        'being fired is no disgrace'

    d. Ontslagen (geworden) zijn (is geen schande)
        fired   been   being (is no disgrace)
        'having been fired is no disgrace'

    e. Iemand   proberen te ontslaan (is niet aardig)
        somebody trying   to fire   (is not nice)
        'trying to fire somebody is not nice'

    f. Iemand   vergeefs geprobeerd hebben te ontslaan
        somebody in vain   tried   having to fire
        (geeft moeilijkheden)
        (raises troubles)
        'in vain having tried to fire somebody raises troubles'

The verbal complexes presented in (13b) to (13f), (13a) representing a simple infinitival nominalization construction, include Passive (13c-13f) and Verb clustering known as Verb raising, along with the different aspectual choices of present and perfect. The availability of these verbal forms on the lowest S projection level is an argument in favour of the impoverished Infl conception discussed earlier. At the same time, we are now in a position to understand why bare S is not just a possible head of an N-projection, but also of an adjective projection. Although one might argue for a sentential underlying structure for Adjective projections in general (cf. Fanselow 1986, Van Gestel 1986), the sentences in (13) containing a passive perfect participle at least consolidate the assumption that this participle (and the present participle as well) is lexically available, along with its argument structure. So in a bare S-construction, with the proper adaptations, we find the adjectival counterpart of nominalization. In (14) a collection of illustrations is presented, the sentential features are taken to be self-evident.

(14)

a. $[_{N''}$ De $[_{S}$ $_{[pass, pres, part]}$ (x) aan de universiteit ontslagen wordende]
             the   at the university fired   being
                                   professor] (is nu met verlof)
                                   professor (is now on leave)
    'the professor who is being fired at the university is now on leave'

b. [$_{N''}$ De [$_S$ [pass, perf] (x) aan de universiteit ontslagen] professor]
      the   at the university fired   professor
                                      (is nu gevierd als goochelaar)
                                      (is now toasted as juggler)
   'the professor who is fired at the university is now toasted
   as a juggler'

c. [$_{N''}$ Dit [$_S$ [pres, part] (x) een professor ontslaande] team]
      this   a   professor   firing   team
                                        (is onmiddellijk op non-actief gesteld)
                                      (is immediately on half-pay placed)
   'this team that is firing a professor is immediately placed
   on half-pay'

d. [$_{N''}$ Dit [$_S$ [perf, part] (x) een professor ontslagen hebbende] team]
      this   a   professor fired   having   team
                                        (had meteen   veel   geld   beschikbaar)
                                        (had immediately much money available)
   'this team that has fired a professor immediately had much
   money available'

The proper morphological adaptations depend on the sentential features: in type (14b) the copula is suppressed, in (14a) to (14d) the relevant verb forms are derived by the features, resulting in present participle forms of the passive auxiliary (14a) combined with the perfect main verb, in just a present participle (14c) and in the active auxiliary combined with the perfect main verb (14d). As compared to Dutch, German appears to be even more liberal in the approval of sentential A-projections, in that even raising verbs seem to be allowed. On this very fact, by the way, Fanselow (1986) based his movement analysis for the empty subject of the adjectival bare S, in competition with the more current PRO-analysis.

(15) [$_{N''}$ Der [$_S$ [$_S$ (x) die Wahlen   verloren zu haben] scheinende]
         the   the elections lost   to have   seeming
                              Kanzler]
                              chancellor
   *de de verkiezingen verloren te hebben schijnende kanselier
   'the chancellor who seems to have lost the elections'

Speculating about binding of empty subjects, we think that it is typical for prenominal sentential constructions that the subject variable is bound by the head of the NP, whereas elsewhere the empty subject is bound by the maximal NP (the external argument or subject of the sentence). We come back to this topic in the next section.

Disregarding the many subtle details, we conclude that the adjectival bare S represents another endocentric projection option. Consequently, it must be possible to create a full NP that contains both the prenominal S and the nominal one. (16) is an acceptable double S-NP fulfilling this expectation.

(16) $[_{N''}$ Het $[_{N'}$ $[_S$ (x) aan de Groningse universiteit beoefende]
        the   at   the Groningen university practized
                       $[_S$ (y) banen afstoten]]]
                            jobs   hiving off
       'the hiving off of jobs that is practized at the Groningen university'

Projecting the object of *afstoten*, which is *banen*, as a prepositional complement, resulting in *afstoten van banen*, certainly would improve the aes-
thetics of the construction, but this is not the topic here. The point is, that
we have to figure out what might be the syntactic status of bare S in
endocentric projections. As we may now conclude on the basis of the
evidence discussed in this section, only infinitival S functions as the head
of an NP, whereas non-infinitival S functions as an N-modifier and projects
as an AP. Rephrasing this analysis in semantic terms, bare S denotes a set
(e,t) or a function from sets to sets, ((e,t),(e,t)), triggered by infinitival or
non-infinitival features. Now since V, N and A are considered to be the major
lexical categories of the language that are positively specified for at least
one of the categorial features [N, V] (Chomsky 1986), we are now in a
position to characterize the three faces of bare S in the following way:

(17)   S = X,   and X = [±N, ±V],
                       with the exclusion of the double negative value

        Application:
        S = [-N, +V], V /finite (INFL)
        S = [+N, -V], N /infinitival
        S = [+N, +V], A /participial

Remarkably absent is the lexical category Preposition-Postposition [-N, -V] (as well as Adverb). This fact emphasizes the deficient treatment of this lexical category in current X-bar theory. We cannot pay enough attention to this question here, but in the light of the prepositional character of the bare S introducing complementizers *om* and *te* 'for', 'to', it looks like an appealing strategy to analyze at least some prepositions as oblique Case markers of NPs, including bare S-headed ones, instead of giving them head status. This idea is firmly rooted in history, for Bloomfield and Jespersen already described prepositional phrases in terms of exocentricity or nexus. We might use this idea in order to explain the absence of prepositions in (17) and to account for the impossibility of nominalizations headed by a complementizer as illustrated by the pattern in (18), specifically (18b).

(18) a.   ?Wijs te zijn is gek (cf. (6c))
      wise to be is crazy
      'to be wise is crazy'
   b.   *Om wijs te zijn is gek
       for   wise to be is crazy
      'it is crazy to be wise'
   c.   Het is gek   om wijs te zijn
      it   is crazy for wise to be
      'it is crazy to be wise'

As a final remark, something must be said about the syntactic function of the nominalizations appearing in the data. They all function as subjects, which means in terms of semantics that in combination with a higher-order predicate (bare S) they are to be interpreted as statements about a property of properties. Consequently, the bare S should be type-raised accordingly.[5] The discussion of how to manage this must wait for another occasion. Nevertheless, it must be admitted that, apart from the prepositional context referred to earlier, nominalization constructions appear in non-subject positions as well. In a few rare cases they function as predicate nominals, thus giving rise to subtle minimal pairs as the following one.

(19) a.   omdat we dat [$_{N''}$ [$_S$ (x) mooi zingen]] vinden
      because we that   nicely singing   find
      'because we find that singing nicely'

b. omdat [$_{S''}$ Infl [$_{S'}$ we [$_S$ (x) dat mooi vinden zingen]]]
    'because we find that singing nicely'
b'. omdat [$_{S''}$ Infl [$_{S'}$ we [$_S$ [$_{N''}$ (x)] [$_{V'}$ [$_{N''}$dat] [$_S$ [$_{N''}$ (y)]
    [$_{V'}$ mooi zingen]] vinden]]]]

In (19a) bare S *mooi zingen* is an instance of syntactic nominalization, hence labelled as N''. Moreover, it is a predicative one, in the sense that it predicates a property of properties of an individual. This implies that here we deal with some higher order predicate, where the subject variable is not bound. In the *accusativus cum infinitivo*-construction (19b), on the other hand, the deepest embedded bare S *mooi zingen* the subject variable *y* is bound by the pronoun *dat*, denoting a contextually given individual that sings nicely. In (19b) the internal structure of the bare S *dat mooi vinden zingen* is reflected in underlying SOV-order, showing that here also *mooi zingen* is a bare S. The difference is that *mooi zingen* in (19a) is an endocentric projection, while in (19b) it interacts with V-Raising, ending up in the bare S *dat mooi vinden zingen*, which is the head of the exocentric sentence S''. In other words, if the external argument of a bare S binds the subject variable, as in (19b), we have V-Raising, and if it does not, we have a higher order predicate nominal.

In conclusion, we have concentrated in this section on the impact of bare S as the head of an endocentric or exocentric construction. In the next section we will investigate the structure-internal properties of this type of projections (for short: SN-projections), a topic that is amply discussed in recent publications but still, if we may say so, poorly understood.

3. Structural properties of syntactic nominalization projections

Most attempts to arrive at some understanding of the distribution of arguments within SN-projections are carried out with reference to the thematic roles of the arguments (cf. van Haaften et al. 1985; Hoekstra 1986). Although we acknowledge the relevance of thematic considerations in these matters, we will pursue the categorial and structural line of investigation and try to work out the basic distinction in specified and non-specified SN-constructions. As is noticed by others, the specifier-less SN-construction displays just verbal properties, whereas the specified SN-construction shows a variety of mixed nominal and verbal properties. This situation is pictured in (20).

(20)

a. Non-specified SN N'' b. Specified SN N''

N

$\parallel$

S

$N''(x) \quad V'$

$(X'') \quad V$

Spec N' (Compl)

$(A'') \quad N$ (Compl)

$\parallel$

S

$N''(x) \quad V'$

$(X'') \quad V$

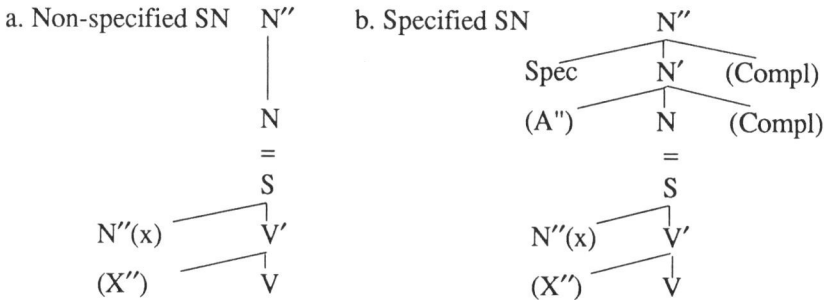

The maximal N-projection of type (20a) expresses the idea that non-specified SN-constructions are non-structured on the N-projection-line. Consequently, it is not possible to incorporate A-modification or N-complementation in this SN-type, as indicated by the starred examples.

(21) a. het mooie zingen
         the nice singing
   a'. *mooie zingen
         nice singing
   b.   het zingen van Frank
         the singing of Frank
   b'. *zingen van Frank
         singing of Frank
   c.   het zingen van ballads
         the singing of ballads
   c'. *zingen van ballads
         singing of ballads

Although the optional V-complement X'' in (20a) is represented as the left sister of the verb, according to the well-established conception of Dutch as an SOV-language, we still find VO-ordering instead of OV, optionally when X'' is a prepositional phrase and obligatorily when X'' is a sentential complement. Under the assumption that a rule of Extraposition has applied in those cases, we can now explain the correctness of the following examples as instances of non-specified nominalizations.

(22) a Werken aan de grenzen (cf. (1))
        working at   the limits
     b. Struikelen over een bananeschil
        stumbling over a   banana skin
     c. Gezoend worden door Mary
        kissed   being by Mary
        'being kissed by Mary'
     d. Teksten laten   vertalen door de computer
        texts   letting translate by   the computer
        'having texts translated by the computer'
     e. Houden van Brigitte Bardot
        loving (of) Brigitte Bardot
        'loving Brigitte Bardot'
     f. Te laat merken   dat je bedrogen bent
        too late realizing that you deceived are
        'realizing too late that you are deceived'
     g. Proberen om iemand   piano te leren spelen
        trying   for somebody piano to teach play
        'trying to teach someone to play the piano'

Thus a prepositional or sentential complement only shows up post-verbally in a non-specified nominalization construction if the verb is subcategorized for these complements. This condition is respected by (22), but not by the starred cases of (21), where the *van*-phrases bind the subject variable. Note that this subcategorization requirement includes the passive argument-structure for transitive verbs (23c). Turning now to the semantics of non-specified nominalizations, we observe first that the subject variable cannot be bound within N''. In other words, a non-specified syntactic nominalization is a property-name, for which the abstraction over the individual bearers of this property is an essential feature. This characteristic is undermined in, for example, (21b'), at the same time denoting an abstract property 'zingen' and the singing individual Frank. Therefore, the non-branching N-line in the non-specified syntactic nominalization is rooted in semantics. We think it to be attractive to identify the semantics of non-specified nominalization constructions with that of the generic bare plurals, as *Bevers bouwen dammen* 'Beavers build dams', for in both cases properties are denoted under abstraction of the possible individuals these properties might be assigned to. As a consequence, the semantic types of the predicates that could be combined with property-denoting subjects, should be of a higher-order type, perhaps like (23), where the type of the subject variable is raised accordingly.[6]

(23)

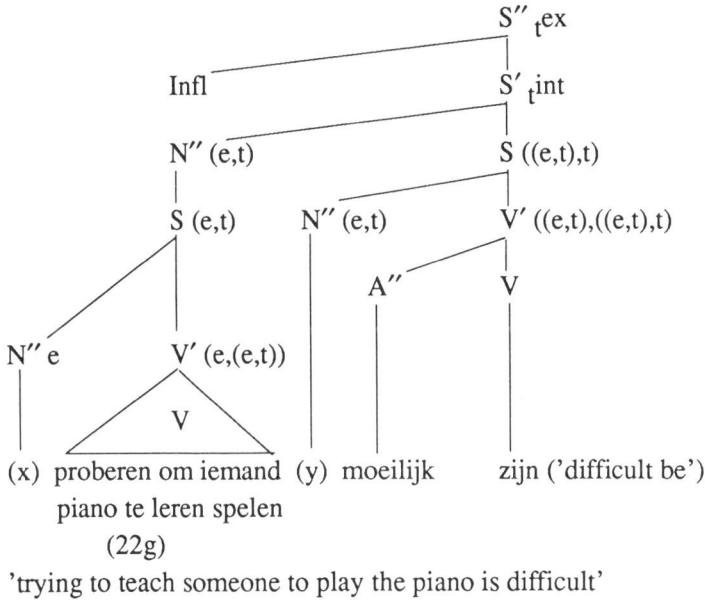

(22g)
'trying to teach someone to play the piano is difficult'

In this analysis, yielding *Proberen iemand piano te leren spelen is moeilijk*, the subject of the construction binds the subject variable (y) on the exocentric line, whereas the subject (x) on the endocentric line remains unbound. The free variable is an essential feature of non-specified syntactic nominalizations, despite the fact that the language offers the possibility to express something like (23) and still restricting the interpretation of the free variable by some sort of pseudo-binding expression, as 'voor mij' in (24). Compare (24a) and (24b), where the sentential complement version appears to be more appropriate for (pseudo-)binding purposes.

(24) a. ?Proberen om iemand   piano te leren spelen is moeilijk
        trying   for somebody piano to teach play   is difficult
        voor mij
        for   me
        'trying to teach someone to play the piano is difficult for me'

    b. Het is moeilijk voor mij om te proberen (om) iemand   piano
       it is   difficult for me   for to try   (to) somebody piano
       te leren spelen
       to teach play
       'it is difficult for me to try to teach someone to play the piano'

Let us switch now to the structural properties of the specified nominalization construction, observing that the subject variable may be bound within its maximal N-projection in two ways, either by a possessive NP in the specifier-position (25a) or by a *van*-phrase in N'-complement position (25b).

(25) a. Jan's recenseren van boeken
        Jan's reviewing of books
    b. Het boeken recenseren van Jan
       the books reviewing of Jan
       'the reviewing of books by Jan'

Instead of a full NP possessive we might use a pronoun, such as *zijn* 'his', in order to bind the subject variable. But the conclusion must be that we are forced to distinguish between two kinds of specifiers of syntactic nominalizations, one being the possessive and the other the determiner, since the *van*-complements in (25a) and (25b) have different interpretations according to the choice of the specifier-type. Moreover, as is shown by the evidence in (26), whatever specifier we choose for the specified nominalization construction, the subject variable normally must be bound, if there is an overt binding argument available. That is why in (26) a must be preferred over a', b over b', and c over c'.

(26) a. Het recenseren van boeken brengt weinig op
          the reviewing of books pays little off '... pays off little'

  a'. Het boeken recenseren brengt weinig op
       the books reviewing pays little off

  b. Jan's boeken recenseren brengt weinig op
      Jan's books reviewing pays little   off

  b'. Het boeken recenseren door Jan brengt weinig op
       the books reviewing by Jan pays little off

  c. Het recenseren van boeken door Jan brengt weinig op
      the reviewing of books by Jan pays little   off

  c'. = b'.

According to our appreciation of the data, the relative unacceptability of the
bar sentences in (26) is due to the fact that they do not reflect the necessary
binding relations. The subject binder is either the *van*-complement or the
possessive specifier, within the specified SN-projection. Outside that projection pseudo-binding is possible, as in (27).

(27) Het boeken recenseren levert Jan weinig op
      the books reviewing pays Jan little   off

  The NP *Jan*, like the PP *voor mij* in (24), may be interpreted as the binder
of the subject variable, in which case Jan reviews books, but since (27) has
another interpretation, such that Jan does not review books, the configuration underlying (27) is referred to as "pseudo-binding". If the analysis of
(26) is correct, then it follows that the subject-variable binding *van*-expres-
sion copies either the subject or the object of the verbal head. In the latter
case, as exemplified in (26a) and (26c), the infinitive is interpreted as
passive, despite of the absence of passive morphology.[7] This conclusion
would explain the near absence of overt passivization in specified nominalizations, as observed by Dik (1985).

(28) a. Het veroveren van de stad door de rebellen was een schok
          the conquering of the city by the rebels was a   shock
          voor de junta
          for the junta

   b. *Het veroverd   worden van de stad door de rebellen was
     the   conquered being of the city by   the rebels   was
     een schok voor de junta
     a   shock for   the junta

In this respect, our passive infinitive might be identified with the one discussed by de Geest (1987), occurring in sentential complement constructions such as (29).

(29) a. Ik zie het huis slopen
        I see the house demolish (i.e., being demolished)
    b. Ik hoor een lied zingen
        I hear a   song sing
        'I hear singing a song'

Like the nominalization construction, such a sentential complement can be extended by a *door*-phrase referring to the agent, which is a good indication for its passive status, or by an NP with accusative case binding the subject variable and then blocking the passive reading.

(30) a. Ik hoor een lied zingen door Marco
        I hear   a   song sing   by   Marco (i.e., being sung)
    b. Ik hoor Marco een lied zingen
        I hear Marco a   song sing
        'I hear Marco singing a song'

There are more common characteristics of syntactic nominalization and sentential complementation, but we must leave this issue here. Keeping to the main track, we must turn to the semantics of the specified nominalizations. The observation that the subject variable of this construction must be bound points in the direction of a closed sentence interpretation. Let us say that the specified nominalization denotes a proposition, whereas the non-specified nominalization denotes a property. Naturally, there are many kinds of propositions, such as situations, activities and states. But if these propositions are linguistically expressed as syntactic nominalizations, they all share the feature of being named by a closed sentence. We suggest that the specified nominalization construction, as opposed to the non-specified one, involves existential quantification.[8] By that we mean that the proposition referred to by the specified nominalization is an entity that is presupposed in the interpretation model. The following texts serve to illustrate this delicate point.

(31) a. Het recenseren van boeken brengt niets op; daarom zijn er maar
the reviewing of books brings nothing in; therefore are there only
weinig recensenten
few   reviewers
'the reviewing of books does not pay; therefore there are
only few reviewers'

   b. ?Het recenseren van boeken brengt niets op; daarom zijn er geen
recensenten
the reviewing of books brings nothing in; therefore are there no
reviewers
'the reviewing of books does not pay; therefore there are no
reviewers'

   c. Boeken recenseren brengt niets op; daarom zijn er maar
weinig/geen recensenten
books reviewing brings nothing in; therefore are there only
few/no reviewers
'reviewing books does not pay; therefore there are only
few/no reviewers'

How can we explain the oddity of (31b), in face of the correctness of (31a) and (31c)? The first sentence of (31b) involves an empirical statement about the reviewing of books, with the implication of actually existing book reviewers, and this implication is contradicted in the second sentence. No such contradiction arises in the case of a non-specified nominalization, because the property-denoting non-specified construction carries no existential presupposition. As we all know, we can easily talk about properties that nobody possesses. A minimal pair expressing this idea is shown in (32).

(32) a. Electronisch garnalen pellen is onmogelijk
electronically shrimps peeling is   impossible
'electronically peeling shrimps is impossible'

   b. ?Het electronisch pellen van garnalen bestaat niet
the electronic   peeling of shrimps exists not
'the electronic peeling of shrimps does not exist'

If we say that a specified nominalization construction denotes a proposition, such as the reviewing of books by someone or the electronic peeling of shrimps by someone, we mean that this construction may pick out all the actual situations that make the sentence 'someone reviews books' or 'someone peels shrimps electronically' true. If the specifier is not the definite article, no such general reading is available. For instance 'this reviewing of books' denotes a particular case of reviewing books and 'most reviewing of books' refers to the majority of book-reviewing cases. So we may very well deal with the denotation of specified nominalizations in the line of the common nouns: without the specifier we denote sets or properties, and in combination with a specifier we denote sets of sets or sets of properties: $((e,t),t)$.

The difference between syntactic nominalizations and common nouns, in this perspective, is not reflected in the type-assignment of the maximal N-projection, but only in the projecting heads: common nouns are lexical items denoting properties and bare sentences, functioning as the head of an N-projection have an internal sentential structure not provided by the lexicon, since sentences are not lexical items.

In conclusion, if we arrange the type assignments along the lines informally discussed in this section, then syntactic nominalization is not in danger of the unlimited process of type-lifting, causing "inflation of levels" and giving rise to "floating types" (Parsons 1979) or, as a safer alternative, to a semantics without type-hierarchies at all (cf. Chierchia 1982). In our account of nominalization, the empty subject of the bare S heading the SN-projection is first-order, and if the non-specified nominalization itself functions as a subject, then the predicate bare S is of a higher type, $((e,t),t)$ instead of regular (e,t). There simply are no higher types. For instance, if we want to nominalize a higher order predicate, such as the one used in (31c), we will find out that we interpret this predicate as a normal non-specified syntactic nominalization, as a property.

(33)   Niets   opleveren is een eigenschap van boeken recenseren
       nothing paying off is a   property   of   books   reviewing
       'not paying off is a property of books reviewing'

Apparently, the internal complexity of properties has no effect on the assignment of types when these properties function as heads of SN-projections.

4. Conclusion

(i)   X-projections are endocentric or exocentric.

(ii)   Exocentric projections are bare S-headed.

(iii) At least some endocentric projections are bare S-headed.

(iv)   Bare S-headed endocentric projections are syntactic nominalization
       (SN) constructions, if S = inf.
       Otherwise, they are adjectival constructions.
       Categorial identity assumptions: S-inf = N, S-part = A.

(v)   There are two kinds of syntactic nominalizations:
       (1) non-specified syntactic nominalizations, where the N-projection
       line is non-branching and where the subject variable must be free,
       (2) specified syntactic nominalizations, where the N-projection line
       is branching and where the subject variable must be bound
       (normally, by the *van*-complement or by the specifier).

(vi)   Non-specified syntactic nominalizations denote properties. Specified
       syntactic nominalizations denotes propositions. The latter involves
       existential presupposition, the former does not.

(vii) X-projections can be matched with semantic types and combined by
       functional application.

Notes

1.   I thank Jan Jullens and Jikke Klaassen for comments and valuable suggestions.
2.   The assumption that Dutch is an SOV-language forces one to account for the
      obligatory post-verbal position of sentential V-arguments in terms of an obliga-
      tory rule of Extraposition. Alternatively, one could argue that in Dutch the verb
      is left-governing for endocentric arguments, but right-governing for exocentric
      arguments. This alternative would be the more attractive one in the line of the
      present article.

3.   For a discussion on NP-interpretation, Partee (1987) gives a useful survey of the issues. Note that in our section 3 some attention is payed to type-changing in the context of syntactic nominalization.

For a suitable analysis of NP-internal syntax and semantics, Verkuyl (1981) is recommended. Verkuyl's type-assignments result, however, in $(((e,t),t),t)$ for NP, since they are mappings from a three level NP projection. Our NP-interpretations, on the other hand, may vary between e, (e,t) and $((e,t),t)$ according to a maximal two level NP projection of an (e,t) type Noun.

4.   We prefer this point of view to the one ascribing nominative case assignments to Infl. According to Akmajian (1984) the accusative case for the subject in so-called 'Mad Magazine Sentences' 'Him wear a tuxedo?!. 'What! Her call me up?!' must be explained by the absence of Infl. For some critical comments, cf. van Zonneveld (1987).

5.   Of course semantic interpretation does not necessarily involve type-theory. For instance, Chierchia (1982) argues for a semantics without types. The main argument is the uncontrollable multiplication of levels in the system of type categories: "there seems to be no upper limit to such a process" (Chierchia 1982: p. 313). We briefly comment on this point in section 3.

6.   The semantic account of non-specified syntactic nominalization along the lines of (23) results in opposite function-argument orderings for sentences with a first-order predicate (cf. 12) and sentences with a second order one, such as (23). We did not investigate the implications of this result. The semantic type of predicates is taken to be a lexical matter. For instance, the predicate *moeilijk zijn* 'to be difficult' applies to e or (e,t) as a subject variable, whereas *hard werken* 'to work hard' and *een prettige eigenschap zijn* 'to be a nice property' only apply to e and (e,t) subject variables, respectively.

7.   Note that a specified nominalization construction without a *van*-complement binding the subject variable, but with a *door*-complement is now, for principled reasons, ruled out (cf. 26b'). This situation is highly comparable to the complement distribution of Dutch *ing*-nominalization (*de verovering van de stad door de vijand*, 'the conquering of the city by the enemy'. See Hoeksema (1986). Further on *van*-complements. If we take a verb introducing a subject-object ambiguity in the *van*-complement, such as *schieten* 'shoot', with *jagers* 'hunters' and *apen* 'apes' as arguments, we see that (i) is ambiguous, (ii) is not and (iii) is impossible.

    (i)   het schieten van de jagers
        'the shooting of the hunters'
    (ii) het schieten van de jagers door de apen
        'the shooting of the hunters by the apes'
    (iii) het schieten van de jagers van de apen
        'the shooting of the hunters of the apes'

In our analysis, the *van*-complement is not ambiguous, since it always binds the subject variable. The infinitive gets an active (i) or a passive (ii) reading. The impossibility of (iii) must be explained by reference to a trivial principle blocking multiple binding of the subject variable.

8. If this claim is correct, then it follows that a specified nominalization might lack an overt subject binding expression, as is the case in (16), where the implicit subject binder is understood as the authorities of the university. This construction would win by projecting the object *banen* as a *van*-complement (*het afstoten van banen*), resulting in a specified nominalization construction with an overt binder, but still in need of information on the understood logical subject of the verb.

References

Akmajian, Adrian
  1984   "Sentence types and the form-function fit", *Natural Language and Linguistic Theory* 2: 1-23

Bloomfield, Leonard
  1933   *Language* (New York: Holt).

Chierchia, Gennaro
  1982   "Nominalization and montague grammar: A semantics without types for natural language", *Linguistics and Philosophy* 5: 303-354
  1985   "Formal semantics and the grammar of predication, *Linguistic Inquiry* 16.4: 417-444

Chomsky, Noam
  1981   *Lectures on government and binding* (Dordrecht: Foris).
  1986   *Barriers* (Cambridge, Mass.: MIT Press).

De Geest, Wim
  1987   "Passive bare infinitive complements in Dutch", Paper presented at the Groningen University, 10/11/87.

Dik, Simon C.
  1985   "Nederlandse nominalisaties in een funktionele grammatika", *Forum der Letteren* 26.2: 81-107

Fanselow, Gisbert
  1986   "On the sentential nature of prenominal adjectives in German", *Folia Linguistica,* Tomus XX/3-4: 341-380 (The Hague: Mouton).

Hoeksema, Jack
  1985   *Categorial morphology* (New York: Garland Press).

Hoekstra, Teun
  1986   "Deverbalization and inheritance", *Linguistics* 24: 549-584

Hoekstra, Teun - Pim Wehrman
1985   "De nominale infinitief", *GLOT* 8.3: 257-274.

Jackendoff, Ray
1977   *X'-Syntax: A Study in phrase structure* (Cambridge, Mass.: MIT Press).

Jespersen, Otto
1933   *Essentials of English grammar* (London: Allen & Unwin).

Lachlan Mackenzie, J.
1986   "Aspects of nominalization in English and Dutch", *Working Papers in Functional Grammar*

Ok Oh, Ye
1988   "Semantik von Nominalisierungen", *Linguistische Berichte* 114: 163-182

Parsons, Terence
1979   "Type theory and ordinary language", *Linguistics, philosophy and Montague grammar*, edited by S. Davis - Marianne Mithun (London: Austin).

Partee, Barbara H.
1986   "Noun phrase interpretation and type-shifting principles", *Studies in discourse representation theory and the theory of generalized quantifiers*, edited by Jeroen Groenendijk - Dick de Jongh - Martin Stokhof (Dordrecht: Foris).

Reuland, Eric J.
1986   "Relating morphological and syntactic structure", *Groningen Papers in Theoretical and Applied Linguistics* 2, [also 1988 in: *Morphology and modularity*, edited by Martin Everaert - Arnold Evers - Riny Huybregts - Mieke Trommelen (Dordrecht: Foris)].

Reuland, Eric J. - Wim Kosmeijer
1989   "Projecting inflected verbs", *Groninger Arbeiten zur germanistischen Linguistik* 29

Stuurman, Frits
1987   "The linguist('s) leveling of English gerunds", *Formal parameters of generative grammar* yearbook III, 1987, edited by Ger de Haan - Wim Zonneveld (Utrecht: University of Utrecht).

Ten Cate, Abraham P.
1985   *Aspektualität und Nominalisierung: Zur Bedeutung satzsemantischer Beziehungen für die Beschreibung der Nominalisierung im Deutschen und im Niederländischen* (Frankfurt/M: Lang).

Van Gestel, Frank
1986   *X-bar grammar: Attribution and predication in Dutch* (Dordrecht: Foris).

Van Haaften, Ton - Simon van de Kerke - Marja Middeldorp - Pieter Muysken
1985   "Nominalisaties in het Nederlands", *GLOT* 8.1: 67-104

Van Zonneveld, Ron M.
1987   "De dubbele bodem van de small clause-syntaxis", *TABU* 17.2: 55-62.

Part 2
Word Order

Word order variation in a configurational language: against a uniform scrambling account in German

Hartmut Czepluch

1. Introduction

It is a pertinent fact of German sentence structure that for the prototypical three-place verb *geben* 'give', neither ordering (1a) to (1f) in the so-called "middle field" is straightforwardly ungrammatical:[1]

(1) a. dann hat die Frau$_N$ dem Jungen$_D$ das Buch$_A$ gegeben
         then has the woman to-the boy   the book   given
     b. dann hat die Frau$_N$ das Buch$_A$ dem Jungen$_D$ gegeben
     c. dann hat dem Jungen$_D$ die Frau$_N$ das Buch$_A$ gegeben
     d. dann hat dem Jungen$_D$ das Buch$_A$ die Frau$_N$ gegeben
     e. dann hat das Buch$_A$ die Frau$_N$ dem Jungen$_D$ gegeben
     f. dann hat das Buch$_A$ dem Jungen$_D$ die Frau$_N$ gegeben

These, and similar, phenomena of apparent free ordering have led to widely divergent conclusions. For proponents of a "flat structure", each structure of (1) would be directly (base-)generated, the textually preferred ordering being determined by pragmatic and/or semantic aspects (theme-rheme, definiteness effects, animacy bias, etc.; cf., e.g., Lötscher 1981; Haider 1982; Zubin – Köpke 1985). On the other hand, even if one assumes a "configurational" middle field showing SU(bject)-OBJ(ect) asymmetries (e.g., Fanselow 1987; Scherpenisse 1986; Tappe 1985; Webelhuth 1985), it is still not clear if there are canonical object orders in the VP. Reviewing arguments for either a basic IO or a DO order (IO = indirect object; DO = direct object), von Stechow and Sternefeld (1988:452ff.) appear to be sceptical that pure syntactical reasons can be given for a fixed *Grundwort-stellung*.[2]

The purpose of the paper is two-fold. Since an analysis of word order variation critically rests upon structural assumptions, we will first give Case-theoretic arguments for a hierarchically structured VP in German, admitting of three *Grundwortstellungen*. This will *a fortiori* forfeit the "flat S hypothesis" (S = IP) of, e.g., Haider (1982). Secondly, as von Stechow and Sternefeld (1988: 470 ff.) point out, there is no descriptively satisfactory theory of scrambling at hand. Although scrambling, as adjunction to a maximal phrase, is powerful enough to derive all word orders, it may be more appropriate not to do so. It seems that there are three distinct processes that may effect word order variations, only one of them being the traditional scrambling mechanism. This will be the topic of the second part of the paper.

2. Preliminary remarks on Case relations

Case is best regarded as a relational notion, i.e., some abstract marking of the relation between a governor g and a dependent d; cf. (2a):

(2) a. $C_j^i (g_i, d_j)$ = a–Case

$\qquad\qquad$ m–Case = affixation on dependent d.[3]

$\quad$ b. $C_1^V (V, NP_1)$ = obj^V

$\qquad$ $C_1^N (N, NP_1)$ = obj^N

$\qquad$ $C_1^P (P, NP_1)$ = obl^P

$\qquad$ $C_1^A (A, NP_1)$ = obl^A

$\quad$ c. $\qquad\quad NP_1 \quad NP_2 \quad NP_3 \quad NP_4 \quad ...$

$\qquad$ V $\quad C_1^V \quad\, C_2^V \quad\, C_3^V \quad\, C_4^V \quad ... \qquad (C_1 = ACC)$

$\qquad\qquad\quad C_{1'}^V \qquad\qquad\qquad\qquad\qquad (C_{1'}^V = DAT)$

$\qquad\qquad\quad C_{1''}^V \qquad\qquad\qquad\qquad\qquad (C_{1''}^V = GEN)$

$\qquad\qquad\quad ...$

P $\quad C_1^P \quad$ ... $\qquad\qquad (C_1^P = \text{DAT})$

$\qquad\qquad$ ... $\qquad\qquad\qquad\qquad\qquad$ cf. Emonds (1985)

A $\quad C_1^A \quad$ ... $\qquad\qquad (C_1^A = \text{DAT})$

$\qquad\qquad$ ... $\qquad\qquad\qquad\qquad\qquad$ cf. van Riemsdijk (1983)

N $\quad C_1^N \quad$ ... $\qquad\qquad (C_1^N = \text{GEN})$

The relation C is called a(bstract)-Case. If C is marked morphologically on a dependent, we speak of m(orphological)-Case. Languages differ as to which categories are Case-assigners g_i and Case-governees d_j. Since C-relations are generally assumed to be structurally defined in terms of government, we may say that C-relations vary with respect to different governors g_i and different d_j's:

1. Different g_i's, i = [±N,±V], yield different C_j^i's: Case-government is generally taken to be some sort of head-feature transmission (e.g. Borer 1984; Travis 1987), and lexical governors normally do not govern alike (e.g. Kayne 1981). This may be expressed in terms of categorial government superscripts as in (2b) (cf. Emonds 1985). Consequently, the Case system consists of category-specific subsystems.

2. Dependent d_j's in a given position with respect to a specific g_i represent different a-Cases if they bear alternating m-Cases (Haider 1983), as depicted in the NP1 column of the V-system in (2c):[4]

(3)   a.   er hat [$_{V'}$ das MädchenA geküßt]
       b.   er hat [$_{V'}$ dem MädchenD geholfen]
       c.   er hat [$_{V'}$ des MädchensG gedacht]

3. Cooccurring d_j's with respect to a given g_i represent different a-Cases; cf. the row in the V-system of (2c) and example (6) below.

In view of (2c), there are generally more distinct a-Case relations than distinct m-Cases in a language. In particular, German having four m-Cases, there cannot be a 1:1-relationship between a- and m-Cases:

(A1) m-Cases are multi-functional in that a particular m-Case represents
       distinct a-Cases within and across categorial domains.

In this respect, the Case model differs both from standard Case theory (Chomsky 1981) and from the alternative of Haider (1983).

3. Morphological and abstract Cases for three-place verbs

Our concern will be with the verbal Case system C_j^V (V, NP$_j$), especially, the Case relations exhibited by three-place verbs.

3.1. M-Case patterns and VP structures

In Czepluch (1987a, 1987b, 1988a, 1988b), three *Grundwortstellungen* with the structures (4a) to (4c) have been motivated for German three-place verbs (PO stands for prepositional object):

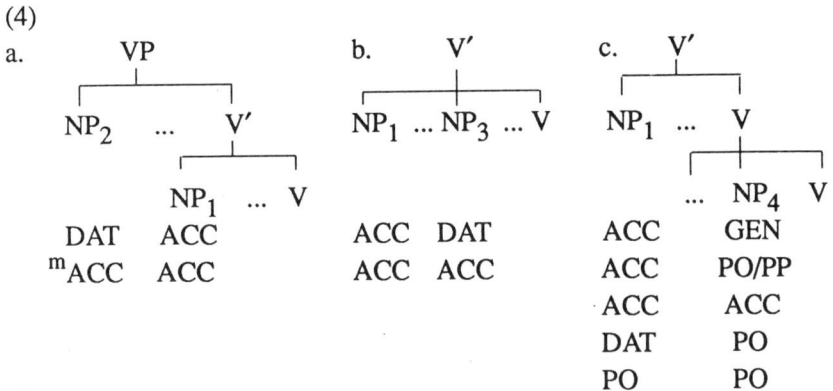

(4)

a.

```
         VP
    ┌─────┴──────┐
  NP₂   ...     V′
              ┌──┴──┐
            NP₁ ... V
```
DAT   ACC
^{m}ACC   ACC

b.

```
        V′
   ┌────┼────┐
 NP₁ ... NP₃ ... V
```
ACC   DAT
ACC   ACC

c.

```
        V′
   ┌────┴────┐
 NP₁  ...    V
         ┌───┴───┐
       ... NP₄   V
```
ACC   GEN
ACC   PO/PP
ACC   ACC
DAT   PO
PO   PO

The structures (4a) to (4c) realize the m-Case patterns (5) as indicated:

(5)

a.	N-D-A-V	daß die Frau dem Jungen	das Buch	gab
b.	N-A-G-V	daß die Frau den Nachbarn	der Lüge	bezichtigt
c.	N-A-A-V	daß die Frau den Jungen	das Lied	lehrte
d.	N-A-D-V	daß die Frau den Wein	dem Bier	vorzieht
e.	N-A-PP-V	daß die Frau das Buch	auf den Tisch	legte
f.	N-A-PO-V	daß die Frau den Mann	an seine Feinde	verriet
g.	N-D-PO-V	daß die Frau dem Mann	für die Hilfe	dankt
h.	N-PO-PO-V	daß die Frau mit dem Mann	über Politik	sprach

Structure (4a) represents the common indirect object-direct object pattern (5a) and also the double accusative (5c).[5] For all other verbs, a second internal argument is realized between the direct object argument (= NP_1) and V.

The reasons for assuming structures (4a) to (4c) are as follows: First of all, the patterns of (5) have to be taken as syntactically "unmarked": These orders obtain whenever semantic and/or pragmatic linearization factors are held neutral. Thus, they represent the pure syntactic projections from lexical structure (cf. Czepluch 1988a, 1988b). Secondly, while single-object dative and genitive represent lexical Cases (henceforth l-Cases), for double-object verbs, only genitive is a l-Case, whereas the accusative in NP_1 and the dative in NP_2 (and NP_3) are structural Cases (henceforth s-Cases).[6] Hence, the distinction of s- and l-oblique corresponds to the left-right asymmetry of second objects, with a proviso for NP_3. Thirdly, in unmarked sentence negation the negation particle delimits the verbal complex (VC = V^0; cf. Thiersch 1978). If so, two post-accusative positions, NP_3 and NP_4, have to be distinguished, since the dative of (5d) is realized outside the verbal complex, whereas genitives, prepositional objects and PP complements turn up inside the verbal complex.[7] Fourthly, adverbial adjuncts may regularly appear between any two A-positions and $NP_{1/3}$ and V without apparent markedness effects that call for a scrambling analysis.[8] This gives rise to assumption (A2):

(A2) thematic arguments and non-thematic material may alternate within the IP:
... [$_{IP}$ NP_0 XP^* NP_2 XP^* NP_1 XP^* V],
where XP^* = one or more adjuncts.

These observations are (and only can be) accounted for if A-positions are distributed over V-projection domains, in which Case-marking is tied to specific structural positions.

3.2. Argument-realization properties

Since, in head-final German, Case is not assigned adjacently by V (cf. van Riemsdijk 1983), the only feasible alternative is that Case is realized at the left periphery of V-projection domains, following Tappe (personal communication, 1985). Generalizing the hypothesis to A-positions, which is called for in view of the categorial possibilities in (4), we have:

(A3) An argument is theta-discharged at the left periphery of its
head-government domain

With respect to the core instance of verbal Case-marking, i.e., the assignment of objective Case to the direct object, the left periphery principle generalizes "at no costs" to head-initial English:

(6) a. Engl.: ... $[_{V'}$V NP$_C$ ...] vs. *... $[_{V'}$ V ... NP$_C$ ...]
b. Germ.: ... $[_{V'}$NP$_C$ ... V] vs. *... $[_{V'}$... NP$_C$ ... V]

The adjacency effect of English is simply the combinatory result of the "head-first" value of the head parameter and the left periphery principle. For German, the head parameter and the left periphery principle yield distant Case-marking and, derivatively, that there is "in-between" space for non-thematic material. Hence, in a head-initial language, arguments should generally be closer to the head than non-arguments, whereas in a head-final language, the distribution of arguments and non-arguments should accord with (A3). This seems to be borne out.[9]

Obviously, a second object cannot satisfy both requirements of (A3): NP$_2$ of (4a) is not head-governed;[10] NP$_{3/4}$ of (4b) and (4c) are not realized at a left periphery. With the left-right asymmetry of second objects in mind, the realization condition (A3) has to be supplemented by the following additions:

(A3) a. Lexically specified arguments may suspend the left periphery
principle.
b. S-Case-marked arguments may suspend head government.

Hence, lexically unmarked oblique arguments are projected to the left of NP$_1$ under the left periphery principle, giving structure (4a). Lexically marked oblique arguments are projected to the right of NP$_1$, where they satisfy head government:[11] Structure (4c) is motivated by (A3a) and the negation data of (21).[12]

Since an extra domain for the NP$_3$ position cannot be independently motivated, we assume (4b) as an option (see note 11).

For the extensions of (A3) a principle is called for, justifying indirect "head-feature transmission" by V'-over-V in (4a) and by V-over-V in (4c), and at the same time constraining this possiblity to exclude unwanted structures like (7):[13]

(7) a. *... $[_{V'}NP^{*}$ ... $[_{V'}NP2$ ... $[_{V'}NP1$ ... V]]]
     b. *... $[_{V}NP^{*}$ ... $[_{V}NP1$ ... $[_{V}NP4$ V]]]
     c. *... $[_{V'}NP2^{*}$ ... $[_{V'}NP1$ ... $[_{V}NP4$ V]]]

To this effect, the notion of governance transmission (Kayne 1981, 1984) may be used to express the realization condition (A4):

(A4) A lexical category X^{0} may transfer its governance property
     if and only if it immediately dominates lexical material.

According to (A4), the starred NPs in (7) are not appropriately head-governed. By virtue of the *if and only if*-clause, both V'-over-V and V-over-V may each be used once for A-realization, cf. (4a) vs. (7a) and (4c) vs. (7b), and both strategies may not be used simultaneously: (7c). Thus, (A4) yields that any verb may realize only *two* of the *four* A-positions within VP.

Apparently, A-positions are not sufficiently licensed by theta-marking for full interpretation (cf. Chomsky 1986a), since languages differ as to how they make use of principles (A3) and (A4). Since one would expect that distinct thematic roles have to be realized distinctively by the projection principle, double objects, in particular those of (4b), pose a problem and even more so for the single-Case condition of government binding theory if both Cases are actually assigned by V. Assume that arguments need to be morphologically licensed (cf. Baker 1985). It follows that languages with/ without Case inflection differ as to the A-realization possibilities:[14] In a language without m-Cases, the single zero Case-form can license only one NP in VP; in a language with m-Cases, two NPs may be licensed distinctively, subject to (A4). This seems to be the function of dative - the default oblique Case of German - which may appear in various configurations where it is not even governed at all.[15]

The present approach need not refer to specific a-Cases.[16] Thus, the theory of a-Case is subsumed under more general principles of A-realization. The essential part of a theory of Case seems to be whether a language has an m-Case system that may distinctively license distinct A-government relations in the syntax.

3.3. Accounting for combinatorial restrictions on double objects

In the two-complement patterns of (5), the non-nominative Cases, prepositional objects and adverbials do not combine freely.[17] The present theory gives the following account: Firstly, the general effect of (A4) is that a verb may realize two internal arguments maximally. Given the independently licensed subject-position [Spec,IP], the (lexical) three-argument restriction follows.[18] Secondly, since government transfer is a structural property, we suppose that V may transfer its governance property only if it Case-governs NP_1 structurally. Hence, there cannot be any Dat-Dat-, Gen-Gen- and Dat-Gen-patterns in German: dative and genitive not being morphological instantiations of the structural objective, neither Case can license a second Case-marked object. Without further stipulation, it also follows that there can be one l-Case or one subcategorized adverbial at most, but not both. The distribution of m-Cases in the V-Case system of (2c) may be depicted as follows:

(8)

V		NP_1	NP_2	NP_3	NP_4	
s-governance		ACC —— DAT				= (5a)
		├————————— DAT				= (5d)
l-governance		├————————————— GEN				= (5b)
		├————————————— PO				= (5e),(5f)
		PO ———————————————┤				= (5h)
		DAT———————————————┤				= (5g), (3b)
		GEN———————┤				= (3c)

Two points deserve mention:
1. The primary function of m-Cases appears to be the distinctive marking

of lexical A-relations in the syntax. Thus, there is no need to associate m-Cases with semantic values.

2. The V-Case system is clearly accusative-centred, as against (traditional) accounts that ascribe the "primary Case" status to the nominative.

Given the distinctive function of m-Cases, it is not necessary to assume that the a-Case module of, for example, English differs substantially from that of German. The reduced realization possibilities can be derived from the interaction of the head parameter, the left periphery principle and morphological licensing.[19] In fact, the null hypothesis would be that English should not have double-NP patterns at all for lack of m-Case distinctions. Except for (9d), this prediction is borne out if we look at the head-initial versions of the three German structures:

(9) a. ...$[_{VP}$ $[_{V'}$ V NP$_1$ NP$_3$] ...]   corr. to (4b)
     b. *...$[_{VP}$ $[_{V'}$ V NP$_1$ NP$_3$] ...]   „   „   „
     c. *...$[_{V'}$ $[_{V'}$ V NP$_i$ ...] NP$_2$ ...]...   „   „ (4a)
     d. ...$[_{V'}$ $[_V$ V NP$_4$] NP$_1$ ...]   „   „ (4c)

(9a) is the normal complementation pattern for two NP arguments: the NP$_3$ position cannot be licensed distinctively relative to NP$_1$ for lack of m-Cases; cf. (9b). Hence the second NP argument must be licensed by a prepositional Case-assigner. In (9c), NP$_2$ does not seem to satisfy the left periphery principle; hence, we do not expect that an argument can be realized outside the minimal c-command domain of V irrespective of Case-marking.[20] English has, though, the head-initial correlate to the German NP$_1$-NP$_4$-V structure: The V-IO-PO pattern is syntactically marked and calls for an explanation anyway.[21] It goes without saying that without m-Cases, l-Cases cannot be specified as a morphosyntactic lexical property.

The cursory comparison of German and English shows that m-Cases cannot simply be regarded as morphonological reflexes of a-Cases. Rather, whether a language has Case morphology or not, is an independent property of grammars that has far-reaching consequences for the syntax of languages.

4. Reordering effects in German

So far, ordering variants have been ignored, taking the patterns of (5) to represent D-structure projections from lexical structures. If so, two questions arise: 1) What are the structures of derived orders that do not conform to the *Grundstrukturen* (4a) to (4c)? 2) Are derived structures associated with specific pragmatic, semantic and/or prosodic properties? As to question 1, I will offer some arguments against a unitary scrambling account. As to question 2, some tentative proposals as to the extra-syntactic properties of derived structures will be put forward.[22]

4.1. Scrambling and projection from the lexicon

Within configurational Case syntax, conditions on reorderings cannot simply be given in linear terms, for example: "Rhematische Elemente tendieren nach rechts, thematische nach links" (von Stechow and Sternefeld 1988: 452), unless reordering is constrained to a single process. Therefore most analyses of scrambling constrain reordering to adjunction to maximal projections (e.g., Thiersch 1982; Fanselow 1987; Webelhuth 1985; den Besten and Webelhuth 1987). In this sense, the well-known scrambling rule of Thiersch (1978), annotated for the rheme condition, is generally assumed to be an instance of adjunction to X''':[23]

(10) ... XP   YP ... $\Rightarrow$ ... YP   XP ..., where XP = [–pron]
     +RH –RH   –RH +RH

From the Dat-Acc structure (11a), rule (10) yields the adjunction structure (11b), but prohibits the rightward movements (11c) and (11d):

(11) a. ... $[_{VP}$ NP2 $[_{V'}$ NP1 V]] = (4a)
       +RH   –RH

    b. ... $[_{VP}$ NP1 $[_{VP}$ NP2 $[_{V'}$ e1 V]]] = VP adjunction
         –RH   +RH

    c. *... $[_{VP}$ e2 $[_{V'}$ NP1 NP2 V]] = (4b): NP2 in NP3 position
           –RH +RH

d. *... $[_{VP}$ e2 $[_{V'}$ NP1 $[_V$ NP2 V]]] = (4c): NP2 in NP4 position
                    −RH   +RH

Although (11b) to (11d) equally affect the pragmatically "natural" [−RH]-[+RH] order, the latter two structures are deviant for independent reasons, as they stand.[24]

The objections against (11c) and (11d) vanish, though, if "reordering" does not leave a trace in NP2, i.e., if the dative argument is directly projected in the NP3 or NP4 position of structures (4b) and (4c) respectively:

(12) a. ... $[_{VP}$ $[_{V'}$ NP1   NP2 V]]   = (4b): NP2 in NP3 position
                        −RH +RH

     b. ... $[_{VP}$ $[_{V'}$ NP1 $[_V$ NP2 V]]]   = (4c): NP2 in NP4 position
                        −RH   +RH

The realizations (12a) and (12b) cannot be eliminated on *a priori* grounds in our theory. Since there are four potential A-positions in which the two internal arguments of a verb may be realized, it should be possible that verbs vary as to which A-positions they make use of.[25]

One would not like to say that the "natural" reordering in (13b) (cf. Lenerz 1977) may just have any of the three structures:

(13)   Wem hat die Frau das Buch gegeben?
     a. Sie hat dem JUNgen das Buch gegeben
              +RH   −RH
     b. Sie hat das Buch dem JUNgen gegeben
              −RH   +RH

If grammatical theory provides "at no costs" for alternative processes that ascribe different structures to the same linear order, unwanted redundancies can only be avoided if the structures are associated with different syntactic and extra-syntactic properties.

4.2. Problems for a uniform scrambling rule

Since scrambling is the established process of reordering, we consider its properties first. On this basis, marked word orders may be identified which do not seem to be analyzable as adjunction to X''.

4.2.1. Adjunction to X''

In von Stechow and Sternefeld (1988:464ff.), the following properties are given, among others:

(14) Scrambling is
    i. Chomsky-adjunction to a maximal phrase that applies
    ii. in IP, VP and AP (but not in NP and PP) *(= 2. Generalisierung)*
    iii. to X'' ≠ VP, IP (AP and AdvP)   *(= 3. Generalisierung)*
    iv. unless X'' is focussed, quantified, or interrogative
                                   (= 4./5. Generalisierung)

A clear instance of scrambling is represented by the "natural" Acc-Nom order for verbs like *überzeugen*:[26]

(15) $[_{CP}$ daß $[_{IP}$ den Lehrer$_A$ $[_{IP}$ die Antwort$_N$ $[_{VP}$ e1 überzeugt]]]]

The Acc-Nom order cannot well be considered a base-generated structure. If the animacy contrast is neutralized, the unmarked Nom-Acc order prevails:

(16) a.   daß den Lehrer die Antwort überzeugt
            [m]daß die Antwort den Lehrer überzeugt
    b.   [m]daß den Lehrer der Schüler überzeugt
            daß der Schüler den Lehrer überzeugt

Accusative and nominative need to be licensed by V and Infl, respectively. Since NP1 is needed for accusative assignment, the nominative phrase cannot be realized within VP, as it is in passive and ergative structures.[27] Hence, the accusative object is moved around NP0 and adjoined to IP, a canonical landing site.[28]

Of particular interest is condition (14iv), as exemplified in (17):

(17) a. ?*weil [$_{IP}$ jede Frau$_1$ [$_{IP}$ der/ein Mann e$_1$ liebt]]
   b. ?*weil [$_{IP}$ viele Frauen$_1$ [$_{IP}$ jeder/ein Mann e$_1$ liebt]]

For the reasons given above, the marked Acc-Nom order must be a scrambled structure. This leads to an unresolvable conflict: Quantified etc. phrases have to appear in operator position at the level of logical form, but an adjunction position is "frozen" for operator movement. Hence, quantified, etc. phrases may not be scrambled.[29]

4.2.2. Exemptions to scrambling?

There are instances of reordering that seem to require a different analysis, though. Firstly, scrambling predicts the existence of adjunctions to VP. Thus, there should be marked Nom-Acc-Dat, Nom-Gen-Acc and Nom-PP-Acc orders with the structures (18a) and (18b), respectively:

(18) a. ... [$_{VP}$ NP$_1$ [$_{VP}$ NP$_2$ [$_{V'}$ e$_1$ V]]]]]   from (4a)
   b. ... [$_{VP}$ XP$_4$ [$_{VP}$ [$_{V'}$ NP$_1$ [$_V$ e$_4$ V]]]]   from (4c)

The VP-adjoined position not being an operator position, the same effects of movement at logical form should show up as for (17).[30] Now, von Stechow and Sternefeld (1988:468) assume the scrambling structure (18a) for (19b):

(19) a. weil der Lehrer [$_{VP}$ allen Schülern$_2$ [$_{V'}$ drei Dramen$_1$ erklärte]]
   b. weil der Lehrer [$_{VP}$ drei Dr.$_1$ [$_{VP}$ allen Sch.$_2$ [$_{V'}$ e$_1$ erklärte]]]

While in (19a) *allen* may have scope over *drei* or vice versa, yielding a "non-distributive" reading ("*it is three plays that ...*") or a "distributive" reading ("*it is to all pupils that ...*"), which does not imply the same three plays to be explained to the pupils, (19b) preferably has a "non-distributive" reading. Hence, in (19b) *drei* ought to have scope over *allen* at logical form, which implies that there is an operator movement from an adjunction position, in contrast to the analysis for (17). If one wishes to maintain condition (14iv)., it seems that (19b) ought to receive a non-scrambling analysis (see 4.3.).

Secondly, double-object structures are not equally susceptible to reordering. Thus, the Acc-Gen pattern hardly admits Gen-Acc reordering under the same conditions of rhematization that yield the Acc-Dat order from a Dat-Acc basis; compare (20) to (13):

(20)   Wen hat die Frau des Diebstahls bezichtigt?
    a. Sie hat einen Angestellten des Diebstahls bezichtigt
        +RH   –RH
    b. ??Sie hat des Diebstahls einen Angestellten bezichtigt
        –RH   +RH

With normal sentence intonation, there is a marked contrast between the answers. The low acceptability of (20b) is quite unexpected if the rheme condition can be satisfied by scrambling a [-RH]-element around a [+RH]-element; cf. (11b). Thus, bringing a [+RH]-element into focus does not seem to be a leftward scrambling.[31] Hence, the unavailability of a rhematic Gen-Acc reordering seems to imply that the direct object-indirect object order of (13b) should be analyzed as either (12a) or (12b), rather than as the leftward scrambling structure (11b).

Thirdly, independent motivation for alternative projections from one lexical structure comes from observations about unmarked object orders. Höhle (1982) and Reis (1986) argue on the basis of "normal intonation" and "focus potential" that Dat-Acc verbs differ as to their unmarked ordering patterns:

(21) a. zeigen: ^{u}Nom-Dat-Acc-V, ^{m}Nom-Acc-Dat-V
    b. schenken: ^{u}Nom-Dat-Acc-V, ^{u}Nom-Acc-Dat-V
    c. aussetzen: ^{m}Nom-Dat-Acc-V, ^{u}Nom-Acc-Dat-V

While *aussetzen* differs from the *geben*-type verbs (21a) and (21b) in that it takes an animate accusative object and an inanimate dative object,[32] the interesting fact is that *schenken* is unmarked for both object orders in contrast to the typical *geben*-type verb *zeigen*. If the Acc-Dat order were derived by VP adjunction of the accusative object, scrambling would be a free option uncorrelated to any extra-syntactic properties and the ordering contrast (21a)/(21b) will be lost. Thus, one would expect that both unmarked object orders for *schenken* are directly base-generated.

Finally, sequences like (1f) might be a problem for a uniform scrambling rule. Given pragmatic and/or contextual conditions under which the sentence is appropriate, the Acc-Dat-Nom sequence would have to be derived by multiple application of adjunction to IP:

(22) ...[$_{IP}$ das Buch$_1$ [$_{IP}$ dem Jungen$_2$ [$_{IP}$ die Frau$_0$ [$_{VP}$ e$_2$ e$_1$ geb-]]]]

Although multiple adjunction occurs at the level of logical form, one may be sceptical about multiple adjunction in the syntax. In English, at least, syntactic adjunction seems to apply only once:

(23) a. [that he has blood on his shirt] proves his guilt [that he is guilty]
   b. it^i proves his guilt [that he has blood on his shirt]^i
   c. *it^i proves [that he is guilty] [that he has blood on his shirt]^i

Traditionally, it is assumed that clausal objects have to be extraposed (string vacuously, in this case; see also Olson 1981). The ungrammaticality of (23c) falls out, then, if there is a prohibition against double adjunction.[33] If so, there must be something else besides adjunction in order to generate multiple reorderings in German at all.

4.3. Projection structures

We have argued *ex negativo* that there are marked syntactic orderings for which a scrambling analysis does not seem appropriate. The alternative is to regard these structures as direct projections from lexical structures, such as (12a) and (12b). This raises the question of how to distinguish between the two options. Since Acc-Gen patterns are restricted anyway, we will be mostly concerned with Dat-Acc verbs.

4.3.1. Lexical focus incorporation

Of the examples discussed above, neither IP adjunction in (15), nor the Acc-Dat projection (21b) for *schenken* are necessarily related to the rheme condition.[34] While the Acc-Nom order is marked syntactically, the Acc-Dat order of *schenken* is unmarked, judging from its focus potential, which is equivalent to that of the Dat-Acc order (cf. Höhle 1982; Reis 1986). On the other hand, there are reorderings with the effect "that the second NP ... must be stressed, more definite than the first, contain new information, etc. ..." (Scherpenisse 1986:105). For reorderings with these properties, Scherpenisse proposed the lexical focus rule (24):

(24) $[_{VP}...x...V] \longrightarrow [_{VP}... [_V x_{[+F]} V]]$

As a lexical rule, focus incorporation, unlike X″ adjunction, does not leave a trace. Scherpenisse apparently analyzes all direct object-indirect object sequences by rule (24). In view of the *schenken*-data, this does not seem to be appropriate for Acc-Dat orders without the assumed prosodic effects. We may assume therefore that only marked Acc-Dat orders are realized in the NP_1-NP_4 structure (4c), whereas unmarked Acc-Dat orders have the NP_1-NP_3 structure (4b).

On the basis of this distinction, the Acc-Dat order of (19b) (cf. 4.2.2.) should have the structure (12b) (cf. Scherpenisse 1986:102ff.):

(25) weil der Lehrer $[_{VP}$ $[_{V'}$ drei Dramen$_1$$[_V$ allen Schülern$_2$ erklärte$]]]$

Structure (25) accounts for the wide scope reading of *drei Dramen* over *allen Schülern*: If the focus incorporation exempts a phrase from (free) operator movement, *allen* may not gain wide scope over *drei* (as it does from the base-generated NP_2 position in the distributive reading for [19a]). Hence, only the base-generated NP_1 element undergoes operator movement, yielding the non-distributive reading.

Further candidates for the focus rule are the verb-adjacent nominative subjects in (1d) and (1f) (cf. 4.3.2.), which necessarily require contrastive intonation and, hence, may bear the focus feature. If the subject NPs are realized as incorporated in the verb, the nominative-V constituents should be available for fronting to [Spec, CP], contrary to the facts:

(26) a. *[die Frau $_{[+F]}$ gegeben]$_i$ hat dem Jungen das Buch e$_i$ (cf. [1d])
     b. *[die Frau $_{[+F]}$ gegeben]$_i$ hat das Buch dem Jungen e$_i$ (cf. [1f])

The deviance of (26a) and (26b) cannot be ascribed to the incompatibility of focussing and topicalization, as Scherpenisse's example (27) shows:[35]

(27) [den Eltern $_{[+F]}$ vorgestellt] hat er seine Freundin noch nicht

The focus rule was designed in view of such examples to provide for the constituency of the dative-V sequence, which normally would not form a constituent excluding the accusative object. The subject-object asymmetry of the examples (26) and (27) is characteristic of effects caused by the empty category principle (ECP). For an account based on this principle, though, one has to assume the existence of empty categories to which lexically incorporated arguments are related. Even if the focus rule does not leave a trace, a gap in a canonical A-position may be warranted. Incorporated accusatives may seem to be Case-marked by the inner V, but incorporated nominatives should be related to the subject position, and incorporated datives to the NP_2 position, the latter position not being available for the "free dative", when emptied by the focus rule; cf. (28a):

(28) a. *daß ich der Frau mein Buch₁ dem Jungen₂ gezeigt habe

    b. daß [$_S$ NP_0 [$_{VP}$ e^i [$_{V'}$ NP_1 [$_V$ NP_2^i V]]]]

Co-superscripting, or theta-coindexing, of the two positions in (28b) may obtain if the Case position that is not assigned a thematic role does not count as an A-position.[36] This gives us assumption (A5):

(A5) Lexically incorporated arguments satisfy the Case filter by virtue of being in a theta-chain with the virtual Case position.

Blocking emptied Case positions for other material, (A5) allows to account for reordered arguments in purely structural terms. The empty category principle accounts for the contrast between (26) and (27) in the following manner: Fronting the incorporated subject and V to the specifier of CP breaks the theta-chain; hence, the empty subject position can be licensed only by lexical government, but Infl is not a proper governor. On the other hand, even though the theta-chain for an empty object position is broken also by fronting an incorporated object and V, object positions are properly governed with respect to the empty category principle by (the trace of the complex) verb.

4.3.2. Reordering accusative and genitive objects

Some remarks on the Acc-Gen pattern seem in order. If rhematic reordering falls under focus incorporation rather than scrambling, the awkwardness of the Gen-Acc order in (20b) (cf. 4.2.2.) may be explained in terms of the properties of the NP_1-NP_4 structure (4c): The NP_4 position has to be realized verb-adjacently; thus, the NP_1 argument cannot be projected between NP_4 and V. Argument incorporation into V seems not to be applicable iteratively (e.g., Baker 1985); i.e., V-within-V may discharge only one thematic role, although it admits complex phrases if these are not theta-marked by the verb (cf. Haegeman and van Riemsdijk 1986).

Reorderings of accusative and genitive objects seem always to have a contrastive reading; cf. (29):

(29) Man hat des Diebstahls den Mann bezichtigt, (nicht die Frau)

Contrastive focus has to be distinguished on independent grounds from normal processes of rhematization and/or focussing (cf. Culicover and Rochemont 1983; Jacobs 1984; von Stechow and Uhmann 1984). Here, only the structure of (29) will be of interest. Again, we contend that (29) does not necessitate scrambling movement. Nom-Gen-Acc probably shows an NP_3-Gen as in (30a) rather than two NP objects internal to the verbal complex as in (30b), in line with the considerations for (20b):

(30) a. $[_S NP_0 [_{VP} [v' e_1 NP_4 [_V NP_1 V]]]]$
   b. $[_S NP_0 [_{VP} [v' e_1 [_V NP_4 NP_1 V]]]]$

Evidence for (30a) as against (30b) comes from the placement of negation:

(31) a. Man hat des Diebstahls nicht den Mann bezichtigt,
       sondern die Frau / *sondern des Überfalls
   b. Man hat nicht des Diebstahls den Mann bezichtigt,
       *sondern die Frau / sondern des Überfalls

Since rule (24) obligatorily assigns focus to the incorporated argument, NP_1 should be in the scope of negation in (31b) if it were incorporated as a sister to NP_4. Instead the sentence shows narrow scope over the genitive NP. In contrast, (31a) behaves as expected: As the continuations of the sentence show, it is the focussed NP_1 that is negated. In the next section, it will be shown that a second genitive object may be realized in NP_3.

4.3.3. Double projections from one lexical structure

If syntactic projection of lexical structure obeys a principle of distinctness, it can be expected that two internal arguments may be realized in different pairs of the four thematic positions within VP. The assumption is supported by the existence of verbs which admit both orders of objects unmarkedly, which should be regarded as alternative projections from one thematic grid, as, e.g., for *schenken*; cf. (21b):[37]

(32) [NOM, DAT, ACC] $\longrightarrow$ a. (4a)   ...–NP_2–NP_1–V
                                        b. (4b)   ...–NP_1–NP_3–V

Vice versa, the verbs of intrinsic comparison (5d), for which structure (4b) was assumed, may well be realized in structure (4a) also.

Another instance of double projection is provided by those double-accusative verbs for speakers who have both passive forms (33a) and (33b):

(33) a.   weil man den Knaben$_A$ das Lied$_A$ lehrte
     b.   weil dem Knaben$_D$ das Lied$_N$ gelehrt wurde
     c.   ?weil der Knabe$_N$ das Lied$_A$ gelehrt wurde

While the passive (33b) is derived from the NP_2-NP_1 structure (4a), (33c) is most easily related to the NP_1-NP_3 structure (4b).

Projection variants for Nom-Acc-Gen verbs seem to exist only for speakers who ascribe unmarked sentence negation to both sentences in (34):

(34) a.   Man hat ihn nicht [$_V$ der Tat überführt]
     b.   Man hat ihn der Tat nicht [$_V$ überführt]

Although no linear reordering of arguments is involved, one would have to assume structures (4b) and (4c) for (34a) and (34b), respectively, in our framework:

(35) [NOM, ACC, GEN] $\longrightarrow$ a. (4c)   ...–NP_1–NP_4–V
                                       b. (4b)   ...–NP_1–NP_3–V

It is likely that individual verbs differ with respect to the possibility of two projection structures.

This does not mean that alternative projections may use any pair of VP-internal theta-positions. Thus, Dat-Acc verbs do not appear unmarked in (4c), and Acc-Gen verbs do not seem to admit (4a) at all. The alternatives of (32) and (35) may be explained as follows: In (32), the oblique argument makes use of the two s-Case positions that are morphologically licensed in the same way; in (35), the genitive-argument makes use of the two Case positions that are equivalent in terms of head government and the left periphery principle for L-marked arguments; cf. (43c). It is implied that double projections do not vary as to their interpretive and prosodic properties.

4.4. Multiple representations

Three processes have been discussed that each seem to be independently justified by grammatical theory: scrambling, focus incorporation, and variable projection. If applied indiscriminately, these mechanisms yield multiple analyses for strings of arguments. To take again the prototypical three-place verb with the unmarked Nom-Dat-Acc order, there are three potential structures for the reordered Nom-Acc-Dat sequence:

(36) a. ... $[_{IP}$ NP0 $[_{VP}$ NP1 $[_{VP}$ NP2 $[_{V'}$ e1 V]]]]] $= (11b)$
     b. ... $[_{IP}$ NP0 $[_{VP}$ e^i $[_{V'}$ NP1 $[_V$ NP$_2^i$ V]]]]] $= (28b)$
     c. ... $[_{IP}$ NP0 $[_{VP}$ $[_{V'}$ NP1 NP3 V]]] $= (4b)$

Since primary sentence stress falls naturally on the last lexical complement, all three structures should have the same focus-pitch accent association. Under what circumstances, then, would either of the structures seem most appropriate?

The structure (36c) should be a viable option only for those verbs that can be shown on independent grounds to have an unmarked Acc-Dat order, e.g., *schenken* and *aussetzen* of (21a)/(21c) and the verbs of intrinsic comparison such as *vorziehen, gleichstellen*. In Höhle (1982) and Reis (1986), this is taken to mean that the structure has the maximal set of potential foci:

(36) c'. Foci: Dat; Dat-V; Nom-Dat-V; Acc-Dat-V; Nom-Acc-Dat-V;
    *Acc-V; etc.

In contrast, there seem to be Acc-Dat orders that do not admit both the direct object and indirect object phrases to be in focus simultaneously (cf. von Stechow and Sternefeld 1988:461, ex. 26). Since reduced possibilities of focus choice are characteristic of marked word orders, this may be indicative of either the scrambling structure (36a) or the focus incorporation structure (36b): If focus spreading (cf. von Stechow and Uhmann 1984) is sensitive to configuration, the exclusion of the direct object from focus may not be plausible if the accusative and dative phrases were sisters as in structure (36c).

It is apparent that scrambling and focus incorporation are freely applicable in the syntax in a modular approach. As for the focus rule, irrespective of its lexical status, there are no lexical restrictions on its application, so that any *geben*-type verb can in principle be realized in the structure (36b). But the resulting structure will only be felicitous if it matches the pragmatic and/or contextual requirements of focus interpretation (cf. Culicover and Rochemont 1983).

What about scrambling, then? Given the expressive power of focus incorporation and variable projection, we may surmise that scrambling operates only if conditions on argument realization leave no other possibility, as discussed for the Acc-Nom order (see 4.3.1.). Scrambling may then be regarded as a "last resort" process, which is in line with the recent characterization of Move Alpha in Chomsky (1986b).

5. Concluding remarks

Sections 2 and 3 have argued for a configurational "Case" syntax, thus yielding a new class of arguments against the flat-structure hypothesis besides the standard arguments from subject-object asymmetries, superiority effects, etc. Apart from arguing for strict configurationality of German sentence structures, the approach greatly reduces the need for lexically specifying Cases, as compared to analyses that do not make use of structurally definable Case positions. The modular approach allows the labour of Case-marking to be divided between a general mode of argument-government (instead of the more restrictive notion of "abstract Case") and the licensing function of Case morphology.

Overall, Case-marking appears to follow a general distinctness requirement. If this view is tenable - which will have to be examined with reference to a larger number of languages - a large number of syntactic differences can be related systematically to the presence/absence of Case inflection.

Thus, languages may be said to differ not so much in the general make-up of the Case module, but rather with respect to the availability of Case morphology for the distinctive identification of NP argument relations,[38] a not too surprising result in view of the tradition.

Configurationality presupposes the existence of "scrambling" mechanisms. Three processes have been proposed that may effect orders of arguments differing from the standard Nom–Dat–Acc–V and Nom–Acc-Dat/Gen–V patterns. There is no question that the reordering processes are powerful enough to capture all possible scrambling phenomena of German. If the structures resulting from the three reordering processes can be distinguished along the lines discussed, the apparent redundancy does not seem to be a serious problem. Obviously, much more work needs to be done to make the conditions more precise under which a particular reordering strategy comes into play. Particularly focussing and intonation properties and their interaction with configurational properties deserve closer scrutiny. Although there seem to be clear cases for each of the proposed reordering processes, so that they seem to be independently justified, it may well turn out that some strategy could be eliminated. If this is so, so much the better. It is a plausible guess, though, that there is no need to bar any of the strategies as such. Rather, if one of them should not be relevant for German this would presumably be an effect of the modular interaction of principles of syntax, prosody and interpretation.

Notes

1.   The so-called "middle field" roughly corresponds to the S=IP-domain of X-bar theory. Controversial views as to the exact nature of the verb-second (V2) position and the "prefield" do not affect the purposes of the paper.

2..   Abraham (1984), for example, appears to hold a flat VP view, while accepting that the prefield and subject position are hierarchically distinct from the VP.

3.   It may be tempting to assume that head-marking languages (cf. Lehmann 1983; Nichols 1986) mark the C-relation on the governor. But see, for example, Speas (1986) for a different approach to head-marking: Affixal morphemes on the head satisfy the theta-criterion and the Case filter in morphological structure, a parametric alternative to licensing in syntactic structure.

4.   Consider also the dative/accusative/genitive alternations for objects of prepositions and adjectives.

5.   Other double-accusative verbs may fall under either (4b) or (4c). The handful of double-accusative verbs are notoriously heterogeneous; compare, e.g., the contrasts in (a) to (c):

   a.   daß sie den Jungen$_A$ das Lied$_A$ lehrte $\Rightarrow$ *daß den Jungen$_A$ das Lied$_N$ gelehrt wurde

                                                $\Rightarrow$?daß der Jungen$_N$ das Lied$_A$ gelehrt wurde

        (daß sie dem Jungen$_D$ das Lied$_A$ lehrte)$\Rightarrow$ daß dem Jungen$_D$ das Lied$_N$ gelehrt worden ist

   b.   ich habe den Mann$_A$ eines$_A$ gebeten $\Rightarrow$ der Mann$_N$ ist eines$_A$ gebeten worden

                                                $\Rightarrow$ *eines$_N$ ist den Mann$_A$ gebeten worden

        ich habe den Mann$_A$ um eines$_{pA}$ gebeten

   c.   das hat den Mann$_A$ das Leben$_A$ gekostet $\Rightarrow$ *der Mann$_N$ ist das Leben$_A$ gekostet worden

                                                $\Rightarrow$ *das Leben$_N$ ist den Mann$_A$ gekostet worden

        das hat dem Mann$_D$ das Leben$_A$ gekostet

   With *lehren*, Acc1 is a "covert" indirect object-dative and Acc2 the direct object argument. With *bitten*, Acc1 appears to be the direct object, and Acc2 may well be a lexical oblique. With *kosten*, Acc1 is again a "covert" dative, hence s-oblique, and the exemption of Acc2 from passivization perhaps allows the Case to be regarded as an l-objective, or, as is more commonly assumed, as an "adverbial" Case.

6.   For German m-Cases, Haider's (1983) criteria for alternating and invariant Cases distinguish s- and l-Case uses:

Gen = l-Case as single and second object: (3c) and (5b)

Dat = l-Case as singular/primary object: (3b), (5g)

= s-Oblique as second object: (5a), (5d);

Acc = s-objective as singular/primary object: (5a) to (5f)

= marked s-Oblique as second object: (5c)

= l-Case as second object

Nom = s-Case throughout

For the s-Case status of the verbal dative, cf. Tappe (1985) and Czepluch (1987a, 1987b, 1988a, 1988b); see note 5 for types of accusative.

7.　　Compare examples (a) to (c):

    a.　daß {sie$_N$ den Mann$_A$ *nicht* der Lüge$_G$ bezichtigte}

       vs. daß sie den Mann der Lüge {*nicht* bezichtigte}

    b.　daß {er$_N$ den Wein$_A$ dem Bier$_D$ *nicht* vorzieht}

       vs. daß er den Wein {*nicht* dem Bier} vorzieht

    c.　daß {er$_N$ das Buch$_A$ *nicht* auf den Tisch$_A$ legte}

       vs. daß er das Buch auf den Tisch {*nicht* legte}

The second examples exclusively (or: preferably) show phrasal negation, as indicated. Although speakers' judgements may vary somewhat as to negation scope interpretation, the tendency appears to be clear enough.

Note also that the single-object l-Cases of (3b) and (3c) are realized outside the verbal complex according to the negation test:

    d.　daß {er$_N$ dem Jungen$_D$ nicht half}

       vs. daß er {nicht dem Jungen} half

    e.　daß {er$_N$ des Gedenktages$_G$ nicht gedachte}

       vs. daß er {nicht des Gedenktages} gedachte

In fact, single objects seem to be realized in the direct object position for Case and thematic role assignment (cf. Czepluch 1987a, 1987b).

8.　　Under the flat-structure hypothesis, the distributional patterns (a) to (f) would seem to show a rather mysterious effect:

    a.　daß die Frau *gestern* dem Jungen *nur zögernd* das Buch gab

    b.　daß die Frau den Nachbarn *vor Gericht* der Lüge bezichtigt

    c.　daß die Frau den Jungen *zwei Wochen* das Lied lehrte

    d.　daß die Frau den Wein *allemal* dem Bier vorzieht

    e.　daß die Frau *im Laden* das Buch *schnell* auf den Tisch legte

    f.　　daß die Frau den Mann *aus Angst* an seine Feinde verriet

We are not concerned with the stylistically appropriate placement of adjuncts; cf. Duden Vol. 4 and Heidolph - Flämig - Motsch (1981) for a distinction between three types of adverbials with respect to their positional preferences. According to (A2), adverbials may cluster.

9.　　If there are head-final languages with adjacent Case-marking, this could be captured by admitting left/right periphery, i.e., the same range of values as are commonly assumed for the head parameter. Such an extension seems to yield unattested languages, though. However, things may turn out empirically, for the present purposes the left periphery principle is sufficient.

10. The term "head-government" expresses the fact that for (the core instances of) Case- and theta-marking "government under sisterhood" is the relevant notion (Davis 1987), in contrast to government within the maximal projection of the governor (Aoun and Sportiche 1983).

11. See Czepluch (1988a, 1988b) for a clarification of the notion "L(exically)-marked argument", which comprises arguments that are specified for l-Case, for not being Case-marked by V (i.e., prepositional objects) and for not being nominal (i.e., adverbials). The post-accusative dative of "verbs of intrinsic comparison", although being structurally Case-marked, may be regarded as L-marked for primarily thematic reasons (see Czepluch 1988a, 1988b and the references cited there). For a similar approach to lexical and syntactic markedness, see Gardner (1980).

12. Note that genitive, prepositional object and adverbial arguments in NP_4 can hardly be separated from the head by intervening lexical material. For the NP_4 position, the left periphery principle does not hold; rather, adjacency seems to be necessary:

    a. er_N hat sie_A gestern   nicht [vor uns *des Diebstahls*$_G$ bezichtigt]
            he has her yesterday not   before us (of) theft   accused
            er_N hat sie_A gestern vor uns nicht [*des Diebstahls*$_G$ bezichtigt]

    b. er_N hat das $Buch_A$ nicht [mit Absicht *nach ihr*$_{PC}$ geworfen]
            he has the book   not   on purpose at   her   thrown
            er_N hat das $Buch_A$ mit Absicht nicht *nach ihr*$_{PC}$ geworfen

Although the first examples may be interpreted for narrow scope negation, the relevant point is that they are also unmarked sentence negations. In contrast, the second variant of (b) only has a narrow scope/contrastive reading.

13. Although projection from lexicon onto syntax will have to relate to lexical theta-grids, only properties of argument realization will be considered here; for our view on lexical A-structure see Czepluch (1984, 1987a, 1988b).

14. For a more detailed account of the relevant Case parameters, see Czepluch (1987b, 1988a).

15. For example, possessive and appositive datives, such as *dem Bundeskanzler seine Mütze* and *wegen seines Romans, dem Bestseller,* do not fall under government at all, if they are to be analyzed as adjunctions to a maximal projection.

16. A-Cases are either derivative in that they are convenient denominations for the amalgamation of the categorial government-feature (in the sense of Emonds 1985) with the (open or lexically filled) Case slot of arguments in lexical grids, or a-Cases can be equated with government-features and hence reduce to the distinction of V-, P-, A- and N-Cases.

17. Pertinent combinatorial constraints on three-place verbs are that they always have:

a. a nominative subject

b. two internal arguments maximally

c. an accusative direct object if the verb takes two NP objects: (5a) to (5d) *Dat-Dat, *Gen-Gen, *Dat-Gen (see Tappe 1984, 1985)

d. maximally one l(exical)-Case: (5b), (5g) (see Czepluch 1982, Zaenen - Maling - Thráinsson 1985, Yip - Maling - Jackendoff 1987)

e. maximally one subcategorized for adverbial (PP/AdvP): (5e)

f. no Gen-prepositional object- or prepositional object-PP patterns (vs. (5g) Dat-prepositional object and (5h) prepositional object-prepositional object)

18.   Fukui (1986) and Speas (1986), for example, assume that all arguments of a verb, including the subject argument, are realized in the V-projection in D-structure. (A4), then, gives a reason why one argument cannot be licensed within VP (= their iterative maximal V'). The obligatoriness of a subject nominative with three-place verbs is not a trivial matter since two- and one-place verbs may appear without an apparent subject; e.g.: *daß den Kranken$_A$ nach Ruhe$_{PO}$ verlangt, daß dem Mann$_D$ (vor der Krankheit$_{PO}$) graut.*

That one- and two-place verbs may not license all their arguments within VP according to (A4), is discussed in Czepluch (1984, 1987b). Note that at least the dative argument of *grauen* seems to have certain "subject" properties if reflexive binding is taken as indication of subjecthood of the antecedent; e.g.: *daß dem Mann$_i$ vor sich$_i$ graute.*

Recently, it has been doubted that Infl assigns nominative under government (cf. Taraldsen 1985; Lamontagne and Travis 1986; Czepluch 1987b). Since agreement sufficiently licenses the subject position, nominative may be considered a zero Case-form.

19.   With respect to morphological licensing, Dutch, for example, would seem to be the "marked" option in that it has the NP$_2$-NP$_1$-V pattern (though not the NP$_1$-NP$_3$-V or NP$_1$-NP$_4$-V patterns).

20.   Thus, the notion of "subcategorization domain" for the minimal V' projection with respect to languages like English seems to be derivative. The benefactive *for*-datives of English, being realized as V'-sisters, are not arguments of verbs.

21.   See Culicover (1976), Stowell (1981) and Czepluch (1987b) for "incorporation" analyses of the indirect object into V. In fact, even authors who prefer variants of a "covert PP" analysis for the prepositionless indirect object (e.g., Czepluch 1982; Kayne 1984; Baker 1985 and Emonds 1985) agree that a flat double-NP structure should be impossible in English.

22.   Taking into account the wealth of potentially influential factors associated with "natural orders", such as the prosodic focus-pitch accent association, the semantic animacy bias, the scope properties of quantified and focussed elements, or the pragmatic theme-rheme distribution, among others, and trying to relate them to reordering processes, is not only beyond my present understanding, but certainly beyond the scope of this paper.

23.   The condition that XP may not be a pronoun, accounts for the contrast:
      a.   daß sie ihm das Buch gab vs.
      b.   *daß sie das Buch ihm gab
      It is not clear, though, whether rule (10) is meant to operate over adjacent constituents or over A-positions.

24.   Structures (11c) and (11d) violate binding principle (C) on R-expressions and the c-command requirement on chain formation.

25.   The basic idea, i.e., that there may be more than one syntactic projection from one lexical structure was first introduced in Czepluch (1982), where it was used to account for the syntactic part of the so-called "dative alternation".

26.   Diverging views as to the position of Infl are of no import for our discussion. Hence, Infl is omitted.

27.   It is not likely that nominative is realized in NP_3, a variant of (12a), if unfocussed VP-internal nominative is restricted to ergative structures, i.e., the NP_1 position. Neither can it appear in NP_4, as a variant of (12b), if V-incorporation is a marked process (as will be argued below).

28.   Webelhuth (in press) assumes adjunction to IP for Dat-Nom sequences with verbs that normally show the Nom-Dat order; cf. (a) and (b):
      a.   gestern hat [$_{IP}$ niemand [$_{VP}$ dem Großvater geholfen]]
      b.   gestern hat [$_{IP}$ dem Großvater$_k$ [$_{IP}$ niemand [$_{VP}$ e$_k$ geholfen]]]
      c.   *[niemand geholfen] hat gestern dem Großvater
      Webelhuth relates the deviance of (c) to the existence of an unbound variable in the preposed IP constituent, which falls out naturally if (c) is derived from (b), but remains mysterious if both the Nom-Dat and Dat-Nom orders were freely base-generated.

29.   Cf., for example, Fanselow (1987:232) and von Stechow and Sternefeld (1988: 466). It is presupposed that adjunction in the middle field does not yield operator positions and that focussed, etc. phrases have to be moved at logical form, because of their scope properties. This would yield a configuration such as (a):
      a.   *[$_{CP}$ XP$_i^{+F/Q}$ [$_{CP}$... [$_{IP/VP}$ e$_i^*$ [$_{IP/VP}$ ...e$_i$...]]]
      According to Fanselow (1987:231), the variable e$_i^*$ violates the empty category principle. It is not clear, though, that this account holds. On the one hand, the variable may satisfy the empty category principle by virtue of antecedent government. On the other hand, intermediate traces of (extended) A-bar-chains do not seem to count in structures at logical form (cf. Lasnik and Saito 1984; Chomsky 1986b:21f.):
      b.   [O$_i$ [... [$_{IP/VP}$ ... t$_i$ ... V]]]
      That is to say, the relevant structure at logical form for the empty category principle is (b) rather than (a). Thus at logical form there is no offending empty category t$_i^*$. Scherpenisse (1986) gives an example, where the left-scrambled NP bears the focus feature:
      c.   daß diesen Mann$_{[+F]}$ ein Auto überfahren hat

d. $[_{CP}$ daß NP_1 $[_{IP}$ NP_0 $[_{I'}INFL$ $[_{VP}$ e_1 V $]]]]$

To account for the contrast with example (15), Scherpenisse proposed to distinguish this case as adjunction to Comp. In the CP-IP analysis, adjunction to heads or to non-maximal projections is not available, though; cf. Chomsky (1986b:6). It is better to analyze (d) as (15) and to take the focus feature as a (pragmatically induced) property of the demonstrative determinator, an effect that can be observed also irrespective of movements.

30. I am not sure that the data confirm the predictions, at least for (c):

a. ?daß er $[_{VP}$ viele Puppen$_i$ $[_{VP}$ dem/einem Mädchen e_i schenkte]]

b. *daß er $[_{VP}$ jeden Anklagepunktes$_i$ $[_{VP}$ den Dieb e_i überführte]]

c. daß er $[_{VP}$ auf jeden Stuhl $[_{VP}$ ein Kissen e_i legte]]

31. Note that the l-Case-marked genitive object is not *per se* unavailable to A-bar movement, since wh-extraction is fine: *wessen hast du den Mann bezichtigt?*

32. Apparently, the projection principle is not sensitive to the animacy contrast, as the *zeigen/schenken* contrast shows. Since Acc-Dat-V is typical of "verbs of intrinsic comparison" (e.g., *gleichstellen, vorziehen* etc.) and seems to be determined thematically (cf. Czepluch 1987a), the unmarked Acc-Dat order for verbs like *aussetzen, unterstellen* etc. may be related to thematic properties also.

33. Compare also the awkwardness of examples (a) and (b), which would be derived as indicated:

a. ??John $[_{VP}$ $[_{VP}$ $[_{VP}$ gave e_1 e_2 at the party] [the book he bought yesteday]$_1$] [to the girl he liked most]$_2$]

b. ??John $[_{VP}$ $[_{VP}$ $[_{VP}$ gave e_1 e_2 at the party] [to the girl he liked most]$_2$] [the book he bought yesterday]$_1$]

34. While this is to be expected for the base-generated Acc-Dat orders of *schenken* or *vorziehen*, the Acc-Nom order of (15) seems to result from the animacy bias rather, i.e., the tendency to have an animate element before an inanimate one. Animacy cannot really be a strong linearization factor, though, since the Acc-Dat order for *schenken* just runs counter to it; cf. also von Stechow and Sternefeld (1988:454f.).

35. Under Scherpenisse's formulation of the focus rule, the subject argument is exempted from V incorporation since it is outside the VP domain of the verb. It is unusual for lexical rules to refer to syntactic structure, in particular if lexical entries contain unordered lists of arguments including the subject.

36. Cf. the rule (a) that Scherpenisse (1986:97) proposed for the VP-internal nominative of ergatives and passives, which was designed as an alternative to the notion of "chain-government" (den Besten 1981):

a. In the structure $[... X_{[-theta,+C]} ... Y_{[+theta,-C]} ...]$, coindex X and Y.

In order to exempt the coindexing relation from the binding theory, a non-theta position has to be regarded as a non-A position. Thus, the lexicalized NP is A-free since it is not bound by a c-commanding argument, and the coindexed empty category is not bound because it has no c-commanding antecedent. This anticipates the recent reduction of the notion of A-position to that of theta-position in Fukui (1986) and Speas (1986). Since the rule is not formally restricted, it extends naturally to structures like (28b), i.e., to reorderings by the focus rule.

37. In the lexical entries, on the left hand side, arguments are designated by their Cases only for expository reasons. In fact, lexical entries are pure thematic grids in the unmarked case (cf. Czepluch 1987a, 1988a, 1988b).

38. If English preposition stranding phenomena depend on V and P subcategorizing and governing in the same way (cf. Kayne 1981), there is a need for a parameter of universal grammar independent of the lack of Case morphology, as the English-French contrasts with respect to P-stranding show. At least, one would expect that P-stranding does not occur, or only limitedly so, in Case-inflecting languages (cf. Czepluch 1987b, 1987c).

References

Abraham, Werner
1984 "Word order in the middle field of the German sentence", *Groninger Arbeiten zur germanistischen Linguistik* 25

Aoun, Joseph - Dominique Sportiche
1983 "On the formal theory of government", *The Linguistic Review* 2.3: 211-236

Baker, Mark
1985 *Incorporation: A theory of grammatical function changing*, doctoral dissertation (Cambridge, Mass.: MIT).

Borer, Hagit
1984 *Parametric syntax* (Dordrecht: Foris).

Chomsky, Noam
1981 *Lectures on government and binding* (Dordrecht: Foris).
1986a *Knowledge of language* (New York: Praeger).
1986b *Barriers* (Cambridge, Mass.: MIT Press).

Culicover, Peter
1976 *Syntax* (New York: Academic Press).
1983 "Stress and focus in English", *Language* 59: 123-165

Czepluch, Hartmut
1982 "Case theory and the dative construction", *The Linguistic Review* 2.1.: 1-38
1984 "Grammatische Relationen und das Projektionsprinzip", *Syntaktische Struktur und Kasusrelation*, edited by Hartmut Czepluch - Hero Janßen (Tübingen: Gunter Narr).

1987a   "Lexikalische Argumentstruktur und syntaktische Projektionen: Zur Beschreibung grammatischer Relationen", *Zeitschrift für Sprachwissenschaft* 6: 3-36

1987b   *Kasus im Englischen und Deutschen: Überlegungen zu einer Theorie des abstrakten Kasus*, Habilitationsschrift (Göttingen: University of Göttingen).

1988a   "Case patterns in German: Implications for a theory of abstract Case", *McGill Working Papers in Linguistics: Special Issue on Comparative Germanic Syntax* (Montreal: McGill University).

1988b   "Kasusmorphologie und Kasusrelationen: Überlegungen zur Kasustheorie am Beispiel des Deutschen", *Linguistische Berichte* 116: 275-310

Davis, Lori
1987   "Remarks on government and proper government", *Linguistic Inquiry* 18: 311-321

Den Besten, Hans
1981   "A Case filter for passives", *Theory of markedness in generative grammar*, edited by Adriana Belletti - Luciana Brandi - Luigi Rizzi (Pisa: Scuola Normale Superiore di Pisa).

Den Besten, Hans - Gert Webelhuth
1987   "Remnant topicalization and the constituent structure of VP in the Germanic SOV languages", *GLOW Newsletter* 18 (Tilburg: Tilburg University).

Emonds, Joseph
1985   *A Unified theory of syntactic categories* (Dordrecht: Foris).

Fanselow, Gisbert
1987   *Konfigurationalität: Untersuchungen zur Universalgrammatik am Beispiel des Deutschen* (Tübingen: Gunter Narr).

Fukui, Naoki
1986   *A Theory of category projection and its application*, doctoral dissertation (Cambridge, Mass.: MIT).

Gardner, Thomas
1980   *Case-Marking in English*, Abhandlungen der Akademie der Wissenschaften und Literatur, Mainz (Wiesbaden: Steiner).

Grebe, Paul et al.
1973   Duden IV: *Der Grosse Duden* Band 4: Grammatik der deutschen Gegenwartssprache (Mannheim: Bibliographisches Institut).

Haegeman, Liliane - Henk van Riemsdijk
1986   "Verb projection raising, scope, and the typology of rules affecting verbs", *Linguistic Inquiry* 17: 417-466

Haider, Hubert
1982   "Dependenzen und Konfigurationen. Zur deutschen V-Projektion", *Groninger Arbeiten zur germanistischen Linguistik* 21
1983   "The Case of German", *Groninger Arbeiten zur germanistischen Linguistik* 22
1985   *Studies in German grammar*, edited by Jindřich Toman (Dordrecht: Foris).
1986   *Parameter der Syntax*, Habilitationsschrift (Vienna: University of Vienna).

Heidolph, Karl Erich - Walter Flämig - Wolfgang Motsch
1981   *Grundzüge einer deutschen Grammatik* (Berlin: Akademie Verlag).

Höhle, Tilman
1982   "Explikation für 'normale Betonung' und 'normale Wortstellung'", *Satzglieder im Deutschen*, edited by Werner Abraham (Tübingen: Gunther Narr).

Jacobs, Joachim
1984   "The syntax of bound focus in German", *Groninger Arbeiten zur germanistischen Linguistik* 25

Jaeggli, Osvaldo
1980   *Topics in Romance syntax* (Dordrecht: Foris).

Kayne, Richard
1981   "On certain differences between French and English", *Linguistic Inquiry* 12: 349-371
1984   *Connectedness and binary branching* (Dordrecht: Foris).

Lamontagne, G. - Lisa Travis
1986   "The Case filter and the ECP", *McGill Working Papers in Linguistics* 3.2

Lasnik, Howard - Mamoru Saito
1984   "On the nature of proper government", *Linguistic Inquiry* 15: 235-289

Lehmann, Christian
1983   "Rektion und syntaktische Relationen", *Folia Linguistica* 17: 339-378

Lenerz, Jürgen
1977   *Zur Abfolge nominaler Satzglieder im Deutschen* (Tübingen: Gunter Narr).

Lötscher, Andreas
1981   "Abfolgeregeln für Ergänzungen im Mittelfeld", *Deutsche Sprache* 9: 44-60

Nichols, Johanna
1986   "Head-marking and dependent-marking grammar", *Language* 62: 56-119

Olson, Susan
1981   *Problems of seem/scheinen constructions and their implications for the theory of predicate sentential complementation* (Tübingen: Niemeyer).

Reis, Marga
1986   "Die Stellung der Verbargumente im Deutschen - Stilübungen zum Grammatik: Pragmatik-Verhältnis", *Lunder germanistische Forschungen* 55: 139-177

Scherpenisse, Wim
1986   *The connection between base structure and linearization restrictions in German and Dutch* (Frankfurt/M: Lang).

Speas, Margaret J.
1986   *Adjunctions and projections in syntax*, doctoral dissertation (Cambridge, Mass.: MIT).

Stowell, Tim
1981   *Origins of phrase structure*, doctoral dissertation (Cambridge, Mass.: MIT).

Tappe, Hans-Thilo
1985   *Struktur und Restrukturierung*, doctoral dissertation (Göttingen: University of Göttingen).

Taraldsen, Tarald
1985   "On the distribution of nominative objects in Finnish", *Features and Projections*, edited by Pieter Muysken and Henk van Riemsdijk (Dordrecht: Foris).

Thiersch, Craig
1978   *Topics in German syntax*, doctoral dissertation (Cambridge, Mass.: MIT).
1982   "A Note on scrambling and the existence of VP", *Wiener Linguistische Gazette* 27/28: 11-34

Travis, Lisa
1984   *Parameters and effects on word order variation*, doctoral dissertation (Cambridge, Mass.: MIT).
1987   "Parameters of phrase structure and V2 phenomena" (Montreal: unpublished manuscript McGill University).

Van Riemsdijk, Henk
1983   "The Case of German adjectives", *Linguistic categories: Auxiliaries and related puzzles*, edited by Frank Heny and Barry Richards (Dordrecht: Reidel).

Von Stechow, Arnim - Wolfgang Sternefeld
1988   *Bausteine syntaktischen Wissens* (Opladen: Westdeutscher Verlag).

Von Stechow, Arnim - Susanne Uhmann
1984   "On the focus-pitch accent relation", *Groninger Arbeiten zur germanistischen Linguistik* 25

Webelhuth, Gert
1985   "German is configurational", *The Linguistic Review* 4.3: 203-246
to appear "More diagnostics for structure" (Amherst: unpublished manuscript University of Massachusetts).

Yip, Moira - Joan Maling - Ray Jackendoff
  1987   "Case in Tiers", *Language* 63: 217-250

Zaenen, Annie - Joan Maling - Höskuldur Thráinsson
  1985   "Case and grammatical functions: The Icelandic passive", *Natural Language and Linguistic Theory* 3: 441-483

Zubin, David A. - Klaus-Michael Köpke
  1985   "Cognitive constraints on the order of subject and object in German", *Studies in Language* 9: 77-99

Verb second, nominative Case and scope[1]

Wim Kosmeijer

1. Introduction

The phenomenon of "verb second" has been extensively discussed during the last ten years. The term refers to the second position finite verbs occupy in declarative main clauses. Many questions are related to this phenomenon. Some of these have a fairly uncontroversial answer. As to the position of the finite verb, for instance, it is generally assumed that the landing site of the moved finite verb in main clauses of the so-called verb-second languages is Comp (see den Besten 1981).

Other questions have been answered in various ways, without one particular answer being generally adopted. For example, the question of what is the trigger of the movement of finite verbs to Comp in main clauses has been answered in terms of nominative Case marking of the subject, scope of [+tense], conditions on government of empty categories, etc., with various properties of Comp, Infl, the V-position, Tense and Agreement interacting.

What all proposals have in common is that the continental Germanic languages, but not for instance English, are analyzed as verb-second languages. English partially shows movement of the finite verb to Comp in main clauses. Only in yes/no questions and in direct questions do auxiliaries and the dummy verb *do* move to Comp.

In this article I will argue that not only English but also Icelandic shows partial verb-second. That is, it is claimed that in Icelandic yes/no questions and in direct questions finite verbs move to Comp. This differs from proposals which analyze Icelandic as a full verb-second language, e.g. Platzack (1986), and from a proposal which analyzes Icelandic as a non-verb-second language (Thráinsson 1986).

Related to this proposal is the question concerning the basic position of the subject. In standard analyses it is assumed that the specifier position of IP is the basic position of the subject. Following e.g. Manzini (1989), Sportiche (1988), I will assume that the basic position of the subject is not in the specifier position of IP but in a VP internal position. In order to receive nominative Case it may then be necessary for the subject to move to the specifier position of IP.

The most important question, however, is the trigger of the movement of the finite verb to Comp in main clauses. I will argue that it is scope of the feature [+tense] that is responsible for this movement. The element determining the finiteness of a clause, i.e. the feature [+tense], must have scope over the entire predication, i.e. over both the VP and the external argument. The domain of this element is defined in terms of c-command. If [+tense] has no scope over the entire predication in its base position it has to move to a position where it has scope over the entire predication. This implies that in main clauses the finite verb, bearing the feature [+tense], has to move. Because nominative Case is also connected to the feature [+tense] and because it is the subject that receives nominative Case, the S-structure position of the subject is dependent on the position of the scope bearing [+tense].

This paper will contain the following sections: in section 2 a number of word order differences between main and subordinate clauses of verb-second languages will be presented by comparing Dutch, Swedish, English and Icelandic. Verb-second and the theory of scope will be the subject of section 3. The position of the subject and nominative Case will be dealt with in section 4. In section 5 we will briefly look at the position of wh-elements and topicalized elements. We will finish with the conclusions in section 6.

2. Word order in main and subordinate clauses

As a consequence of the movement of the finite verb from its basic position in subordinate clauses to the Comp-position in main clauses, a number of differences in the word order of main and subordinate clauses in verb-second languages can be observed.

When the finite verb moves to Comp (in main clauses), another constituent may or must be moved to the left of Comp. Whether these constituents actually move to the specifier position of CP or to a topic-position outside the CP, is a problem to which I will briefly return in section 5. For present purposes it suffices to assume that these constituents move to the specifier position of CP. Subjects, objects and wh-elements are among the types of constituents that can be moved to the left of the finite verb in Comp. Observe that only wh-elements can be moved to a position to the left of complementizers in subordinate clauses. E.g., the order "subject-complementizer" is not allowed.

We will now look at the word order differences between main and subordinate clauses in Dutch, Swedish, English and Icelandic. In previous analyses Dutch and Swedish have been shown to be verb-second languages. English has been analyzed as only partly a verb-second language. In yes/no questions and wh-questions, auxiliaries move from Infl to Comp. If the subject is in first position or e.g. a direct object is topicalized, no movement to Comp takes place. For Icelandic proposals have been made in which this language is analyzed as a full verb-second language or as a non-verb-second language.

Consider the facts. In Dutch it is easy to see that finite verbs have different positions in main and subordinate clauses. Since Koster (1975) it has been generally accepted that the SOV order of subordinate clauses is the basic word order. So in subordinate clauses the finite verb is to the right of the object, whereas in main clauses with the subject in first position the finite verb precedes the direct object. Examples are given in (1).

(1)   a.   Jan *kocht* gisteren   een boek
              John bought yesterday a book
      b.   Ik weet dat Jan gisteren   een boek *kocht.*
              I know that John yesterday a book   bought.

Another difference is that where in main clauses the order "topic-Vf-subject" can be found, this order is excluded in subordinate clauses; even the order "topic-subject-Vf" is not allowed. This is illustrated in (2).

(2)   a.   Dit boek kocht Jan gisteren
              This book bought John yesterday

b. *Ik weet dat dit boek Jan gisteren kocht
   I   know that this book John yesterday bought

A third difference is the occurence of verb-first structures, as in yes/no questions. In Dutch verb-first structures can only be found in main clauses. Examples are given in (3).

(3) a. Kocht Jan gisteren een boek?
         Bought John yesterday a book
     b. *Ik vraag me af of   kocht Jan gisteren een boek
          I   wonder   whether bought John yesterday a book

A final difference shows the complementary distribution of complementizers and finite verbs. In main clauses, a wh-element is followed by a finite verb, whereas in subordinate clauses it is followed by the complementizer.

(4) a. *Wat kocht* Jan gisteren?
         What bought John yesterday?
     b. Ik weet niet *wat of* Jan gisteren gekocht heeft
         I   know not   what if John yesterday bought has

In Swedish the different position of the finite verb in main and subordinate clauses is not as clear as in Dutch, because Swedish is an SVO-language. The mutual order of finite verbs and sentence adverbials, however, illustrates the different positions of finite verbs. In subordinate clauses the finite verb follows the sentence adverbial, whereas in main clauses the finite verb precedes the sentence adverbial.[2] This is illustrated in (5).

(5) a. Jan *köpte inte* denna bok igår
         John bought not this book yesterday
     b. Jag undrar om Jan *inte köpte* denna bok igår
         I wonder whether John not bought this book yesterday

In other respects, Swedish behaves like Dutch. In normal subordinate clauses, topicalization of e.g. objects is excluded, whereas in main clauses it occurs freely. Verb-first-structures are only found in main clauses, not in subordinate clauses. In Swedish, the complementary distribution of finite verbs and complementizers in Comp is most easily seen on the basis of wh-sentences. In main clauses, we find the order "wh-Vf-subject" and in subordinate clauses the order "wh-complementizer-subject".

Contrary to Swedish and Dutch, English is not a full verb-second language but has only restricted movement of finite verbs in main clauses. That is, verb movement to Comp is restricted to auxiliaries and takes place only in yes/no questions (i.e. verb-first structures) and in wh-sentences.

With respect to these two structures, English is like Swedish and Dutch if we look at the differences between main and subordinate clauses. Verb-first structures are allowed in main clauses only. This is illustrated in (6).

(6) a. Will John buy this book?
    b. *I know that will John buy this book

In main clauses we find the order "wh-Vf-subject". In subordinate clauses the order "wh-(complementizer)-subject" can be observed. This is the same as we found in Dutch and Swedish.

In the other two sentence types, i.e. sentences with the subject in first position and sentences with a topicalized element, no verb movement seems to have taken place. In sentences with the subject in first position, the order is exactly the same in main and subordinate clauses. In main clauses with a topicalized element we find the order "Topic-subject-Vf". This is a difference between English and e.g. Dutch, which has the finite verb between the topicalized element and the subject. It seems that in these two cases no verb movement has taken place. Examples are given in (7) and (8).3

(7) (I wonder whether) John will not buy this book

(8) a. This book John will never buy
    b. *I wonder whether this book John will never buy

Let us now consider Icelandic. With respect to verb-second, Icelandic has been analyzed in two different ways. In Platzack (1986) it is analyzed as a full verb-second language. Thráinsson (1986), however, proposes that there is no movement of the finite verb to Comp in main clauses at all. The finite verb is in Infl both in main and in subordinate clauses. I will argue, however, that neither of these proposals is correct. Rather, Icelandic is like English, in a sense.

In sentences with the subject in first position and in sentences with another non operator in first position, no movement of the finite verb to Comp takes place. The word order of these two types of sentences is exactly the same in main and subordinate clauses. This is illustrated in (9).

(9) a. (Hann spurði hvort)   ég hefði ekki keypt   bókina
        (He wondered whether) I   had   not bought the book
    b. (Hann spurði hvort)   þessa bókum hefði ég ekki keypt
        (He wondered whether) these books had I   not bought

Therefore in these sentence types Icelandic is closer to English than it is to the verb-second languages Dutch and Swedish.

In yes/no questions and in wh-sentences there is movement of the finite verb to Comp in main clauses. So, with respect to these sentences Icelandic seems to follow the other languages.

In main clauses we find the order "wh-Vf-subject". In subordinate clauses we find the order "wh-subject-Vf". A complementizer between them is not allowed here. Examples are given in (10)

(10) a. Hvern   hefur María kysst?
        Whom (A) has   María kissed?
    b. Ég veit   ekki hvern   María hefur kysst
        I   know not whom (A) María has   kissed

If we look at verb-first structures the picture is somewhat diffuse. We can observe two types of verb-first structures. In main clauses a sentence as in (11) can have two readings.

(11)   Hitti hann þá   einhverja útlendinga?/.
       Met he   then some   foreigners
    a. Did he meet then some foreigners?
    b. He met then some foreigners

The second type of verb-first structures is often referred to as narrative inversion. In subordinate clauses only narrative inversion-structures can be observed. In section 4, I will show that the two verb-first structures are different in nature. Yes/no questions have the finite verb in Comp, whereas in narrative inversion-constructions, the finite verb is situated in Infl.

3. Verb second and the scope of tense

In this section I will sketch a proposal that accounts for the movement of the finite verb to Comp in main clauses in verb second languages and the absence of this movement in non verb second languages. This proposal is based on the scope analysis given in Evers (1982).

The central idea is that in all the languages discussed the element that determines the finiteness of a finite clause must have scope over the entire predication, i.e. the VP and the external argument. The following questions arise: (i) Which element determines the finiteness of a clause and (ii) how is the domain of this scope bearing element defined?

The element that determines whether a clause is finite or not, is the feature [tense]. If this feature has the positive value, i.e. [+tense] the sentence is finite. If its value is [-tense] the result is an infinitival. This feature [+tense] can be situated in the Comp-, Infl-, and V-position. To become an element that has scopal properties it has to be lexically suppor- ted.[4] The domain of the scope bearing [+tense] will be defined in terms of c-command, as defined in Chomsky (1981).

(12) C-Command

α c-commands β if and only if

(i) α does not contain β

(ii) Suppose that G^1.....G^n is the maximal sequence such that

(a) $G^n = \alpha$

(b) $G^i = \alpha^j$

(c) G^i immediately dominates G^{i+1}

Then if δ dominates α then either

(I) δ dominates β or

(II) $\delta = G^i$ and G^i dominates β

We will now look at the languages we were dealing with in the previous section, starting with Dutch as an example of the Germanic SOV-languages. Without discussion I am adopting the proposal developed in Reuland - Kosmeijer (1988). For justification, I refer to that article. The basic structure for Dutch is then given in (13).

(13)

```
                    CP
                  /    \
            SPEC        C′
                       /  \
                  COMP     IP
                          /  \
                     SPEC     VP/I′
                             /    \
                         SPEC      V′/I′
                                  /    \
                                DO      V/I
                                         |
                                         Vf
                                      [+tense]
```

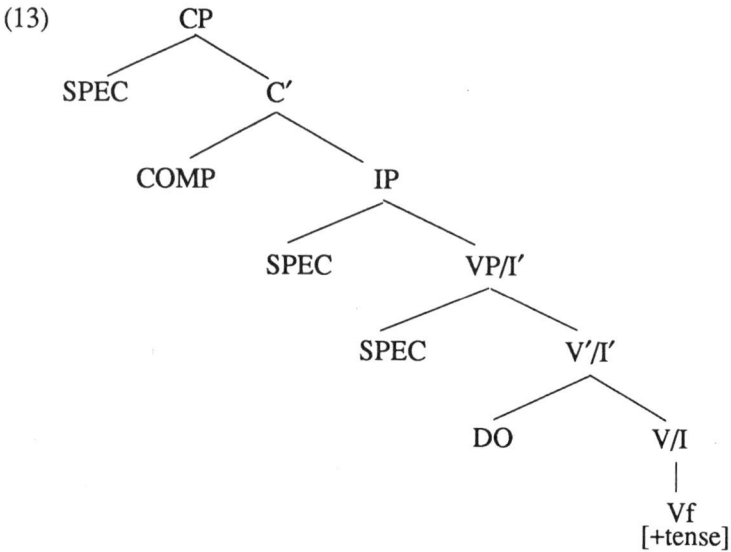

In this structure we have a joined V/I-projection. Such a joined projection is only possible under certain conditions: e.g. the two heads of the joined projections must govern in the same direction. Also note, that in Dutch the morphological structure of the finite verb (v-infl) is reflected in the syntax (V-I). (For the theory of phrase structure this requires see Reuland - Kosmeijer 1988 and Lasnik - Kupin 1977).

The feature [+tense] contained in the finite verb in the joined V/I-position does not have scope over the entire predication (subject + VP). Since it is contained in the VP, this would imply that it would c-command itself which is excluded. To have the entire predication in its scope [+tense] must be in a position where it c-commands both the VP and the external argument. In the absence of an independent I-position, the only available place is Comp.

The feature [+tense] in Comp must be lexically supported. In subordinate clauses Comp is filled by the complementizer. In main clauses, however, Comp is not lexically filled. Hence, the verb bearing [+tense] must move along to provide lexical support.

When [+tense] is in Comp, its domain is the CP, so even elements in the specifier position of the CP are its scope; these are the operators like wh-elements.[5]

A main clause in Dutch will now have a structure as in (14).[6]

(14)

```
              CP
           ╱      ╲
       SPEC        C′
                 ╱    ╲
             COMP      IP
               │     ╱    ╲
              Vfᵢ  SPEC   VP/I′
            [+tense]    ╱      ╲
                     SPEC     V′/I′
                            ╱    ╲
                          DO      V/I
                                   │
                                   eᵢ
```

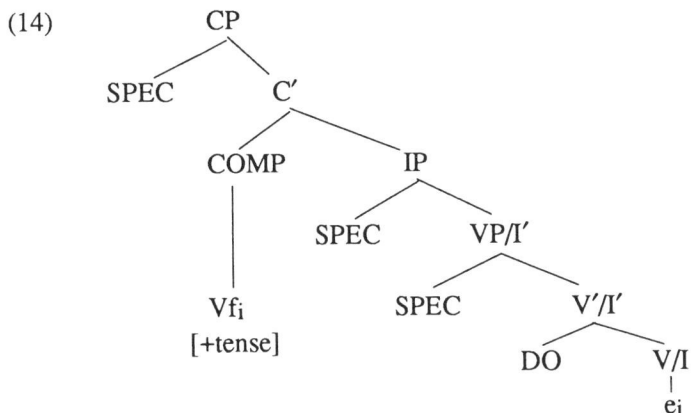

This accounts for the movement of the finite verb to Comp in main clauses and thus for the complementary distribution of finite verbs in main clauses and complementizers in subordinate clauses.

For the SVO-languages the picture is different. Here we do not have a joined V/I projection but two seperate projections of V and Infl.

As a consequence finite verbs are not two-headed but have only one head. In Kosmeijer (1987) it is argued that finite verbs in Swedish are of category V. So for Swedish we find a base structure as given in (15).

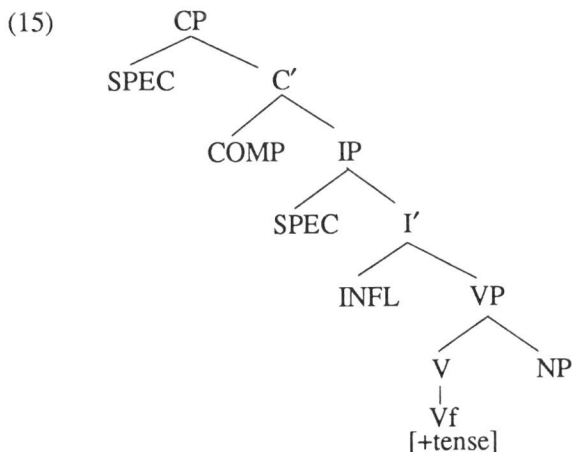

(15)

```
          CP
       ╱      ╲
   SPEC        C′
             ╱    ╲
         COMP      IP
                 ╱    ╲
             SPEC     I′
                    ╱    ╲
                INFL     VP
                        ╱   ╲
                       V     NP
                       │
                      Vf
                   [+tense]
```

In Swedish, as in Dutch, [+tense] in V cannot have scope over the entire predication, because [+tense] is contained in the finite verb in V. When it would c-command the VP it would c-command itself, which is excluded. So, like in Dutch, the finite verb has to move.

However, contrary to Dutch, not only Comp but also Infl is a possible position of [+tense]. The facts, however, indicate that it is the Comp-position to which the finite verb moves in main clauses to give [+tense] lexical support (see e.g. Platzack 1986).

The question is why the scope requirements of [+tense] is are met in Comp and not in Infl. In a proposal made by Holmberg - Platzack (this volume) it is claimed that for independent reasons Infl may not be lexically filled in Swedish.

In Holmberg - Platzack the emptiness of Infl is accounted for in the following way: An operator [+F], similar to the scope bearing [+tense] in this article, has to be licensed. This operator can be licensed in two ways: 1) by nominal agreement in Infl or 2) by (free) co-indexing between Comp and Infl.

Swedish lacks verbal agreement and nominal AGR in Infl, as they show, excluding the first option. Movement of the finite verb to Infl would block the indexing between Comp and INFL, excluding the second option; so the operator [+F] cannot be licensed either way.

It now follows that the scope bearing [+tense] must be in Comp, where it can be lexically supported and has the entire predication in its scope. Like in Dutch, [+tense] is lexically supported by a complementizer in subordinate clauses; in main clauses it is lexically supported by the moved finite verb. A main clause in Swedish then has the following S-structure:

(16)

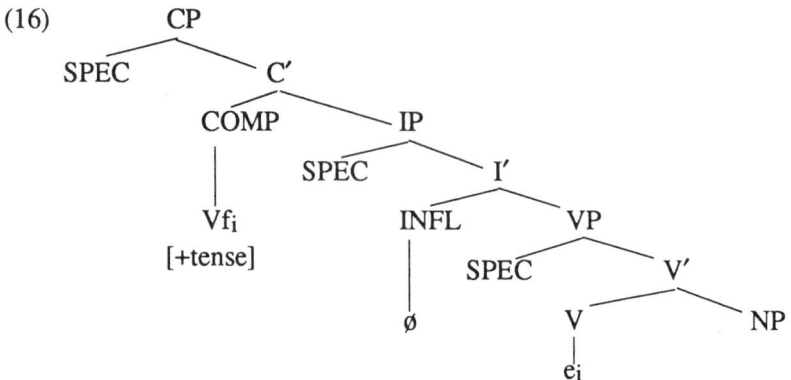

Before we turning to Icelandic we will first deal with English. As we saw in section 2, sentences with the subject in first position or sentences with a fronted non-operator do not show movement of the finite verb in main clauses. In sentences with an operator in first position, subject-aux inversion is observed. Operators are among others wh-elements, negation-elements and the abstract question marker Q.

Contrary to Swedish we can distinguish between two classes of verbs: main verbs and auxiliaries.[7] Main verbs are situated in V and auxiliaries are situated in Infl. (In terms of Holmberg and Platzacks analysis this requires that English auxiliaries contain an abstract nominal AGR, see e.g. Chomsky 1981.) We will assume this can be justified. So, [+tense] in Infl is lexically supported and can bear scope over the entire predication. This is the canonical sentence pattern exemplified in (17) and (18), with the subject or another non-operator in first position.

(17) a.   John will never buy this book
     b.   This book John will never buy

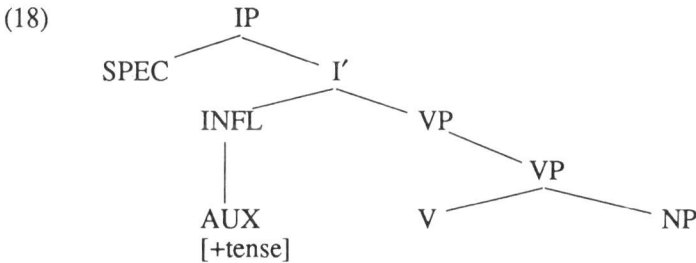

(18)

IP

SPEC   I′

    INFL   VP

                    VP

    AUX   V   NP
    [+tense]

In English the subject is always to the left of the AUX in Infl (in the specifier position of the IP), where it is in the scope of [+tense] in Infl. If the fronted non-operator must be in the scope of [+tense] in Infl it can not be in the projection of Comp but has to be adjoined to the IP. In this way it is in the c-command domain of [+tense] in Infl if c-command is defined as in Chomsky (1981). The structure of (17b) is then [$_{IP}$ TOPIC [$_{IP}$ Su....]]. For English, however, one additional assumption must be made. Infl has to be lexically filled at S-structure to give [+tense] lexical support. If Infl contains no auxiliary it is filled by the dummy verb "do". In the phonological component this dummy verb is deleted (for this type of "do-deletion" see e.g. Koster 1986). In this way the absence of the movement of the finite verb to Comp is accounted for.

In sentences headed by an operator-like element we find subject-aux inversion. Under the standard analyses that these elements are in the specifier position of the CP it will be clear why subject-aux inversion occurs. The operator in the specifier position of CP is not in the scope of the [+tense] in Infl. In order for these operator elements to be in the scope of [+tense], this element must be situated in Comp. In main clauses this [+tense] must have lexical support. It gets the lexical support from the auxiliary verb that moves from Infl to Comp. In subordinate clauses Comp is filled by the complementizer, as in the other languages discussed. In these sentences we get a structure as in (19).

(19)

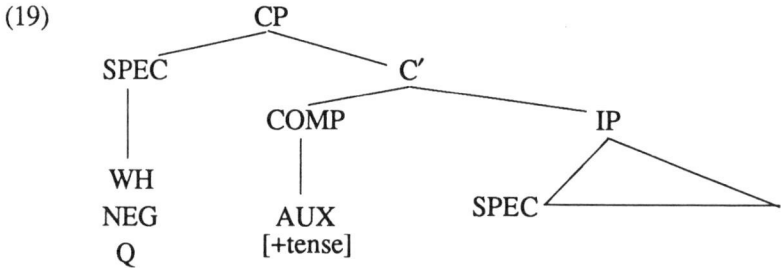

If we now look at Icelandic we see a picture resembling that of English. It will be argued that Icelandic is neither a full verb-second language nor a non verb-second language. There is movement of the finite verb to Comp in main clauses with operator-like elements in the specifier position of the CP. But in other sentences the finite verb remains in Infl. This makes our analysis of Icelandic rather different from previous ones.

Let us now consider it in more detail.

In Icelandic, contrary to Swedish, finite verbs contain verbal inflection. This inflection agrees with the subject in person and number. In other words, in Icelandic we have overt AGR-features. Under the analysis of Holmberg and Platzack (this volume), this implies without further assumptions that finite verbs can stay in Infl and that like in English the scope bearing [+tense] can be in Infl.[8]

This implies that in sentences with the subject in first position or in sentences with a fronted non-operator no movement needs to take place.

That this is actually the case can be seen by the similar word order of these sentence types in main and subordinate clauses. The examples are repeated here.

(20) a. (Hann spurði hvort)   ég keypti ekki þessum bókum
      (He wondered whether) I   bought not these   books
   b. (Hann spurði hvort)   þessum hring hefðu þeir lofað   mér
      (He wondered whether) this   ring had   they promised me

Note that the subject in (20b) is to the right of the finite verb. That we do not have a subject with quirky case to the left of the finite verb can be seen by the agreement of the verb with the plural pronoun "þeir". If we have a subject with quirky case, in (20b) the element "þessum hring" the verb would have a third person singular form.

So sentences as in (20) have a structure like in (21).

(21)

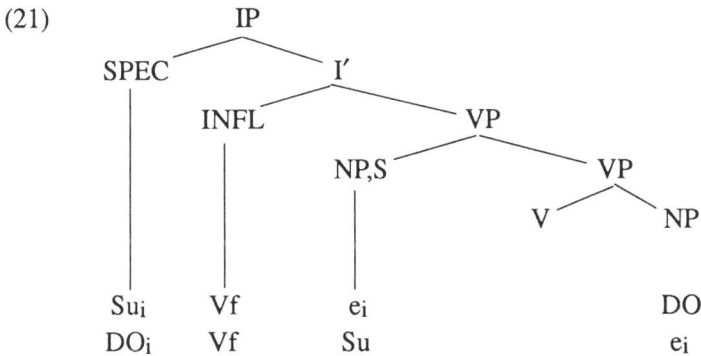

Narrative inversion also fits into this structure. In that case the specifier position of the IP is empty.

In sentences where we have an operator in the specifier position of CP, the finite verb has to move from Infl to Comp in main clauses to lexicalize the [+tense] there which then will become the scope bearing [+tense]. As was already argued for with respect to English, operators are situated in the specifier position of the CP and are not in the domain of [+tense] in Infl. In these constructions the subject is always immediately to the right of the finite verb in main clauses or to the right of the complementizer or the wh-element in subordinate clauses. In the next section we will see that this is so for reasons of nominative Case.

4. Nominative Case and the position of the subject.

In Platzack (1986) it is proposed that the movement of the finite verb to Comp in main clauses of verb second languages can be accounted for by nominative Case assignment. The feature [+tense] in Comp assigns nominative Case to the adjacent subject in the specifier position of the IP. This [+tense] can only assign its Case if Comp is lexicalized. In subordinate clauses we have the complementizer in Comp but in main clauses Comp is empty. The finite verb now moves to Comp to give [+tense] lexical support. In Platzack's proposal the position of the finite verb is determined by the position of the subject.

In the proposal outlined here we propose the opposite. The position of the subject is dependent on the position of the scope bearing [+tense]. I will assume that this element is the nominative Case assigner. Nominative Case is like other structural Cases assigned under government, government being defined in terms of minimality as in Chomsky (1986).

(22) Minimality Condition
τ is a barrier for β if τ is the immediate projection of δ, a zero level category distinct from β

Government in terms of minimality implies that a head governs inside its complement. So in a structure as in (23) the head Y governs X''.

(23)

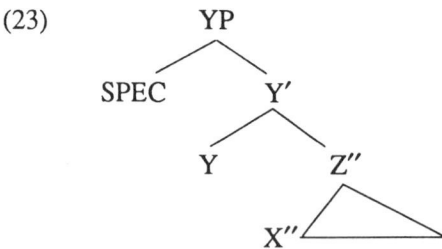

So Comp can govern the specifier position of the IP and Infl can govern the specifier position of the VP or a VP-adjoined position.

In section 3 we have seen that the scope bearing [+tense] can be either in Infl or in Comp. This implies that nominative Case is assigned either from Comp or from Infl, so the subject has to be in a position in which it is governed by the nominative Case assigner.

In standard analyses the specifier position of the IP is said to be the basic position of the external argument; in some recent analyses it is, however, a VP-adjoined position that serves as the basic position of the subject (see e.g. Manzini 1989, Sportiche 1988). The two possibilities are given in (24).

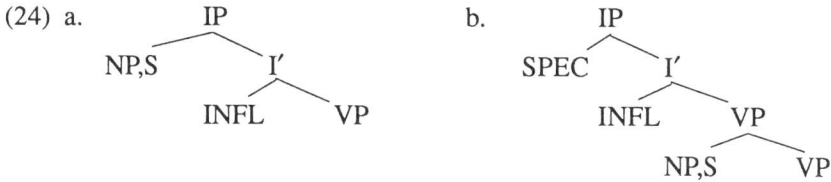

(24) a.

```
            IP
         /     \
    NP,S        I'
              /    \
          INFL      VP
```

b.

```
            IP
         /     \
    SPEC        I'
              /    \
          INFL      VP
                  /    \
               NP,S     VP
```

As we will see below the VP-adjoined position of the subject is to be preferred to the specifier position of the IP, even though in most examples the subject will be in the specifier position of the IP.

So, if we now examine the languages we are dealing with, the following picture arises: in Swedish and Dutch the scope bearing feature [+tense] is in Comp. If this [+tense] is the nominative Case assigner, the subject has to move because it would be Caseless in the VP-adjoined position, the VP being a barrier to government. If the subject does not move, the sentence will be ruled out by the Case-filter. The subject now moves to the specifier position of the IP. In this position the subject is governed by Comp, which contains the scope bearing [+tense] and can also get nominative Case. In Swedish and Dutch a sentence will have the following S-structure:

(25) $[_{C'}\text{COMP} [_{IP} \text{NP,S}_i ... [_{VP} e_i [_{VP}...]]]]$

In Icelandic and English the same is true for wh-sentences and yes/no questions. If not the subject, but another element is questioned, we find the word order "wh-Vf-subject" in main clauses and the order "wh-(complementizer)-subject" in subordinate clauses. Of course, this is a consequence of the fact that the scope bearing [+tense] is situated in Comp, and is, in main clauses, lexically supported by the finite verb. From this position nominative Case is assigned, which can only be received by the subject when it is in the specifier position of the IP.

Let us now consider sentences with the subject in first position and sentences with e.g. a topicalized object in English and Icelandic. Both in Icelandic and English it is the Infl node which contains the scope bearing

[+tense]. In this case the structural subject is in the domain of [+tense], both in the specifier position of the IP and in a VP-adjoined position. Yet it seems that Icelandic and English differ in the position of the subject at S-structure.

In Icelandic, topicalization structures result in the order "topic-Vf-subject" both in main and in subordinate clauses. Contrary to e.g. Swedish and West-Frisian this is not restricted to the complementizer *að* and to matrix verbs that select assertions, but it also occurs in a sentence like (26).

(26) Hann spurði   hvort   þessum hring hefðu þeir lofað   mér
      He   wondered whether this   ring   had   they promised me

I will assume that topicalization structures in Icelandic are IPs.[9] This implies that the topic is in the specifier position of the IP, the finite verb in Infl and the subject in its basic position adjoined to the VP. So the finite verb and the subject give rise to the following structure:

(27) $[_{I'}$ Vf $[_{VP}$ NP,S $[_{VP}...$

The position of the subject in (27) is governed by the finite verb and also by the scope bearing [+tense] under minimality. The subject can receive nominative Case from Infl. The subject can remain in its basic position and may optionally move to the specifier position of the IP, as it does in clauses with the subject in first position.

It will also be clear why having both wh-movement and topicalization in the same clause is impossible in Icelandic. In this case the subject would have to move to the specifier position of the IP to receive nominative Case. If another constituent would remain in this position, blocking the movement of the subject to the specifier position of the IP, the subject in the VP-adjoined position would be Caseless and the sentence ruled out by the Case-Filter.

A final remark on Icelandic: in section 2 it has been mentioned that besides yes/no questions there is another type of verb-first structure, viz. narrative inversion. This type of verb-first structure is also found in subordinate clauses. Now we can distinguish these two types of verb-first. In yes/no questions we have the question marker Q in the specifier position of the CP. The finite verb moves to Comp to get this question marker into the scope of [+tense]. To receive nominative Case, the subject has to move to the specifier position of the IP. Narrative inversion-structures, on the other hand, have the finite verb in Infl and the subject in the VP-adjoined position.

For English, as we saw in section 3, no verb movement to Comp takes place in sentences with the subject in first position and in topiccalization constructions. There is, however, a remarkable difference between English and Icelandic. It seems that in English the presence of the subject in the specifier of IP is obligatory. The order "topic-Vf-subject" is not found, neither in main nor in subordinate clauses. In main clauses we find the order "topic-subject-Vf". In subordinate clauses, these constructions are restricted to sentences with the complementizer *that* and matrix verbs that select assertions (see Hooper - Thompson 1973). This suggests that in English the subject has to move to the specifier of IP to receive its Case. The question is: Why? The only possibility would be that Infl assigns nominative Case to the left, not to the right. To get Case the subject can not remain in a VP-adjoined position. A possible explanation for this somewhat strange picture would be an underlying SOV structure for English (see Koster 1988, Hoekstra 1988). Not only V but also Infl governs to the left, which accounts for the obligatory movement of the subject to the specifier of IP.

In this section I have tried to account for the several positions subjects have in the languages we are dealing with. The positions are determined by nominative Case assignment, which by itself is connected to the position of the scope bearing [+tense].

In the last section I will briefly discuss the position of wh-elements and topicalized elements.

5. The position of wh-elements and topics

Given the assumption that the VP-adjoined position is the basic position of the subject, it might appear at first sight that two positions are available for operators and fronted non-operators. Both the specifier position of the IP and the specifier position of the CP are available for fronted elements.

Considering operators, for instance wh-elements, we see that they do not occur in the specifier position of IP but in the specifier position of CP. For the verb-second languages Swedish and Dutch it was argued that the scope bearing [+tense] is situated in Comp, implying that in main clauses Comp is filled by the finite verb and in subordinate clauses by the complementizer. Both in main and in subordinate clauses we find wh-elements to the left of Comp.

In Chomsky (1986) it is argued for that adjunction to arguments is excluded for reasons of theta-marking. The CP as a subordinate clause can function as an argument and thus, adjunction to this position is excluded. The only position available for wh-elements is the specifier position of the CP. We will assume that this holds true for other operators as well. That this is correct is not as clear for English and Icelandic as it is for Swedish and Dutch. For English we argued that the subject has to be in the specifier of IP for reasons of nominative Case. In English direct questions we find the order "wh-aux-subject. So both the auxiliary and the wh-element are to the left of the specifier of IP. As the auxiliary is situated in Comp, we are forced to say that the wh-element is to the left of Comp. Since we also find embedded wh-sentences, it is reasonable to assume that for English like for Swedish wh-elements are in the specifier position of CP.[10]

For Icelandic, too, ons must assume that wh-elements are in the specifier position of CP. This cannot be made visible in main clauses, but in subordinate clauses we find both the subject and the wh-element to the left of the finite verb. Because the finite verb is in Infl in subordinate clauses both the subject and the wh-element are to the left of Infl. This gives us the specifier position of the IP for the subject and the specifier position of the CP for the wh-element.

Thus for operators we get the following structure.

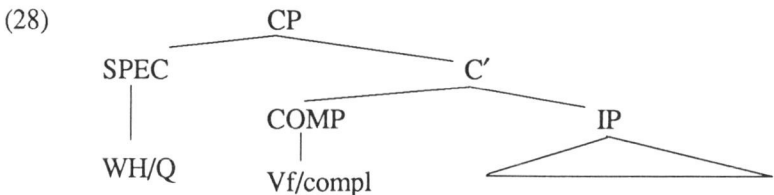

(28)

```
                    CP
        _____/  _____
      SPEC                        C'
        |                _____/  _____
        |              COMP                  IP
        |                |                __/  \__
      WH/Q            Vf/compl          /_____\
```

If the specifier position of CP is reserved for operators, only the specifier of IP would remain as a possible landing site for fronted non-operators. This is exactly what we find in a number of Icelandic sentence types. As we have already oberved there is a similarity in the word order of main and subordinate clauses if we have the subject in first position or if we have another

fronted non-operator in first position. It was already argued that in these
sentence types the finite verb and the scope bearing [+tense] are in Infl.
Because the subject receives its Case in the VP-adjoined position and can
remain there, the specifier of IP is available as a landing site for fronted
non-operators. This can be the object but also the subject itself.

For the Dutch, Swedish and English this picture is too simple. In these
languages not only is the specifier position of CP reserved for other
constituents but the specifier of IP is not available for fronted non-operators
because this position is needed for the subject. Only here can it receive its
Case from the scope bearing [+tense].

I will propose that a fronted non-operator is adjoined to the minimal
domain of the scope bearing [+tense].
In English the minimal domain of the scope bearing [+tense] is the IP. A
fronted object would then be adjoined to the IP, resulting in a structure as
in (29).

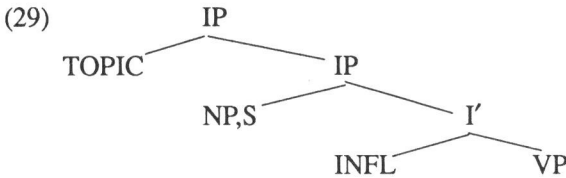

(29)

```
              IP
           ╱      ╲
      TOPIC        IP
               ╱       ╲
            NP,S         I′
                      ╱      ╲
                  INFL        VP
```

The fronted non-operator is still in the scope of the [+tense] in Infl because
the head of a projection has the entire projection in its scope.

In Dutch and Swedish the minimal domain of [+tense] is the CP. Because
the specifier position of CP and the specifier of IP are not available for
fronted non-operators, such an element should be adjoined to the CP, giving
a structure like (30).[11]

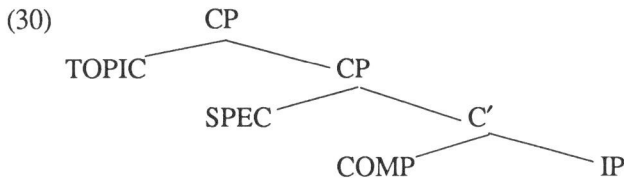

(30)

```
               CP
            ╱      ╲
      TOPIC         CP
                 ╱      ╲
             SPEC        C′
                      ╱      ╲
                  COMP        IP
```

It will now be clear why fronted elements are excluded in subordinate clauses. A subordinate clause has the status of an argument and adjunction is excluded for reasons of theta-marking (see Chomsky (1986).

Summarizing I will claim the following: the specifier position of CP position is the basic operator position and the specifier of IP is the basic position for fronted non-operators. If the specifier of IP is not available for fronted non-operators, these elements are adjoined to the minimal domain of [+tense], i.e. to the IP in English and to the CP in Swedish and Dutch.

That the topic-position has another status in Dutch, Swedish and English than it has in Icelandic can be supported by the following arguments: (i) whereas in Dutch, Swedish and English topics can license parasitic gaps, like operators, in Icelandic only true operators can license a parasitic gap, but topics cannot; (ii) embedded main clauses (i.e. a complementizer followed by a sentential structure with main clause word order) should be permitted without restrictions if they are IPs; this is what one sees in Icelandic. If the construction represents a CP (i.e., a complementizer followed by a CP) restrictions are to be expected. This is what one finds in English where these embedded main clauses are in fact restricted. In Swedish, embedded main clauses are restricted in the same way as they are in English. In Dutch such sentences are even totally excluded. This is in keeping with the way we described the difference between Icelandic and English. In Icelandic we have a bare IP whereas in English we have an adjunction to the IP. (Note, that we do need a further restriction, though, to the effect that adjoined structures are excluded or minimally restricted as embedded main clauses; I will not discuss this here.) For discussion of the restrictions on embedded main clauses in English I refer to Hooper - Thompson (1973) and for embedded main clauses in Swedish to Andersson (1975).

6. Conclusions

In this article I discussed several questions concerning word order in main and subordinate clauses of Dutch, Swedish, English and Icelandic. All these questions were related to the notion verb-second.

The most important issue was the trigger of the movement of the finite verb to Comp in main clauses of verb-second languages and the restrictions on this movement in other languages. The assumption that the element [+tense] must have scope over the entire predication has been shown to account for the movement or absence of movement of finite verbs to Comp. In Swedish and Dutch this scope bearing [+tense] element occurs either on V or on Comp. If [+tense] is generated on the verb, the [+tense] verb cannot stay in the V position, because from its base position it does not have scope over the predication (given the standard definition of c-command). In the Comp position, on the other hand, it does have the predication in its scope. In subordinate clauses where Comp is lexically filled and supports [+tense] nothing has to move. In main clauses (and some other clause types), Comp is not lexically filled. Hence, the finite verb moves to this position. This accounts for the movement of the finite verb in main clauses.

In English the restriction of movement to Comp, namely to auxiliaries, is accounted for in the following way: [+tense] is base generated in Infl. From this position it has scope over the predication as required. Hence, no movement is needed unless the specifier of CP is filled. Wh-elements, the question marker Q and other operator-like elements in the specifier position of CP can only be in the scope of [+tense] if this feature is situated in Comp. Hence in that case [+tense] and the auxiliary supporting it move to Comp. Icelandic is neither a full, nor a non-verb-second language. As in English the [+tense] contained in Infl has scope over the entire predication, provided that the sentence has no operator elements in the specifier position of CP. Therefore, in sentences with the subject or another topicalized element in first position, no movement of V to Comp is required. The difference is that not only auxiliaries, but also main verbs are admissible in Infl position. This accounts for the similarity in word order of these sentence types in main and subordinate clauses. If there is an operator in the specifier position of CP, as in the other languages movement of the finite verb to Comp in main clauses is necessary to get these elements in the scope of [+tense].

Connected to the position of the scope bearing [+tense] is the position of the subject. It has been proposed that the basic position of the subject is a VP-adjoined position, but that for reasons of nominative Case, assigned from the position containing the scope bearing [+tense], the subject has to move to the specifier of IP. Therefore, if the scope bearing [+tense] is in Comp, the subject has to move to that specifier of IP, because it would be Caseless if it remained in the VP-adjoined position, which would rule out the sentence. With respect to [+tense] in Infl, the following picture has been developed. In Icelandic, the VP-adjoined position of the subject receives Case from Infl, which, we take, governs to the right. In this way the specifier of IP is available for topicalization. In yes/no questions and wh-sentences, the subject has to move to the specifier of IP for reasons of Case assignment. In English, we assume, Infl governs only to the left; hence, despite the fact that [+tense] is in Infl, the subject always has to move to the specifier of IP. In the last section we briefly discussed the position of topicalized elements. A few arguments have been given, favoring a topic-position for these elements instead of the specifier position of CP. In this way wh-elements and topicalized elements have different positions.

In this article I could only give a brief sketch of the set of problems. A more extensive discussion of several complications is necessary but is not possible here for reasons of space.

Notes

1. I would like to thank Eric Hoekstra, Helen de Hoop, Jan Koster, Eric Reuland, Christer Platzack, Halldor Sigurðsson and Höskuldur Thráinsson for their useful comments on earlier versions of this paper

2. In Swedish subordinate clauses are found in which the mutual order of sentence adverbials and finite verbs is the same as in main clauses. These sentences, however, are highly restricted and also differ in other respects from real subordinate clauses. In this article I will not take these sentences into account. For a more extensive discussion of these sentence types I refer to Kosmeijer (in prep.).

3. Under certain conditions, a sentence as in (8b) is allowed. I will ignore these sentences, as I did for Swedish.

4. The idea that the feature [+tense] has to be lexically supported can also be found in other analyses of verb-second (see Platzack 1986, Holmberg & Platzack (this volume).

5. In section 5 we will assume that topicalized elements in Dutch are adjoined to the CP, the minimal domain of the scope bearing [+tense]. These adjoined elements are in the scope of [+tense] too.

6. The subject is not given here. To the matter of the position of the subject we will return in the next section.

7. The verbs "have" and "be" are a separate case. On the one hand they can be moved to the sentence initial position in yes/no questions just like auxiliaries and "do". On the other hand we find these verbs together with other auxiliaries. A combination of two real auxiliaries, however, is excluded. This way "have" and "be" function like main verbs. It is often proposed that these two verbs can be moved from the canonical V-position to the INFL-position (see e.g. Akmajan, Steele & Wasow 1979).

8. In this respect my proposal differs from the one given in Holmberg & Platzack (this volume). In their proposal the operator [+F], which is similar to the scope bearing [+tense] in my proposal, is always situated in Comp, whereas in my proposal [+tense] can remain in Infl if it has the entire predication in its scope from there.

9. For arguments favoring the IP-status of Topicalization structures in Icelandic I refer to Kosmeijer (in prep.)

10. Some other problems, however, arise if we assume that in a sentence as in (i) the wh-element is in the specifier position of the CP.

  (i) I knew what he would buy yesterday

In a sentence as in (i) the wh-element is not in the scope of [+tense] in Infl. At this moment I find it hard to account for this fact.

One way to account for the absence of the movement of the finite verb to Comp in this sentences can be found in the proposal made in Taraldsen (1986). An embedded clause has a Comp that is nominal in nature because the whole clause is an argument. Movement of a verb to Comp would made CP verbal.

This, however, does not solve our problem of getting the wh-element in the scope of [+tense] in Infl. The only thing I can suggest is that the complementizer in Comp is deleted and that when not visible the wh-element is in the scope of the [+tense] in Comp.

11. In e.g. Koster (1978) an analysis is given in which topicalized elements are situated under an E-node, a sort of extension of the matrix-S. Translated in our terms this gives a structure like in (i).

  (i) [_E_TOPIC [_CP_SPEC [

References

Akmajan, Adrian - Susan Steele - Tom Wasow
  1979   "The category AUX in universal grammar", *Linguistic Inquiry* 10: 1-64

Andersson, Lars Gunnar
  1975   *Form and function of subordinate clauses*, Göteborg Monographs in Linguistics II (Göteborg: University of Göteborg).

Chomsky, Noam
  1981   *Lectures on government and binding* (Dordrecht: Foris).
  1986   *Barriers* (Cambridge, Mass.: MIT Press).

Den Besten, Hans
  1981   "Government, syntaktische Struktur und Kasus", *Sprache: Formen und Strukturen, Akten des 15. Linguistischen Kolloquiums Münster 1980*, Volume I, Linguistischen Arbeiten 98, edited by Manfred Kohrt - Jürgen Lenerz (Tübingen: Niemeyer).

Evers, Arnold
  1982   "Twee functionele regels voor de regel VERSCHUIF HET WERKWOORD", *GLOT* 5: 11-30

Hoekstra, Eric
  1988   "Binding objects and the structure of the English VP" (Groningen: unpublished manuscript University of Groningen).

Hooper, Joan B. - Sandra A. Thompson
  1973   "On the application of root transformations", *Linquistic Inquiry* 4.4: 465-497

Kosmeijer, Wim
  1987   *Remarks on word order in the Scandinavian languages*, master's thesis (Groningen: University of Groningen).
  in prep. "The categorial status of embedded main clauses"

Koster, Jan
  1975   "Dutch as an SOV language", *Linguistic Analysis* 1: 111-136
  1978   *Locality principles in syntax* (Dordrecht: Foris).
  1986   "The relation between pro-drop, scrambling and verb movement", *Groningen Papers in Theoretical and Applied Linguistics (TTT)* 1
  1988   "The residual SOV-structure of English", *Groningen Papers in Theoretical and Applied Linguistics (TENK)* 5

Manzini, Rita
  1989   "Constituent structure and locality", *Constituent structure*, edited by Anna Cardinaletti - Guglielmo Cinque - Giuliana Giusti (Dordrecht: Foris).

Platzack, Christer
1986   "COMP, INFL and Germanic word order", *Topics in Scandinavian syntax*, edited by Lars Hellan - Kirsti Koch Christensen (Dordrecht: Reidel).

Reuland, Eric J. - Wim Kosmeijer
1988   "Projecting inflected verbs", *Groninger Arbeiten zur germanistischen Linguistik 29*

Sportiche, Dominique
1988   (Los Angeles, unpublished manuscript University of Southern California).

Taraldsen, Tarald
1986   "On verb second and the functional content of syntactic categories", *Verb second phenomena in Germanic languages*, edited by Hubert Haider - Martin Prinzhorn (Dordrecht: Foris).

Thráinsson, Höskuldur
1986   "V1, V2, V3 in Icelandic", *Verb second phenomena in Germanic languages*, edited by Hubert Haider - Martin Prinzhorn (Dordrecht: Foris).

Functional uncertainty and verb-raising dependencies[1]

Ineke Schuurman

1. Introduction

This paper is about cross-serial dependencies as occurring in the Dutch verb raising construction and the way in which they are handled within the framework of lexical-functional grammar. First of all I will make some remarks on lexical-functional grammar itself.[2] Next, the lexical-functional treatment of Dutch verb raising constructions will be dealt with. As a point of departure I shall take the traditional approach of Bresnan-Kaplan-Peters-Zaenen (1982), this being one of the most well-known lexical-functional approaches. As we will see, the results are satisfactory, in that the different behaviour of verb raising constructions and extraposition constructions can be accounted for. However, some objections are to be raised against this proposal, for example with respect to the lack of descriptive adequacy. Therefore, another approach is formulated, in which recent lexical-functional principles regarding long-distance phenomena are transferred to the short-distance constructions we are interested in, leading up to a new analysis of verb raising constructions. The approach suggested has several substantial consequences, if the line of reasoning is followed to its logical conclusion. These consequences, however, can only be briefly touched on, as they lay outside the scope of the present paper.

2. Some remarks on lexical-functional grammar

Lexical-functional grammar is a kind of extended unification-based grammar and as such it makes extensive use of features. In lexical-functional grammar these features, together with their values, are represented in matrices: the functional structures. An essential characteristic of unification grammar is that these feature-value pairs are not necessarily simplex (the value of a feature may be complex) and that reentrance is allowed (more features may have the same value; for example in *Marie has fallen* the subject of both *has* and *fallen* is *Marie*).

The syntactic rules, in lexical-functional grammar called constituent structure rules, are context-free and annotated with equations, as in (1).[3]

(1)   S   →   NP   VP
              (↑SUBJ)=↓   ↑=↓

Unlike many other unification grammars, the constituent structure rules are subject to well-formedness conditions. First, the restrictions formulated in Kaplan - Bresnan (1982) should be mentioned. These are meant to ensure the decidability of lexical-functional grammar by reducing its computational complexity: only a finite number of constituent structures can be assigned to a particular string of elements. To attain this goal, vacuous derivations are excluded in a valid constituent structure. Thus an upper bound is set on the generative capacity of lexical-functional grammar.[4] Other well-formedness conditions on constituent structure rules are given in Bresnan (1982). These refer to both categories and grammatical functions. With respect to the categories, the constituent structure rules are of the familiar X'-type (configurational encoding):

(2) $X^{n+1} \rightarrow$ $C_1...X^n..C_m$ $(n \geq 0 ;$ C   either minor category or maximal projection)

With respect to the grammatical functions, in the constituent structure rules a function-assigning equation (↑G)=↓ is associated with each C_i if and only if C_i is a maximal projection, and an equation ↑=↓ elsewhere. Furthermore it is stated that each phrase should have a (unique) head, a major category bearing an equation ↑=↓.

The functional equations specify the relations that must hold between nodes by means of the features they contain. In lexical-functional grammar functional features involving grammatical functions like subject and object are very important. By means of functional equations a complex feature structure for a sentence can be built up, the functional structure. The functional description, a tree structure in which the metavariables ($\uparrow$ and $\downarrow$) of the constituent structure rules are replaced by actual variables,[5] functions as an intermediary between the constituent structure and the functional structure.

The functional structure is the heart of lexical-functional grammar. On this structure all the necessary conditions are formulated (cf. note 18). And because there is no isomorphism between the constituent structure on the one hand and the functional structure on the other hand,[6] these conditions are not trivially exchangeable for conditions on constituent structures.

3. The traditional approach

In Bresnan-Kaplan-Peters-Zaenen (1982) the following constituent structure (4), functional description (5) and functional structure (6) are proposed for sentence (3) (cf. their sentence [26] and structures [37] and [38]).

(3)   ..., dat Jan_i $Piet_j$ $Marie_k$ zag_i $helpen_j$ $zwemmen_k$
         'that Jan saw Piet help Marie to swim'

(4)

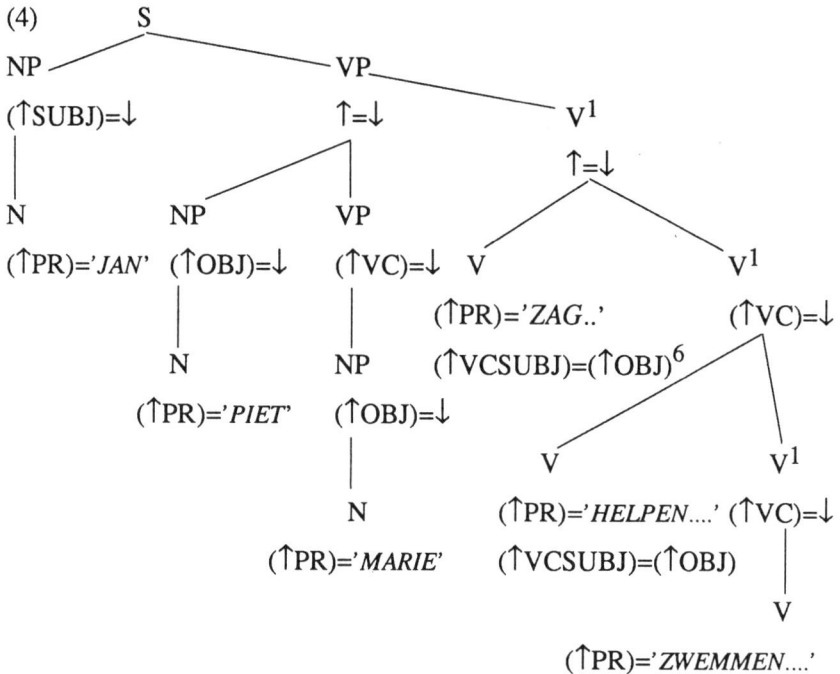

Accepting the tree-structure (4) for the time being, this analysis turns out to be an adequate one - that is, it accounts for the particular properties of verb raising constructions as opposed to extraposition constructions. This can be illustrated with the help of the pair of sentences in (7), containing a pure verb raising construction and a pure extraposition construction, respectively.[8] The corresponding functional descriptions and functional structures are given in (8) and (9).

(5)

```
                S
         ___/ 1 _____
       NP                        VP_____
     (1SUBJ)=2                    1=3          \
                                               V¹
                                               3=7
       N         NP         VP           __/      \__
    (2PR)='JAN'  (3OBJ)=4  (3VC)=5      V             V¹
                                     (7PR)='ZAG...'  (7VC)=8
                                     (7VCSUBJ)=(7OBJ)
                   N          NP                 __/    \
                (4PR)='PIET'  (5OBJ)=6          V        V¹
                                             (8PR)='HELPEN.' (8VC)=9
                              N              (8VCSUBJ)=(8OBJ)  |
                           (6PR)='MARIE'                       V
                                                         (9PR)='ZWEMMEN..'
```

(6)

$$
\begin{bmatrix}
\text{SUBJ} & 2 & [\text{PR 'JAN'}] \\
\text{PR} & & \text{'ZAG} <(\uparrow\text{SUBJ})(\uparrow\text{OBJ})(\uparrow\text{VC})>\text{'} \\
\text{OBJ} & 4 & [\text{PR 'PIET'}] \\
\text{VC} & & \begin{bmatrix}
\text{SUBJ} & \\
\text{PR} & \text{'HELPEN} <(\uparrow\text{SUBJ})(\uparrow\text{OBJ})(\uparrow\text{VC})>\text{'} \\
\text{OBJ} & 6 & [\text{PR 'MARIE'}] \\
\text{VC} & \text{SUBJ} \\
& 9 & \text{PR 'ZWEMMEN} <(\uparrow\text{SUBJ})>\text{'}
\end{bmatrix}
\end{bmatrix}
$$

1 3 7   5 8

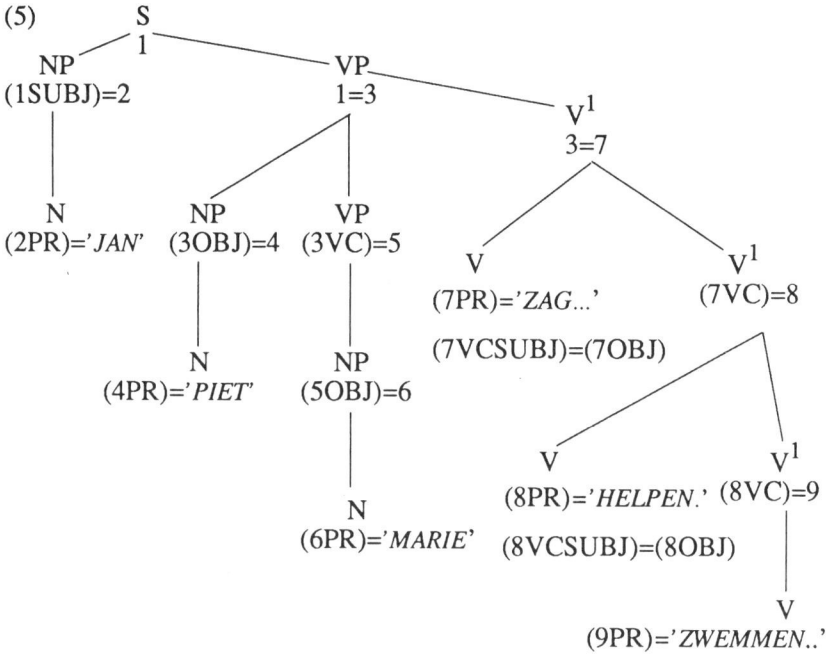

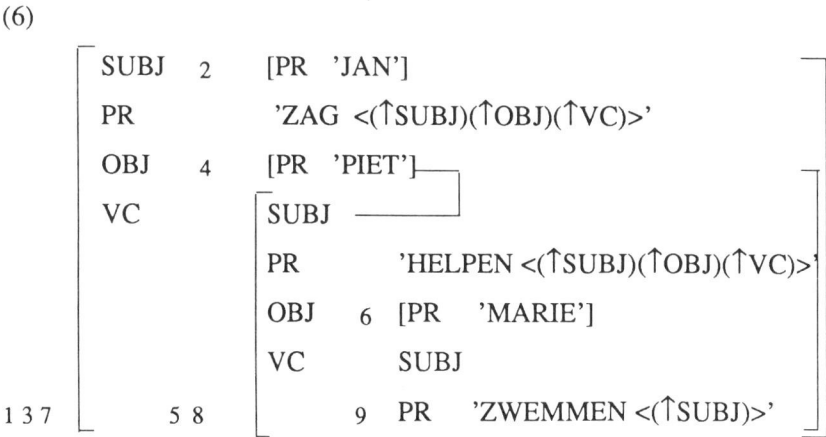

(7) a. ..., dat Jan Marie placht te plagen
         'that Jan was in the habit of teasing Marie'

     b. ..., dat Jan ophield Marie te plagen
         'that Jan stopped teasing Marie'

(8)   a.

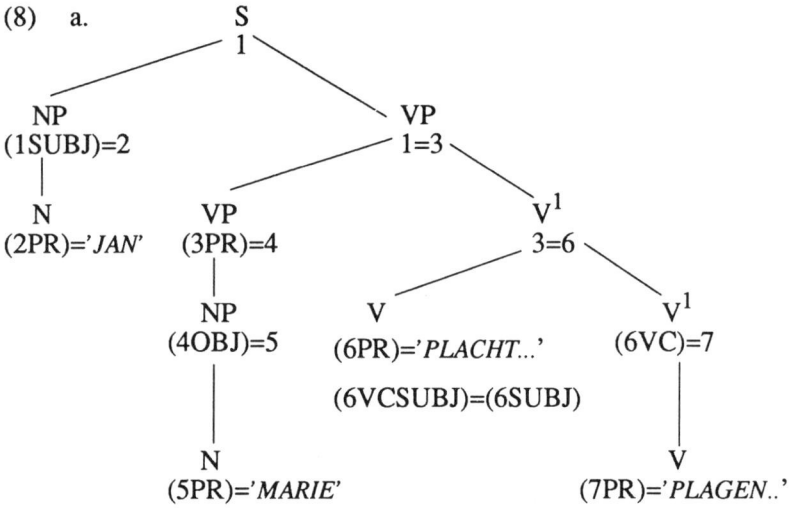

(9)   a.

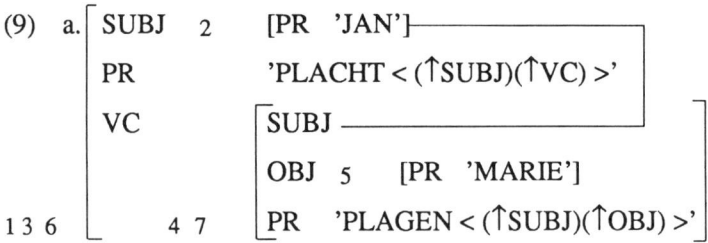

(8)   b.

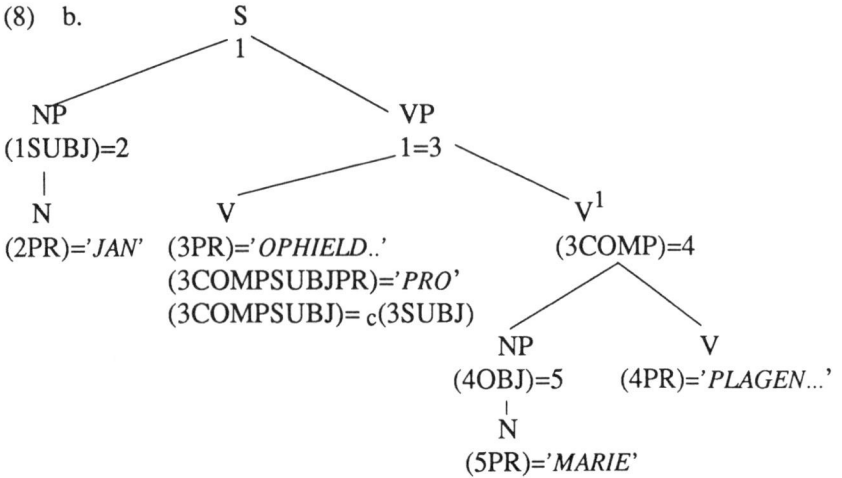

(9) b.
$$
\begin{bmatrix}
\text{SUBJ} & 2 & [\text{PR} \quad \text{'JAN'}] \\
\text{PR} & & \text{'OPHIELD} < (\uparrow\text{SUBJ})(\uparrow\text{COMP}) >' \\
\text{COMP} & & \begin{bmatrix} \text{SUBJ}_2 & [\text{PR} \quad \text{'PRO}_{+u}\text{'}] \\ \text{OBJ}_5 & [\text{PR} \quad \text{'MARIE'}] \\ \text{PR} & \text{'PLAGEN} < (\uparrow\text{SUBJ})(\uparrow\text{OBJ}) >' \end{bmatrix}_4
\end{bmatrix}_{13}
$$

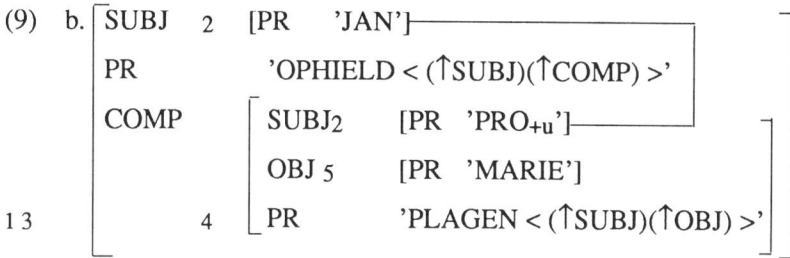

The analysis of the verb raising construction (7a) is in the spirit of Bresnan-Kaplan-Peters-Zaenen (1982); the analysis of the extraposition construction (7b) is inspired by Netter (1988). It should be noticed that Netter, primarily interested in functional uncertainty, regards both a verb raising complement and an extraposition complement as V^1s with the function VCOMP[9] assigned to them. To the contrary, I do prefer to regard an extraposition complement as associated with the function COMP.[10] Such a function COMP is mostly attached to a full sentence (S or S^1), not to an infinitival complement (VP or V^1). Some syntactic arguments for the combination V^1 - COMP in case of extraposition constructions are to be found in the possible occurrence of a complementizer (10a), of two negations (11a), and of two time adverbs (12a). These are no possibilities with respect to the verb raising constructions (the b sentences). This shows that an extraposition complement functions as if it were a full sentence, contrary to a verb raising complement.

(10) a.   ..., dat Jan ophield (om) Marie te plagen
         'that Jan stopped teasing Marie'
      b. *..., dat Jan placht om Marie te plagen
         'that Jan was in the habit of teasing Marie'

(11) a.   ..., dat Marie niet rondbazuint Jan niet te mogen
         'that Marie does not proclaim to dislike Jan'
      b. *..., dat Marie Jan niet niet leert schaken[11]
         'that Marie does not not teach Jan to play chess'

(12) a.   ..., dat Marie ons vandaag meedeelde morgen het geld over
         te maken
         'that Marie let us know today to transfer the money tomorrow'

 b. *..., dat Marie Jan vandaag morgen durft bellen
   'that Marie dared Jan today to call tomorrow'

The difference between VCOMP and COMP is vast. A VCOMP is an open grammatical function, a COMP a closed one. An open grammatical function goes with functional control, expressed by equations as $(\uparrow VCSUBJ)=(\downarrow G)$, where G = OBJ2 (indirect object), otherwise OBJ, otherwise SUBJ (in that order; so if there is an OBJ2, G = OBJ2). Functional control means that the referential dependency between the subject of the VCOMP and G is such that they are identical, or rather their functional structures are. Note that functional control is a form of obligatory, unique control - that is, there always is an, in fact structurally fixed, controller. VCOMP is a grammatical function going with a property; at functional structure level it is transparant.

In (9a), the functional structure belonging to (7a), the subject in the functional structure indexed {4,7} is not directly associated with a predicate. But, functional control (by means of the equation (6VCSUBJ)=(6SUBJ)) makes this subject identical with the subject of {1,3,6}, reflected by the continuous line between both subjects, and thus the first subject gets its predicate.

On the other hand, a COMP is a closed grammatical function and therefore functional control is excluded. The control relations in COMP are anaphoric. This implies no complete identity of the relevant functional structures (as with functional control), but only "identity of reference". Anaphoric control depends on the presence of a PRO at the level of functional structure, which is [+unexpressed] at the level of constituent structure, a PRO_{+u}. Therefore, such a PRO must be inserted from the lexicon. This PRO_{+u} has to be bound within a certain domain. Within this domain, for example the functional structure which contains the functional structure of which PRO is the subject, there may be more than one category available for controllership ; for the only other restriction is that the controller has to f-command[12] its controllee. So in principle there is no unique control associated with anaphoric control, in contrast with functional control. Nevertheless, sometimes further restrictions are to be formulated. This is, for example, the case with the so called obviative clauses in which certain control relations would lead to ungrammaticality. The restrictions are to be formulated in the lexicon and there are several ways of doing this (cf.

Simpson - Bresnan 1983; Zec 1987). In this paper I will make use of constraining equations attached to the extraposition trigger. Such an equation (of the form $(\uparrow VCSUBJ)=_c (\downarrow G)$[13] is distinct from other equations. It is not used to build up a functional structure, but it expresses a condition that must be satisfied by the functional structure. It plays its role when the functional structure is completed: a functional structure is yet declared deviant if it does not go with the constraint formulated by the equation. So functional control is not involved. COMP is a grammatical function going with a proposition; at the level of functional structure it is not transparant.

In (9b), the functional structure belonging to (7b), the subject of the functional structure {4} has a predicate of its own (the functional structure {5}), containing an unexpressed pronoun PRO_{+u}. It is introduced by the defining equation $(3COMPSUBJPR)='PRO'$. This PRO is a semantic form lacking real content. Therefore it is to be bound. Functional control is excluded, for otherwise the subject would receive two different values (PRO and something else), so a weaker form of control is needed: anaphoric control. Anaphoric control allows for identity of reference of PRO with the subject of {1,3} and the object of {4}. Suppose that, as in (9b), referential identity of the subject of {4} and that of {1,3} exists, reflected by a broken line. Evaluating the functional structure, it will be considered well-formed, for the constraint as formulated in the constraining equation $(3COMPSUBJ)=_c(3SUBJ)$ is satisfied. On the contrary, the functional structure would have been considered ill-formed if there had been referential identity with the object of {4}.

That "accusative plus infinitive" and "subject raising" verbs demand functional control, whereas verbs permitting so called "split antecedents" require anaphoric control, is to be traced back to the kind of identity relation between controller and controllee. As stated before, with functional control, controller and controllee are completely identical, as opposed to the weaker form, identity of reference, occurring with anaphoric control. The lexical entries of accusative plus infinitive and subject raising verbs differ from those of most other verbs in that not all their arguments have "semantic status". In lexical entries the latter occur outside the brackets. Some examples are given below, (13d) and (13e) being the lexical entries of an accusative plus infinitive and a subject raising verb, respectively.

(13) a. main verb
   zingen (to sing)   '< (SUBJ) (OBJ) >'
   geven (to give)   '< (SUBJ) (OBJ) (OBJ2) >'
  b. verb raising verb
   plegen (to tend)   '< (SUBJ) (VCOMP) >'
  c. extraposition verb
   ophouden (to stop)   '< (SUBJ) (COMP) >'
   dwingen (to force)   '< (SUBJ) (OBJ) (COMP) >'
  d. accusative plus infinitive verb
   horen (to hear)   '< (SUBJ) (VCOMP) > (OBJ)'
  e. subject raising verb
   blijken (to seem)   '< (VCOMP) > (SUBJ)'

In (13d) and (13e) an object and a subject, respectively, are stated to fulfil no semantic roles with respect to their matrix verbs. They represent the very functions one intuitively regards as the controllers in sentences like (14a) and (14b).

(14) a. ..., dat Jan Marie$_1$ een liedje hoort zingen$_1$
      'that Jan hears Marie sing a song'
  b. ..., dat Jan$_1$ Marie blijkt te kennen$_1$
      'that Jan appears to know Marie'

If there were only "identity of reference" with the controllees, the controllers would not be bound to a (semantic) argument position and therefore the constructions would have to be declared ill-formed. So, "complete identity" is needed and therefore functional control has to occur.

The phenomenon of "split antecedents" as it may occur in (15) requires an explanation the other way round. For "complete identity" between controllers and controllees in these cases would result in two or more distinct values of the controllee, and thus the functional structure is to be declared deviant.

(15) ..., dat Jan$_1$ Marie$_2$ overreedt naar Amsterdam te gaan$_{1,2}$
      'that Jan persuades Marie to go to Amsterdam'

Differences between a verb raising construction and an extraposition construction are to be traced back to differences between VCOMP and

COMP, as is shown below by means of *transparancy* (16), *adverbial scope* (17), and *passive* (18).

(16) a. ..., dat Jan$_i$ Marie naast zich$_i$ zag lopen
   'that Jan saw Marie walking next to himself'
   b. *..., dat Jan$_i$ Marie dwong (om) naast zich$_i$ te lopen
   'That Jan forced Marie to walk next to himself'

(17) a. ..., dat de directeur hem waarschijnlijk dient te ontslaan
   'that the manager probably ought to fire him'
   b. ..., dat de directeur zegt hem waarschijnlijk te ontslaan
   'that the manager says to fire him probably'

(18) a. *..., dat Marie werd geweten te vinden$_1$ door Jan$_1$
   'that Marie was managed to be found by Jan'
   b. *..., dat Marie een liedje werd zingen gehoord door Jan
   'that Marie was heard singing a song by Jan'
   c. *..., dat Marie werd gebleken te kennen door Jan
   'that Marie was seemed to be known by Jan'
   d. ..., dat Marie door Jan werd gedwongen een nieuwe jas te kopen
   'that Marie was forced by Jan to buy a new coat'

The difference between infinitival complements being COMP or V-COMP accounts for the different possibilities regarding reference of *zich*. *Zich* has to be bound by the first f-commanding[14] subject. In the case of an extraposition construction, as in (16b), this is the only possible binding relation, for COMP is a closed function. Whenever this relation is out of the question, for example for semantic reasons, the construction is ruled out. On the other hand, in a verb raising construction, as in (16a), there may be an alternative possibility to bind *zich*, since VCOMP is an open function. So, another f-commanding subject in another functional structure may bind *zich*.

An adverbial like *waarschijnlijk* selects for a function representing a proposition, for example COMP (but not VCOMP!). In (17a), a verb raising construction, the minimal proposition is in fact the whole sentence, so *waarschijnlijk* has to take matrix scope. On the other hand, in (17b), an extraposition construction, the infinitival complement is the minimal proposition. Therefore *waarschijnlijk* takes complement scope in such cases (cf. Cremers 1983).

In the verb raising constructions (18a), (18b) and (18c) passivization gives bad results, but not in (18d), an extraposition construction. The a-sentence is bad because *weten* triggers functional control by the subject. When passivization of this lexical entry applies, the new controller would be the "by-phrase", an oblique function (as indicated in [18a]). But this is not a possible functional controller (only OBJ2, OBJ, and SUBJ are) and therefore the sentence is deviant. It appears that only object control verbs are to be passivized. Therefore, (18c) is ruled out for the same reason as (18a). One would expect that constructions with passivized accusative plus infinitive verbs (which go with object control) are correct. They are not, as is to be seen in (18b). The reason is that in this case the object is not a semantic argument with respect to the accusative plus infinitive verb, only semantic arguments being affected by passivization. (So this restriction too would prevent a subject raising verb from being passivized.)

In (18d) nothing prevents passivization, anaphoric control being the relevant control relation. F-command constitutes the principal restriction on control relations in such constructions. In (18d) it prevents *door Jan*, not *Marie,* from being a possible controller.

Thus far, the results of the traditional approach are satisfactory. At the level of functional structure the relations between the verbs and their arguments (the predicate-argument relations) are shown in a perspicuous way. The differences between verb raising and extraposition constructions can also be accounted for at this level.

A close look at the level of constituent structure, the shape of which we neglected thus far, makes clear that there are important failures. These are of both theory-independent and theory-dependent nature and one cannot always escape the impression that the wish has been the father to the thought: the functional structure has to be sound.

4. Some problems

Theory-independently the weak point of the argument is that the object-spine has such a rich structure (cf. [4]). Bresnan-Kaplan-Peters-Zaenen (1982) claim that their structure is supported by the constituency of the relevant object-VPs. Their line of argumentation is, however, not convincing, being based on a difference in acceptability between (19) and (20). In constructions with cross-serial dependencies only the last NP may form a constituent with the PP. So in (19) *een pop* may form a constituent together with *aan Henk*; the same holds for *een treintje* and *aan Piet*. The new constituents may be conjoined, as indicated below, resulting in a correct sentence (according to the authors). On the other hand, in (20) *de meisjes* does not form a constituent together with *een treintje aan Piet*, neither does *de jongens* with *een pop aan Henk*, and therefore (20) should be bad.

(19) ...dat Jan de kinderen *een treintje aan Piet en een pop aan Henk* zag geven voor Marie
 '...that Jan saw the children give a toy train to Piet and a doll to Henk for Marie'

(20) ??...dat Jan *de meisjes een treintje aan Piet* en *de jongens een pop aan Henk* zag geven voor Marie
 '...that Jan saw the girls give a toy train to Piet and the boys give a doll to Henk for Marie'

Most of my informants think (19) and (20) to be unacceptable because of the PP *voor Marie* and, what is of more importance, do not find them to differ substantially with respect to grammaticality without this PP.[15] The authors on the other hand do claim that (19) is better than (20) and therefore that *een treintje aan Piet* is a constituent (a VP), contrary to *de meisjes een treintje aan Piet*. Their position is untenable. The same holds for their argumentation with respect to the positions in which a PP may occur, for they compare apples with oranges, in this case a locative modifier and a prepositional indirect object. My informants state that for the position of both a locative modifier and a prepositional indirect object it is not important whether this construction is simplex or complex, contrary to the claim in

Bresnan-Kaplan-Peters-Zaenen (1982). However, a difference exists with respect to their respective freedom of ordering but this is not relevant to the question whether or not the object spine has to have a rich structure.

As far as I can see, the authors were forced to assume such a rich structure, for otherwise the correct verb-argument dependencies could not be expressed.

(21)   dat Jan dat boek zou kunnen beginnen te lezen
         'that Jan could start reading that book'

(22)

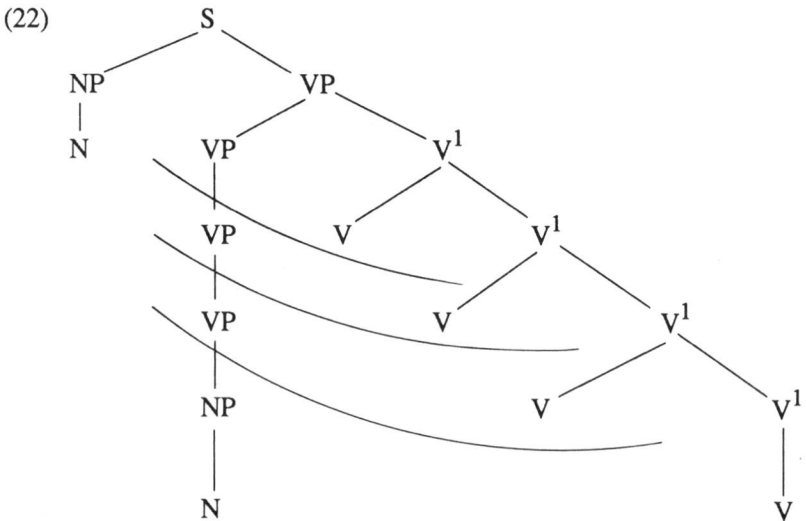

In (22) the different functional levels are indicated by drawn lines. So it can be demonstrated that less nodes in the object spine would have ended in an ill-formed result.[16]

No real justification being found pro a rich structure, such a structure has to be rejected because we are always looking for the most simple and elegant analysis.

Theory-dependently, there are several problems with structures like (4): in Bresnan-Kaplan-Peters-Zaenen (1982), a version of lexical-functional grammar is made use of which is in several respects in conflict with the basic assumptions of this theory. Therefore, their constituent structures have several suspicious properties. One of these concerns the kind of equation associated with non-maximal projections. As mentioned above, function-assigning equations are to be associated only with maximal projections, never with heads; moreover, every phrase has to have a unique head.

These principles have several consequences. Firstly, the association in (4) of a function VCOMP[17] with a V^1 should be avoided, since V^1 cannot be regarded as a maximal projection. This problem could be solved by replacing the V^1 by VP, which would be justified by the fact that the format of the (endocentric) constituent structure rules is such that the non-head is either a maximal projection or a minor category. V^1 does not meet this restriction, VP does. Secondly, note that the traditional structure makes crucial use of two spines, an object spine and a verb spine. Both spines produce "partial" functional structures that are unified at the level of the VP dominating both spines by means of its equation $\uparrow=\downarrow$, connecting the arguments to the appropriate verbs. Note that both spines contain potentially infinite functional structures (Johnson 1986). Not counting the arguments mentioned before, in fact the proposed layered structure runs into problems when the sentences (and consequently the spines) are more complex, as in (23) and (24). For one of the constituent structure rules that one will need in order to derive (26), a constituent structure like it is to be found in Bresnan-Kaplan-Peters-Zaenen (1982), will be (25), which has no head and therefore is to be rejected (Unique Head Constraint).

(23) ..., dat Jan$_i$ Piet$_j$ Marie$_k$ een tas zag$_i$ helpen$_j$ kopen$_k$
'that Jan saw Piet help Marie to buy a bag'

(24) ..., dat Jan$_i$ Piet$_j$ Marie$_k$ de kinderen$_l$ zag$_i$ helpen$_j$ leren$_k$ zwemmen$_l$
'that Jan saw Piet help Marie teach the children to swim'

(25) VP $\rightarrow$ NP   VP
           ($\uparrow$OBJ)   ($\uparrow$VC)=$\downarrow$

(26)

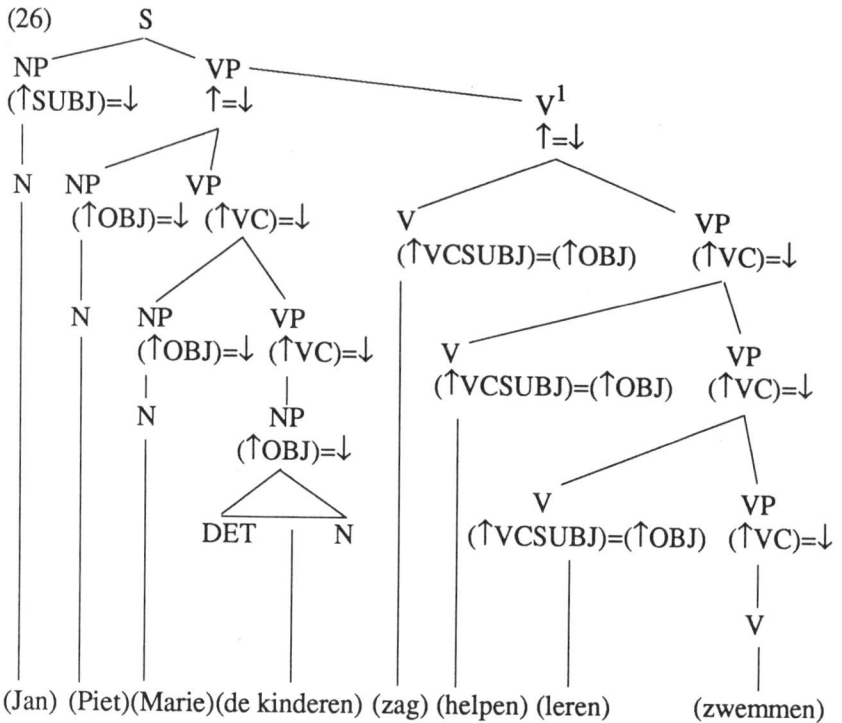

So far, one can but conclude that at the level of constituent structure lexical-functional grammar meets serious problems in treating the Dutch verb raising construction correctly. Recall that at the level of functional structure the results were quite satisfying. Thus a new proposal has to be formulated in which the constituent structure has to meet the theory-internal and external requirements, nevertheless being strongly functional equivalent with the traditional analysis.

5. Another proposal

Functional uncertainty, originally meant to treat long-distance dependencies properly[18], may also apply to phenomena that are traditionally not thought of as falling into the same class as long-distance dependencies but nevertheless seem to involve some degree of uncertainty. Netter (1986), for example, uses functional uncertainty to cover the extraposition-construction in German, claiming that German word order yields a large number of phenomena that may be classified as "unbounded" or "long-distance" dependencies without necessarily involving wh-constituents or "movement" across sentence boundaries. In my opinion,[19] functional uncertainty could also be very useful with regard to the treatment of the cross-serial dependencies in Dutch verb raising constructions, functions with an uncertain number of embeddings being essential in these cases. Recent research by Kaplan and Zaenen seems to confirm this view (cf. Cooper 1988).

Note that the problems mentioned in section 3 can all be traced back to the level of embedding in the constituent structure[20] and also that functional uncertainty in effect allows elements to be deeper embedded on functional structure than on constituent structure.

In our cases the Kleene star operator * (the use of which *in equations* indicates functional uncertainty) occurs as in (27). The concrete rules needed to derive a constituent structure (29) for (3) are those in (28):

(27) $(\uparrow XC*Y)=\downarrow$ (where Y is any subcategorizable category).

(28) constituent structure rules

S	→	NP	VP	
		$(\uparrow SUBJ)=\downarrow$	$\uparrow=\downarrow$	
VP →		(NP)	(NP)	V^1
		$(\uparrow OBJ)=\downarrow$	$(\uparrow XC*OBJ)=\downarrow$	$\uparrow=\downarrow$
NP→		N		

(29)

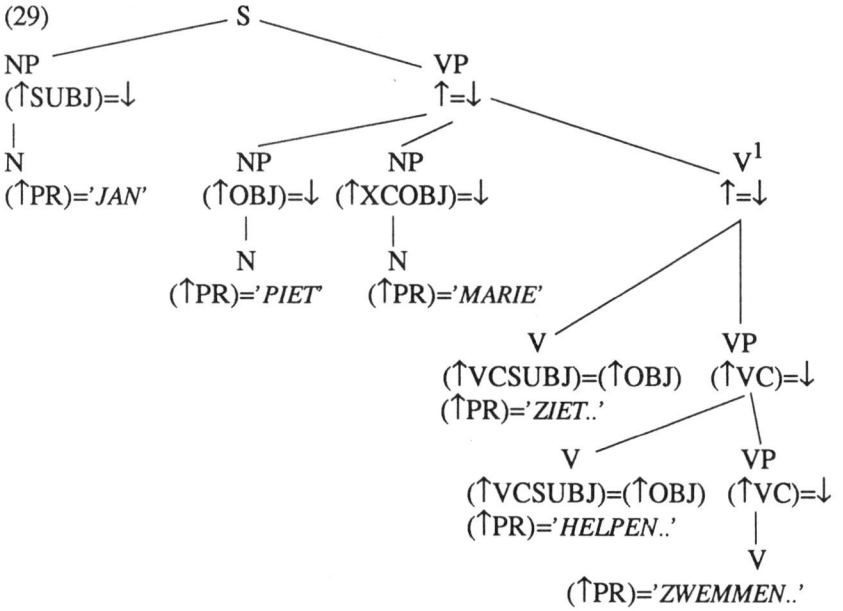

(30)

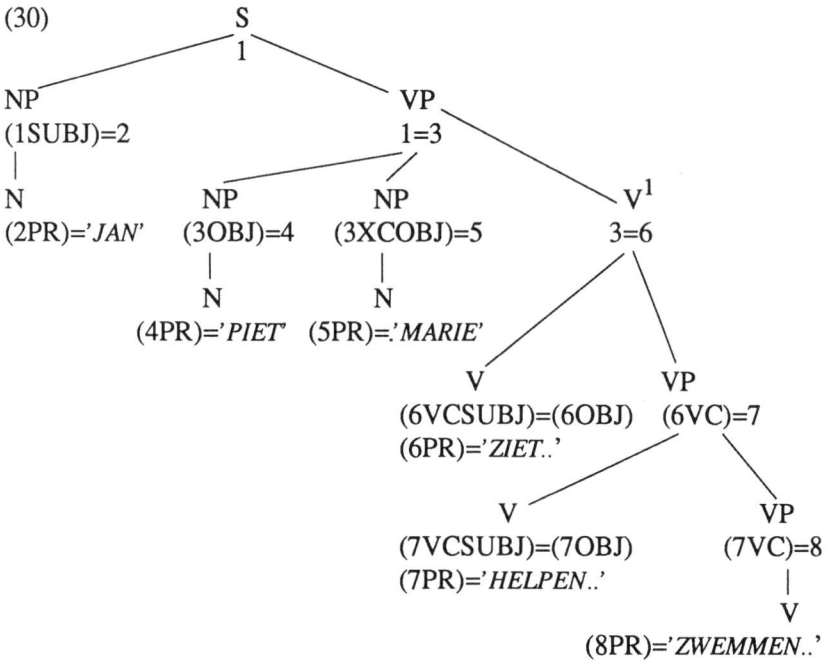

(31)

$$
\begin{bmatrix}
\text{SUBJ} & 2 & [\text{PR} \quad \text{'JAN'}] \\[4pt]
\text{PR} & & \text{'ZAG} < (\uparrow\text{SUBJ})(\uparrow\text{OBJ})(\uparrow\text{VC}) > \text{'} \\[4pt]
\text{OBJ} & 4 & [\text{PR} \quad \text{'PIET'}] \\[4pt]
\text{VC} & & \begin{bmatrix}
\text{SUBJ} \\
\text{PR} \quad \text{'HELPEN'} < (\uparrow\text{SUBJ})(\uparrow\text{OBJ})(\uparrow\text{VC}) > \text{'} \\
\text{OBJ} \; 5 \quad [\text{PR} \quad \text{'MARIE'}] \\
\text{VC} \quad \begin{bmatrix} \text{SUBJ} \\ \text{PR 'ZWEMMEN} < (\uparrow\text{SUBJ}) > \text{'} \end{bmatrix}
\end{bmatrix}
\end{bmatrix}
$$

1 3 6   7   8

It can easily be seen that (4) and (29) are strongly functional equivalent. A comparison of (6) and (31) shows that these are the same, apart from the numbers identifying the various functional structures. Therefore, it is no bold expectation that under the new analysis a verb raising construction has all the properties it had under the traditional analysis (section 3).

With help of functional uncertainty, a construction such as (24), which was problematic for the traditional analysis, can be treated in a straightforward way. In fact only the VP constituent structure rule has to be adapted with an extra NP category:

(32) VP $\rightarrow$(NP)   (NP)   (NP) V^1

          ($\uparrow$OBJ)=$\downarrow$ ($\uparrow$XC*OBJ)=$\downarrow$ ($\uparrow$XC*OBJ)=$\downarrow$ $\uparrow$=$\downarrow$

(33)

(verbal spine as in (26))

(Jan)   (Piet) (Marie)   (de kinderen)   (zag helpen leren zwemmen)

In (33) there is no more object spine to be found, so the unmotivated larger constituents (cf. [26]), non-branching argument-chains (cf. [22]), and VPs only dominating non-verbal elements (cf. note 15) are abandoned. The constituent structure of the non-verbal part of a verb raising construction resembles that of a simple sentence. A nice result, for in several respects a verb raising construction behaves like a simple sentence (cf. section 3).[21]

In fact the same functional equation is attached to all the NPs in the constituent structure rule for VP used in (32): the Kleene star may have any value, including zero. Therefore, a more elegant formulation of this rule is given below, resulting in exactly the same constituent structure. It is important that both Kleene stars (the one attached to the category-label and the one in the equation) in principle have independent values:

$$(34)\ VP \rightarrow \quad NP^* \qquad\qquad V^1$$
$$(\uparrow XC^*OBJ){=}{\downarrow} \qquad \uparrow{=}{\downarrow}$$

There are good reasons for stating that in the verb string, too, the principle of functional uncertainty applies, for example in languages in which the order of the verbs is not strictly left to right or vice versa. The verb raising construction in the Groningen dialect gives us a clear example of such a situation.

In this dialect, functional uncertainty, and therefore functional equations with Kleene stars seems to be necessary in those cases where a "*te+inf*" is involved. In constructions of this kind all verbs are positioned to the left of the finite verb, except the *te+inf* verb (and the verbs selected by this *te+inf*). Consequently, this verbal chain is essentially discontinuous, although the whole chain is still a verbal cluster (cf. Schuurman - Wierenga 1987; Schuurman 1988, 1989).[22]

(35) ..., dat e$_1$ meester$_2$ zien kinder$_3$ perbaaiern$_2$ loaten$_{11}$ wol$_1$ te leren$_{22}$
zwemmen$_3$ [23]

'that he wanted to make the teacher try to teach his children to swim'

When the partial chain "te leren zwemmen" is treated without the new mechanism, and yet is to meet the principle that every phrase has a head without a functional equation (see above), there is no way to avoid wrong derivations: in (36) the spines dominated by the boxed VP and its sister VP are both said to have the same functional structure (compare their functional equations), resulting in a situation in which a PRED has two values, for example *loaten* en *te leren*. Such a structure violates the uniqueness condition and has to be declared deviant.

It would be ad hoc to replace (through a constituent structure rule) the boxed functional equation directly by a more complex one (6XCXCXC)=9, an instantiation of $(\uparrow XCXCXC)=\downarrow$, since the use of functional uncertainty is more generalizing; see (37).

(36) Partial functional description (without functional uncertainty)

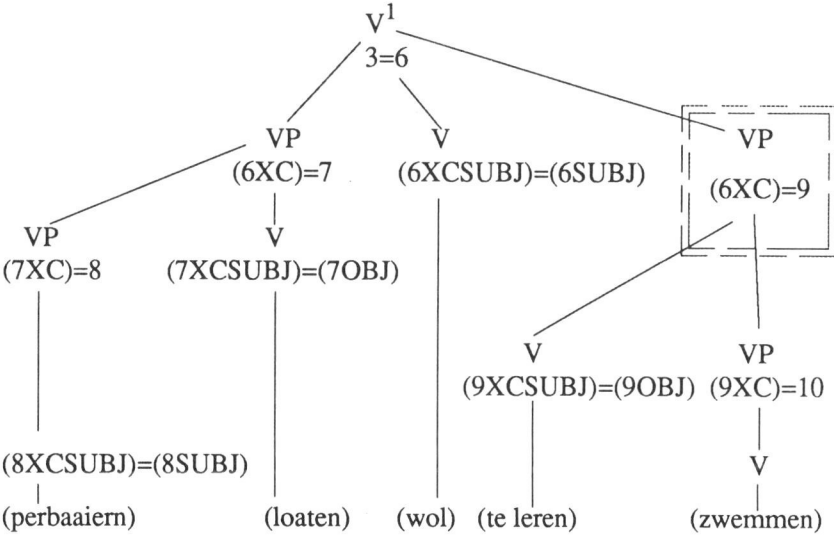

(37) Partial constituent structure (with functional uncertainty)

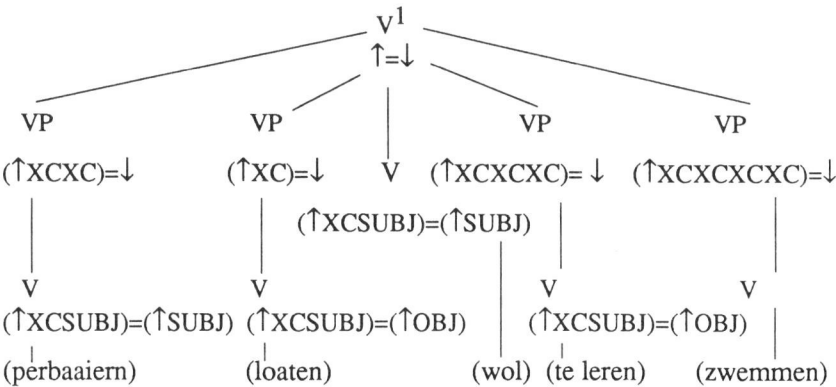

Of course the use of a functional equation $(\uparrow XC^*XC)=\downarrow$ only in the *"te+inf"* - category would have been sufficient to derive a sound functional structure; however, uniformity is to be preferred. Another point is that in (37) there are no spines, whereas in the alternative there would have been two, one [-te] and one [+te]. A structure with all VPs as sisters of each other, as in (37), is given preference if there is no independent motivation favouring a more layered structure. On the contrary, the resemblance between a cluster of verbs and a separable particle verb (for instance with respect to verb-second) is such that a structure is desirable in which the only difference in level is the one between the tensed part and the rest. Consequently, a structure as in (37) is to be preferred also in languages in which the verbal chain is not discontinuous.[24]

6. Conclusion

Extensive use of the Kleene star operator gives rise to constituent structure rules as in (38).

$$(38) \quad VP \rightarrow \quad NP^* \qquad\qquad V^1$$
$$\qquad\qquad\qquad (\uparrow XC^*OBJ)=\downarrow \qquad \uparrow=\downarrow$$
$$\qquad V^1 \rightarrow \quad VP^* \qquad\qquad V \qquad\qquad VP^*$$
$$\qquad\qquad\qquad (\uparrow XC^*XC)=\downarrow \qquad \uparrow=\downarrow \qquad (\uparrow XC^*XC)=\downarrow$$

Note that as a consequence these constituent structure rules permit much more ordering than the original constituent structure rules; for each Kleene star may have any value, including zero. Therefore some restrictions have to be formulated.

Kleene stars attached to category-labels refer to the number of elements dominated by the mother-node, whereas the Kleene stars in the equations refer to relations between the daughter-nodes. So first of all it seems to be useful to distinguish in (38) two kinds of constituent structure rules; immediate dominance rules and linear precedence rules. Doing such, the use of functional uncertainty in verb raising constructions means that the format of the constituent structure rules has to be changed.[25]

Of course, the eventual consequences of their new format in other parts of the grammar have to be carefully investigated. There is some hope, however, for in some recent versions of generalized phrase structure grammar (GPSG) such a splitting up has proved to be very useful in order to treat languages with different degrees of word order freedom.

Notes

1	I would like to thank Gosse Bouma, Theo Janssen, Eric Reuland, Ron van Zonneveld, and Frans Zwarts for helpful discussions after the presentation of my paper at the workshop and comments on earlier versions of this paper.
2.	For a more detailed introduction, see for example Wescoat - Zaenen (1985).
3.	The mother ($\uparrow$) and ego ($\downarrow$) metavariables in an equation ($\uparrow$G)=$\downarrow$ are to be interpreted in the following way: the value of G, a grammatical function, in the functional structure associated with the mother category, is the functional structure associated with the ego category. An equation $\uparrow$=$\downarrow$ means that the functional structures of the mother and the ego category are identical.
4.	Nevertheless, lexical-functional languages are included in the context-sensitive languages (and properly include the context-free languages). This is not undesirable, since at least some context-sensitive power is needed to treat certain phenomena in natural languages. A convincing formal proof of this with respect to the Dutch verb raising construction is given in Huybregts (1984). As Bresnan-Kaplan-Peters-Zaenen (1982) argue that Dutch cannot be strongly context-free, Huybregts argues that Dutch (and Swiss German) cannot even be weakly context-free (see also Shieber 1985).
5.	Roughly: the metavariables (arrows) are replaced by actual variables (numbers) by attaching to the top-node some actual (daughter) variable and subsequently replacing each $\uparrow$ by the actual daughter variable of the dominating node and replacing each new $\downarrow$ by a distinct actual variable.
6.	For example, the category VP has no (functional) counterpart in the functional structure (see [5]).
7.	To be read as: the subject of the verbal complement of $\uparrow$ is the same as the object of $\uparrow$. (Verbal complement is shortened as VCOMP or even VC).
8.	Den Besten-Rutjes-Veenstra-Veld (1988) give evidence that there are constructions to be distinguished in between the pure verb raising and the pure extrapo-

sition construction. I will take for granted that the verbs in (k) trigger the pure forms.

9. In fact Netter makes use of the category VP instead of V^1. I consider this to be correct. However, in the present section I will use the traditional category V^1.

10. Two different types of infinitival complementation, whether or not explicitly related to verb raising complements and extraposition complements, were among others suggested by Williams (1980) and Cremers (1983).

11. Note that under certain circumstances (11b) may be correct. But under these circumstances two negations are also allowed in a simplex sentence. The same holds for (12b).

12. For any occurrences of the functions α, β in an functional structure F, α *f-commands* β if and only if α does not contain β and every functional structure of F that contains α contains β.

13. Note that such an equation is marked by a subscript c, in contrast with the usual, defining, equations.

14. In a more precise formulation, which is not relevant in the present paper, *functional precedence* is likely to play an important role.

15. Note that a slight difference in acceptability is to be expected, the latter verbal string being longer than the first one.

16. There is another problem with this part of the structure. It concerns the quite unmotivated VP-nodes, dominating only non-verbal elements: what justifies VP?

17. Especially in constituent structures, VCOMP (or better the overall term XCOMP) will be abbreviated as VC (or XC).

18. In the original (1982) formulation of lexical-functional grammar constituent structures instead of functional structures were used to state generalizations about long-distance dependencies, the essential notion being *constituent-control*. In recent work (e.g. Kaplan-Zaenen in press), however, it is claimed that the constraints with respect to these dependencies are functional rather than phrasal and therefore should be formulated at functional structure, using the formal device of *functional uncertainty*, a formal device permitting an infinite set of functionally constrained possibilities to be finitely specified in individual rules and lexical entries. In effect, equations on arguments may contain string-*sets*, specified by the Kleene star operator *, as in $(\uparrow TOPIC)=(\uparrow COMP^*GF)$.

19. For the mathematical and computational properties of functional uncertainty, see Kaplan - Maxwell (in press). In this paper I will give some linguistic evidence for the use of the principle of functional uncertainty with respect to verb raising.

20. With the exception of the association of a function-assigning equation with a non-maximal projection. A way out is suggested in the text itself (section 4).

21. The fact that this 'simplex' sentence contains more than one object is not *a priori* to be considered improper. In German the simplex verbs *kosten* (to cost) and *lehren* (to teach), for example, both happen to select for two objects.

22.   A somehow complicating factor is that in the Groningen dialect the first projection of V may be V-raised (restricted verb projection raising). I will ignore this phenomenon in this paper (but see Schuurman 1988).

23.   The numbers indicate that for example *e* (he) is the subject of *wol* (wanted) and also, one level below, of *loaten* (made). Incidentally, the *te+inf* and the verb(s) depending on it may also appear in its mirror image:

i) dat de e meester zien kinder perbaaiern loaten wol *zwemmen te leren*

24.   In Schuurman (1988), however, evidence is given for a more structured verbal string whenever an *inf+te* is involved. Such an *inf+te* string is said to constitute a cluster within the overall cluster, both in the Groningen dialect and in Dutch. Functional uncertainty still plays a very important role.

The shape of the verbal string of the constituent structure of sentence (35):

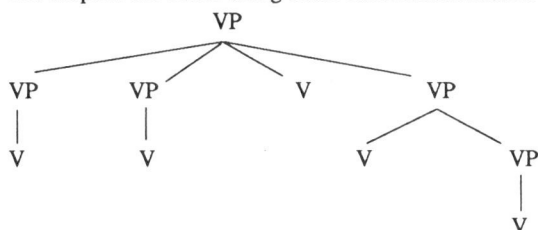

It might be surprising that the resemblance with the behaviour of particle verbs is maintained.

25.   Functional precedence might be an alternative possibility. At the moment I cannot calculate the consequences of this principle with respect to the situation depicted in this paper.

References

Bresnan, Joan
  1982   "Control and complementation", *The mental representation of grammatical relations*, edited by Joan Bresnan (Cambridge, Mass. - London: MIT Press).

Bresnan, Joan (ed.)
  1982   *The mental representation of grammatical relations* (Cambridge, Mass. - London: MIT Press).

Bresnan, Joan - Ronald Kaplan - Stanley Peters - Annie Zaenen
  1982   "Cross-serial dependencies in Dutch", *Linguistic Inquiry* 13.4: 613-635

Cooper, Kathrin E.
1988   *Word Order in bare infinitival contructions in Swiss German*, master's thesis (Edinburgh: university of Edinburgh).

Cremers, Crit
1983   "On two types of infinitival complementation", *Linguistic categories: auxiliaries and related puzzles* Volume 1, edited by Frank Heny - Barry Richards (Dordrecht: Reidel).

Den Besten, Hans - Jean Rutten - Tonjes Veenstra - Jacques Veld
1988   "Verb raising, extrapositie en de derde constructie", (Amsterdam: unpublished manuscript University of Amsterdam).

Huybregts, Riny
1984   "The weak inadequacy of context-free phrase structure grammars", *Van periferie naar kern*, edited by Ger de Haan - Mieke Trommelen - Wim Zonneveld (Dordrecht: Foris).

Johnson, Mark
1986   "The LFG treatment of discontinuity and the double infinitive construction in Dutch", report 86-65 (Stanford: Center for the Study of Language and Information).

Kaplan, Ronald - Joan Bresnan
1982   "Lexical-functional grammar: a formal system for grammatical representation", *The mental representation of grammatical relations*, edited by Joan Bresnan (Cambridge, Mass. - London: MIT Press).

Kaplan, Ronald - John Maxwell
1988   "Functional uncertainty" (unpublished manuscript).

Kaplan, Ronald - Annie Zaenen
in press "Long-distance dependencies, constituent structure, and functional uncertainty", *Alternative conceptions of phrase structure*, edited by Mark Baltin - Anthony Kroch.

Netter, Klaus
1986   "Getting things out of order", *Proceedings of COLING 1986* (Bonn).
1988   "Nonlocal-dependencies and infinitival constructions in German", *Natural language parsing and linguistic theories*, edited by Uwe Reyle - Christian Rohrer (Dordrecht: Reidel).

Schuurman, Ineke
1989   "Verb Raising [+te]: a cluster in itself?", *Sprechen und Hören*, Akten des 23. Linguistischen Kolloquiums (Berlin 1988), edited by Norbert Reiter (Tübingen: Niemeyer).
in press "A lexical-functional treatment of cross-serial dependencies", *Proceedings of the XIVth International Congress of Linguists* (Berlin 1987).

Schuurman, Ineke - Annet Wierenga
in press "Het Gronings: 'Verb-raising' in soorten en maten", *Taal en tongval* special
issue.

Shieber, Stuart
1985 "Evidence against the context-freeness of natural language", *Linguistics and Philosophy* 8: 333-343

Simpson, Jane - Joan Bresnan
1983 "Control and obviation in Warlpiri", *Natural Language and Linguistic Theory* 1: 49-64

Wescoat, Michael - Annie Zaenen
1985 "Lexicaal-functionele grammatica", *Stromingen in de hedendaagse linguistiek*, edited by Flip Droste (Leuven - Assen: Van Gorcum).

Williams, Edwin
1980 "Predication", *Linguistic Inquiry* 11: 203-238

Zec, Draga
1987 "On obligatory control in clausal complements", *Working papers in grammatical theory and discourse structure*, edited by Masayo Iida - Stephen Wechsler - Draga Zec (Stanford: Center for the Study of Language and Information).

Some implications from an analysis of German word order[1]

Bonnie D. Schwartz and Alessandra Tomaselli

1. Introduction

In this paper we will compare two different proposals for the structure of the German sentence, both of which are formulated within a *Barriers* (Chomsky 1986) framework. The data we will rely on come from two very different areas of research, namely:
a) the syntactic behavior of pronominal elements in German (in particular the facts related to topicalization);
b) the stages of acquisition of German word order by native speakers of Italian, Portuguese and Spanish.

2. The position of Infl° in German: Two possibilities

Given the analysis of the structure of the sentence as proposed in *Barriers*, no problem exists with respect to the internal ordering of the VP; in fact, there is general agreement in the generative literature that VP is head-final in German (see, e.g., Bach 1962; Bierwisch 1963; Koster 1975; Thiersch 1978; etc.). However, with respect to IP, two different analyses have been argued for, as illustrated in (1) and (2). Travis (1984) has proposed that IP is "head-medial", with the subject position to the left of I^o (corresponding to the specifier position) and VP to the right of I^o (corresponding to the complement position):

(1) $[_{CP} \text{ (XP) } [_{C'} C^o [_{IP} NP_{(subj.)} [_{I'} I^o [_{VP} NP \ V^o]]]]]$

Den Besten (1986), among others, has, in contrast proposed that IP, like VP, is a head-final projection in German.

(2) $[_{CP} (XP) [_{C'} C^0 [_{IP} NP_{(subj.)} [_{I'} [_{VP} NP V^0] I^0]]]]$

3.1. The crucial data for Travis (1984): Pronominals and stress

The data we first reconsider concern the topicalization of pronominal elements, these being the crucial facts Travis relies on to argue for IP as head-medial. Look at (3) and (4):

(3)   *Ihn_{acc} hat die Mutter_{nom} geküßt.
       him   has the mother   kissed
       'The mother has kissed him'

(4)   IHN hat die Mutter geküßt

These examples show that the object pronoun can occur in sentence-initial position only with stress. The facts are even clearer when we consider the behavior of the object pronoun *es*, the third-person singular neuter pronoun (i.e., *it* in English). Since the object pronoun *es* can never occur with stress, it must be replaced by the corresponding demonstrative pronoun *das* when it appears in sentence-initial position, as shown in (5) and (6):

(5)   *Es_{acc} hat das Pferd_{nom} gefressen
       it   has the horse   eaten

(6)   Das_{acc} hat das Pferd_{nom} gefressen
       that   has the horse   eaten
       'The horse has eaten that'

Crucially, however, the subject pronoun *es* can appear unstressed in sentence-initial position:

(7)   Es_{nom} hat das Gras_{acc} gefressen
       it   has the grass   eaten
       'It has eaten the grass'

3.2. Travis' (1984) analysis

The question is, then, how can this "stress"-asymmetry between subject and object pronouns in sentence-initial position be explained? Travis (1984) accounts for this phenomenon by postulating that object pronouns undergo (for obvious reasons) "topicalization", i.e., movement to the specifier position of CP, whereas subject pronouns remain in their base position, i.e. the specifier position of IP. The examples in (3) to (7) are then easily explained, assuming some sort of constraint, working at the level of phonological form, like (8):

(8)   A pronominal element which has moved to the specifier position of CP, cannot remain in its weak form.

The structures in (9) and (10) illustrate how Travis' analysis works:

(9)   *[Ihn$_i$[$_{C'}$ [$_{C^o}$ hat$_v$][$_{IP}$ [$_{NP}$ die Mutter] [$_{I'}$[$_{I^o}$ e$_v$][$_{VP}$ [$_{VP}$ e$_i$ ....

geküßt e$_v$]]]]]

In (9), the object pronoun *ihn* has moved from its argument position inside VP to the specifier position of CP, a process which given the constraint in (8), rules out the possibility of *ihn* remaining unstressed. According to Travis, movement to the specifier position of CP forces the movement of the finite verb from I^o to C^o, in order to avoid violating the empty category principle (note in fact that otherwise the head of CP would remain empty). The same analysis explains (5) and (6). As for (7), Travis assumes that a matrix clause with a sentence-initial subject must be represented as an IP, i.e., the subject does not topicalize to the specifier position of CP, as shown in (10):

(10)   [$_{IP}$ [$_{NP}$ es] [$_{I'}$ [$_{I}$^{o} hat$_v$][$_{VP}$ [$_{VP}$ [$_{NP}$ das Gras] gefressen] e$_v$]]]

The head of the higher VP (*hat*) moves to I^o to realize inflection (or alternatively, to avoid a violation of the empty category principle[2]) and stops. The subject pronoun stays in its argumental base position, where it may remain unstressed. Note, of course, that this solution relies crucially on the idea that IP is head-medial.

4.1. An IP-final analysis: Tomaselli (1987)

What we would like to propose, however, is that in fact these data do not necessarily argue for the superiority of a head- medial IP structure; they can also be explained in terms of a structure in which IP is head-final (cf. [2]). Note that if IP is assumed to be head-final, then even in matrix clauses where the pronominal subject is sentence-initial, a double-movement analysis must be postulated (I^0 to C^0; XP to the specifier position of CP). But then we still need to explain how the subject pronoun can remain unstressed in sentence-initial position.

Maintaining the constraint in (8), we propose the following (cf. Tomaselli 1987): The subject pronoun can cliticize to the head of CP both at S-structure and at the level of phonological form (cf. Kayne 1984 for a similar analysis of subject clitics in French).

4.2. The Wackernagel position

In order to argue for the plausibility of this solution, we will first show that a cliticization process must be assumed in the grammar of German at the level of S-Structure.

Note first that examples (11) to (14) show that pronouns may intervene between Comp and a full NP subject, occupying a position traditionally referred to as the "Wackernagel" position (cf. e.g., Thiersch 1978; Lenerz 1985).[3]

(11) $[_{C'} C^0 \quad [_{IP} W \quad [_{IP} NP_{(subj.)} [_{I'} VP I^0]]]]$

,	daß		der Mann	ihm	ein Buch geschenkt hat
			Nom	Dat Acc	
	that		the man	to-him a book	given has
	'that		the man	has given a book to him'	
(12) ,	daß	ihm	der Mann	t	ein Buch geschenkt hat
		Dat	Nom		Acc
	that	to-him	the man		a book given has
(13) ,	daß		der Mann	dem Jungen es	geschenkt hat
			Nom	Dat Acc	
	that		the man	to-the boy it	given has

(14),	daß	es	der Mann	dem Jungen t geschenkt hat
		Acc	Nom	Dat
	that	it	the man	to the boy given has

However, when the subject is a pronoun nothing can intervene between it and Comp.[4] (15) and (16) show precisely this:

(15) a ..., daß er   ihm   ein Buch geschenkt hat
                  Nom   Dat   Acc
          that he   to-him a book   given   has
    b *..., daß ihm   er   t ein Buch geschenkt hat (cf. [12])
                   Dat.   Nom.   Acc.
          that to-him   he   a book   given   has

(16) a ..., daß er   es   dem Jungen t geschenkt hat
                  Nom   Acc   Dat
          that he   it   to-the boy   given   has
    b *..., daß es   er   dem Jungen t geschenkt hat (cf. [14])
                   Acc   Nom   Dat
          that it   he   to-the boy   given   has

In fact, examples such as these argue for the idea that a nominative subject pronoun has some sort of "privileged" relation with Comp, in that they must be immediately adjacent. Following Kayne's (1984) analysis for French, we suggest that the subject pronoun in German cliticizes to Comp^{o} (from right to left) at S-structure, schematized as in (17):[5]

(17)   C′ (cf. (16a))

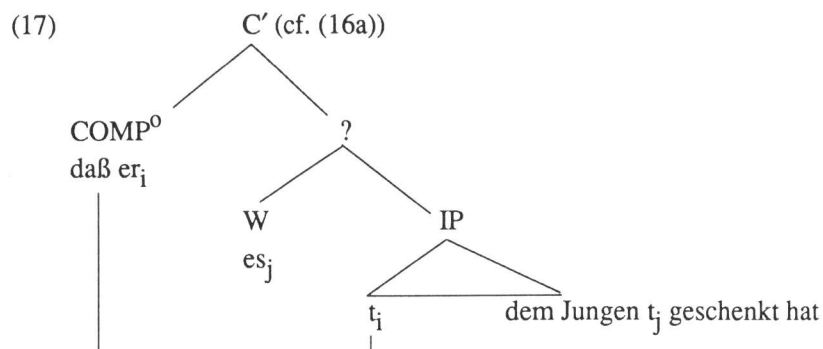

COMP^{o}

daß er$_i$

                    W   IP

                    es$_j$

                              t$_i$ dem Jungen t$_j$ geschenkt hat

4.3. Cliticization at the level of phonological form

Summarizing thus far, we have seen that unstressed pronominal elements may appear in one of two places: their base argument position or the Wackernagel position. Additionally, the sentences in (15) and (16) argue for the privileged status of the subject pronoun in relation to Comp. We accounted for this by saying that it cliticizes to $Comp^0$. Since we have motivated a process of cliticization for subject pronouns at S-structure, it seems justified to posit the same process at another level of grammar, i.e., at the level of phonological form. And it is precisely this process that accounts for the fact that the subject pronoun can appear unstressed in sentence-initial position (cf. [7]). As we have seen, given a head-final IP, one has to assume that at S-structure the subject pronoun moves to the specifier position of CP where it cannot remain in its unstressed form (cf. [8]). The structure in (18) depicts this:

(18) $[_{CP}$ ES$_i$ $[_{C'}$ $[_{C^0}$ hat $]$ $[_{IP}$ $[_{NP}$ e$_i$ ....

However, the subject pronoun may escape the constraint in (8) by cliticizing to Comp at the level of phonological form (from left to right), as in (19):

(19)

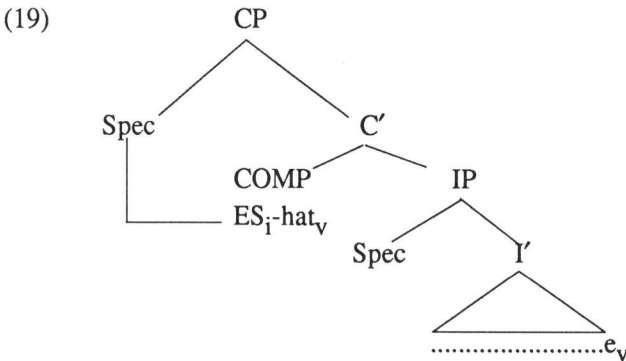

4.4. First conclusion

We have come to the following conclusions about the position of the head of IP in German: We have shown that the data concerning topicalization of pronominal elements (the "stress"-asymmetry facts) do not constitute an empirical counter-argument against an analysis of IP as head-final. In fact, on the contrary, these data can be easily explained by positing, at the level of phonological form, a process of cliticization of subject pronouns (which we showed to be independently motivated at the level of S-structure). We suggest, moreover, that there are several reasons, both theoretical and empirical, that argue for the superiority of a head-final analysis of IP, which we now briefly sketch:

a) All matrix declaratives are CPs, i.e. there is a uniform characterization of verb-second as V^o to I^o to C^o.

b) There is no difference between the way inflection is realized on the verb in matrix as opposed to subordinate clauses.

c) One can maintain that the infinitival marker *zu* is base- generated in I^o (Giusti 1986) (cf. Kayne 1984 for *to* in English, and Reuland 1983 for *te* in Dutch).

d) One can easily account for the different behavior of dummy *es* (whose occurence is limited to the sentence-initial position in matrix clauses) and of *es* coindexed with an extraposed sentential subject (whose occurence is obligatory) (cf., e.g., Safir 1985; Bennis 1986; Tomaselli 1986; Grange 1987).

Apart from these arguments based purely on the syntax of German, which, unfortunately, we will not have space to develop here, we would like to maintain that data from a distinct area of research, namely, second language acquisition, may be relevant.

In what follows, we will discuss some well-known facts concerning the development of word order by native speakers of Italian, Portuguese or Spanish acquiring German as a second language.

We will show that our analysis of the second language acquisition data constitutes an independent argument both for the assumption of an IP projection in German and, moreover, for its head-final status.

5.1. Word order stages of German as a second language by native speakers of Romance languages

The second language acquisition of word order in German is one of the more thoroughly studied areas in non-native language acquisition. It has, in fact, been the focus of much debate among students of second language acquisition, for the data have been used as evidence both supporting and attacking the hypothesis that principles of universal grammar are at work in second language acquisition. For the sake of brevity we will henceforth use L1 for the native language and L2 for the target language,.

Although there is disagreement as to what it is that underlies the explanation for the L2 German stages, there is general agreement as to what the description of these stages is (see e.g., Clahsen and Muysken 1986 and the references cited there). The description of the six stages found for native speakers of Italian, Portuguese or Spanish acquiring German is presented in (20):

(20) (S-structure) description: L1 Romance, L2 German stages

   i. SVO

   ii. (Adv/PP) SVO

   iii. $SV_{[+fin.]} OV_{[-fin.]}$ Particles, participles and infinitives in final position

   iv. $XP V_{[+fin.]} SO$ Verb-Second/subject-inversion)

   v. $SV_{[+fin.]} (Adv) O$

   vi. daß $SOV_{[+fin.]}$ Distinction made between matrix and subordinate clauses

5.2. Clahsen and Muysken (1986)

A well-known attempt to explain these stages comes from Clahsen and Muysken (1986). These researchers argue that second language acquisition by adults is not due to the same processes exploited in L1 grammar construction.

As support they offer evidence, from word order developmental sequences, that child L1A of German produces a different developmental sequence from adult L2A of German. It is argued in Schwartz (1988), however, that the comparison between child L1 and adult L2 may not be the appropriate comparison, for only in second language acquisition is there the possibility of a previously acquired grammar affecting the construction of the target language grammar.

In fact, it has been shown (Clahsen 1984)[6] that the stages in (20) appropriately characterize the L2 German stages for children (whose mother-tongue is Italian) as well. If the stages for non-native German grammar construction are the same for both children and adults, then the fact that these stages differ from the L1 German stages is not a convincing argument for concluding that second language acquisition by adults falls outside of the domain of principles of universal grammar.[7]

A second reason Clahsen and Muysken conclude that second language acquisition by adults is completely different from native language acquisition concerns their analysis of the stages, given in (21) (from 1986:114):

(21) Clahsen and Muysken's analysis of adult L2 German stages

I.   S → NP VP
     VP→ V...

II   The PS rules in I + Adv-Prep

$$X \begin{Bmatrix} PP \\ Adv \end{Bmatrix} Y \rightarrow \begin{Bmatrix} PP \\ Adv \end{Bmatrix} X \, e \, Y$$

III The rules in II + Particle

i. $X [_{V'} P V_{[+tns]}] Y \Rightarrow X [_{V'} e V_{[+tns]}] Y + P$

ii. $X [_{V'} V_{[+tns]} \begin{Bmatrix} \text{V-inf} \\ \text{V-part]} \end{Bmatrix} Y \rightarrow X [_{V'} V_{[+tns]} e] Y + \begin{Bmatrix} \text{V-inf} \\ \text{V-part} \end{Bmatrix}$

IV   The rules in III + Inversion
     $X \; Subj \; V \; Y \Rightarrow X \; V+Subj \; e \; Y$

V   The rules in IV + Adv-VP
     $X \; V \; NP \; AdvP \Rightarrow X \; V+AdvP \; NP \; e$

VI   The rules in V + V End
     $X \; V_{[+tns]} \; Y \Rightarrow X \; e \; Y+ V_{[+tns]}$

Clahsen and Muysken conclude that some of the rules posited in (21) are not definable in terms of current linguistic theory.

Before going into detail, it is important to stress that they posit an underlying SVO word order at all stages; notice that, from our perspective, this is due to the fact that, crucially, their structure of the sentence lacks an IP projection. We will address this important issue later.

Let us return now to the idea of "unnatural" rules; two stages in particular warrant discussion: stages III and VI. As for stage III, they claim that the fix-up rule that transforms the base SVO order to surface $SV_{[+fin]}OV_{[-fin]}$, by moving particles, participles and infinitivals into sentence-final position, is not a rule that current linguistic theory allows.

The same argument is used for the rule they posit at stage VI, postposing the finite verb to sentence-final position in embedded clauses.[8] Hence, their logic is that although adult L2 German acquirers are creating rules for German which may end up with target-like results, these rules themselves cannot be captured by current theories of syntax. Thus, their general conclusion is that second language acquisition by adults is not effected by principles of universal grammar.

5.3.1. DuPlessis, Solin, Travis and White (1987)

In opposition to Clahsen and Muysken's approach, duPlessis, Solin, Travis and White (1987) have argued that second language acquisition by adults does result from processes involving universal grammar. In a reanalysis of the L2 German data, they have convincingly illustrated that the six stages fall out from independently motivated principles and parameters of universal grammar.

We shall outline their analysis in what follows.

According to duPlessis et al., at stage 1, the underlying order is SVO or more accurately SIVO, like Romance, and this is the order realized in the surface.

At stage 2, PP/Adv is optionally adjoined to IP, this type of adjunction being allowed in Romance but not in German, following work by Travis (1986).

It is at stage 3 where duPlessis et al.'s analysis really starts to diverge from that of Clahsen and Muysken. Two things happen: First, the value of the headedness parameter for VP is changed, which makes the underlying order SIOV (verb-final); secondly, movement of V^0 to I^0 consequently results in the surface order $SV_{[+f]}OV_{[-f]}$ (both in matrix and subordinate clauses).[9] The structure that depicts this movement is in (22):

(22) $[_{IP}$ NP $[_{I'}$ I^0 $[_{VP}$ $[_{VP}$ NP $V^0_{[-f]}$ $]$ V^0 $]]]$

We suggested earlier that a crucial problem in Clahsen and Muysken's account stems from the fact that their structure of the sentence lacks an independent IP projection. Now we can see how important the positing of IP is: without it, there is only one place for V to occupy at this stage, namely, the head of VP. This is why Clahsen and Muysken cannot allow the order head-complement to be reversed.

Stage 4 is where the acquirers get verb second, i.e., what looks like subject-inversion. By combining (1) and (2), i.e., (1) moving an XP into the specifier position of CP and (2) moving the finite Verb (through I^0) into Comp, we get the desired surface order $XPV_{[+f]}S$ .... Note that (2) is a standard example of head-to-head movement, as discussed in Travis (1984), Chomsky (1986) and Baker (1988), whose effect is verb second in matrix clauses. Since in subordinate clauses Comp is filled by a complementizer, it prevents the verb from moving to Comp; and so the surface order there will be as in the previous stage, namely, daß $SV_{[+f]}O$.

DuPlessis et al. note that the second language acquirers may have given up adjunction to IP at this stage but that the data are not conclusive.

As for the fifth stage, namely, V (Adv) O, duPlessis et al. claim that it is not relevant for a parameter-changing account of the L2 data, and hence they do not discuss it. We would like to point out, however, that a full analysis should be able to account for all the data and, more importantly, that this stage may indeed have significant consequences in relation to the positioning of AdvP, particularly in view of the differences between the first and second languages involved here.[10]

At stage 6, by virtue of acquiring that Comp can be a proper governor of Infl in German, the second language acquirers now get the word order in subordinate clauses correct, namely *daß* SOV. Hence, at stage 6 their grammar produces target German word order in both main and subordinate clauses.

Before turning to our proposal, we would like to discuss very briefly Travis' (1984) idea of Comp being a proper governor of Infl. According to Travis, there is a parameter that distinguishes, e.g., Romance languages in which Comp is not a proper governor of Infl, from German, in which it is. For German, when Comp is filled with a complementizer, Travis assumes it is able to properly govern the empty Infl, thereby satisfying the empty category principle; in fact, however, Travis uses this idea to prevent the verb from moving into Infl.[12]

(23) shows the analysis they propose for stage 6:

(23) $[_{C'} [_C^0 \text{ daß}] [_{IP} \text{NP}_{(subj)} [_{I'} [_I^0 \text{ e}] [_{VP} \text{NP V}^0]]]]$
$\llcorner$ proper government $\lrcorner$ $(*V^0 \text{ to } I^0)$

5.3.2. Preliminary summary of German L2A

Summarizing thus far, in duPlessis et al.'s analysis, three different parameters have to be invoked: First, an adjunction to IP parameter which is claimed to distinguish Romance languages from German; second, a headedness parameter, where VP is head-final in German but head-initial in Romance languages; and third, a parameter concerning Comp as a proper governor of Infl.

And not only are duPlessis et al. able to account for the same stages of second language acquisition that Clahsen and Muysken's analysis can, they do so by making use of parameters and movement rules already known in the syntax literature. Thus, the important conclusion to be drawn from the work in duPlessis et al. is that, contrary to Clahsen and Muysken's general conclusion, the rules needed to explain the stages are indeed definable in terms of universal grammar.

5.4. The last German L2A stage: IP as head-final

Although we basically agree with duPlessis et al.'s analysis up to stage 5,[11] we now want to propose a different analysis of the last stage. Our suggestion has the positive consequence of allowing all of the L2 data to be accounted for by making use of only two parameters instead of three, as we shall see.

What we say that is crucially different from duPlessis et al. is that at stage 6, the L2 German acquirers analyze IP as being head-final, just like VP. This gives a structure like (24):

(24) $[_{IP}$ NP$_{(subj)}$ $[_{I'}$ $[_{VP}$ NP$_{(obj)}$ V^0 $]$ I^0 $]]$

By analyzing German with Infl in clause-final position, we are relying on the headedness parameter: VP, the complement of Infl, is now to the left of Infl. In matrix clauses, the V still first moves to I^0, in order to acquire inflection, and then to C^0. When something moves into the specifier position of CP, this will give verb second effects in matrix clauses. However, in embedded clauses with a complementizer in C^0, the V cannot move there. Thus the essence of our analysis is that at stage 6, the second language acquirers are completing the setting of the headedness parameter, which makes Travis' "Comp as a proper governor of Infl" parameter unnecessary.

6.1. Diachrony and acquisition: English evolution and L2 German

An additional advantage of our analysis comes from the historical development of English. It is interesting to note that, with respect to the relative ordering of S,V,O and Infl, English went through the same stages of development in precisely the opposite direction from those we posited in our analysis of L1 Romance, L2 German acquisition. That is, according to Steele et al. (1981:285 ff.), the evolution of English is as follows:

(25) i.   SOVI (Old English)
    ii. SIOV (Early Modern English)
    iii. SIVO (Modern English)

This is the mirror-image of the stages we hypothesized in our analysis of the German L2 facts: At stages 1 and 2, the L2 acquirers' order was SIVO; at stages 3, 4 and 5, SIOV; and at Stage 6, SOVI.

Notice, moreover, that if these three stages given for the historical development of English are the correct description, (what is crucial here, of course, is the relative order of the stages and not the absolute chronology)[13], then necessarily the stages are definable in terms of universal grammar. Thus, if the opposite order to these stages correctly describes the developmental sequence of L1 Romance speakers acquiring L2 German, then it seems reasonable to assume that the grammar changes required to move from one stage to the next are also possible in terms of universal grammar.

6.2. Ruling out possibilities: Theoretical superiority

If the main point here can be maintained, then a single, yet crucial, question remains: Of the three word order stages, why is the second stage realized as SIOV rather than SVOI? In other words, why do the second language acquirers first set the headedness parameter for VP and then IP rather than first for IP and then secondly VP? If they did this, it would give rise to an underlying order of SVOI. One partial answer to this question comes from Den Besten (1986:250), who points out that the underlying order SVOI is not attested among natural language grammars. It seems reasonable to expect that Den Besten's observation should find an explanation relying on a principle of universal grammar. For now, however, notice that if SVOI is not a possible underlying word order, and if it is the case that the second language acquirers are making use of universal grammar in building their L2 German grammar, then we would in fact expect that they would not even be able to hypothesize SVOI as an intermediate grammar stage. Hence we have an answer to why the second language acquirers first set the headedness parameter for VP, realizing the second word order stage as SIOV rather than as the unattested SVOI: They can not.

In this answer also lies another reason for preferring our account of the second language developmental sequence data to that of duPlessis et al. In fact, the two accounts seem to be empirically equivalent, and, importantly, both lead to the same conclusion that universal grammar does underly second language acquisition by adults. However, it is also important to note that duPlessis et al. have no explanation for why parameter change should happen in this order. In contrast, by exploiting the idea that SVOI is an impossible underlying order, we can explain why the headedness parameter is first set for VP rather than for IP. For this reason our account is theoretically superior to theirs.

6.3. A universal grammar explanation for *SVOI

Let us return now to the observation of den Besten that SVOI is an impossible base word order. Before proposing an explanation, we need to elaborate on the theory of non-lexical categories, in particular on Infl. First, let us start with an intuitive division concerning Infl: It seems that a correct observation is that some languages allow independent lexical material to be base-generated in Infl whereas in other languages, Infl is simply characterized by a set of abstract features. An example of the first type is English, where, for example, modals and *do* are base-generated in Infl. An example of the second type is German, where no lexical material can occur in (tensed) Infl at D-structure. There also seems to be a third type, characterized as generating independent non-verbal lexical material in Infl, for example, pronominal and negative clitics. An example of such a language is Italian. The table in (26) is intended to give a typology of the three different instantiations of tensed Infl: "fully autonomous", "semi- autonomous", or "non-autonomous".

(26) Typology of Infl: fully, semi-, and non-autonomous[14,15]

$Infl_{[+T]}$	is fully autonomous only if it contains a morphologically independent Verb	$[+V]_{[+lex]}$	*do*, English
$Infl_{[+T]}$	is semi-autonomous only if it contains morphologically independent material	$[-V]_{[+lex]}$	clitics Italian
$Infl_{[+T]}$	is non-autonomous otherwise	$[-V]_{[-lex]}$	∅ German

Although languages like Italian are similar to languages like German in that no verbal material is base-generated in tensed Infl, for our concerns, the important split is between the base- generation of lexical material in Infl vs. base-generating a lexically empty Infl. Let us refer to this difference in terms of [non-autonomous] Infl, where a lexically empty Infl is [+ non-autonomous].

In order then, to capture the main intuition in this three- way typology and account for den Besten's observation, we propose the following two principles of universal grammar, at least one of which must be satisfied in all languages:

(27) [+ non-autonomous] Infl must be adjacent to V^o

(28) [- non-autonomous] Infl must be adjacent to the subject

The result is that only in languages where Infl is non-autonomous must the verb and Infl be adjacent; in all other cases, the verb must be adjacent to the subject. Notice, furthermore, that den Besten's observation falls out nicely if something like (27) and (28) are assumed: SVOI is impossible because Infl must be adjacent either to the verb or to the subject.[17]

To describe briefly the two situations in question here, we would say that with respect to the evolution of English, Infl started out as non-autonomous with the underlying order SOVI, the verb and Infl necessarily being adjacent. However, when English began to base-generate some "verbs" directly in Infl (the so- called "pre-modals", cf. Lightfoot 1979; Steele et al. 1981; and Roberts 1985), Infl was no longer non-autonomous, and a reordering was forced to take place, given (28). Infl was thus forced to be head-medial. The result is the order SIOV.[16]

Secondly, with respect to the L2 German acquisition stages, we assume that the first stage represents the effect of the L1 grammar, namely, Romance's SIVO. Combining 1) the positive evidence from German input (the object precedes, in matrix clauses, the non-finite verb, and, in subordinate clauses, the whole verbal complex) with 2) the principles in (27) and (28), we see that the only possible compatible parameter change at the second stage is for VP, giving SIOV, where Infl remains adjacent to the subject. We furthermore speculate that the deeper explanation for the second change in headedness (IP as head- final) comes from the acquirers no longer analyzing Infl in German as [- non-autonomous] (as in Italian) but rather as [+non-autonomous] (as in the target language). From this (and [27]), Infl must be adjacent to the verb, and hence we arrive at the order SOVI.

7.1. Summary and conclusion

In this paper we have tried to argue for an analysis of German with IP as head-final. We first looked at pronominal topicalization facts in German, these being the crucial data that Travis originally used to argue for the empirical superiority of an analysis of IP as head-medial over head-final. We provided an alternative analysis, which follows from an independently motivated cliticization process concerning the subject pronoun; our account shows that the "stress"-asymmetry facts can be just as adequately handled with a head-final IP structure.

We then turned to data from the second language acquisition of German, which we approached from a universal grammar perspective. We argued that the final acquisition stage finds a straightforward solution by positing IP as head-final in German. The advantages of our analysis are:

a) two parameters are invoked, rather than duPlessis et al.'s three;
b) an explanation is provided for the particular order of parameter changes;
c) when compared to the historical evolution of English, the mirror-image development is noted; observing that SVOI needs to be excluded both in the second language acquisition stages and the English evolution stages, we propose that its impossibility falls out from two seemingly natural principles of universal grammar.

We would like to close with one final remark: Although the principal domain of universal grammar is typically perceived to be native-speaker syntactic knowledge, we would like to suggest that it is not unreasonable to consider data of second language acquisition to be relevant to theories of universal grammar, in the sense that the so-called "interlanguage" syntax of second language acquirers can indeed be used as an additional data source where hypotheses are either refuted or supported.

Notes

1.   Many people were of great help to us in bringing this paper into its current state, in particular Ian G. Roberts in many hours of discussion and criticism. We would also like to thank the following people for listening, reading and commenting: Harald Clahsen, Georgio Graffi, Liliane Haegeman, Steve Krashen, Andrea Moro, Luigi Rizzi, Ramona Römisch, Bill Rutherford, Beatrice Santorini and Sten Vikner.

   This paper was written while both authors were at the University of Geneva in the winter semester 1987-1988, and we would like to extend our appreciation to Prof. Luigi Rizzi and to the Dean of the Faculty of Letters, M. André Hurst, for making this collaboration possible.

2.   In Travis (1984) Infl can be base-generated either empty or with inflectional morphology; the verb is forced to move to I^o, in the first case, in order to avoid a violation of the empty category principle, and in the second, to acquire inflection.

3.   For ease of explanation we use embedded examples to avoid complications relating to verb movement; it should be noted that exactly the same facts obtain in matrix clauses.

4   The grammatical sentence below is an apparent counter- example:

    i)   , daß mir's gelungen ist

           that to me it succeeded is

           'that I succeeded in doing it'

The nominative pronoun (*'s*) is cliticized to the dative pronoun (*mir*). However, note that 1) the reduced form of *es* (*'s*) indicates that a process of cliticization at the level of phonological form is at work (this is in fact a peculiarity of *es*); and 2) this example can be regarded as an ergative construction: this means that the nominative NP is generated inside VP (where, following den Besten [1985], it receives nominative Case):

    ii)

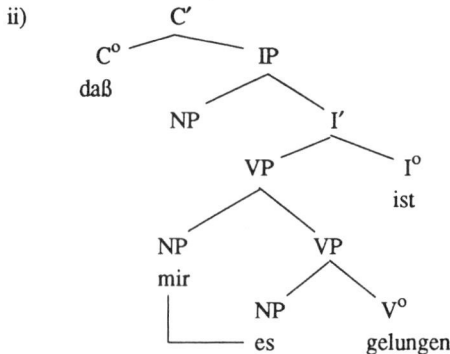

Therefore, the pronoun *es* seems to have cliticized from its object position to the adjacent dative pronoun. Note, furthermore, that the cliticization of (nom.) *es* gives an ungrammatical result if *es* is the subject of a transitive sentence:

    iii)   *, daß mir's einen Kuß gegeben hat

                that to me it a kiss given has

5.   Assuming a process of subject cliticization in German, other important facts about German syntax also fall away, notably the existence of null subject phenomena. The hypothesis that the subject pronoun cliticizes to Comp supports the idea that Comp in German is characterized by pronominal features; this leads to an analysis attributing to Comp licensing properties, similar to Infl in a null-subject language like Italian (cf. Platzack 1987; Tomaselli 1987).

6.   It should be pointed out that Clahsen offers a very different explanation of these facts.

7.   In fact, in Schwartz (1988) precisely the opposite conclusion is argued for. The logic used is the following: It is often assumed that the division concerning the activation of the principles of universal grammar in second language acquisition lies between children and adults, that is, that the "critical period" for language acquisition stops around puberty (cf. Lenneberg 1967; it should be noted, however, that this claim has been contested, and that if it exists at all, it may be much earlier -cf., e.g., Krashen 1973). However, assuming that something like a critical period exists (even in a weakened form), then the fact that the (L1 Italian) children acquiring L2 German went through the same stages as the adults (L1=Italian, Portuguese or Spanish) is evidence that adult second language acquirers make use of universal grammar. This follows because 1) one can safely assume that the children (whose age, importantly, was eight) are relying on universal grammar, and so 2) since both groups evidenced equivalent second language developmental sequences, the adults, then, must be making use of the same underlying process, namely, principles of universal grammar. In fact, looked at from Clahsen and Muysken's perspective, they should necessarily predict that the developmental sequences in the two cases should differ, unless they resort to hypothesizing that universal grammar does not underlie the child L2 stages either. Although a logical possibility, such an account falls short in many ways, one of the most obvious being to provide an explanation for why children, who are known to be less able with respect to problem-solving skills should surpass adults only in the domain of non-native language acquisition.

8.   Note also that Clahsen and Muysken also point to the unnaturalness of the rule posited at stage IV, saying that the inversion rule in stage IV is hard to formulate because the X in the left context is not simply an arbitrary variable which can either be present or absent, but a preposed constituent triggering the rule. The trouble is that the class of objects here is hard to state as a natural class in terms of syntactic categories. (Clahsen and Muysken 1986: 115)

However, this is precisely the situation that exists in the Scandinavian languages which are both SVO and verb-second. Hence stage 4 must be describable in terms of universal grammar.

9.   Notice that it is not the case that one needs to assume that the second language acquirers have "acquired" movement from V° to I°, or in other words to assume that the Romance languages differ from German with respect to V° to I° movement. In fact, even in the previous two stages one can assume that the acquirers move from V° to I°; however, its results are string vacuous. (Cf. Emonds 1978; Pollock 1987; and Belletti 1988 for ideas on V° to I° movement in Romance languages.)

In addition, notice that if one assumes that the L1 grammar is originally invoked in second language acquisition (as we do), then it seems very unlikely that in the early stages these second language acquirers would produce sentences in which the finite verb is in sentence-final position since Infl$^\circ$ is to the left of V°. More generally, one would in fact expect no such cases until the final acquisition stage (see our account below). Moreover, this allows us to question the main criterion Clahsen and Muysken (1986) rely on to reject duPlessis et al.'s (1987) analysis of stage 3, namely, that there are no "cases of finite verbs occuring in final position at this point" (Clahsen and Muysken 1986: 115).

10.   Several hypotheses about a possible explanation for the stage 5 facts are available. For one idea, see Tomaselli - Schwartz (in prep.).

11.   Notice that this is an unorthodox use of the empty category principle. In fact, this proper government relation (between C° and I°) has nothing to do with movement, e.g. the relation between an antecedent and its trace - this being the standard case where the empty category principle is pertinent. On the contrary, Travis' proposal for German merely stipulates that a lexical complementizer properly governs (the base-generated empty) I°. Moreover, even if one were to interpret her proposal in terms of licensing, it still remains a mystery as to why lexical material is prevented from filling the empty I°.

12.   But cf. the discussion concerning duPlessis et al.'s treatment of stage 5. It may also be the case that there is no adjunction to IP parameter, distinguishing the Romance languages from German. The following grammatical example seems to indicate that adjunction to IP is available:

i)   , daß gestern der Mann dem Jungen ein Buch geschenkt hat
       that yesterday the man the boy a book gave has

We do not mean to imply that the analysis that duPlessis et al. offer for the stage 2 facts is wrong, but rather that it needs some refinement, in particular some precision as to what the parameter responsible for verb second in stage 4 is.

13.   See, for example, van Kemenade (1987), who argues that English was already VO in Middle English (by around 1200).

14.   Given standard assumptions, Infl is characterized by both tense and agreement features (cf. Chomsky 1981:52, where Infl is rewritten as [tense (AGR)]). Note, however, that it could be argued from this typology that [+V, +lx] is the lexical

instantiation of tense features and that [-V, +lex] the lexical instantiation of agreement features. If tenable, then the fact that both Tense and AGR can be independently lexicalized may provide indirect support for recent theories of Infl, where Tense and AGR each head their own projection (see Moro 1987; Pollock 1987; Rizzi 1987; and Belletti 1988).

15. These ideas about the autonomy of Infl owe much to discussions with Ian Roberts.

16. We should point out that Travis (1984:147) also notes this tension between I^{o} being adjacent either to the verb (for morphological-dependency reasons) or to the subject (for nominative Case reasons). Notice, however, that she states this observation only as a tendency, rather than having it follow from principles of universal grammar.

17. It should also be pointed out that Old English evidenced quite regular verb raising and verb-projection raising, especially with modal, perception, and causative verbs (van Kemenade 1987). The effect of verb projection raising is to give the surface order $SV_{[+f]}OV_{[-f]}$. Hence positive evidence existed for an underlying order SIOV, and this too may have helped the resetting of the headedness parameter for VP.

References

Bach, Emmon
1962   "The order of elements in a transformational grammar of German", *Language* 38: 263-269

Baker, Mark
1988   *Incorporation: A theory of grammatical function changing* (Chicago: The University of Chicago Press).

Bayer, Josef
1984   "Comp in Bavarian syntax", *The Linguistic Review* 3: 209-274

Belletti, Adriana
1988   "Generalized verb movement: On some differences and similarities between Italian and French", Paper presented at the GLOW Conference, Budapest.

Bennis, Hans
1986   *Gaps and dummies* (Dordrecht: Foris).

Bierwisch, Manfred
1963   *Grammatik des deutschen Verbs* (Berlin Ost: Akademie-Verlag).

Chomsky, Noam
1981   *Lectures on government and binding* (Dordrecht: Foris).
1986   *Barriers* (Cambridge, Mass.: MIT Press).

Clahsen, Harald
1984   "The acquisition of German word order: A test case for a cognitive approach to
        L2 development", *Second languages: A cross-linguistic perspective*: 219-242,
        edited by Roger Andersen (Rowley, Mass.: Newbury House).

Clahsen, Harald - Jürgen Meisel - Manfred Pienemann
1983   *Deutsch als Zweitsprache, Der Spracherwerb ausländischer Arbeiter* (Tübin-
        gen: Gunter Narr).

Clahsen, Harald - Pieter Muysken
1986   "The availability of universal grammar to adult and child learners - A study of
        the acquisition of German word order", *Second Language Research* 2: 93-119
1988   "The universal grammar paradox in L2 acquisition", (unpublished manuscript
        Universität Düsseldorf/Universiteit van Amsterdam).

Den Besten, Hans
1985   "The ergative hypothesis and free word order in Dutch and German", *Studies
        in German grammar*: 23-64, edited by Jindřich Toman (Dordrecht: Foris).
1986   "Decidability in the syntax of verbs of (not necessarily) West-Germanic langu-
        ages", *Groninger Arbeiten zur Germanistischen Linguistik* 28: 232- 256

duPlessis, Jean - Doreen Solin - Lisa Travis - Lydia White
1987   "Universal grammar or not universal grammar, that is the question: A reply to
        Clahsen and Muysken", *Second Language Research* 3: 56-75

Emonds, Joseph
1978   "The verbal complex V'-V in French", *Linguistic Inquiry* 9: 151-175

Giusti, Giuliana
1986   "On the lack of wh-infinitives with *zu* and the projection of Comp in German",
        Groninger Arbeiten zur Germanistischen Linguistik 28: 115-169

Grange-Stott, C.
1987   "Selected aspects of the syntax of expletive constructions", *Mémoire de licence*
        (Geneva: université de Genève).

Haider, Hubert
1984   "Topic, focus and verb-second", *Groninger Arbeiten zur Germanistischen Lin-
        guistik* 25: 1-48

Kayne, Richard
1984   *Connectedness and binary branching* (Dordrecht: Foris).

Koster, Jan
1975   "Dutch as an SOV language", *Linguistic Analysis* 1: 111-136

Krashen, Steve
1973   "Lateralization, language learning and the critical period", *Language Learning*
        23: 63-74

Lenerz, Jürgen
1985   "Diachronic syntax: Verb position and Comp in German", *Studies in German
        grammar*:103-132, edited by Jindřich Toman (Dordrecht: Foris).

Lenneberg, Eric
1967   *Biological foundations of language* (New York: Wiley and sons).

Lightfoot, David
1979   *Principles of diachronic syntax* (Cambridge: Cambridge University Press).

Meisel, Jürgen, Harald Clahsen - Manfred Pienemann
1981   "On determining developmental stages in natural second language acquisition",
        Studies in Second Language Acquisition 3: 109-135

Moro, Andrea
1987   *Tempo e predicazione nella sintassi delle frasi copulari*, tesi di laurea (Pavia:
        università di Pavia.

Pienemann, Manfred
1980   "The second language acquisition of immigrant children", *Second language
        development: Trends and issues*: 41-56, edited by Sascha Felix (Tübingen:
        Gunter Narr).
1981   *Der Zweitspracherwerb ausländischer Arbeiterkinder* (Bonn: Bouvier).

Platzack, Christer
1987   "The Scandinavian languages and the null subject parameter", *Natural Langu-
        age and Linguistic Theory* 5: 377-401

Pollock, Jean-Yves
1989   "Verb movement, universal grammar and the structure of IP", *Linguistic Inquiry*
        20: 365-424

Reuland, Eric
1983   "Government and the search for AUXes: A case study in cross-linguistic
        category identification", *Linguistic categories: Auxiliaries and related puzzles*
        Vol.I: 99-168, edited by Frank Heny - Barry Richards (Dordrecht: Reidel).

Rizzi, Luigi
1987   "Three issues in Romance dialectology", Paper presented at the GLOW Work-
        shop, Venice.

Roberts, Ian
1985   "Agreement parameters and the development of English modal auxiliaries",
        Natural Language and Linguistic Theory 3: 21-58

Safir, Ken
1985   "Missing subjects in German", *Studies in German grammar*: 193-230, edited
        by Jindřich Toman (Dordrecht: Foris).

Schwartz, Bonnie D.

1987   *The modular basis of second language acquisition*, doctoral dissertation (Los Angelos: University of Southern California).

1988   "Testing between universal grammar and problem-solving models of SLA: Developmental sequence data" (Geneva: unpublished manuscript université de Genève).

Steele, Susan et al.

1981   *An encyclopedia of AUX: A study of cross-linguistic equivalence* (Cambridge, Mass.: MIT Press).

Thiersch, Craig

1978   *Topics in German syntax*, doctoral dissertation (Cambridge, Mass.: MIT).

Tomaselli, Alessandra

1986   "Das unpersönliche *es* - Eine Analyse im Rahmen der generativen Grammatik", *Linguistische Berichte* 102: 171-190

1987   "On the pronominal nature of Comp in German" (Pavia: unpublished manuscript università di Pavia).

Tomaselli, Alessandra - Bonnie Schwartz

(in prep) "Negation in L2 German: Sequence data as support for universal grammar in adult SLA" (unpublished manuscript Università di Pavia/Université de Genève).

Travis, Lisa

1984   *Parameters and effects of word order variation*, doctoral dissertation (Cambridge, Mass.: MIT).

1986   "Parameters of word order and verb second phenomena", Paper presented at the Princeton Workshop on Comparative Syntax, Princeton (to appear in the proceedings).

Van Kemenade, Ans

1987   *Syntactic Case and morphological Case in the history of English* (Dordrecht: Foris).

Part 3
Binding

.

Nominative anaphors in Icelandic: morphology or syntax?[1]

Martin Everaert

1. Introduction

It is a well-known fact that Germanic languages do not have nominative reflexives or reciprocals as is illustrated in (1).

(1)   *They$_i$ think that each other$_i$/themselves(they selves)$_i$ bought
      the book

Within generative grammar this observation has been treated as either the result of morphological principles or syntactic principles.

Brame (1977:388) (and a similar approach is taken in Koster 1978:132) seems to suggest that a morphological approach must be advocated. The examples in (1) are excluded because anaphors like *themselves* or *each other* are intrinsically marked <+objective> and the subject position in English requires a <–objective> pronominal. That is, (1) is excluded for the same reason as *Him reads the book* is excluded. Clearly such a proposal misses the point. Although it might seem uncontroversial to assume that *himself* is, like *him*, intrinsically marked objective, the question, however, is why personal pronouns do have a "nominative - non-nominative" opposition like *him - he* while reflexive pronouns do not have this opposition, *himself - *heself*. The only meaningful interpretation of Brame's proposal is that there is some morphological principle that excludes the potential availability of nominative reflexives, or reciprocals for that matter. We could call this the morphological gap theory (cf. Maling 1984; Anderson 1986).

We can distinguish two types of syntactic approaches. In the first type the non-existence of nominative anaphors is attributed to that module of grammar that is responsible for the distribution of anaphors and pronominals, the binding theory (cf. Chomsky 1981; Rizzi 1982; Everaert 1986). The second type tries to explain this phenomenon by means of an independently motivated principle of grammar (cf. Kayne 1984; Johnson 1984; Chomsky 1986).

In Chomsky (1981), for instance, the ungrammaticality of (1) is the result of a violation of binding condition A of the binding theory. This condition requires that anaphors have to be bound within a limited domain, their governing category:

(2) α is a governing category for β if and only if α is the minimal
      category containing β, a governor of β and a subject accessible to β

For our purpose the notion "accessible subject" in (2) can be summarized as: subject of clause or a <+Tense, AGR>-marked Infl-node. For (1), this will mean that the anaphors *themselves/each other* must be bound in the embedded clause as (3), part of the structure of the embedded clause in (1), will make clear why:

(3)   that [$_S$ [each other/themselves]$_{NP}$ INFL   VP]
                              <+Tense, AGR>

In (3), S is the governing category for an anaphor in subject position because S is the minimal category that contains the anaphor, the governor of the anaphor and an accessible subject for the anaphor - in both cases the <+Tense, AGR>-marked Infl node. The anaphor is not bound by an argument NP within this governing category and, thus, the binding theory is violated.

Crucial in this analysis is that a finite Infl-node is taken as an accessible subject, thus limiting the domain of interpretation of the anaphor. In Chomsky (1986:175-176) it is suggested that one should drop this extended notion of accessible subject, limiting oneself to "real" subjects. As a consequence, the matrix clause in (1) will be the governing category for the anaphor because only the matrix subject *they* will count as an accessible subject. It is now, wrongly, predicted that (1) would be grammatical. Chomsky, therefore, assumes that sentences like (1) are not excluded as a violation of the binding theory but as a violation of another principle of grammar, the empty category principle (ECP), partly following a line of reasoning first advocated by Kayne (cf. Kayne 1984). He argues that anaphors undergo movement at logical form (LF) to an Infl-node, leaving a trace subject to the empty category principle. The empty category principle requires that empty categories are properly governed where proper government could be defined as either i) lexical government or ii) antecedent government. Under such a scenario, the relevant part of the representation of (1) in logical form would be as in (4):

(4)   They$_i$ each other$_i$/themselves$_i$-INFL [$_{VP}$ think [$_{S'}$ that [$_S$ e$_i$ INFL VP]]]

The empty category in the embedded subject position in (4) is neither antecedent governed nor lexically governed and, hence, the empty category principle is violated. Clearly, this is an example of the second type of approach where a principle separate from binding theory is held responsible for the non-existence of nominative anaphors.

For an example as in (1), the morphological and the syntactic approaches sketched above make the same predictions. The reason is that, in English, subject NPs are always nominative NPs of tensed clauses. Suppose, however, that a language has nominative objects or non-nominative subjects. In that case the syntactic approaches would predict that the former but not the latter could be an anaphor while the predictions are reversed for the morphological approach. Such a language would, thus, offer us decisive evidence to choose between the morphological and the syntactic approaches sketched above. Icelandic seems to be a case at hand.

2. Icelandic reflexivization

Within the version of the government-binding framework in Chomsky (1981), the distribution of lexical anaphors is solely accounted for by the binding theory. The binding theory states that an anaphor must be bound within a limited domain, i.e. its governing category (cf. 2), while a pronominal is free in that same domain:

(5)   a. An anaphor must be bound in its governing category
      b. A pronominal must be free in its governing category

As a result, anaphors and pronominals should be in complementary distribution. In simplex sentences, this prediction is borne out as is, for instance illustrated by the examples from Icelandic in (6):[2]

(6)   a. Jón$_i$ elskar sig$_i$
      b. *Jón$_i$ elskar hann$_i$
         (John loves himself/him)

As a rule, Icelandic has clause-bound reflexivization, (cf. 7a), but the domain of interpretation for bound anaphors is extended in the case of subjunctive clauses, (cf. 7b), and in these cases the complementary distribution between anaphors and pronominals is neutralized (cf. Thráinsson 1979):

(7)   a. Jón$_i$ veit   að María elskar   *sig$_i$/hann$_i$
         John knows that Mary loves [ind] himself/him
         (John knows that Mary loves him)
      b. Jón$_i$ segir að   María elski   sig$_i$/hann$_i$
         John says that Mary loves [subj] himself/him
         (John knows that Mary loves him)

On the basis of (7) it can be concluded that, for Icelandic, the notion governing category is sensitive to the distinction indicative vs. subjunctive. However, a reformulation of this kind faces at least one serious observational problem: extending the domain of anaphoric interpretation for subjunctive complements will permit every NP-position in these complements to be accessible to reflexivization. As a result, one would wrongly predict that (8) would be grammatical:

(8)   *Jón$_i$ segir að REFL$_i$ elski   Maríu
       John says that REFL [nom] loves [subj] Mary

This problem has been noted in Kayne (1984) who suggests a way out. In his view, the so-called nominative reflexive in (8) is not excluded by means of some condition on the binding theory but by means of the "connectedness condition", a condition on the distribution of empty categories. Roughly speaking, the analysis boils down to the following: empty categories and lexical anaphors must be connected with their antecedents. In order to be "connected", empty categories and lexical anaphors must at least be canonically governed. For the discussion here, it is sufficient to note that (nominative) subjects are not canonically governed but that all objects are. Thus, (8) is excluded by the connectedness condition, while (7b) is not. Kayne's analysis presupposes i) a parallel between anaphors and bound variables and ii) a subject/object asymmetry for the connectedness requirement. Everaert (1986:171-172) discusses the viability of the former assumption; Maling (1984:215-219) questions the second assumption.

   Maling presents several arguments against Kayne's syntactic proposal to account for the non-existence of nominative anaphors by means of his connectedness analysis (and the same arguments would hold against Chomsky's analysis based on the empty category principle). She points out that, although (8) is correctly excluded in the connectedness analysis, it is not clear why non-nominative anaphors in subject position are not disallowed in such an analysis:[3]

(9) Hún_i   sagði að sér_i   þætti   vænt um mig
     She [nom] said   that herself [dat] was [subj] fond of me
     (She said that she was fond of me)

Moreover, Icelandic allows nominative NP's in what appears to be an object position. A reflexive in that position is excluded:

(10) *Henni_i finnst REFL_i   veik
     Her [dat] finds REFL [nom] sick
     (She considers herself sick)

Within a syntactic analysis, one would expect (10) to be grammatical since the nominative reflexive seems to be canonically governed by the verb; but in fact it is ungrammatical. Maling, furthermore, observes that the non- existence of nominative anaphors does not hold for possessive reflexives. Compare, for instance, (10) with (11):[4]

(11) Honum_i líkar bíllinn sinn_i /*hans_i
     Her [dat] likes his own [nom]/his [nom] car
     (She likes his car)

She argues that, for Icelandic, there is no syntactic approach available that can account for the non-existence of nominative anaphors and that the locus for an explanation for this phenomenon should be morphology. The non-existence of nominative non-possessive reflexives in Icelandic might be simply a gap in the reflexive paradigm.

Whatever the right solution may be, the examples above make clear that the discussion is about nominative vs. non-nominative anaphors and not about anaphors in subject position vs. object position. Any approach that is based on that same subject/object asymmetry is bound to fail.

3. Reciprocals in Icelandic

We have just seen that one might account for the observation that Icelandic does not have nominative (non-possessive) reflexives by means of the assumption that the reflexive paradigm has a gap. This immediately raises the question of what is to be expected in the case of reciprocals; does Icelandic have nominative reciprocals or does the reciprocal paradigm also have a gap? Before we can answer that question properly, something more needs to be said about the behaviour of reciprocals in Icelandic.

First of all it must be noted that reciprocals do not allow extension of their binding domain as is the case with reflexives (cf. 9), but are always clause-bound (cf. Thráinsson 1979; Anderson 1986).

(12) *þeir$_i$ telja   að hvorum   öðrum$_i$ þyki vænt um mig
     They [nom] believe that each [dat] other [dat] feels fond of me

This is important, because it means that nominative reciprocals are only to be expected in nominative object positions and not in nominative subject positions of tensed clauses (cf. 8). In the latter case the clause-boundedness constraint on the binding of reciprocals would be violated.

According to Thráinsson (1979:326, fn. 24), the Icelandic reciprocal consists of two indefinite demonstrative pronouns, *hvor* and *annar*, roughly meaning "one of (both)" and "the other, another". Both parts have their own agreement restrictions. As far as number and gender are concerned, they agree with the antecedent. Case marking, however, is different. For some native speakers the *hvor* part agrees in Case with the subject and the *annar* part takes the Case of the position the reciprocal occupies, the "split Case reciprocal" as I will call it (cf. 13a). Other native speakers, however, do not allow Case agreement with the antecedent and take the same Case for both *hvor* and *annar*, the "like Case reciprocal" (cf. 13b) (cf. Thráinsson 1979:129, fn. 23). The split Case reciprocal variant is usually taken as standard.

(13) a. The split Case reciprocal
             hvor   *annar*
         (Case agreement with antecedent)   (variable Case)
               (number agreement with antecedent)
               (gender agreement with antecedent)

b The like Case reciprocal
>   *hvor*   *annar*
>   (variable Case)   (variable Case)
>   (number agreement with antecedent)
>   (gender agreement with antecedent)

So, for instance, both (14a) and (14b) can be used:

(14) a. þeir$_i$ elska hvor   annan$_i$
     They love one [nom] another [acc]
   b. þeir$_i$ elska hvorn   annan$_i$
     They love   one [acc] another [acc]
     (They love each other)

All native speakers who I consulted accepted both variants in (14) but most of them seemed to prefer the like Case reciprocal variant (14b).

It is important to note that these variants seem to be equivalent from a semantic point of view, but can be distinguished syntactically. For instance, if the verb takes a prepositional object the two forms behave differently. Schematically, the distribution of the reciprocal parts is as in (15) (the example is given with a nominative subject and a preposition governing accusative Case):[5]

(15) a. NP   V   hvor   prep   annan
       [nom]   [nom]   [acc]
   b. *NP   V   prep   hvor   annan
       [nom]   [nom]   [acc]
   c. *NP   V   hvorn   prep   annan
       [nom]   [acc]   [acc]
   d. NP   V   prep   hvorn   annan
       [nom]   [acc]   [acc]

From a distributional point of view, the split Case reciprocal seems to behave like French *l'un ..l'autre* or Italian *l'uno..l'altro* (cf. Belletti 1983) and the like Case reciprocal more like English *each other*.

For the issue under discussion the relevant question is: can a reciprocal occupy the nominative object position, i.e., does Icelandic have a nominative reciprocal? Judgements vary. Most native speakers seem to make a distinction between the two reciprocal variants:[6] the split Case reciprocal is excluded (cf. 16a,17a) while the like Case is accepted (cf. 16b,17b).[7,8]

(16) a. *þeim$_i$ leiðist   hvorum annar$_i$
        Them [dat] find boring one [dat] another [nom]
        (They find each other boring)
     b. þeim$_i$ leiðist   hvor   annar$_i$
        Them [dat] find boring one [nom] another [nom]
        (They find each other boring)

(17) a. *þeim$_i$ finnst hvorum annar$_i$ (vera) skrýtinn
        Them [dat] find   one [dat] another [nom] (be) strange
     b. þeim$_i$ finnst hvor   annar   skrýtinn
        Them [dat] find   one [nom] another [nom] strange
        (They consider each other to be strange)

What might be the reason that the two reciprocal variants behave differently? Observe that both reciprocal variants seem to behave the same in other contexts (cf. Thráinsson 1979:439, fn.13) so it seems justified to say that both are subject to something like the binding condition A restriction.[9] In a binding theory based syntactic approach it is thus to be expected that both variants are ungrammatical. Condition A applies to both reflexives and reciprocals and if nominative reflexives are to be excluded as a condition A violation, the same should hold for reciprocals, contrary to fact in the case of (16a) and (17a). The only way to explain in a syntactic approach why most native speakers make a difference between (16a,17a) and (16b,17b), is to assume that all these sentences are excepted as far as binding theory is concerned (for instance by the hypothesis that reciprocals as such are *not* anaphors and thus not subject to binding condition A (cf. Heim-Lasnik-May 1988) but that the a-sentences in (16) and (17) are excluded on independent grounds. I will briefly sketch such a hypothetical analysis.

Above I noted that the Icelandic split Case reciprocal, but not the like Case reciprocal, might be analyzed as a discontinuous reciprocal in the sense of Belletti (1983). In such an analysis the second conjunct *annar* in (16a) and (17a) is an anaphor which is locally bound by the first conjunct *hvorum*, while both conjuncts taken together form a small clause. *Hvorum*, in its turn, would have the status of a quantified NP and be obligatorily moved at logical form to a nearby subject. This would result in the representations (18):

(18) a. [hvorum_i [þeim_i] [leiðist [e_i [annar_i]]]
      one [dat]   them [dat] find   boring another [nom]
    b. [hvorum_i [þeim_i]] finnst [e_i [annar_i]]   skrýtinn
      one [dat]   them [dat] find   another [nom] strange

Now suppose, contrary to Belletti's analysis, that (18a) and (18b) are not the representations of (16a) and (17a) at logical form but, in fact, the D(eep)-structure representations, and that (16a) and (17a) are the result of "quantifier-float" of *hvorum* (cf. Dougherty 1970). Such an analysis would give a straightforward account for the fact that the *hvor*-part of the split Case reciprocal agrees in Case with the antecedent. The ungrammaticality of these examples might then be attributed to a violation of the conditions on quantifier-float (and Case agreement, cf. fn. 9). I will not pursue this approach here any further.

Are the grammaticality judgements in (16) and (17) to be expected in a morphological gap theory? This depends on the answer to the question why nominative reflexives do not exist. Suppose one would suggest that there was little "need" for clause-bound nominative *reflexives* because very few verbs take nominative objects as in (16) and (17). If that is so, there is, at first sight, no reason to expect nominative reciprocals to behave differently from reflexives. However, since both *hvor* and *annar* have nominative forms, independently, all the ingredients for a nominative reciprocal are there, for free so to speak. Thus, the like Case variant is certainly not unexpected in a morphological gap theory. But the same is predicted for the split Case variant, contrary to fact.[10]

For the moment, I am reluctant to draw firm conclusions with respect to the different morphological and syntactic theories, because what is said above touches only the surface of the complex semantics and distributional peculiarities of reciprocals in Icelandic which I have not been able to study in detail.

4. The reflexive paradigm

Let us, for the moment, ignore the observational problems for the different approaches and compare them in view of the consequences they have for the reflexive paradigm. This will allow us to discuss an approach that has been ignored up untill now, the suppletion approach.

What does it mean to say that Icelandic does not "have" a non-possessive nominative reflexive if we look at the reflexive paradigm? In both types of syntactic approaches it means: a nominative reflexive might "exist" but it is generally filtered out, just as, for instance, a lexical pronominal anaphor is always filtered out by a combination of binding theory and Case theory. If, for some reason, the filter does not work in a particular construction or in a particular language, nominative reflexives should appear. So, there is no absolute barrier against the presence of nominative reflexives (or reciprocals).

(19) Syntactic   nominative   accusative   genitive   dative
     approaches

                    REFL   sig   sin   sér

In any morphological gap approach it is clear what the reflexive paradigm in Icelandic looks like: there is simply no nominative form available.

(20) Morphological nominative   accusative   genitive   dative
     gap approach
                    ——   sig   sin   sér

The morphological gap approach moves the burden of explanation to morphology and leaves the explanation to future research. The best one can do is to give a plausibility argument for why the gap is there, as, for instance, Maling (1984) has done. In a footnote she suggests a functional explanation which runs as follows: i) It may have been the case that in an earlier stage of Icelandic reflexivization was clause bounded, i.e., was limited to the minimal finite clause (but cf. Sigurðsson 1986); ii) there were only a few verbs taking nominative objects and, as a consequence, there was little or no need for a reflexive form in the nominative Case; iii) with the appearance of non-clause-bounded reflexivization - a new grammatical function in Maling's view - the need for a nominative reflexive increased, in principle; (iv) still, the use of the incomplete reflexive paradigm for clause-bounded reflexivization was extended to this new grammatical function.

This reconstruction is unsatisfactory in several respects. Johnson (1984) has pointed out, correctly to my mind, that since there appear to be no nominative reflexive pronouns across so many languages, it seems unlikely that this morphological gap re-occurs.[11] Moreover, although it is difficult to find plausible examples of nominative objects, they do exist all the same (see section 5). The question of "need" could therefore better be rephrased as a question "how marked" this morphological gap is in a morphological theory. Furthermore, a crucial assumption in the discussion of Icelandic reflexivization is the distinction between (clause-bounded) reflexivization and (non-clause-bound) logophoricity, both making use of the same defective paradigm. Exactly this distinction between clause-bounded and non-clause-bounded "reflexivization" weakens the functional explanation. One could very well imagine a situation where the introduction of a new grammatical function in the grammar of Icelandic, i.e., logophoricity, gave rise to a logophoric pronoun paradigm, in many respects equal to the reflexive paradigm but including a newly created nominative form. The very fact that reflexivization and logophoricity are distinct strategies makes it unlikely that logophoricity did not create a nominative form. Finally, one might wonder why nominative possessives do exist in view of the functional explanation sketched above.

The morphological gap approach still seems to be the best we have if other, syntactic, approaches fail on an observational level. As it stands, this seems to be the case, but in section 7 we will show that a syntactic approach that is observationally adequate is feasible.

In the approaches just discussed it is taken for granted that nominative reflexives in Icelandic (or any other Germanic or Romance language) "do not exist". But is it correct to say that Icelandic does not have a nominative reflexive? The statement is true in the sense that there is no nominative (non-possessive) reflexive form that is somehow morphologically recognizable as "reflexive". But that does not necessarily mean that there is no nominative reflexive form. Suppose that the nominative position in the reflexive paradigm is "filled" by a suppletive form, for instance the nominative form of the personal pronoun paradigm, as is suggested in Sigurðsson (1986). We would then have a reflexive paradigm as in (21):

(21) Suppletion
approaches

	nominative	accusative	genitive	dative
	hann/hun/etc	sig	sin	ser

Sigurðsson argues that such a proposal is supported by the fact that the first and second person reflexive paradigms also show suppletion (cf. also Thráinsson 1976b). Observe, for instance, the examples below from Sigurðsson (1986) where *mig* is used as an anaphor (22a) or a pronominal (22b):

(22) a. Ég meiddi mig
(I hurt myself)
b. Jón meiddi mig
(John hurt himself)

Is it possible to distinguish the approaches discussed above on an observational level and determine whether one of these is on the right track? Up untill now the discussion was concerned with the distribution of reflexives and reciprocals. However, as we will see below, the approaches discussed in this section make different predictions in the case of the distribution of pronominals, i.e., the behaviour of pronominals with respect to condition B. The following section will make clear that, at first sight, a syntactic binding theory-based approach and a suppletion approach are superior to a morphological gap approach and other syntactic approaches on this point.

5. Condition B

Thráinsson (1979) has shown that, in general, anaphors and pronominals in Icelandic are in perfect complementary distribution in simple sentences (cf. also 5b) and small clause complements:

(23) a. *Henni$_i$ virðist hana$_i$ vanta peninga
Her [dat] seems her [acc] lack   money
b. Henni$_i$ virðist sig$_i$ vanta peninga
Her [dat] seems herself [acc] lack money
(She seems to herself to lack money)

(24) a. *Jón$_i$ lét   mig raka hann$_i$
John [nom] made me   shave him [acc]
b. Jón$_i$ lét   mig raka   sig$_i$
John [nom] made me   shave himself [acc]
(John made me shave him)

Suppose we have a structure where a nominative anaphor has to be "close"- bound, that is, in configurations comparable to (23) and (24):

(25) *Honum_i finnst REFL_i   veikur
     Him [dat] finds   REFL [nom] sick
     (He considers himself sick)

(26) *Honum_i sýndist REFL_i   vera að tapa
     Him [dat] seemed REFL [nom] be   to lose
     (It seemed to him that he was losing)

(27) *Maríu_i   leiðist REFL_i
     Maria [dat] finds boring REFL [nom]
     (Maria finds herself boring)

(28) *Jón_i telur   mér finnast REFL_i   skrýtinn
     John believes me find REFL [nom] strange
     (John believes me to consider him strange)

As we have already noted, these sentences are ungrammatical. But what will
happen if we put a pronominal coreferent with the designated subject in the
position of the nominative anaphor in (25) to (28)? The fact is that in such cases
pronominals are possible:[12,13]

(29) Honum_i   finnst ?hann_i/hann sjálfur (vera) skrýtinn
     Him [dat] finds he/he himself [nom] (be)   strange
     (He considers himself strange)

(30) Honum_i   sýndist hann_i/(?)hann_i sjálfur vera að tapa
     Him [dat] seemed he/he himself [nom] be   to lose
     (It seemed to him that he was losing)

(31) Maríu_i   leiðist   *hún_i/hún_i   sjálf
     Maria [dat] finds boring she/she   herself [nom]
     (Maria finds herself boring)

(32) Jón_i telur   mér   finnast hann_i/?hann_i sjálfur skrýtinn
     John believes me [dat] find he/he himself [nom]   strange
     (John believes me to consider him strange)

How is one to account for this apparent violation of condition B? In a morphological gap approach, the binding theory is rendered inoperative in the case of
nominative anaphors but not with respect to nominative pronominals. So, without

additional principles, it is to be expected that these sentences are ungrammatical because of a condition B violation of the binding theory, as was the case in (23) and (24).[14] For syntactic approaches no uniform answer can be given, it depends on the precise formulation of the theory. In an approach based on binding theory the grammaticality of (29) to (32) is to be expected. If a nominative reflexive in object position is excluded as a violation of binding condition A, a nominative pronominal in that position will automatically be permitted under the assumption of complementary distribution between anaphors and pronominals (cf. section 7). If a principle of grammar separate from binding theory (empty category principle/connectedness constraint) is to be held responsible for the non-existence of nominative anaphors it is not clear whether the pronominal variants will be excluded. If the principle only applies to anaphors, as was the case in Kayne's connectedness analysis and Chomsky's ECP-approach, (29) to (32) are predicted to be ungrammatical due to a violation of condition B of the binding theory. Finally, in a suppletion approach there is, at first sight, no difference between the reflexive variant, i.e., (25) to (29) with *hann* substituted for REFL, and the (supposedly) pronominal variant (29) to (32). We are free to choose either the pronominal or the anaphor, which happen to have the same form. Parallel to (23) and (24), the pronominal *hann* would be excluded and, consequently, the anaphoric *hann* would be accepted by the binding theory.

We can, thus, conclude that the grammaticality of (29) to (32) contradicts the morphological gap approach and a Connectedness/ECP-type syntactic approach but might support a binding theory-based syntactic approach or a suppletion approach. In the next section we will compare the latter two.

6. Hann/hún/etc.: pronominals or anaphors in disguise?

Observe that the binding theory-based syntactic approach and the suppletion approach both predict (29) to (32) to be grammatical, but for different reasons. In a suppletion approach (29) to (32) contain an anaphor *hann/hann sjálfur* while the binding theory approach predicts that these sentences contain a pronominal *hann/hann sjálfur*. In 6.1. to 6.4. we will discuss some phenomena that should allow us to choose between the conflicting hypotheses.

6.1. Bound variable versus pragmatic coreference interpretation

Reinhart (1983,1986) observes that regular pronouns in the c-command domain of a definite NP allow a bound variable interpretation with respect to that NP, while, in such a configuration, a pragmatic coreference interpretation is also possible for these pronouns; of course, anaphors allow only a bound variable interpretation. What is meant by bound variable interpretation and pragmatic coreference interpretation can be best illustrated with the help of a VP-deletion context as in (33):

(33) John hopes that I like him and Peter does too
    a. bound variable interpretation
       = John hopes that I like John and Peter hopes that I like Peter
    b. pragmatic coreference interpretation
       = John hopes that I like John and Peter hopes that I like John

Reflexives allow a bound variable interpretation only:

(34) John likes himself and Peter does too
    a. bound variable interpretation
       = John likes John and Peter likes Peter
    b. pragmatic coreference interpretation
       ≠ John likes John and Peter likes John

Let us now turn to the examples under discussion here. It appears that in the case of nominative object pronouns, native speakers either allow only a pragmatic coreference reading (cf. [35b] and [36b]) or allow both a bound variable interpretation (35a) and (36a) and a pragmatic coreference reading (35b) and (36b):[15]

(35) Jóni$_i$ finnst hann$_i$ (sjálfur)   vera skrýtinn og Haraldi$_j$ líka
    John [dat] finds he (himself) [nom] be   strange and Harald [dat] too
    (John thinks he is strange and Harald thinks it too)
    a. bound variable interpretation
       = John thinks John is strange and Harald thinks Harald is strange
    b. pragmatic coreference interpretation
       = John thinks John is strange and Harald thinks John is strange

(36) Jóni$_i$ sýndist hann$_i$ (sjálfur)   vera að tapa og Haraldi$_j$ líka
    John [dat] seems he (himself) [nom] be   to lose and Harald [dat] too
    (It seemed to John that he was losing and it seemed to Harald too)

a. bound variable interpretation
  = It seemed to John that John was losing and it seems to Harald that
  Harald was losing
b pragmatic coreference interpretation
  = It seemed to John that John was losing and it seems to Harald that
  John was losing

This clearly indicates that the nominative pronoun in (35) and (36) is a pronominal and not an anaphor because if it were an anaphor the pragmatic coreference reading should not have been available. The fact that some speakers allow a pragmatic interpretation only still has to be explained but it is not incompatible with the pronominal-hypothesis.

6.2. The position of the emphatic pronoun[16]

It is a well-known fact in the grammar of Icelandic that the emphatic pronoun *sjálfur* (self) follows an ordinary pronominal but precedes a reflexive (example from Thráinsson 1979:83):

(37) a. Haraldur rakaði hann sjálfan
        (Harald shaved him)
    b. Haraldur rakaði sjálfan sig
        (Harald shaved himself)

If the pronouns in (29) to (32) were actually "reflexives in disguise" it would require a separate statement to account for the fact that the emphatic element has to follow the (reflexive) pronoun in these cases.

6.3. Split antecedents

It is generally accepted that anaphors do not have split antecedents, while pronominals do. If this is so, an object nominative pronoun should allow split antecedents if it is really a pronominal, but not if it is a reflexive in disguise.

In sentences like (38a), the third person plural nominative pronoun *þeir* (masculine) can refer (in principle) to either the matrix subject or the embedded subject; a split antecedant reading as in (38b) is excluded, however.

(38) a. Feður$_i$ telja   sonum$_j$ finnast þeir$_{i/j}$ skrýtnir
Fathers [nom] believe sons [dat] find   they [nom] strange
(Fathers believe that sons consider them/themselves strange)

     b. *Feður$_i$ telja   sonum$_j$ finnast þeir$_{i+j}$ skrýtnir
Fathers [nom] believe sons [dat] find   they [nom] strange
(Fathers believe that sons consider them (=fathers and children)
strange)

Only three native speakers were consulted on this point but none of them accepted the split antecedent reading, which would point in the direction of an anaphoric status of þeir.

However, it is not clear how much value must be attached to this conclusion. It is very hard to come up with the right environment to test the predictions. Several factors interfere. First of all people tend to disambiguate. For instance, one native speaker allowed þeir in (38) to corefer with the matrix subject but not with the embedded subject (cf. [39a] and [39b]) although the same native speaker found the latter reading possible in isolation (cf. 39c):

(39) a. Feður$_i$ telja   að   sonum$_j$ finnist þeir$_i$ skrýtnir
     b. *Feður   telja   að   sonum$_j$ finnist þeir$_j$ skrýtnir
Fathers [nom] believe that sons [dat] find   they [nom] strange
(Fathers believe that sons consider them/themselves strange)

     c. ?Honum$_i$ finnst hann$_i$ (vera) skrýtinn
Him [dat] finds he [nom] (be)   strange)
(He considers himself strange)

Furthermore, people tend to prefer one of the pronominal options (cf. fn. 10) and that can vary for "close" or "non-close" antecedents:

(40) a. Honum$_i$ finnst ?hann$_i$/hann$_i$ sjálfur (vera) skrýtinn
Him [dat] finds he [nom]   (be)   strange)
(He considers himself strange)

     b. Jón$_i$ telur   mér   finnast hann$_i$/?*hann$_i$ sjálfur (vera) skrýtinn
John believes me [dat] find   he [nom]   (be)   strange
(John believes me to consider him strange)

6.4. Topicalization

It has been frequently observed that there is a difference in acceptability in the case of topicalization of anaphors or pronominals. Anaphors can in general be topicalized without change in grammaticality, while topicalization of a pronominal usually gives a less grammatical outcome compared to the non-topicalized version. For the sentences that I have checked one can state that topicalization of a reflexive reduces grammaticality but is still acceptable, while topicalization of a pronominal leads to complete ungrammaticality (see also Zaenen 1980:23 on this point).[17]

(41) a. Ég sagði að   Jóni$_i$ virtist sig$_i$ (sjálfan) vanta peninga
      I   said that John [dat] seemed himself [acc] lack money
      (I said that John seemed to himself to lack money)

    b. ?Sig$_i$ sjálfan virtist   Jóni$_i$ e$_i$ vanta peninga
      Himself [acc] seemed John   lack money

    c. ??Sig$_i$ (sjálfan) sagði ég að   Jóni$_i$ virtist e$_i$ vanta peninga
      Himself [acc]   said I that John seemed lack money

(42) a. Ég heyrði frá   Jóni$_i$ að   María hefði kysst hann$_i$
      I   heard from John that Maria has kissed him [acc]
      (I heard from John that Maria has kissed him)

    b. *Hann$_i$ heyrði ég frá   Jóni$_i$ að   María hefði   kysst e$_i$
      Him [acc] heard I from John that Maria has [subj] kissed

Now observe what happens in the case of topicalization of nominative objects:

(43) a. Jóni$_i$ syndist hann$_i$ (sjálfur)   vera að tapa
      John [dat] seemed he (himself) [nom] be   to lose
      (It seemed to John that he was losing)

    b. *Hann$_i$ (sjálfur)   syndist Joni$_i$ e$_i$ vera að tapa
      He (himself) [nom] seemed John [dat] be   to lose

(44) a. Maríu$_i$ leiðist   hún$_i$ sjálf
      Maria [dat] finds boring she   herself [nom]
      (Maria finds herself boring)

    b. *Hún$_i$ sjálf   leiðist   Maríu$_i$ e$_i$
      She   herself [nom] finds boring Maria [dat]

In all cases, topicalization of the nominative object results in unacceptability, which seems to indicate that they are pronominals and not anaphors. However, the difference in unacceptability between (42b) on the one hand and (43b) and (44b) on the other does not warrant any firm conclusions on this point.

6.5. Conclusions

Our point of departure was the observation that nominative pronouns in object position can be clause-bound in apparent violation of condition B of the binding theory. What had to be determined was whether these pronouns were real pronominals or perhaps anaphors in disguise. Recall that the suppletion approach predicts that nominative object pronouns are anaphors (subject to condition A of the binding theory) while the binding theory-based approach predicts that they are pronominals (subject to condition B of the binding theory). The results indicate that these nominative object pronouns behave as pronominals. We can conclude from this that the suppletion approach cannot be the right approach. We had already concluded that the apparent condition B violations argue against a morphological gap approach or a Connectedness/ECP-type syntactic approach. This leaves us with the option of a binding theory-based syntactic approach.

7. A revised binding theory

In Everaert (1986) a binding theory has been developed which incorporates some of the insights of Kayne's connectedness approach into binding conditions of the type proposed in Chomsky (1981). The essentials of the theory are summarized in (45) to (47):

(45) a. An anaphor must be bound
      b. A pronominal must be free

(46) a. α is bound by β if and only if α and β are connected by a
government chain C, $C=(\tau_1,...,\tau_n)$, such that (i) the head τ_1 of C
governs β, (ii) the foot τ_n of C governs α, and (iii) α and β are
coindexed

b. α is free if and only if not bound

(47) Every link in the government chain connecting the anaphor/
pronominal to the antecedent is subject to a licensing requirement

I will now show that this particular version of the binding theory makes the right
predictions with respect to the Icelandic facts discussed above.

First we must say something more about the notion "licensing" in (47). We
propose that the lowest governor in a government chain - the one that governs the
anaphor/pronominal - is licensed if it is a c-governor. C-government is defined in
(48):

(48) α c-governs β if and only if α assigns Case to β, either directly or
indirectly

What is meant by indirect or direct Case-assignment can be illustrated by means
of (49a) to (49c):

(49) a. Hann$_i$ skaut sjálfan sig$_i$ með þessari byssu
He   shot   himself himself [acc] with shotgun this
(He shot himself with this shotgun)

b. Hann$_i$ hjálpaði aðeins sjálfum sér$_i$
He   helped   only   himself himself [dat]
(He helped only himself)

c. Hún$_i$ sagði að   sér$_i$ þætti   vænt um mig
She   said that herself [dat] was [subj] fond of me
(She said that she was fond of me)

In (49a) the object is assigned accusative Case as a result of structural Case-assignment and in (49b) the object is assigned dative Case lexically (cf. Maling -
Zaenen - Thráinsson 1985). In (49a) the verb is a c-governor for the object because
it assigns Case to it directly. Suppose that lexical Case-assignment is really
Case-assignment linked to the thematic role of a NP (cf. Aoun 1979). In (49b),
then, the verb will participate in assigning Case to the object because it is the
element that assigns the theta-role to the object. The same holds for (49c) under

the assumption that the subject is assigned dative Case lexically where this dative Case is linked to the external theta-role of the verb lexically. In Everaert (1986) it is argued that the external theta-role is assigned via the Infl-position and this will mean that, in our view, Infl will be a c-governor in such a case. Consequently the reflexive is properly connected to its antecedent via a government chain (cf. Everaert 1986 for further details).

Let us now turn to the examples mentioned in section 5 with a nominative object position:

(50) a. *Henni$_i$ finnst REFL$_i$ veik
       Her [dat] finds REFL [nom] sick
    b. Henni$_i$ finnst hún$_i$ veik
       Her [dat] considers she [nom] sick
       (She considers herself sick)

It has been argued that assignment of nominative Case in Icelandic actually signals lack of Case (cf. Andrews 1982,1988; Odijk 1984; see also Zwart 1988 and Weerman 1988 for the claim that nominative Case in (older versions) of Dutch signals lack of Case). That is, an NP is assigned nominative Case if not governed by a Case-assigner. If nominative Case in Icelandic is really lack of Case, it is evident that the governor of the nominative anaphor/pronominal does not count as a c- governor. As a result, the verb in (50) cannot be part of a government chain connecting the anaphor/pronominal to the subject, because it is not licensed. If it is not possible to create a legitimate government chain connecting the nominative anaphor to its antecedent in (50a), such an anaphor will never be bound according to the definition in (46a) and binding condition A is violated. In this approach nominative reciprocals are predicted to be ungrammatical if they are subject to the binding theory (but see also section 3). For nominative pronominals, the opposite will hold: since no legitimate government chain can be formed, the nominative pronominal is always free by definition (46b), which explains the grammaticality of (50b).

We are now left to explain why nominative possessives as in (51) do exist:

(51) a. Sigga$_i$ telur að mér líki vel nýja hjólið sitt$_i$
       Sigga thinks that me [dat] like [subj] a lot new bike [nom] her own [nom]
       (Sigga thinks that I like her new bike a lot)

b. Haraldur~i~ segir að bókin   sín~i~   sé   ennþá til sölu
   Harald   says   that book [nom] his own [nom] is [subj] still   for sale
   (Harald says that his book is still for sale)

Notice that the possessive in Icelandic agrees with its head in Case. Somehow the Case, or the lack of Case, of the head of the noun is transmitted to the possessive:

(52) a. Maríu líkar nýja penninn   minn
        Maria likes new pen [nom] my [nom]
        (Maria likes my new pen)
     b. María bað   Ólaf pennans míns
        Maria asked Olaf pen [gen] his [gen]
        (Maria asked Olaf his pen)

We will take this agreement phenomenon to indicate that nouns in Icelandic act as indirect Case-assigners. This will mean that the nouns in (51) in fact c-govern the possessive anaphors, even though no real Case is assigned in these cases, establishing a government chain between the anaphors and their antecedents.

8. Nominative Case

Whatever analysis is chosen, it seems that, for the present discussion, nominative Case assignment has to be set apart from all other types of Case-assignment and, above, this was a result of the assumption that nominative Case meant "lack of Case". In this section I shall discuss why.

In the generative literature diverse positions have been taken with respect to nominative Case-assignment. Babby (1980) and Andrews (1982), for instance, adopt the Jakobsonian view that nominative Case signals lack of Case. They differ slightly, though, on how nominative Case is related to accusative Case. For Babby both nominative and acccusative Case mark the absence of Case, i.e., depending on its structural position, a Caseless NP is marked nominative or accusative. Andrews seems to make a distinction between the two Cases; accusative Case is introduced by an elsewhere condition while nominative Case is put in if no Case feature is assigned to an NP by any other Case-assigning mechanism, including the accusative-elsewhere rule. In Case theories of the government binding type there seems to be no fundamental difference between nominative Case or accusative Case (and oblique Case for that matter). In the Case-theory of Chomsky (1981,1986) nominative Case is assigned to an NP if governed by Infl and objective (=accusative) Case if governed by a [-N]-governor, in the case of verbs subject to subcategorization restrictions. Zaenen - Maling - Thráinsson (1985), working within a framework of lexical functional grammar, also seem to adhere to such a position. They assume that both nominative and accusative Case are assigned by a similar looking (universal) mechanism that is interpreted as an elsewhere condition. A fundamentally different position is taken in van Riemsdijk (1983) where nominative Case is predicted to be the unmarked and accusative Case the marked non-oblique Case form, just as dative Case is the unmarked oblique Case.

For the present discussion it is crucial that a fundamental difference is made between nominative Case on the one hand and all other Cases on the other. This excludes the Case theories of Babby, Zaenen et al. and van Riemsdijk, and Case theories along the lines of Chomsky (1981). Only in the position taken in Andrews (1982,1988), nominative Case is set apart as a case of "lack of Case", the "no Case hypothesis".[18]

One must still answer the question why it is reasonable to assume that nominative Case in Icelandic is "lack of Case". There seem to be at least two reasons for this assumption (cf. also Zwart 1988). First, it is generally taken that the left dislocated element in left dislocation structures is in a position of non-Case-assignment and in Icelandic, this NP is assigned nominative Case (cf. Thráinsson 1979, Zaenen 1980). Secondly, it seems to be the case that prepositions can assign any Case verbs can assign, except nominative Case (cf. Odijk 1983, Babby 1987). This is to be expected under the assumptions that prepositions are always there to assign some Case and nominative Case would be equivalent to no Case. Icelandic has prepositions governing accusative, dative and genitive Case but no prepositions that govern nominative Case.

It is important to note that it is not a priori the case that, in every language, nominative Case is a manifestation of no Case. In a language where it can be argued that nominative Case is a "normal" Case, one would expect nominative anaphors to exist; Albanian may be such a language (cf. Everaert in preparation). The other way around, if, for instance, it could be argued that dative Case is a manifestation of no Case in a particular language, it is predicted in this analysis that such a language would not have dative anaphors. See Everaert (in preparation) for a discussion of these predictions.

9. Conclusion

In this article several theories that try to account for "the non-existence" of (non-possessive) anaphors in Icelandic (and other Germanic languages) have been reviewed. Although none of them is fully observationally adequate, a binding theory based approach seems to be the best available. The binding theory approach introduced in Everaert (1986) and further developed above is one way to give a straightforward account for the (non-)distribution of nominative reflexives and pronominals.[19] This proposal makes crucial use of the Case-assigning properties of the governor of a reflexive/pronominal. However, reference to Case-assignment - or in fact the lack of Case-assignment - in this binding theory based approach does not seem to follow from independently needed considerations. This remains a desideratum.

Notes

1.　　I would like to thank the following people for helpful discussions and/or comments: Avery Andrews, Peter Coopmans, Erik Hoekstra, Joan Maling, Tanya Reinhart, Halldór Sigurðsson, Höskuldur Thráinsson. I am grateful to Helgi Bernódusson, Jona van Buren - Hjartar, Sigríður Sigurjónsdóttir, Halldór Sigurðsson and Höskuldur Thráinsson for their help in gathering data, their native judgements and their patience with my limited knowledge of Icelandic grammar. This paper was presented at the 5th workshop on Germanic syntax, Groningen University, May 18-20 1988; I would like to thank the organizers Werner Abraham and Eric Reuland for creating an inspiring atmosphere. Parts of this paper were presented at seminars of the University of Utrecht (25.9.1987) and Tilburg University (19.1.1988). I thank the audiences for critical and insightful remarks.

This research was made possible by a grant from the Niels Stensen foundation, which is hereby gratefully acknowledged.

2.   Maling (1986) observes that the complementary distribution between anaphors and pronominals in simplex sentences is neutralized in certain contexts.

3.   Cf. Thráinsson (1979), Zaenen et al. (1985) and Sigurðsson (1989) for arguments that these oblique NPs are subjects.

4.   In what follows I will continue to use the phrase "the non-existence of nominative reflexives" for convenience.

5.   There seems to be some variation as to the ungrammaticality of (15c). Some native speakers found examples as in (i) and (ii) acceptable:

         (i)   þeir töluðu um   hvor   annan

             They talked about one [nom] another [acc]

             (They talked about each other)

         (ii)   þeir lömdu í hvor   annan

             They hit   one [nom] another [acc]

6.   Five out of the six native speakers who were consulted made a clear difference between the two reciprocal variants; the one native speaker who did not make a difference between the two variants seemed to reject both.

7.   Höskuldur Thráinsson drew my attention to the fact that there seems to be some sort of semantic restriction on what counts as a "reciprocal enough" action for the Icelandic reciprocal to be possible. This might influence judgements on this point. Perhaps such a restriction is responsible for the fact that only three out of six native speakers accepted (ib).

         (i)   a.   *þeim$_i$ sýndist hvorum annar$_i$ vera að tapa

                They [dat] seemed each [dat] other [nom] be   to lose

                (They seemed to each other to be losing)

            b.   (*)þeim$_i$ sýndist hvor   annar$_i$ vera að tapa

                They [dat] seemed each [nom] other [nom] be   to lose

                (They seemed to each other to be losing)

8.   Observe that the restriction on the binding domain of reciprocals cannot be the explanation for the ungrammaticality of (17a) - where the reciprocal occupies the subject position of a small clause - because that would leave the ungrammaticality of (16a) unaccounted for.

9.   In an earlier version of his (1986)-paper Sigurðsson observed that the like Case reciprocal, but not the split Case reciprocal, might be long distant bound.

         (i)   þeir$_i$ skipuðu mér að raka hvorn   annan   /*hvor annan

             They [nom] ordered me to shave one [acc] another [acc] /one [nom] another [acc]

             (They ordered me to shave each other)

         (ii)   ?þeir$_i$ sögðu mér að ég ætti að raka hvorn annan   /*hvor annan

             They [nom] told me that I ought to shave one [acc] another [acc] / one [nom] another [acc]

             They told me that I ought to shave each other

     If we accept his judgements, the like Case reciprocal is not a clause-bounded anaphor as we assumed above (cf. 12). Sigurðsson suggests that the distributional differences between the two reciprocal variants might be attributed to Case theory.

10. Of course, a morphological gap theory also has resource to a quantifier movement analysis to account for the difference in grammaticality between the like Case variant and split Case variant.

11. I do not want to claim that no languages can be found that might have nominative anaphors (cf. Keenan 1988 and Everaert in preparation). But as far as the Germanic, Romance and Slavic languages are concerned the statement holds (and makes sense).

12. See also Maling (1984: ex. 53b).

13. In (29) to (32) I have given two readings, *she/he* and *she herself/he himself*, the latter a variant with an emphatic pronoun. As was pointed out in Thráinsson (1979:83), addition of an emphatic pronoun does not change grammaticality judgements in (i) and, for the moment, I assume the same holds for the examples in the text, i.e., addition of an emphatic pronoun does not have any fundamental effect on the status of the pronoun being subject to binding condition B (or A in the case of *sig*):

  (i) a. *Hann$_i$ rakaði hann$_i$
      b. *Hann$_i$ rakaði hann$_i$ sjálfan
        (He shaved him/him himself)

There is some variation across speakers about which form, the emphatic or the non-emphatic, is to be preferred. There is also variation across the examples, as will become clear in the text.

14. In a morphological gap approach one might take refuge to the view that binding condition B should be dispensed with and that, instead, some pragmatic principle is used to make the right choice between reflexives and pronominals (cf. Reinhart 1983:167). In such an analysis a pronominal would not have been chosen in a context where one could have chosen a reflexive. But for a nominative pronominal there is no reflexive variant so that the pragmatic principle does not apply and the pronominal is freely interpreted "as if it was a reflexive". However, as Reinhart (1983,1986) has argued, this is only a viable approach for the pragmatic coreference interpretation of pronominals. Binding condition B still holds in the case of a bound variable interpretation of pronominals.

Observe that the nominative pronouns in (i) and (ii) allow a bound variable interpretation only, and still there is an apparent condition B violation:

  (i) Hverjum$_i$/Engum$_i$ finnst hann$_i$ (sjálfur)   (vera) veikur
    Who/No one [dat] finds he   (himself) [nom]   sick
    (Who/No one considers himself sick)
  (ii) Hver$_i$/Enginn$_i$ telur   mér   leiðast   hann$_i$ (sjálfur)
    Who/No one believes me [dat] find boring he   (himself) [nom]
    (Who/No one believes me to find him boring)

15. There seems to be one exception. In the case of (35), three out of six native speakers seem to have a bound variable interpretation only for the emphatic variant *hann sjálfur*.

16. This argument was pointed out to me by Joan Maling.

17. I am not really concerned here with the reason why this would be so.

18.   This mechanism had better not be called default-Case (as I called it in Everaert 1986) because default Case assignment is often interpreted as unmarked Case assignment.

19.   It seems that the same results can be obtained by incorporating the licensing requirement into the standard binding theory (which would then have to be limited to lexical elements). All we have to do is change the standard definition of governing category as presented in (i) into (ii):

> (i) α is a governing category for β if and only if α is the minimal category containing β, a governor of β and a subject accessible to β
>
> (ii) α is a governing category for β if and only if α is the minimal category containing β, a proper governor of β and a subject accessible to β

The problem would then be that in such an approach a nominative anaphor does not have a governing category and will thus not be excluded by the binding theory. A similar problem occurs with sentences like *For each other to win would be unfortunate*. In Chomsky (1981) this was salvaged by adding the ad hoc principle (iii).

> (iii) A root sentence is a governing category for a governed element

This particular formulation would not work for the sentences under discussion, but a statement as in (iv) would do the job:

> (iv) The minimal S containing α is the governing category of α if α is not properly governed

Note, though, that (iv) does not offer a solution for the observed "condition B violation" in (29) to (32). The nominative pronominal in these sentences will have a governing category because of (iv) and, as a result, will cause a condition B violation.

References

Anderson, Stephen, R.
1986   "Types of dependency in anaphors: Icelandic (and other) reflexives", *Topics in Scandinavian Syntax* edited by Lars Hellan - Kirsti Koch Christensen (Dordrecht: Reidel).

Andrews, Avery
1982   "The representation of Case in modern Icelandic", *The mental representation of grammatical relations*, edited by Joan Bresnan (Cambridge, Mass.: MIT Press).
1988   "Case structures and control in modern Icelandic" (unpublished manuscript Australian National University).

Aoun, Joseph
1979   "On government, Case-marking and clitic placement" (Cambridge, Mass.: unpublished manuscript MIT).

Babby, Leonard
1987 "The syntax of surface Case marking", *Cornell Working Papers in Linguistics* 1
"Case, prequantifiers, and discontinuous agreement in Russian", *Natural Language & Linguistic Theory* 5, 91-138

Belletti, Adriana
1983 "On the anaphoric status of the reciprocal construction in Italian", *The Linguistic Review* 2: 101-138

Brame, Michael
1977 "Alternatives to the tensed S and specfied subject condition", *Linguistics & Philosophy* 1: 381-411

Chomsky, Noam
1981 *Lectures on government and binding* (Dordrecht: Foris).
1986 *Knowledge of language: Its nature, origin, and use* (New York: Praeger).

Everaert, Martin
1986 *The Syntax of reflexivization* (Dordrecht: Foris).
in prep. "Nominative Case and binding theory" (Tilburg: unpublished manuscript Tilburg University).

Hellan, Lars
1986 "Anaphora in Norwegian and theory of "binding", *Topics in Scandinavian syntax*, edited by Lars Hellan - Kirsti Koch Christensen (Dordrecht: Reidel).

Johnson, Kyle
1984 "Some notes on subjunctive clauses and binding in Icelandic", *MIT Working Papers in Linguistics* 6

Kayne, Richard
1984 *Connectedness and binary branching* (Dordrecht: Foris).

Keenan, Ed
1987 "On semantics and the binding theory" (Los Angeles: unpublished manuscript UCLA).

Koster, Jan
1978 *Locality principles in syntax* (Dordrecht: Foris).

Maling, Joan
1984 "Non-clause bounded reflexives in Icelandic", *Linguistics and Philosophy* 7: 211-241
1986 "Clause-bounded reflexives in modern Icelandic", *Topics in Scandinavian syntax*, edited by Lars Hellan - Kirsti Koch Christensen (Dordrecht: Reidel).

Odijk, Jan
1983 "On the non-existence of nominative anaphors" (Utrecht: unpublished manuscript University of Utrecht).

Reinhart, Tanya
1983 *Anaphora and semantic interpretation* (London: Croom Helm).

1986 "Center and periphery in the grammar of anaphora", *Studies in the acquisition of anaphora*, vol. 1, edited by Barbara Lust (Dordrecht: Reidel).

Sigurðsson, Halldór
1986 "Moods and (long distance) reflexives in Icelandic", *Working Papers in Scandinavian Syntax* 25

Thráinsson, Höskuldur
1976a "Some arguments against the interpretive theory of pronouns and reflexives", *Harvard Studies in Syntax and Semantics* 2
1976b "Reflexives and subjunctives in Icelandic", *Proceedings of NELS* 6 (Amherst: GLSA).
1979 *On complementation in Icelandic* (New York: Garland).

Van Riemsdijk, Henk
1983 "The Case of German adjectives", *Linguistic categories: Auxiliaries and related puzzles* Vol. 1, edited by Frank Heny - Barry Richards. (Dordrecht: Reidel).

Weerman, Fred
1988 "The V2 conspiracy: A synchronic and a diachronic analysis" (Utrecht: manuscript university of Utrecht).

Zaenen, Annie
1980 *Extraction rules in Icelandic*, doctoral dissertation (Cambridge, Mass.: Harvard University).

Zaenen, Annie - Joan Maling - Höskuldur Thráinsson
1985 "Case and grammatical functions: The Icelandic passive", *Natural Language & Linguistic Theory* 3: 441-483

Zwart, Jan Wouter
1988 "The first Case: The nominative as a default Case and consequences for control theory", master's thesis (Groningen: University of Groningen).

"To be" and indices[1]

Elly van Gelderen

In this paper, I discuss the indexing of pre-verbal and post-verbal NPs around the verb *to be* as in:

(1) It is me/It is them.

(2) There's John, Mary, me ...

(3) a. There's three men in the room.
     b. There are three men in the room.

In a government binding framework (cf. Chomsky 1981; 1986), a finite verb has a collection of features (person, gender and number) which is called AGR(eement). AGR assigns nominative Case to the subject it governs. There is a question as to how this assignment takes place. There are additional questions as to what element or position AGR co-indexes with for number agreement (cf. 1, 2 and 3a versus 3b) to be correct and how and which Case is assigned to the post-verbal NP.

In section 1, I outline some recent proposals (Borer 1983, 1986 and Chomsky 1981, 1986) on AGR-indexing and nominative Case assignment. In section 2, I discuss Safir's (1985) account of certain kinds of *to be* and in section 3, I examine two constructions that do not fit with Safir's proposal. On the basis of such constructions, I argue in section 4 that there are three kinds of *to be*, and account for their respective properties. In section 5, I show how some problematic sentences can be explained in this way.

1. Agreement and nominative Case: Borer (1983, 1986) and Chomsky (1981, 1986)

In this section, I give an overview of various recent proposals on subject-verb agreement as they are relevant to English. A lot of controversy has centered around the question how Case is assigned to post-verbal NPs (with unaccusative verbs): either it is assigned directly to the post-verbal NP or it is transmitted via the pre-verbal one, i.e. the [Spec, IP] position.

Chomsky (1981: 259) formulates a well-known rule that co-superscripts AGR(eement) with the NP it governs. Case assignment to the subject makes use of this co-indexation: nominative Case is assigned to an NP governed by and co-superscripted with AGR. (Later, Case assignment is replaced by Case checking, but that distinction is irrelevant here).

Borer (1983) assumes most of Chomsky's (1981) system (e.g. co-superscripting of AGR and [Spec, IP] and nominative Case assignment) but argues that a post-verbal NP as in (4a) and (4b) can freely pick an index:

(4) a. There's at least seven people in the garden (cf. 3)
     b. There are at least seven people in the garden

(Borer 1983: 242)

She assumes that the superscripting of the post-verbal NP is random. If the index of the post-verbal NP is not the same as that of the AGR (and of the pleonastic *there*), *be* will assign accusative Case to the post-verbal NP and will not agree with this NP. This is the situation in (4a). Construction (4a) violates Burzio's (1981) generalization (which states that a verb only assigns an accusative Case if it has an external argument) because *be* assigns accusative even though *there* is not an argument, but a pleonastic. If the index of the post-verbal NP is the same as the index of the AGR (and of *there*), then the form of *be* will agree with the post-verbal NP and the post-verbal NP will be assigned nominative Case. This is the case in (4b). *There* needs no Case since it forms an A-chain with the NP.

In Borer (1986: 401), the rule co-indexing the subject position and the AGR (as in Chomsky) is replaced by an obligatory rule requiring some NP (not necessarily the NP in [Spec, IP] to be co-indexed with the Infl position. Borer accounts for sentences such as (4a) where no agreement exists between the verb and the post-verbal NP by co-indexing the pleonastic with AGR. The latter receives nominative Case because it is co-indexed with AGR. The post-verbal NP receives accusative from *be*, since it is not co-indexed with AGR. She argues that the [Spec, IP] position in (4a) is not a theta-position even though claiming this violates Burzio's generalization (since accusative is assigned by the verb, it should have an external argument). In (4b), the post-verbal NP is co-indexed with AGR and will get nominative Case. This means that *there* in Borer (1986), unlike Borer (1983), is without Case in (4b), because no chain is formed. She does not comment on that problem, but one might say that Case is always needed for visibility reasons. As is obvious, there are quite a number of problems with Borer's account of (4) and in section 5 I propose a different solution to (4).

Following Safir (1985), Borer replaces co-superscripting with co-subscripting. Chomsky (1981) uses superscripts, because (unlike co-subscripts) they are exempt from binding relations. If they did enter into binding relations, sentences such as (4b) would be ungrammatical, since *seven people* would be bound to *there*. Borer (1986:388) argues that binding theory (i.e. condition C) only applies to NPs with i-features. *There* lacks such features and therefore is not relevant for binding relations. (*It* has i-features and cannot co-occur with a post-verbal co-indexed NP).

Apart from assuming certain elements to have i-features, there are other solutions to the possible binding violations in (4b). If reconstruction takes place at the level of logical form, and binding theory applies afterwards, there is no problem either. Rizzi (1982) argues that the binding of an argument by a non-argument is not subject to condition C. Safir (1985) argues that indefinite NPs (the only ones supposed to occur in sentences such as [4]) escape condition C at s-structure. Chomsky (1986: 75) no longer assumes superscripting either: the co-indexation of subject and Infl position is of the same kind as the one involved in movement. In sections 2 and 3, I outline some binding theory problems.

Chomsky (1986: 24) extends the relation between subject and AGR to the relation between the specifier of Infl and the Infl-position. This is referred to as specifier-head agreement. It means that the specifier of Infl and Infl share features (and I assume are co-indexed) regardless of the presence of AGR in Infl. When AGR is present, it shares with the subject its features person, number, gender, Case, etc; when AGR is missing, it shares with the subject an abstract feature. For Chomsky (1986), the subject position, i.e. the spec(ifier) of IP, is required perhaps by the extended projection principle. It is the position that is assigned the external theta-role in Williams (1981). Borer (1986) defines the notion of subject as the element that has a relationship with the Infl node. This element need not be the specifier of IP.

In section 1, I have sketched some differences between Borer and Chomsky with respect to the indexing of subject and Infl/AGR. In section 4, I account for some data involving indexing and Case marking by AGR. The data are first discussed in sections 2 and 3. I will conclude that AGR and [Spec, IP] are co-indexed.

2. Safir (1985)

As has often been noted, *to be* in one construction can be very different from *to be* in another construction. I will examine certain differences in syntactic properties, e.g. Case marking by *to be* and number of arguments. In this section, I discuss a classification as made, for instance, by Safir.[2]

Safir (1985: 116ff.) distinguishes between predicational and identificational *to be*, as in (5) and (6) respectively:

(5) a. John is a president
     b. John and Mary are presidents
     c. *John and Mary is president(s)
(6) a. John is the president
     b. John and Mary are the presidents
     c. *John and Mary is the president(s)

Unlike in sentences such as (4), in (5) and (6) number agreement between pre-verbal NP, post-verbal NP and the verb is obligatory. This will be discussed later. Safir, following Stowell (1978), argues that the structure of sentences such as (5) is (7), where *to be* subcategorizes for a S(mall) C(lause):

(7)   John$_i$ is [$_{SC}$ t$_i$ a president]

In (7), *John* moves because it needs Case (the Case filter or the visibility principle requires this, cf. Chomsky 1981). Sentences with existential *there* are analyzed similarly in that *to be* has one argument (an internal one) but does not assign Case.

Unlike *to be* in (5), *to be* in (6) has two arguments: an internal one (*the president*) and an external one (*John*). In (6), *John* gets Case from the AGR and *the president* gets Case from *to be*. So far, two differences between the *to be*'s were indicated: in (5), *to be* has one argument and assigns no Case, whereas in (6), it has two arguments and assigns one Case (as predicted by Burzio's generalization).

Safir (1985: 118) considers the *be* in sentences such as (8) as an instance of identificational *to be* and in fact uses the construction as evidence that identificational *be* assigns Case to the post-verbal NP. Since most speakers use *me, them*, etc., instead of *I, they*, etc., Case must be assigned by *be*. Safir argues:

(8)   a.   It is me
      b.   It is them
      c.   It is John[3]

With respect to 'list'-sentences with *there* and *to be* as in (9), Safir (1985: 119) argues as well that *to be* is identificational and not predicational. This means that sentences such as (8) and (9) have roughly the same analysis:

(9)   a.   There's John, Mary, me ...
      b.   There's (always) John

There, like *it* in (8), functions as an argument and not as a pleonastic. I come back to sentences (8) and (9) below and analyze them differently.

A third difference is that indefinites as in (5) do not refer and can only be used predicatively. Safir discusses this problem. The NP following an identificational *to be* as in (10a) can be definite, whereas the NP following a predicational *to be* as in (10b) cannot be definite:

(10) a.   I thought Shakespeare to be the author of *The Tempest*.
      b.   *I thought Shakespeare the author of *The Tempest*.

                         (Safir 1985: 118, examples 60a and 60b)

Safir argues that the two complements of *thought* are different. The *be* in (10a) is an identificational one that assigns Case to *the author of the Tempest*. *Shakespeare* gets Case from *thought*. The complement in (10b) consists of two NPs, one of which is the predicate that needs no Case (cf. the visibility principle, which requires only arguments to receive Case) and one that is subject to the predicate, but which is Case-marked by *thought*. Since a predicate cannot be definite, sentence (10b) is ungrammatical.

A fourth difference (cf. Safir 1985: 117) is that with identificational *to be* the two NPs can be reversed, while retaining their meaning, as in (11), but not with predicational *to be*, as in (12):

(11) The president is John

(12) *A president is John

So far, I have described four differences that Safir shows to exist between identificational *to be* and predicational *to be*. I now examine (5) and (6) in more detail.

3. *It is me* and *there's* ...

Safir argues that sentences such as (1) and (2) above are instances of identificational *to be*. I will argue that even though some properties are the same, others are different. In 3.1. I examine what kinds of elements *it* and *there* are (pronouns or expletives). This will not go against Safir's analysis. In 3.2. I look at the argument structure and Case marking abilities of *to be*; at whether or not in (1) and (2) the post-verbal NP can be definite; and whether or not the post-verbal NP agrees with the verb and the subject in number. Here, *to be* will be shown not to be identificational in sentences (1) and (2).

3.1. *It* and *there*

Are *it* and *there* pronouns or expletives in (1) and (2)? As noted above, Burzio (1981) points out that verbs Case mark their object if and only if they theta-mark a subject. This means that if one analyses (1) as in (13) below, i.e. without external argument, *be* would not assign Case and hence, an expletive (*it*) would be required to transmit Case to *me* as in (14). The post-verbal NP could also move as in (15). It would then be Case marked directly in subject position:

(13) e be I

(14) It is me

(15) I_i am t_i

One problem is that (14) and (15) are not variations of each other with the same basic meaning. Sentence (15) states that someone (*I*) exists, whereas sentence (14) answers the question: "Who is there?". If structure (13) were a possible d-structure, both sentences (14) and (15) would have to be possible derivations.

Another major problem with (13) is that (14) would be predicted to be ungrammatical. If *it* transmits its (nominative) Case, one would expect *I* instead of *me*.

There are other arguments to show that *it* is a pronoun. For instance, *it* can be questioned as in (16):

(16) Who t is me.   (e.g. a question in response to "it is me")

This extraction is impossible in sentences with expletives as in (17) or semi-arguments as in (18):

(17) a.   It was mentioned that she left
      b.   *What t was mentioned that she left

(18) a.   It rains
      b.   *What t rains

Because the trace in (17b) and (18b) is taken as a variable (and as having a thematic role), the theta-criterion is violated. A last difficulty with *it* as expletive in these sentences is that in other instances of expletive *it*, *it* forms a chain with a CP and not with an NP as in (1).

If *there* in sentences such as (2) were an expletive, the d-structure would be as in:

(19) e be [John, Mary, me ...]

Again following Burzio's observation (if verbs lack external arguments, they do not Case mark their object), the post-verbal NP must move in (19) or get Case from *there*. If expletive *there*, unlike expletive *it*, formed a chain with the NP argument, *there* would transmit its nominative Case to the post-verbal complex. Instead, the Case on *me* is clearly accusative and must therefore be assigned by *to be*. Sentences in which the post-verbal NP is nominative are ungrammatical:

(20) *There's I, John, ...

The conclusion is that *it* in (1) and *there* in (2) are not expletives, but pronouns, i.e., full-fledged arguments.

3.2. *To be*

What is the status of *to be* in (1) and (2)? Assuming *it* is not a pleonastic, there are two possible underlying structures for (1), namely (21) or (22):

(21) e be [it me]

(22) it be me

In (22), *be* is identificational, whereas in (21), it is predicational and *me* is the predicate of *it*. It is often assumed that only indefinite NPs can occur as part of a predicate (e.g. Safir) and that would rule out (21) because *me* is definite. Here, I show that there are syntactic reasons why structure (21) is ungrammatical and why, if *be* is identificational in (22), structure (22) is also. Sentence (1) would be derived from (21) as in:

(23) it$_i$ AGR be [$_{SC}$ t$_i$ me$_i$]

Since *it* is an argument of *me*, it is co-indexed with *me* (cf. Williams 1980, 1983). It is possible to argue that binding theory holds only of arguments, not of predicates. Thus, *me* in (23) does not violate condition (C). Assuming

[Spec, IP] to be co-indexed with AGR (but the co-indexation of any NP would have the same result), the verb would agree in number with the post-verbal NP because their indices are the same.

However, with sentences such as (1), number agreement does not occur:

(24) a   It is them.
   b. *It are them.

The data are the same with "list"-*there*:

(25) a. There's John, Mary, me, ...
   b. *There are John, Mary, me, ...

Therefore, *be* in these sentences is not predicational.

For sentences such as (22), Hornstein (1984: 92-93) argues that copular co-indexing co-indexes pre-verbal and post-verbal NP. One of his arguments is that this rule explains the ungrammaticality of (26), as opposed to the grammaticality of (27):

(26) a. *John$_i$ is his$_i$ cook
   b. *John$_i$ is $_{NP}$ [his$_i$ cook]$_i$

(27) a. John's$_i$ father is his$_i$ cook
   b. [John's father]$_j$ is [his cook]$_j$

If *John* and *his cook* are co-indexed in (26), an i-within-i violation will occur if *his* refers to *John* as shown in (26b). There is no such violation in (27), shown in (27b).

Perhaps related to copular co-indexing is the phenomenon shown in (11) and (12) above. In sentences without pronominals (i.e. where c-command is not relevant), the post-verbal and pre-verbal NPs are reversible without change in meaning. Also, the two arguments in (11) and (12) refer to the same person and it is not unexpected that this is somehow indicated.

I will assume copular co-indexing. One of the problems with copular co-indexing that Hornstein does not discuss is that sentences with identificational *to be*, such as (6) and (11), violate the binding theory (C): an R-expression must be free (A-free). *His cook* is not free in either (26) or in (27) because it is co-indexed with *John*. There are other violations of (C) involving names and NPs (cf. Higginbotham 1985; Lasnik 1976; Reinhart 1983a, 1983b). Intuitively, there is a difference between variables which must be bound to an element in an A'-position on the one hand and names and NPs which are generally not bound on the other. Condition C holds for variables, but not always as straightforwardly for names and NPs ("let Reagan be Reagan", "keep the mayor the mayor", etc.).[4]

I now return to the analysis of sentences such as (1) and (22). Assuming copular co-indexing takes place, the result, after AGR co-indexation, is as in:

(28) It$_i$ AGR$_i$ be me$_i$

However, in (1), *me* does not refer to *it* in the same way that *his cook* refers to *John* or to *John's father* in (26) and (27). Neither are the NPs in sentences such as (1) and (2) reversible:

(29) *Mary is it

(30) *John, Mary, me's it

If one wants to emphasize the post-verbal NP, this must be done as in:

(31) Mary, it is t

It is not possible to test j-within-i violations as in (26) and (27), since the pre-verbal *it* cannot serve as an antecedent for a pronominal in the post-verbal NP. Since the explanation for the ungrammaticality of (26) was one of the motivations for copular co-indexing, in sentences such as (1) and (2) there is no motivation to co-index the pre-verbal and post-verbal NPs.

The only result would be a binding theory violation, but without the advantages of explaining (26) and (27). In addition, as noted in section 2, there is a major difference between (1) and (2) on the one hand and identificational *to be* on the other, with respect to number agreement. If pre- and postverbal NPs are co-indexed, one would expect number agreement. I therefore assume *to be* in (1) and (2) to be neither identificational nor predicational *to be*. I will come back to this in section 4 in more detail.

A property that (5) and (6) share with identificational *to be* is that both can have a definite post-verbal NP:

(32) It is the merchant of Venice

(33) There is the vicar, the mayor, and the actor

In section 3, I have shown that *it* and *there* in sentences such as (1) and (2) are arguments and not pleonastics and that *to be* in these constructions is neither identificational nor predicational, but of a third variety. In section 4, I examine the indexing properties of the three kinds and account for the number agreement and Case marking.

4. *To be* and indexing

In this section, I discuss the indexing, agreement and Case marking properties of different *to be*'s in a more systematic way.

In sentences with identificational *to be* such as (34) and (35), the pre- and post-verbal NPs must agree in number:

(34) John is the president

(35) These men are the presidents

Assuming copular co-indexing takes place, the structure for (34) is as in (36). In (36), it makes no difference whether AGR is co-indexed with the subject position (i.e. with *John, these men*) or just with some NP as Borer (1986) argues. The result is as in (37) and number agreement follows:

(36) $[NP]_i$ AGR be $[NP]_i$

(37) NP_i AGR_i $[_{VP}$ be $NP_i]$

Assuming AGR Case marks an NP governed and co-indexed by it, nominative can be assigned to either of the two NPs. How can one make sure AGR assigns Case to the NP in [Spec, IP] position and not to the post-verbal NP, which gets accusative Case from *be*:

(38) The president is him. (while pointing out someone)

(39) You are me. (poetic)

If nominative Case were assigned to the post-verbal NP, Case conflict would rule the sentence ungrammatical. Hence, one solution is to allow free assignment of Case by AGR to any NP it governs and with which it is co-indexed. If AGR assigns Case to its right, the sentence is ungrammatical because of Case conflict; if AGR assigns Case to its left, the sentence is grammatical. This solution may be too cumbersome if one thinks of grammar as a production or parsing model. In that case, Case assignment by AGR must be restricted, perhaps directionally (cf. Koopman 1984; Travis 1984).

The second kind of *to be* I discuss is the predicational one, as in:

(40) John is a president

(41) They are presidents

A representation of the structure of (40) is:

(42) John$_i$ AGR$_i$ be $_{SC}$ [t$_i$ a president$_i$]

In (42), for number agreement, it makes no difference whether AGR is co-indexed with the [Spec, IP] position or with the post-verbal NP. The indexation would remain the same. (The small clause could not bear the i-index, as otherwise an i-within-i violation would arise.)

Case marking, however, is different from (37) above. The only argument in (42) is *John* and hence only *John* needs Case. *John* moves to subject position. The only reason for *John* to move would be that otherwise *John* would be without Case at s-structure. Sentence (42) therefore provides evidence that (at least in English) Case must be assigned to [Spec, IP]. If this position was not assigned Case, *John* would have no reason to move.

The third kind of *to be* is as in (1) and (2). The pre- and post-verbal NPs are not co-indexed (not by copular co-indexation as I argue above and not by movement). Hence, sentences (1) and (2) can be used to test what AGR co-indexes with in English because that NP will determine the number. Sentences (1) and (2) are singular, regardless of the number of the post-verbal NP. Therefore, AGR co-indexes with [Spec, IP] as in:

(43) it$_i$ AGR$_i$ [be me].

AGR assigns Case to *it* (or to *there*) and *be* assigns Case to the post-verbal NP. Because the pre- and post-verbal NPs are not co-indexed, it is impossible to reverse them, as (29) and (30) above show.

Assuming specifier-head agreement (as in 1.), number agreement and Case marking with various kinds of *to be* can be accounted for with no extra stipulations. Specifier-head agreement is used elsewhere and hence is independently motivated. In this system, Case assignment by AGR is to the NP co-indexed with AGR and need not be restricted to the NP to the left of AGR (otherwise a Case conflict or visibility principle violation would occur).

In section 5, I examine sentences such as (3). Borer (1983, 1986) uses these as examples that either the pre-verbal or the post-verbal NP is co-indexed with AGR. I have argued in this section that AGR is co-indexed with the Specifier of IP, i.e. the pre-verbal NP, and hence I must account for (3).

5. "There are/'s pictures on the wall"

As I mentioned above, Borer's analysis of (4) is problematic. Native speakers seem to feel that the two variants repeated here with slightly different words do not really mean the same, which one expects if they are variants on the same structure:

(44) a.   There's pictures on the wall.[5]
      b.   There are pictures on the wall.

Sentence (44a) is relevant when one is discussing the value of a house. In (44a), there is something (i.e., pictures on the wall); it does not mean that something (i.e., pictures) is somewhere (i.e., on the wall):

(45) There's the pictures on the wall, the furniture in the attic...

Sentence (44b) provides information as to where the pictures are, namely "on the wall":

(46) There are pictures on the wall; they are not on the floor or in the basement

The same can be said of sentence (4), Borer's example. Sentence (4a) can be the answer to the question "Who can lift the piano for me?", i.e., who is available. Sentence (4b) provides information as to where the seven people are, namely "in the garden".

With this interpretation, the (a) sentences are similar to sentences such as (2) above: *there* is an argument with nominative Case and there is a post-verbal NP rather than a small clause, which gets accusative from *to be*. The (b) sentences have a structure as in (47); the PP is a predicate to the NP:

(47) e be $_{SC}$[NP PP]

In (47), NP can move to [Spec, IP] to get nominative Case or *there* can be inserted.

What syntactic evidence exists to show that (2) and (47) are the correct analyses for the (a) and (b) structures respectively? The post-verbal NP gets accusative Case in (2), but nominative in (47). If one replaces the full NP by a pronoun, the pronoun in (4a), if the structure is as in (2), is expected to show accusative Case, whereas the pronoun in (4b), if the structure is as in (47), is not. This is the case:

(48) There's (just) us in the garden

(49) *There are (just) us in the garden

Even though (48) is not perfect, it is grammatical compared to (49), especially if (48) is an answer to "Who's in the garden?"[6]

Another piece of evidence is that definites should not be able to occur as post-verbal NPs in the (b) sentences. Sentence (45) above shows that definites can occur in the (a) sentences, but (50) is not judged grammatical:

(50) *There are the pictures on the wall, not on the floor

It is almost as if *the* in (50) forces the sentence to be read as in (2). This is not possible because of *are*.

Constructions such as (4a) and (44a) on the one hand and as (4b) and (44b) on the other have different underlying structures. The (a) sentences are analysed as (26) and the (b) sentences are analysed as (47). This means that Borer's sentence (4) is not a problem for the account of indexing, number agreement and Case marking that is presented in section 4.

There is other evidence that the (a) sentences have an analysis different from the (b) sentences. I have argued that the former are like (1) and (2): *it* and *there* are nominative arguments and the post-verbal NP is accusative. In a language without sentences such as (1) and (2), one would not expect (4a) or (44a). This prediction is borne out: Swedish is a language without (1) and (2):[7]

(51) *Det är mig
      "It is me"

(52) *Det finns/är borgmästaren, pastorn,   mig...
      "There's   the mayor,   the minister, me..."

Swedish is a language without number agreement on the verb, and a sentence such as (4) would just have one form:

(53) Det   finns några barn   i trädgården
     "There are   some children in the garden"

However, (53) is not ambiguous in meaning. It implies that the children are in the garden as in the English (b)-type sentence, but it is not an answer to "Who could have eaten the chocolate?", as in the English (a)-type sentence. That is also the reason one can have (54) but not (55):

(54) Det   finns en kvinna i trädgården
     "There is   a woman in the garden"

(55) *Det   finns kvinnan   i trädgården
     "There is   the woman in the garden"

In English, when *there* agrees with the verb, it is possible to say (56):

(56) There is the (nasty) woman in the garden and the man
     in the house...

Summarizing, in English, there is a kind of *to be* as in (1) and (2) that assigns accusative and can have a definite post-verbal NP. This *to be* agrees in number with the *it/there* in [Spec, IP] position. Sentences such as (4a) and (44a) in which the verb agrees with *there* and not with the post-verbal NP are instances of this construction as well. Sentences such as (4b) and (44b) are not.

In Swedish, number agreement is not present and a sentence such as (4) or (44) has one form only and could be understood either as (a) or as (b). However, as shown in (52) and (55), such structures cannot have an accusative or definite post-verbal NP. Therefore their structure is as in (b). The meaning is also as in the English (b) structures. Sentences such as (4a) do not exist in Swedish. Neither do sentences such as (1) and (2) that would be similar.

6. Conclusion

My main focus in this paper has been on sentences such as (1), (2) and (3). I have given an analysis of these sentences. I show that Chomsky's (1986) specifier-head agreement rule, the often used nominative Case assignment rule (Case is assigned to the element governed and co-indexed by AGR), Williams' predicate-subject co-indexing and Hornstein's copular co-indexing are the only rules necessary to account for number agreement and Case assignment in *to be* constructions.

I argue that there are three kinds of *to be*: (a) identificational, (b) predicational, and (c) *to be* as in (1), (2) and (3a). The basic structures are given in:

(a) NP_i AGR *be* NP_i (copular co-indexing).

    ↑___↓ ↓_↑

    Case   Case

(b) e AGR *be* [NP_i NP_i]   (predicate-subject co-indexing).

    ↑_↓

    Case

(c) $\begin{vmatrix} there \\ it \end{vmatrix}$ AGR *be* NP

                    ↓_↑

                     Case

            Case

(The arrows indicate Case assignment.)

After specifier-head agreement, the AGR is co-indexed with the [Spec, IP] position and the correct number agreement follows.

It is also shown that Swedish is different from English in that it does not have the third kind of *to be*. As a result, the absence of constructions such as (1), (2) and (3a) is accounted for.

Notes

1. I wish to thank Jose Bonneau, Harry Bracken and Evelyn Styan for comments on this paper.
2. Rapoport (1987) argues there is only one kind of *to be* which is inserted after d-structure. The main problem with her approach is Case marking (Rapoport 1987: 163ff.). She argues that in English, "the distinction between nominative and accusative pronouns is being lost in many contexts" (Rapoport 1987: 164). Accusative pronouns are possible in many "nominative positions" (e.g. *Him and me left*). However, a nominative is still possible, whereas in sentences with identificational *to be* and in sentences (1), (2) and (3a) a nominative is not possible.
3. Speakers tend to avoid cleft constructions with a pronoun as in:
    (i)   It is me/I who will cook dinner tonight.
    (ii) It was us/we that stole the statue.
    As indicated in (i) and (ii), speakers are unsure as to what Case to use. Many, however, feel that the construction with the post-verbal nominative sounds stilted. If it is no longer common, *to be* in (i) and (ii) can be analyzed as in (1). In a language such as Swedish which, as will be shown in section 5, does not have constructions as (1), it is impossible to have a post-verbal accusative in (i) and (ii):
    (iii) Det är jag som ska åka,
          "It is I   who will go".
    (iv) *Det är mig som ska åka,
          "It is me who will go".
4. Reinhart (1983a, 1983b), for instance, argues that part of binding theory is not included in the grammar, but can be seen as dealt with by a pragmatic strategy.
5. It seems that *'s* must occur here for most speakers. In constructions such as (1) and (2) either *'s* or *is* can be used.
6. *Us* cannot be replaced by *we* because definite NPs are not allowed in this construction.

7.   With thanks to Karin Edström Gadelii for checking the Swedish.
          An earlier version of this section appears in *Working Papers on Scandinavian Syntax* (1988).

References

Borer, Hagit
  1983   *Parametric syntax* (Dordrecht: Foris).
  1986   "I-subjects", *Linguistic Inquiry* 17.3: 375-417

Burzio, Luigi
  1981   *Intransitive verbs and Italian auxiliaries*, doctoral dissertation (Cambridge, Mass.: MIT).

Chomsky, Noam
  1981   *Lectures on government and binding* (Dordrecht: Foris).
  1986   *Barriers* (Cambridge, Mass: MIT Press).

Higginbotham, Jim
  1985   "On semantics", *Linguistic Inquiry* 16.4: 547-594

Hornstein, Norbert
  1984   *Logic as grammar* (Cambridge, Mass.: MIT Press).

Koopman, Hilda
  1984   *The syntax of verbs* (Dordrecht: Foris).

Lasnik, Howard
  1976   "Remarks on coreference", *Linguistic Analysis* 2.1: 1-22

Rapoport, Tova
  1987   *Copular, nominal and small clauses*, doctoral dissertation (Cambridge, Mass.: MIT).

Reinhart, Tanya
  1983a   *Anaphora and semantic interpretation* (London: Croom Helm).
  1983b   "Coreference and bound anaphora", *Linguistics and Philosophy* 6.1: 47-88

Rizzi, Luigi
  1982   *Issues in Italian Syntax* (Dordrecht: Foris).

Safir, Ken
  1985   *Syntactic chains* (Cambridge, UK: Cambridge University Press).

Stowell, Tim
  1978   "What was there before there was there", *Papers from the Fourteenth Regional Meeting of the Chicago Linguistic Society* (Chicago: Chicago University).

Travis, Lisa
  1984   *Parameters and effects of word-order variation*, doctoral dissertation (Cambridge, Mass.: MIT).

Williams, Edwin
  1980   "Predication", *Linguistic Inquiry* 11.1: 203-238
  1983   "Against small clauses", *Linguistic Inquiry* 14.2: 287-308

The syntax of floating *alles* in German[1]

Giuliana Giusti

1. Introduction

The distribution of the neuter singular quantifier *alles* in German is not only limited to obvious cases in which it clearly refers to a neuter singular NP. In certain cases it seems to refer to NPs with other features. Since this phenomenon has mostly passed unnoticed in the literature, as far as I know, this study tries to offer a fair description of it along with a theoretical analysis. Its marginal status and the significant variation in acceptability of a part of the corpus makes it an interesting field of research from the point of view of generative grammar. In fact, since the speaker can hardly learn the relevant rules from direct exposure to the data, it is reasonable to suppose that this phenomenon can be derived from independent principles of the core grammar of German.

This phenomenon can be found in three constructions, as far as I can see: infinitival imperatives, as in (1), copular constructions, as in (2), and wh-constructions, as in (3):

(1) Alles aussteigen, bitte!
     all   get off   please

(2) Das sind alles arme Leute
     that are all   poor people

(3) Wer ist heute abend alles da?
     who is tonight   all   here?

At first sight, one could assume that these three cases can be reduced to a single property of German, but after careful investigation it becomes clear that the appearance of neuter singular features on the quantifier *alles* in (1) to (3) is due to the interaction of different principles of the grammar of German and that there is no way of unifying this phenomenon. On the other hand, this is not too surprising, given the marginality of the usage which correlates with the difficulty in collecting clear judgements in this area. This conclusion will not result in a complication of the system of the grammar. In fact, I will claim that it is possible to reduce the three constructions to independent principles of the core grammar of German, without recourse to any ad hoc assumption.

In section 2 I will examine a recent proposal made by Sportiche (1987) for floating[2] quantifiers in French and (partially) in English and formulate some suggestions as to how to extend it to German. In section 3 we will see in some detail how the syntax of quantifiers interacts with some properties of German, such as the possibility of expressing a "generalized imperative" with an infinitive (or a past participle), as in (1); the possibility of a neuter presentative subject for copular constructions as in (2), and the property of wh-elements of being modified by a right-adjoined constituent, as in (3). In section 4 we will see how the analysis for the wh-construction carries over to that of other pronouns.

2. Floating quantifiers in German

There is no extensive literature about the so-called "floating" quantifiers in German. The most significant studies can be found in Link (1974), Vater (1980, 1986), Reis and Vater (1980), Bayer (1987). In this section I will present a recent theory proposed by Sportiche (1987) for French and try to extend it to German, which displays different behaviour in certain respects.

2.1. Sportiche's theory

Sportiche (1987) assumes an independently motivated structure like (4) for French and English, in which the subject of the sentence is generated in the

NP* position and then moved (for reasons of case assignment) to the specifier of IP. He further assumes that a modifier is generated (left-)adjacent to the element which is modified by it:[3]

(4)

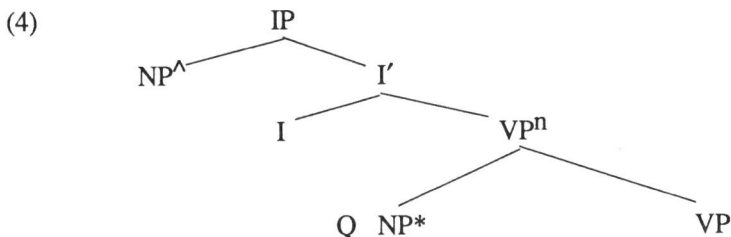

In assuming (4), Sportiche can account for the anaphoric behavior of distant quantifiers, which ends up being a mere effect of the movement of NP*, and for their adverbial position, which is now due to the assumption that subjects, as well as adverbs, are generated in a "higher" position inside the VP. In so doing, he dismisses two mysterious properties previously attributed to floating quantifiers: their downward movement into an adverbial position and their anaphoric behavior, neither of which would be allowed in the present framework.

The structure in (4) entails that distant quantifiers can only refer to a subject, since the grammatical function "subject" is the only grammatical function that receives its theta-role and Case in two different positions in English and French or, maybe in universal grammar.[4] (4) also entails that the quantifier is left-adjacent to NP* in English and French. In what follows I will investigate how German behaves with respect to the theory outlined.

2.2. Floating *alle*

In this section I will limit my study to the syntax of *alle* ('all'), since the syntax of *beide* ('both'), although very similar to *alle*, presents some differences, as discussed in Reis - Vater (1980), while indefinite quantifiers such as *keine* ('none'), *einige* ('some'), etc., in my opinion, enter a completely different construction.

Sportiche notices that in French non-distant quantifiers never follow their NP, as shown in (5), while in English they can do so only in subject position, as shown in (6):

(5)   a.   *les enfants tous sont partis
      b.   *j'ai vu les enfants tous

(6)   a.   the children all will leave
      b.   *I saw the children all

He reduces the contrast between (5a) and (6a) to the possibility in English vs. the impossibility in French of topicalization. In (6a) *the children* should be topicalized leaving *all* in the specifier of IP. The only problem with this proposal is the lack of the typical topicalized intonation in (6b), as Sportiche himself notices.

In German, in which topicalization is the standard structure in verb second clauses,[5] the NP *die Kinder* in (7) clearly forms a separate constituent. There is a light pause between the NP and *alle*, and the quantifier is not heavily stressed, as it would be normal for distant quantifiers.[6]

(7)   a.   die Kinder, alle werden wegfahren
      b.   *?ich sah die Kinder alle
      c.   ich habe die Kinder alle gesehen

The counterpart of (7a) without a pause is unacceptable, showing that *die Kinder alle* do not form a constituent. The same is shown by the contrast in (7b) and (7c). In (7b), in which no other element follows the quantifier, it is more difficult to make a pause between *die Kinder* and *alle*, and the sentence is (almost) impossible, while (7c), which is minimally different from (7b), is perfect.

Our first finding, therefore, is that the quantifier is always generated left-adjoined to the NP. All other word orders must be derived transformationally.[7]

The examples in (8), taken from Link (1974), confirm that the quantifier can appear as deeply embedded into VP as its base position, assuming a structure such as (4) for German as well. (8b) would be correct with a pause between the NP and the Q, as we have noticed for (7a). In (8e) the Q is in its VP-adjoined base-position. In (8c) and (8d), it is adjoined to some projection of I.[8] The ungrammaticality of (8f) is not due to the distance between Q and the source NP, as Vater (1980) and Reis and Vater (1980) claim, but to the fact that the subject position in which the Q is stranded is higher than that of the (indefinite) object, as we can see in (9a). In (9b) this fact is obscured by the possibility of scrambling the definite direct object:

(8) a. alle Mitglieder des Hockeyteams   haben gestern   nach
         all   players   of the hockey team have   yesterday after
         der Niederlage vom Vorsitzenden einen Trostpreis   erhalten
         the defeat   of   the president a   booby-prize obtained
     b. *die Mitglieder des Hockeyteams alle haben gestern nach
         der Niederlage vom Vorsitzenden einen Trostpreis erhalten
     c. die Mitglieder des Hockeyteams haben alle gestern nach
         der Niederlage vom Vorsitzenden einen Trostpreis erhalten
     d. die Mitglieder des Hockeyteams haben gestern alle nach
         der Niederlage vom Vorsitzenden einen Trostpreis erhalten
     e. die Mitglieder des Hockeyteams haben gestern nach
         der Niederlage vom Vorsitzenden alle einen Trostpreis erhalten
     f. *die Mitglieder des Hockeyteams haben gestern nach
         der Niederlage vom Vorsitzenden einen Trostpreis alle erhalten

(9) a. *die Kinder haben gestern einen Trostpreis alle erhalten
     b. die Kinder haben gestern den Trostpreis alle erhalten

What remains to be discussed is the contrast between French and English on the one hand, and German on the other, with regard to the grammatical function to which a distant quantifier may refer. As noticed by Link (1974), and as already anticipated in (7b) and (7c), a distant quantifier can also refer to direct and indirect objects:

(10) a. der Lehrer hat die Schüler gestern   alle gelobt
         the teacher has the students yesterday all   praised
     b. der Lehrer hat den Schülern   gestern   allen eine Fünf gegeben
         the teacher has to the students yesterday all   a   five given

This property of German can be reduced to one that is well-known and has been independently studied, namely scrambling in the *Mittelfeld*. As we have seen in (9) above, scrambling can move a definite NP to the left inside the *Mittelfeld*. It can therefore move the source NP, which is always definite. This property of German (and Dutch) has been studied by Lenerz (1977), de Haan (1979), Hoekstra (1984), Bennis and Hoekstra (1984), Thiersch (1985), den Besten and Webelhuth (1987) among others, and it consists in moving elements from inside the VP to adjoin them maybe to projections of I. It is interesting to notice that Q can "go along" some steps with its source NP, as shown in (8c) to (8e), suggesting that scrambling is a very local movement, more local than wh-movement. Since this kind of transformation appears to interact with the informational structure of German, which concerns issues such as thema/rhema distribution, the definitness effect, etc., I will not go into that here.[9]

My findings are different from Link's (1974) and Vater's (1980) judgements on objects of prepositions. They both give (11a) as good, but none of my informants agree on that:

(11) a. *Caesar wurde von den Soldaten allen gehaßt
       Caesar was   by the soldiers all   hated
    b. *von den Soldaten wurde Caesar allen gehaßt

Even more delicate is the case of selected PPs, as in (12) and (13). Some speakers judge them as completely unacceptable, others assign them one or two question marks. What is clear is the unacceptability of a distant quantifier referring to an adverbial PP:

(12) a. */?? ich habe über meine Probleme (gestern) alle gedacht
    b. */? über meine Probleme habe ich (gestern)   alle gedacht
         on   my   problems have I   yesterday all thought

(13) a. */?? ich habe mit meinen Freunden (gestern) allen getanzt
    b. */? mit meinen Freunden habe ich (gestern)   allen getanzt
         with my   friends   have I   yesterday all   danced

(14) a. *ich habe aus diesen Gründen gestern allen die Stadt verlassen
    b. *aus diesen Gründen habe ich gestern   allen die Stadt verlassen
         on   these grounds have I   yesterday all   the town left

This area of uncertainty shows a significant degree of underspecification in the grammar of adjoined modifiers. For the speakers who do not completely exclude (12) and (13), it seems marginally possible for the Q to (right-)ad-join to a selected PP, but not to adverbial PPs, as in (14). The "??" vs. "?" judgements for the (a) and (b) examples respectively appear to be consistent, and suggest once more that wh-movement involved in topicalization in (b) gives different results from scrambling in (a). This is something to be taken into account in investigating the nature of scrambling, but this does not concern us here. For those who exclude (12) and (13) we can say that in a structure like (15) the Q left-adjoined to NP cannot move to right-adjoin to PP, so that the sequence P NP cannot be scrambled alone:

(15)

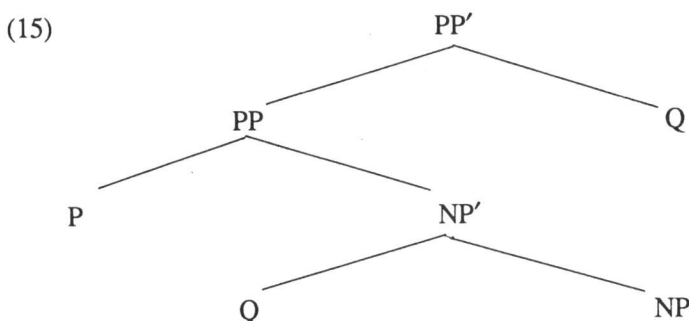

This is not very surprising since it is well-known that a violation of the left-branch condition usually gives very bad results. We will come back to this in 2.3.

Let us finally address the problem of the internal structure of the source NP. In (8a) Link gives *alle Mitglieder* as the basic string from which the quantifier is floated. If this were correct, the obligatory presence of the article in the specifier of NP when the quantifier is distant would be a problem (as it is, in fact for Link), unless we assume some sort of N'-mo-vement plus regeneration of the kind proposed for distant *keine* by Van Riemsdijk (1987). But, as opposed to *keine*, *alle* in its pre-NP position is not incompatible with a definite article. Furthermore, when the article is present, *all* need not be declined, supporting two assumptions: that Q is base-generated outside the NP, as Sportiche (1987) claims for French and English, and that the starting structure for distant quantifiers has a definite article, as in (16a), as opposed to (16b):[10]

(16) a.   all(e) die armen Studenten, die ich kenne, haben einen Ferienjob
    b.   alle Studenten, die ich kenne, haben einen Ferienjob
       'all the students I know have a summer job'

3. Neuter *alles*

With Sportiche's theory extended to German, let us now turn to our initial topic. In section 3.1. I will examine the possibility of a quantifier being adjacent to an empty pronoun subject of an infinitival. In 3.2. we will see, following Reis (1982), that a presentative neuter singular pronoun can be the subject of a copular verb in German. In this case the quantifier agrees with it, getting neuter singular features. In 3.3. I will investigate some special properties of wh-pronouns.

3.1. The imperative construction

In German it is possible to express an imperative (with what I will informally call a "generalized subject") with an infinitive, as in (17a), or a past participle. The "generalized subject" of the imperative is not arbitrary in reference, since it refers to all the people present at the time of the utterance, but it is more general than a simple second person plural. As for all non-finite tenses, the subject of this construction must be empty. I will also assume infinitives without *zu* and past participles to be bare VPs, not CPs or IPs, given the lack of the infinitival marker *zu*.[11] Therefore, the empty subject will not be in the specifier of IP, but adjoined to VP, as in (4); and, as a consequence, it will be *pro* rather than PRO. However, no part of the analysis crucially relies on this.

    The only exception to the emptiness of the subject is the occurrence of the quantifier *alle, alles*:

(17) a.   (jetzt) rausgehen
       now   go out
    b.   (jetzt) alle(s) rausgehen

c. *(jetzt) die Kinder (alle) rausgehen
    now   the children all   go out

In Sportiche's theory, which we have applied to German, this is immediately accounted for. In fact, since a quantifier is not part of the (small) NP, it can be lexical even when its source NP is an empty category. The French examples are taken from Sportiche (1987), the German example (19a) from Bayer (1987):

(18) a. Il aurait fallu tous PRO$_{arb}$ partir
         it will (be) need(ed)   to leave
         'it will be necessary to leave'
     b. Ils$_i$ ont décidé de tous PRO$_i$ partir
         they have decided *de* all   to leave

(19) a. der König befahl den Dienern PRO schleunigst   beide/alle
         the king   ordered to the servants   immediately both/all
         Flöte zu spielen
         flute to play
         'The king ordered the servants that they both/all
         should immediatly play the flute'
     b. es ist nötig PRO$_{arb}$ alle wegzufahren
         it is necessary   all to go away

In (19a) and (19b) I assume that both PRO and t respectively have been moved from the specifier of VP to the specifier of IP in a structure like (4), as we have assumed all the way through. The corresponding sentences with the Q moved along are expected, correctly, to be acceptable as well. Notice that the fact that Q can left-adjoin to an empty category such as PRO is more indirect evidence for the assumption that Q is base generated outside the NP, given the full NP-status of PRO.

An interesting property of the infinitival imperative construction is that, in some cases, the "generalized subject" can display neuter singular features:

(20) a. alles/alle umsteigen/weitergehen
                   change   go further

    b. (*?alles)/ alle Maria anrufen
           call Maria
    c. (*?alles)/alle die Fahrscheine zeigen
           show the tickets
    d. (*?alles)/alle telephonieren/tanzen
           telephone   dance

(21) a. alles/(alle) aufgewacht
           get up
     b. alles/(*alle) sich erhoben und salutiert
           raise oneself and salute

The descriptive generalizations are the following: past participles always prefer neuter *alles*, as in (21), with the impossibility of plural *alle* in transitives and unergatives, as in (21b). On the other hand, infinitives always permit plural *alle*, as in (20), with (almost) impossible neuter *alles* in the subject of transitives, as in (20b) and (20c), and unergatives, as in (20d).

Eric Reuland (personal communication) suggests that *alles* appears if the quantifier is adjoined to the external subject, when this does not receive a theta-role. In this case the external subject position is probably filled by an expletive pro which appears to display neuter singular features. The correlation expletive pro/neuter singular features is empirically motivated in German by the observation that the overt expletive in this language is the neuter singular pronoun *es*.[12]

The external subject of past participles is always without a theta-role, since past participles have the property of absorbing the external theta-role. Therefore, *alles* is always permitted with past participles. *Alle* is permitted only by ergative past participles, as in (21a), since in this case the theta-role of the subject is assigned internally, and is not absorbed; but *alles* is not excluded, since there is still an external subject position without a theta-role. In infinitives we find exactly the opposite situation: *alle* is always possible, since there is always one position to which the theta-role is assigned. Ergative verbs, as in (20a), assign a theta-role to the VP-internal subject position; in this case *alles* is possible, since the theta-role is assigned VP-internally and the external subject position does not receive a theta-role; transitives, as in (20b) and (20c), and unergatives, as in (20d), assign a theta-role to the external subject and the features are those of the referent, therefore only *alle* is possible.

This proposal is in line with the syntactic results provided by participial constructions in Italian, in which transitive verbs receive passive interpretation, as in (22a), ergative verbs receive active interpretation, as in (22b), and unergative verbs give bad results, as in (22c), since they assign no theta-role to the structural object:

(22) a. chiamata Maria
        called   Maria
     b. arrivata Maria
        arrived Maria
     c. *ballata/o Maria
        danced   Maria

(21) and (22) show that past participles in both languages cannot assign a theta-role to the structural subject. If the object position is available to take over the theta-role of the subject as in passives or ergatives, the construction is possible in Italian, and the features are referential in German. If there is no object, the construction is out in Italian, while in German the subject must be non-referential (i.e., an empty expletive). If I am correct, we can derive an independently well-known difference between null subjects in German and in Italian: in German they must be non-referential (they cannot have a theta-role), while in Italian they can.[13]

3.2. The copular construction

The neuter presentative subject *das* can appear in German only with a copular verb, as studied by Reis (1982). She notices that "if in German two Nominatives Nom_i and Nom_j with different reference of person and number are in the same sentence, (...) when Nom_i is *das/es* ('that/it'), *wer/was* ('who/what') verbal agreement is oriented towards Nom_j" (my translation)[14] as in (23); (cf. Reis 1982: ex. 35):

(23) a. das — Tatsachen ('facts')   a'. Tatsachen — das
     b. es/das — Meiers   b'. Meiers — das
     c. Wer — die Leute da drüben? c'. die Leute — wer?
         'the people over there'

In (23) the hyphen stands for the copula which, following Reis's generalization, in all cases agrees with the plural NP.

The presentative can be quantified:

(24) a. all(es) das sind arme Leute
         all   that are poor people-[plur]
     b. das sind alles arme Leute

(25) a. das ist alles saure Milch
         that is all   sour milk-[fem.]
     b. das werden alles große Bäume
         that become all   big   trees
     c. das bleiben alles reiche Leute
         that remain all   rich   people
     d. das scheinen alles reiche Leute
         that seem   all   rich   people

The condition for *alles* to appear is that the subject is the presentative *das* and that the predicate is a referential NP. The presentative gains some kind of referential property from the predicate NP in order to be quantified. That this is a matter of syntactic and not pragmatic reference is shown by the fact that in (26) *alles* is out even in pragmatically unambiguous contexts:

(26) a. das sind (*alles) schön
         that are   all   beautiful
     b. das sind (*alles) auf dem Tisch
         that are   all   on the table

On the other hand, if the neuter presentative is not present, *alles* cannot appear, showing that *alles* refers to the presentative pronoun:

(27) *alles diese Leute sind arm

Alles can refer to the expletive subject of the cleft construction, but only marginally to the expletive *es* that can appear only in the *Vorfeld* in certain constructions:

(28) a. es sind alles arme Leute, die   hier   wohnen
         it are   all   poor people who   here live
     b. OK/* es kamen alles arme Leute

This suggests that for some speakers this expletive *es* in (28b) cannot receive enough referential features from the subject, in order to be able to be quantified, while for others it may.

The syntax of *alles* provides evidence for the presence of an empty expletive in two cases: in the case of a locative adverb in copular constructions, as in (29), and in the case of the empty resumptive pronoun, as in (30):

(29) a. (das) alles hier sind arme Leute
     b. (das) hier sind alles arme Leute
     c. (das) alles sind hier arme Leute
     d. all das hier sind arme Leute
         all that here are poor people

(30)   Johann, Maria, Karl und Therese sind alles/alle arme Leute

(31) J., M., K., und T.,
     a. das sind alles/*alle arme Leute
     b. die sind *alles/alle arme Leute

When *das* is missing in (29a) to (29c), the adverb licenses a (presentative) *pro*, to which *alles* refers. I do not consider *alles* to refer directly to the locative, since I do not see how a locative adverb could be quantified.[15] In (30), in which the resumptive pronoun is non-overt, it can assume either plural or neuter singular features, as the overt resumptive pronouns show in (31a) and (31b). The quantifier must agree, as always, with its source NP, the resumptive pronoun.

Up until now we have seen that a marginal fact like the apparently idiosyncratic appearance of the neuter singular quantifier *alles* in certain constructions in German, can not only be explained with independent principles of the core grammar of this language, but can also provide empirical evidence for certain hypotheses formulated in recent literature, such as the existence of an expletive *pro* in German, although German is not a null subject language in the usual sense (cf. Tomaselli 1988, Cardinaletti 1988), and the existence of an empty resumptive pronoun in topicalization constructions (cf. Cardinaletti (1986)).

3.3. The wh-construction

In the previous two constructions *alles* displayed all the properties of floating quantifiers that we have discussed in section 2: it was base-generated at the left of its source and it agreed with an (overt or empty) neuter singular pronoun. The wh-construction presents some differences and some similarities:

(32) a. Mit wem   alles hast du   gestern   über deine Dissertation
        with whom all   have you yesterday about your   dissertation
        freimütig gesprochen?
        freely   talked
     b. Mit wem hast du alles gestern über deine Dissertation freimütig gesprochen?
     c. Mit wem hast du gestern alles über deine Dissertation freimütig gesprochen?
     d. mit wem hast du gestern über deine Dissertation alles freimütig gesprochen?
     e. *Mit wem hast du gestern über deine Dissertation freimütig alles gesprochen?

The most apparent similarity in (32) is that the quantifier can appear as deeply embedded as its source could be in the base. *Alles* can be left in its base position or higher in the *Mittelfeld* (32b) to (32e), showing local scrambling in (32b) and (32c) together with wh-movement.

The fact that scrambling also interacts with this construction should not obscure two crucial differences with respect to the two previous ones. *Alles* appears right-adjoined to the w-pronoun, as shown in (32a), and its ending does not appear to refer to any neuter singular element, either overt or non-overt. The two characteristics are connected to each other. a w-pronoun in German can be modified by different kinds of right-adjoined maximal projections, or by particles, as in (33) to (37), which naturally do not have to agree with it. The quantifier is one of these:

(33) a. ich habe (et)was   Gutes gegessen
        I   have something good eaten
     b. Was hast du Gutes gegessen?[16]
        what have you good   eaten
     c. ich habe jemanden Fremdes/Fremden gesehen
        I have somebody foreign   seen
     d. Wen hast du Fremdes/Fremden gesehen?
        who have yoù foreign   seen

(34) a. Was für Bücher hast du gelesen?
        what for books have you read
        'what kind of books have you read'
     b. Was hast du für Bücher gelesen?

(35) a. Was auch immer hast du machen wollen?
        'what on earth did you want to do?'
     b. Was hast du auch immer machen wollen?

(36) a. Wer in diesem Haus ist Artzt?
        who in this   house is a doctor?
     b. Wer ist in diesem Haus Artzt?

The constructions in (33) to (36) are somewhat heterogeneous, but they all share the property of having a right-adjoined element modifying a pronoun. Furthermore, in most of them the modifier has a partitive meaning. Werner Abraham (personal communication) points out that *alles* in this construction probably has the ending of an old (partitive) genitive and not the neuter singular ending that we have found in the two previous constructions. The same, I think, is true of the adjective in (33), given that in (33c) and (33d) the adjective does not necessarily agree with the human features of the pronoun. The preposition *für* also introduces a partitive projection. The special status of this construction (the preposition transmits rather than assigns Case; the head of the construction appears to be the noun and not *was*) does not concern us here. What is important again is that a right-adjoined modifier has partitive meaning and can be left stranded, as happens to the PP in (36b).[17]

Since we have found sufficient evidence to support the existence of a structure with a modifier right-adjoined to a pronoun, there is no difficulty in admitting that a Q can take part in this construction. Neither is there a contradiction in assuming two structures as the base for floating quantifiers, given that floating has been recognized as a mere surface effect of movement of the source NP. The structure for the copular and the imperative construction is represented in (37a), while the structure for the wh-construction is shown in (37b):

(37) a.

NP?
Q(P)   NP*

b.

NP?
NP   XP
wh-

This structural difference is responsible for the different results that *alles* produces when it is left stranded from a PP with a wh-pronoun or with an NP:

(38) a. mit wem   alles/allem hast du gestern   gesprochen?
         with whom all   have you yesterday spoken
     b. mit wem hast du alles/allem gesprochen?

(39) a. *mit meinen Lehrern allen habe ich gestern   gesprochen
          with my teachers   all   have I yesterday talked
     b. *mit meinen Lehrern habe ich allen gesprochen

As we have noticed above, (39a) shows that Q cannot be right-adjoined to an NP and (39b) shows that the left-branch condition is very difficult to violate. In a parallel fashion, (38a) shows that the wh-pronoun forms a constituent with the right-adjoined quantifier and (38b) shows that a right branch can be left stranded more easily.

A quantifier cannot always be stranded from a wh-pronoun. A marginal result is produced by the neuter *was*, and an unacceptable one is given by the clitic *wo*:[18]

(40) a. an   was alles hast du   gestern   gedacht?
      about what all have you   yesterday thought?

   b. ??an was hast du alles gestern gedacht?

   c. ?an was hast du gestern alles gedacht

(41) a. *woran alles hast du gedacht?

   b. *?woran hast du alles gestern gedacht?

   c. ??woran hast du gestern alles gedacht

In (40) and (41) a process of (obligatory) cliticization of *was* to the P interacts with the properties of the distant quantifier. In (40a) the constituent *was alles* is "heavy enough" to resist cliticization. But in (40b) and (40c) the quantifier is distant and cliticization can hardly be prevented. On the other hand, *wo* cannot be quantified even when it is not cliticized, as shown in (42):

(42) a. *wo   alles bist du   gewesen?
      where all   have you been

   b. *wo bist du alles gewesen

The unacceptability of (41a) is completely parallel to the acceptability of (40a), if we assume that in this context cliticization cannot apply due to the "heaviness" of the constituent formed by the wh-pronoun and the quantifier. In the (b) and (c) examples of (40) and (41) we observe the competition between distant quantifiers and cliticization. In the (b) examples, in particular, scrambling intervenes to move the quantifier to a higher position in the structure, yielding an even worse result.

4. One related issue

The structural difference in (37a) and (37b) can also explain certain differences between full NPs, which do not permit the so-called "backwards floating", and pronominals. The following examples are given by Reis and Vater (1980: [33],[34]):

(43) a. Jetzt sind alle die Gäste gegangen
       Now are   all the guests gone
    b. *alle sind die Gäste gegangen

(44) a. Jetzt sind sie   alle gegangen
       Now are   them all gone
    b. alle sind sie jetzt gegangen
    c. *jetzt sind alle sie gegangen

Reis and Vater's generalizations are the following: "Only pronominal NPs can be source NPs for backwards floating (...). Only the first sentence position can be the ultimate position for backwards floating" (my translation).[19] If we assume a structure like (37b) for pronominal source NPs, justified in any case by the contrast between (44a) and (44c), we can explain why the quantifier can be topicalized alone only when it relates to a pronoun. In structure (37b), the quantifier builds an autonomous maximal projection that can be topicalized, being a right branch.

Structure (37b) for pronouns is also confirmed by d-pronouns in left dislocation (cf. Altmann 1981):

(45) die Kinder, die   alle/*alle die sind gekommen
    the children those all/*all   those have come

There are two apparent counterexamples to this analysis also given by Reis and Vater. One is that the pronoun *sie* appears to prefer a distant quantifier when it is moved to the *Vorfeld*, as in (46a), although we have just seen in (44a) that it can be adjacent to its quantifier in the *Mittelfeld*. But this appears to be an idiosyncratic property of *sie*, which is not shared by other pronouns, as (46b) shows:

(46) a. ?sie alle   haben der Mutter beim Waschen geholfen
    b. wir alle   haben der Mutter beim Waschen geholfen
       ?they all/we all have the mother in the washing helped

The other problem is that, as opposed to wh-pronouns, personal pronouns cannot have a distant quantifier when they are embedded in a PP:

(47) a. an uns alle hat man diesmal einen Brief geschrieben
       to us all has one this time a   letter written

   b. *an uns hat man alle diesmal einen Brief geschrieben

   c. *an uns hat man diesmal alle einen Brief geschrieben

   d. *alle hat man an uns einen Brief geschrieben

This would be a serious counterexample to my theory if I had motivated the possibility of a distant quantifier out of a wh-PP as a direct consequence of (37b), but I did not. Above, I had postulated movement of the Q to a PP-adjoined position. This does not happen when a pronominal is the modified NP. Neither can the quantifier be topicalized in this case, as shown in (47d).

That (even selected) PPs are islands of some sort, is well-known. My opinion is that it is the wh-construction that is deviant in this respect. One way to motivate this larger "freedom" of the wh-construction is to use the independently needed mechanism of percolation of the wh-features to the PP to motivate the adjunction of the quantifier to the PP, assuming that it is a property of wh-elements, regardless of their categorial status, to be modified by a right-adjoined maximal projection. A deeper analysis of this problem would be beyond the scope of this paper and should be left for future research.

5. Conclusions

Work in generative grammar usually tries to unify apparently unrelated phenomena on the assumption that, given a parameter, several surface phenomena depend on it. In this article we have gone through the inverse process. We have observed an apparently unitary phenomenon, the appearance of neuter singular features on the quantifier *alles* in certain cases in which it refers to non neuter singular NPs, and we have shown that this is the surface effect of different, independently motivated properties of German. This procedure, although not very common among works based on the assumption of an underlying modular system of principles and parameters, is completely in line with it. In fact, there is no reason to believe that the surface can hide not only similarities but also interesting differences.

In analyzing the three constructions in which the phenomenon under consideration appears, we have touched several properties of German and their interaction with principles of universal grammar. In section 2. we have assumed following Sportiche (1987) that quantifiers are generated outside the (small) NP, which can be either moved from the specifier of VP to the specifier of higher functional categories for Case assignment reasons, or scrambled, or else topicalized, according to the language. The fact that German displays more "freedom" in the distribution of distant quantifiers than English and French is straightforwardly accounted for by the possibility of these three types of movement in this language. In sections 3.1 and 3.2, we have seen how the neuter singular features on the quantifier depend on the presence of a presentative pronoun in copular constructions, and of a non-overt expletive in the imperative construction, both of which share the neuter singular features with the quantifier. In section 3.3. we have recognized that both the features and the structure of the source NP were different from those in the other two constructions, although the quantifier still maintained the property of being able to be left stranded in its base position.

The assumption of two different structures from which a quantifier can be stranded is not only motivated by the empirical evidence but also by at least some of the peculiar properties of quantified pronouns.

Notes

1   I thank Anemone Müller for having collaborated with me at the first stages of this study during my stay at the University of Konstanz in Spring 1987. I thank colleagues, staff and visitors at the University of Venice during the academic year 1987/1988, especially Guglielmo Cinque, Giuseppe Longobardi, Anna Cardinaletti, Arnim von Stechow, Bruna Radelli, Adrian Battye and Martin Prinzhorn for discussions and comments. I am also grateful to all the participants of the Germanic Syntax Workshop in Groningen for criticism and support; among them I would like to mention in particular Werner Abraham, Eric Reuland, Hubert Haider and Günther Grewendorf. Needless to say, I alone am responsible for this paper.

2   The term "floating" in Sportiche's and in our framework has completely lost its meaning, since it is not the Q that floats rightwards, but it is the NP which moves leftwards, leaving the Q in place. For this reason I will sometimes talk of "stranded" quantifiers, parallel to stranded prepositions. A more neutral term from the theoretical point of view is "distant quantifier". In this paper all three terms appear depending on what we are referring to: in references of previous analyses the old "floating" will be kept, in the descriptive part "distant quantifiers" will be used, while "stranded" will be used in the formulation of my hypotheses.

3   Sportiche (1987) does not take a position on the status of VP^n, or on the status of the node dominating Q NP*, if there is one. He proposes that the generation of the Q undergoes the Adjunct Projection Principle (his [7]):

        If X "modifies" some (semantic) type Y, and X and Y are syntactical-
        ly realized as a and b, a is projected as adjacent to b, or to the head of
        b.

For ease of exposition, however, I will refer to Q as (left or right) adjoined to NP, although I have nothing to say about the unclear notion of "adjunction". In any case, the node dominating Q NP*, would have to be transparent for theta-role assignment and, as is evident for German, for Case assignment to NP*.

4   We will see in the next subsection that this observation does not hold for German, in which other grammatical functions can host a distant quantifier. This property of German, however, will not represent a counterexample to Sportiche's theory.

5   Cf. Cardinaletti (1986) for this analysis of verb second structures, and the literature mentioned there.

6   Link (1974) and Vater (1980) notice that *alle* in this case is not stressed, but they take this to be evidence for right-adjunction inside NP. This is disproved by the fact that the pause between the NP and Q is also obligatory in the *Mittelfeld*. Furthermore, Altmann (1981) points out that the resumptive pronoun can be modified by a quantifier in the *Vorfeld*, yielding sentences such as (i):

        (i)   die Kinder, die alle werden wegfahren

which I assume to be the left-dislocation counterpart of (7a) with the overt operator *die*. For the right-adjoined position of the quantifier cf. section 4. below.

7   The fact that a quantifier can appear right-adjoined to pronouns, as in *wir alle* ('we all'), *sie alle* ('they all'), *die alle*, ('those all' cf. note 6), etc., is not a counterexample to our claim here, since pronouns behave differently in this respect not only in German, as we will claim in 3.3. and 4., but also in English, as one can conclude from the glosses.

8   If one assumes that Infl is actually split into two maximal projections TP (Tense) and AGRP (Agreement), it would be reasonable to assume that the subject moves from one specifier position to the next. This would hold only for the subject position. However, other positions can host a distant quantifier, that can

also be "moved along" in the *Mittelfeld*. I will explain this by recourse of an independent property of German, namely scrambling of definite NPs. It is difficult and indeed not crucial to decide whether the subject is scrambled or moved from specifier position to specifier position.

9   For a treatment of these problems see Lenerz (1977) and subsequent work. That sentence stress (as a consequence of informational prominence) interacts with quantifier floating has already been noticed by Vater (1980), although Vater does not connect this property with scrambling.

10 Vater (1980) also suggests something similar, but notices as a problem that generic statements cannot have an underlying form with an article, since (i) and not (ii) has the generic interpretation corresponding to (iii):

(i)   alle Hunde haben eine gute Nase
      all dogs have a good nose
(ii) alle die Hunde haben eine gute Nase
(iii) die Hunde haben alle eine gute Nase

I do not regard this as a problem since interpretive rules apply after syntax anyway.

11 Cf. Giusti (1986) and Schwartz - Tomaselli (1988) on this issue.

12 Anna Cardinaletti pointed out to me that it could be a contradiction for an expletive to be quantified, since an expletive is non-referential by definition. We may suppose that, when a referential subject is present, the expletive assumes its reference, although it is not coindexed with it and it does not assume its features. This is also supported by the data in (27) below. I will leave open the question of how the expletive can receive "some" referential features in order to be able to be quantified but "not too many", in order not to lose its expletive nature.

13 On this issue see Tomaselli (1988); Cardinaletti (1988).

14 "...befinden sich im Deutschen zwei person- bzw. numerus-verschiedene Nominativ-NPs Nom$_i$, Nom$_j$ im gleichen Satz, so gilt (...) Wenn Nom$_i$ *das/es* ist oder *wer/was*, richtet sich die Verbalkongruenz nach Nom$_j$." (Reis 1982: ex. 37).

15 We will see below that the locative interrogative *wo* cannot be quantified, although wh-pronouns enter a quantified construction, as we have seen in (3).

16 The corresponding sentences with the modifying adjective fronted together with the wh-pronoun are not completely acceptable, perhaps because the string *was Gutes* is not analysed as interrogative, as shown in (33a).

17 For a more detailed analysis of the *was für* construction cf. den Besten (1985) and the literature quoted there.

18 The neuter *was* almost always cliticizes to the left of the P, in which it is embedded, becoming *wo(r)*.

19 "Nur pronominale Elemente NPs kommen als Quell-NPs für Rückwärts-Floating in Frage (...). Nur die Spitzenposition des Satzes kommt als Endposition für den Quantor in Frage." (Reis and Vater 1980: 371)

References

Altmann, Hans
1981   "Formen der "Herausstellung" im Deutschen", *Rechtsversetzung, Linksverset-*
       zung, Freies Thema und verwandte Konstruktionen (Linguistische Arbeiten
       106) (Tübingen: Niemeyer).

Bayer, Josef
1987   "The syntax of scalar particles and so-called floating quantifiers" (Nijmegen:
       unpublished manuscript Max Planck-Institut für Psycholinguistik).

Bennis, Hans - Teun Hoekstra
1984   "Gaps and parasitic gaps", *The Linguistic Review* 4.1: 29-87

Cardinaletti, Anna
1986   "Topicalization in German: movement to Comp or base-generation in Comp?",
       Groninger Arbeiten zur Germanistischen Linguistik 28: 202-231
1988   "On *es*, pro and sentential arguments in German" (Venice: unpublished manus-
       cript university of Venice).

De Haan, Ger J.
1979   *Conditions on rules: The proper balance between syntax and semantics* (Dord-
       recht: Foris).

Den Besten, Hans
1985   "The ergative hypothesis and free word order in Dutch and German", *Studies*
       on German grammar, edited by Jindřich Toman (Dordrecht: Foris).

Den Besten, Hans - Gert Webelhuth
1987   "Remnant topicalization and the constituent structure of VP in the Germanic
       SOV languages", paper delivered at the GLOW Conference, Venice 1987.

Giusti, Giuliana
1986   "On the lack of wh-infinitives with *zu* and the projection of Comp in German",
       Groninger Arbeiten zur Germanistischen Linguistik 28: 115-169

Hoekstra, Teun
1984   *Transitivity: Grammatical relations in government-binding theory* (Dordrecht:
       Foris).

Lenerz, Jürgen
1977   *Zur Abfolge nominaler Satzglieder im Deutschen* (Studien zur deutschen Gram-
       matik 5) (Tübingen: Gunter Narr).

Link, Godehard
1974   "Quantoren-Floating im Deutschen", *Syntax und Generative Grammatik*, vol.
       2: 105-127, edited by Ferenc Kiefer - David M. Perlmutter (Frankfurt/M:
       Athenaion).

Reis, Marga
   1982   "Zum Subjektbegriff im Deutschen", *Satzglieder im Deutschen* (Studien zur deutschen Grammatik): 171-211, edited by Werner Abraham (Tübingen: Gunter Narr).

Reis, Marga - Heinz Vater
   1980   "Beide", *Wege zur Universalienforschung*, Sprachwissenschafliche Beiträge zum 60. Geburtstag von Hansjakob Seiler (Tübinger Beiträge zur Linguistik 145): 360-386, edited by Günther Brettschneider - Christian Lehmann (Tübingen: Gunter Narr).

Sportiche, Dominique
   1987   "A theory of floating quantifiers" (unpublished manuscript University of Southern California).

Thiersch, Craig
   1985   "VP and scrambling in the Mittelfeld" (unpublished manuscript University of Köln and University of Connecticut).

Tomaselli, Alessandra
   1988   "On the pronominal nature of Comp in German" (Pavia: unpublished manuscript university of Pavia).

Van Riemsdijk, Henk
   in press   "Movement and regeneration", *Dialect variation and the theory of grammar*, edited by Paola Benincà (Dordrecht: Foris).

Vater, Heinz
   1980   "Quantifier floating in German", *The semantics of determiners*: 232-249, edited by Johan van der Auwera (London: Croom Helm).

Vater, Heinz (ed.)
   1986   *Zur Syntax der Determinantien* (Studien zur deutschen Grammatik 31) (Tübingen: Gunter Narr).

Binding, ditransitives and the structure of the VP[1]

Eric Hoekstra

1. Introduction

In this paper I will introduce an analysis of double objects within the framework of government and binding of Chomsky (1981). Double objects, or more generally the dative alternation, have been investigated by Green (1974) and Oehrle (1975), among others. The dative alternation is illustrated by the following pairs of sentences:

(1) a. John gave Mary a book
     b. John gave a book to Mary

(2) a. Jan gaf Marie een boek
     b. Jan gaf een boek aan Marie[2]

The indirect object *Mary* is a NP in the (a)-sentence; in the (b)-sentence it is expressed in a PP with the preposition *to*.

The dative alternation is an interesting area of research because of the theoretical problems associated with it. Neither Chomsky (1955) nor Chomsky (1965) explicitly deals with this construction, although a suggestion as to its analysis is made in Chomsky (1955). This suggestion is taken up and further developed in Larson (1987).[3] Chomsky (1981) contains a few references to the dative alternation but no analysis is developed.

One of the main problems associated with the dative alternation is the problem of defining indirect objects. Is it possible to give a universal definition of the indirect object in terms of X-bar theory? A second problem: how should the two alternating forms be related? Within the framework of government binding the answer to this question depends partly upon the outcome of the debate about representation versus derivation. Closely related to this issue is the debate about the interaction between the lexicon and syntax. Thirdly, there is the issue of Case theory: how do double objects get Case? We will return to these questions in the course of this paper.

The particular analysis of the dative alternation proposed here will have some consequences for the analysis of the English VP. These consequences will be discussed in the course of this paper.

2. Analyses of the dative alternation

2.1. Summary

In this section we will investigate various analyses of the dative alternation, focusing on the problem of how to define indirect objects and direct objects.

2.2. Chomsky (1981), the definition of objects and X-bar theory

Chomsky (1981) proposes to define grammatical functions in terms of a phrase structure based on X-bar theory, essentially following Chomsky (1965), although he concedes (1981:10) that the actual definition of grammatical functions may be more complex. Nevertheless, the subject is defined as [NP,S] and the object as [NP,VP] (Chomsky 1981:42). How can the distinction between direct and indirect objects be defined?

Chomsky (1981:48) proposes to use the notation $[NP^1,VP]$, $[NP^2,VP]$ for indirect object and direct object, respectively. He notes that a pure X-bar notation does not suffice for the distinction between direct and indirect objects, and that this particular notation does not distinguish between objects and cases of adjunction. Chomsky (1981:48) suggests:

> The problem can easily be resolved by means of a more careful development
> of theory and notations in terms of heads, complements and adjuncts.

The notion *head* can be defined in X-bar structure but the distinction between complements, adjuncts and (we may add) specifiers is not without discussion in X-bar theory. Let us adopt the idea, implicit in much recent work, that specifiers are daughters of maximal projections whereas adjuncts are not only daughters but also sisters of maximal projections.

Whatever variation may exist with respect to the precise definition of these concepts, most linguists would agree that complements and adjuncts must be defined in terms of X-bar theory. Similarly, it would seem that the distinction between direct and indirect objects must be defined in these terms. Yet there are some non-trivial problems. Chomsky (1981:171) suggests that the verb and the indirect object form a small VP which is sister to the direct object. This proposal obeys the requirement that tree structures are binary-branching, cf. Kayne (1984). Notice that this proposal does not directly give us adequate definitions of indirect and direct object. The indirect object is in the [NP,V'] position, which is reserved for direct objects with monotransitive verbs. Similarly the direct object is in the [NP,VP] position. With monotransitives the direct object also occupies this position. Yet there is a difference. With monotransitives the direct object is a sister of V, but not with ditransitives. Presumably the actual definition of grammatical functions is more complex, cf. the reference above.

An alternative to these suggestions by Chomsky has been proposed by Kayne (1984a).

2.3. Kayne (1984a): an empty preposition

Kayne (1984a) attempts to analyze the dative alternation by means of an empty preposition, relating the analysis of the double object construction to that of preposition stranding. The representation of a sentence like (1) would be as below:

(3)   ... [V [PP [$_p$e NP]] NP]

The indirect NP-object is preceded by an empty preposition adjacent to V. Movement of the PP entails spelling out the preposition in a suitable form. The preposition is spelled out not as *of* but as *to*.

The chief problem with Kayne's analysis is that it predicts that direct objects should be able to bind indirect objects and not vice versa; the direct object c-commands the indirect object in (3), regardless of whether c-command is defined as extended c-command or strict c-command. Consider, for instance, the following. Kayne predicts (4a) to be out and (4b) to be okay:

(4) a. I [[[$_V$ showed] [$_P$e [$_{NP}$ the men]]] [$_{NP}$ each other]]
     b. *I [[[$_V$ showed] [$_P$e [$_{NP}$ each other]]] [$_{NP}$ the men]]

(5) a. Ik toonde de mannen elkaar
     b. *Ik toonde elkaar de mannen

This prediction is wrong. As Barrs & Lasnik (1987) have shown, there is a binding asymmetry between the indirect object and the direct object to the effect that the indirect object may bind the direct object.

Kayne proposes that the empty preposition must occur adjacent to V. This works out nicely for English because it forces the indirect object to be adjacent to V. In Dutch, however, the indirect object is separated from V by the direct object. This is particularly clear in nominalizations:

(6) a. Kinderen snoepjes geven is onverstandig
         children candies give   is not smart
     b. *Snoepjes kinderen geven is onverstandig

Compare also the sentences above, abstracting from the distorting effects of verb-second plus topicalization in Dutch.

It is more promising to hypothesize that the indirect object is of the category NP and not of the category PP. The postulation of an empty preposition necessitates quite a few stipulations. For instance, Kayne (1984a: 197) must assume there are verbs in French which may take either a PP with *à* or an NP to which they cannot assign Case. This typically occurs with verbs without a direct object. If such dual subcategorization (NP/PP) is needed anyhow, then what is the use of reducing the V-NP-NP construction elsewhere to a V-PP-NP construction? A similar objection holds against Larson's (1987) analysis, which I will not discuss here (cf. note 3).

3. Binding

In this section I will more extensively introduce the binding facts about the double object construction and discuss their implications.

3.1. Anaphor binding

Reconsider the following facts:

(7) a. I showed the men themselves
    b. *I showed themselves the men

(8) a. Ik toonde de mannen zichzelf/hunzelf
    b. *Ik toonde zichzelf/hunzelf de mannen[4]

The binding asymmetry holds for both English and Dutch, (cf. also Blom - Daalder 1977). What do these facts indicate? Following Belletti - Rizzi (1988) we assume that binding must be defined in terms of minimal c-command, not L-command. This implies that both in English and in Dutch the indirect object is in a position where it c-commands the direct object but not vice versa. Hence we are proposing that both English and Dutch have the same structure for the double object construction, order aside:

(9) $[_{VP}$ IO $[_{V'}$ DO V]

We will develop our analysis further in section 5 in order to account for the surface word order. Notice that the word order of Dutch is no problem. The standard word order in Dutch is IO-DO-V, which follows directly from the assumption that V governs leftward.

3.2. Other binding configurations

If our analysis so far is correct, then we predict that the asymmetry between direct and indirect objects will appear whereever some form of binding is involved, assuming that all forms of binding rely on c-command.

3.2.1. Reciprocal binding

Consider the following examples:

(10) a. I showed the men each other
     b. *I showed each other the men

(11) a. Ik toonde de mannen elkaar
    b. *Ik toonde elkaar de mannen

(12) a. I showed the professors each other's students
    b. *I showed each other's students the professors

(13) a. Ik toonde de professoren elkaars studenten
    b. *Ik toonde elkaars studenten de professoren

These facts speak for themselves.

3.2.2. Bound variable binding

The same holds true of the examples in (14) to (17):

(14) a. I gave back every owner his car
    b. *I gave back its owner every car

(15) a. Ik gaf elke eigenaar z'n auto terug
    b. *Ik gaf z'n eigenaar elke auto terug

(16) a. Which owner did you give back his car
    b. *Which car did you give back its owner

(17) a. Welke eigenaar heb je z'n auto teruggegeven
    b. *Welke auto heb je z'n eigenaar teruggegeven

3.2.3. Negative polarity

I will assume that the trigger for negative polarity must be in a position where it c-commands the negative polarity item. This is clear from the familiar subject-object asymmetry associated with negative polarity:

(18) a. Nobody did anything
    b. *Anybody did nothing

(19) a. Niemand heeft ook maar iets gedaan
    b. *Ook maar iemand heeft niets gedaan

Analogously we find the by now familiar asymmetry between indirect and direct objects:

(20) a. I showed nobody anything
     b. *I showed anybody nothing

(21) a. Ik heb niemand ook maar iets getoond
     b. *Ik heb ook maar iemand niets getoond

This indicates that it is quite plausible to propose that the indirect object c-commands the direct object and not vice versa. This proposal is independently supported by evidence from idiom constructions.

4. Idiom formation

Marantz (1980:49) notes that "just about every simple transitive English verb expresses a wide range of predicates depending on the choice of direct objects". To exemplify this he presents examples like the following:

(22) a. throw a party
     b. throw a fit
     c. take a nap
     d. take a bus
     e. kill a conversation
     e. kill an audience

The above examples may be considered to a greater or lesser extent idiomatical.

No such variation exists in the opposite direction; there is not a wide range of predicates depending on the choice of subject. To illustrate this, consider the following:

(23) a. the policeman threw NP
     b. the aardvark throws NP
     c. Harry killed NP
     d. cars killed NP

The meaning of the predicate is not so much affected by the choice of subject. Again we have a case of a subject-object asymmetry.

In the normal case, then, the verb plus its object is predicated of the subject and not vice versa. In other words, object idioms abound whereas subject idioms are rare. The reason for this is that the object is contained in a constituent predicated of the subject.

We propose that the indirect object gets its theta role by predication of V + direct object. Given that our analysis supposes that V forms a constituent with the direct object, this is a natural hypothesis.

Hence we make the following prediction:

(24) Given the configuration $[V\ NP^1\ NP^2]$, an idiom will fix the direct object and leave the indirect object free.

The relevant facts can be found in Larson (1987:49) who draws them from Green (1974):

(25) a. Mary gave John a cold
   b. *Mary gave a cold to John

(26) a. Mary gave John a broken arm
   b. *Mary gave a broken arm to John

(27) a. Mary gave John a black eye
   b. *Mary gave a black eye to John

(28) a. Mary gave John a bath
   b. *Mary gave a bath to John

(29) a. Mary gave John a kiss
   b. *Mary gave a kiss to John

(30) a. Mary gave John a punch in the nose
   b. *Mary gave a punch in the nose to John

(31) a. Max gave linguistics his all
   b. The count gives me the creeps
   c. I gave him the boot
   d. Mary showed Oscar the door

The unmarked format for double object idiom formation is that the indirect object is free whereas the direct object is fixed. Put differently, the meaning of the predicate depends much on the content of the direct object, much less on the content of the indirect object. Conversely, there are hardly idioms in which the indirect object is fixed whereas the direct object is free, in the double object construction. This situation is parallel to the one pertaining to subject and direct objects.

In Larson's analysis V forms a constituent with the indirect object. Hence he is forced to treat these idioms as being discontinuous. In our analysis V forms a constituent with the direct object and not with the indirect object. Hence we need not analyse these idioms as discontinuous constituents: they are just V′ in the normal case.

Larson proposes to account for these idioms by entering them in the lexicon, with the indirect object directly in the specifier position. Now, if Larson in any case needs to enter some structures in the lexicon with the direct object in the specifier position, why then bother to derive indirect objects in other cases from positions sister to the verb?! Then we might just as well enter all indirect objects in the lexicon in the position which they occupy at S-structure.

5. The structure of the English VP

I will propose that English has the following D-structure:

(32)

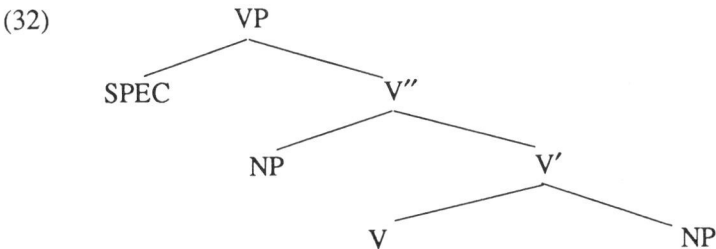

In order to derive the correct word order it is proposed that V must move to the specifier position of VP.[5] In Dutch such movement cannot occur because V must anyhow move to INFL, which is only allowed from a head position (cf. Koopman 1984).

Following Stowell (1981) I assume that structural Case, at least in English, must be assigned under adjacency. According to our proposal (33a) receives a (simplified) structure as in (33b), where *t* indicates the trace of the moved verb:

(33) a. I gave John the book
     b. [$_{VP}$ gave [$_{V''}$John [$_{V'}$ [t] the book]]]

Evidence for this analysis comes from double object verbs taking a particle. Consider the following facts (cf. Emonds 1972; Kayne 1985):

(34) a. I handed John [t] down the tools
     b. *I handed John the tools down

The particle indicates the base position of the moved V; cf. Koster (1987).

Independent evidence that particles form a constituent with V comes from Dutch. In Dutch, verbs may undergo a process known as verb raising; cf. Evers (1975); Haegeman - van Riemsdijk (1986). Consider the following facts:

(35) a. Omdat ik je op [t] wil bellen
     b. Omdat ik je [t] wil opbellen

(36) a   Omdat ik deze jongen wil zien
     b. *Omdat ik wil deze jongen zien

(37) a. Omdat ik op een wonder wil hopen
     b. *Omdat ik wil op een wonder hopen

The generalization is that only particles may be raised along with the verb. This follows if particle and verb form a constituent. We will assume that particle and V form a V again and that rules may refer to the lower V (such as verb-second) or to either V (such as verb-raising).

Further evidence for the constituenthood of V and particle also comes from Dutch. We observe that the order [Prt NP V] never occurs in Dutch. Evidence for the constituenthood of V and Prt can also be found in English. Consider the following facts:

(38) a. the calling up of John
    b. *the calling of John up

Nominalizations indicate that V and Prt belong together, contrary to the claims of the proponents of a small clause analysis.[6]

6. Independent evidence for a left-branch position

Following Chomsky (1986) we assume that Case is assigned under minimal c-command. This means that indirect objects can be structurally Case-marked because V has been moved to the specifier of VP. The adjacency condition on Case-assignment is likewise satisfied at S-structure.[7] I have proposed that VP-internal NPs in English may appear on a left branch in English. Evidence for this claim comes from morphology:

(39) a. man-eater vs. *eater-man
    b. spy-catcher vs. *catcher-spy

The possibility of these N-V compounds strongly suggests that there is an argument position within the English VP to the left of V.

7. Conclusion

In the first part of this paper it was shown that the indirect object occurs in a position where it asymmetrically c-commands the direct object. In the second part of this paper we explored some of the consequences of our proposal about indirect objects. To summarize, there are four arguments in favour of the structure we have proposed for the English VP. There is an argument from binding, an argument from idiom formation, an argument from particle stranding and an argument from morphology. Diverse facts follow from one hypothesis, which is encouraging.

Although some specifics of the analysis we suggest for the English VP might well be wrong, we believe that future analyses of the English VP will have to start off with a D-structure in which the indirect object asymmetrically c-commands the direct object. If this claim can be maintained, my paper has served its main purpose.

Notes

1.   I would like to thank the following people for discussing with me the ideas presented in this paper: Helen de Hoop, Mark Kas, Wim Kosmeijer, Eric Reuland, and especially Jan Koster. This paper was presented at the Fifth Workshop on Comparative Germanic Syntax, Groningen, May 1988. I thank the participants for their questions and comments.

   This research was supported by the Foundation for Linguistic Research, which is funded by the Netherlands organization for the advancement of pure research (N.W.O.), project number 300-163-030, which is gratefully acknowledged.

2.   Unless otherwise indicated, the English sentences are followed by their Dutch equivalents.

3.   For reasons of space we will not discuss Larson's analysis in any detail.

4.   Some speakers cannot have the anaphor *zichzelf* referring to non-subjects. As far as I know, everybody agrees that the anaphor '*mzelf* and its variants behave as indicated in the text (see also Koster 1985).

5.   The motivation for this movement might well reside in the directionality of government. It is well-known that the Germanic languages are all moving towards a head-initial phrase structure. The English VP, under our analysis, is head-initial at S-structure but not at D-structure.

6.   Kayne (1985) argues that particle constructions should be analyzed as small clauses. The general problem for his analysis is that it offers no plausible account of the fact that the configuration [V Prt NP] seems basic and the configuration [V NP Prt derived.

7.   I assume that the direct object in the double object construction in Standard English gets lexical Case in some way. Presumably lexical Case in general cannot be absorbed, accounting for the ungrammaticality of (i) and (ii) below:

       (i)   *The book was given John

       (ii)   *Er wird geholfen (cf. Ich helfe ihm)

             he is   helped   I   help him-DAT

References

Barrs, Andrew - Howard Lasnik
1986   "A note on anaphora and double objects", *Linguistic Inquiry* 17: 347-354

Belletti, Adriana - Luigi Rizzi
1988   "Psych-verbs and theta theory", *Natural Language and Linguistic Theory* 6: 291-352

Blom, Alied - Saskia Daalder
1977   "De strukturele positie van reflexieve en reciproke pronomina", *Spektator* 5: 397-414

Chomsky, Noam
1955   *The logical structure of linguistic theory* (New York 1975: Plenum Press).
1965   *Aspects of the theory of syntax* (Cambridge, Mass.: MIT Press).
1981   *Lectures on government and binding* (Dordrecht: Foris).
1986   *Barriers* (Cambridge, Mass.: MIT Press).

Emonds, Joseph
1972   "Evidence that indirect object movement is a structure-preserving rule", *Foundations of Language* 8: 546-561

Evers, Arnold
1982   "Twee functionele principes voor de regel VERSCHUIF HET WERKWOORD", *GLOT* 5.1: 11-30

Green, Georgia
1974   *Semantics and syntactic regularity* (Bloomington: Indiana University).

Guéron, Jaqueline - Hans-Georg Obenauer - Jean-Yves Pollock
1985   *Grammatical representation* (Dordrecht: Foris).

Haegeman, Liliane - Henk van Riemsdijk
1986   "Verb projection raising, scope and the typology of rules affecting verbs", *Linguistic Inquiry* 17: 417-466

Kayne, Richard
1984a   "Datives in French and English", *Connectedness and binary branching* (Dordrecht: Foris).
1984b   *Connectedness and binary branching* (Dordrecht: Foris).
1985   "Principles of particle constructions", *Grammatical representation*, edited by Jaqueline Guéron - Hans-Georg Obenauer - Jean-Yves Pollock (Dordrecht: Foris).

Koopman, Hilda
1984   *The syntax of verbs* (Dordrecht: Foris).

Koster, Jan
   1987   *Domains and dynasties* (Dordrecht: Foris).

Larson, Richard
   1987   "On the double object construction", *MIT Lexicon Project Working Papers* 16

Marantz, Alec
   1980   *On the nature of grammatical relations*, doctoral dissertation (Cambridge, Mass.: MIT).

Oehrle, Richard
   1975   *The grammatical status of the English dative alternation*, doctoral dissertation (Cambridge, Mass.: MIT).

Stowell, Tim
   1981   *Origins of phrase structure*, doctoral dissertation (Cambridge, Mass.: MIT).

Be is selected over *have* if and only if it is part of an A-chain

Sten Vikner

1. Introduction.

In this paper, I propose to describe the facts of *have/be* selection in Germanic and Romance in the following way: *Be* is selected over *have* if the V^o in question is part of an A-chain (i.e., if *be* governs a coindexed A-bound NP).[1]

I furthermore want to depart from previous accounts such as Hoekstra (1984), Haider (1985), and Burzio (1986) by attempting to assimilate the analysis of the perfect auxiliary *have/be* to that of other occurrences of *have/be*, including *have/be* of passive constructions and *have/be* of predicative adjective constructions. Such a step will furthermore allow more languages to be included in the analysis, as the languages so far considered not to have "auxiliary selection", e.g., English, Swedish, and Spanish, will also be accounted for.

2. *Be*-selection as an A-chain membership requirement

The leading idea of the analysis is that *have* and *be* are alike in that they represent the lexicalisation of an empty V^o node. *Have* and *be* are different in that *be* is selected when V^o governs an NP with which it (and its subject) are coindexed, and *have* is selected otherwise. The underlying intuition is that *be* is a reflex of a relation of identity.

The coindexed NP that triggers *be* is a trace in the specifier position of the maximal projection that is the complement of *be*. This trace is required by the empty category principle, reduced by Chomsky (1986:77) to a requirement that traces be antecedent governed. Contrary to Chomsky (1986), it is assumed here that coindexation does not obtain between an auxiliary and a main verb, and thus there is no such coindexation in the cases where *have* or *be* occur. The VP (or V') of the main verb is a barrier, and an intermediate trace is therefore needed which is antecedent governed and which antecedent governs the trace in object position, in, e.g., ergatives or passives. This intermediate trace (italicized below) is taken to be in the specifier of VP:

(1) Engl. Peter$_i$ ... [$_{V'}$ was$_i$ [$_{VP}$ *t*$_i$ [$_{V'}$ photographed e$_i$]]]

The intermediate trace is motivated by the relativized minimality condition on government of Rizzi (1987). Assuming that the specifier of VP is a position which is always present, it is a "potential antecedent governor", and must itself govern the object trace, to save this from violating the empty category principle. In other words, A-movement out of any XP must go through the specifier of XP.

To sum up: (1) has *be* and not *have* because *be* is part of an A-chain in that it governs a coindexed A-bound NP (i.e., the italicized trace), "(head)-governs" as there is no intervening governor, "co-indexed" as *be* is co-indexed with the subject and the trace is a trace of the subject, and A-bound as it is a trace of the subject which is an A-position.

A'-bound NPs do not count for the selection of *be*, as *be* is not selected when the relevant trace is A'-bound, even if it is both coindexed with and governed by *have/be*. This is shown by the following examples, where the trace is A'-bound (it is the trace of a topicalization), coindexing obtains (the moved NP is a reflexive), and government obtains (no intervening governors/barriers) (cf. the partial structure in [4]). Government holds, irrespective of whether the relevant trace is in the specifier of VP, as assumed in (5), or adjoined to VP.

(2) Ital. a. Se stessa, Maria ha sempre odiato
           b. *Se stessa, Maria è sempre odiata/odiato
               Herself, Maria has/is always hated

(3) Dan. a. Sig selv har Peter aldrig kritiseret
          b. *Sig selv er Peter aldrig kritiseret
              REFL self has/is Peter never criticised

(4) $[_{CP}$ NP$_i$ C $[_{IP}$ NP$_i$ ... *have/be$_i$* $[_{VP}$ t$_i$ *hated* t$_i$]]]

The variation in *be*-selection observed across (some of) the Germanic and Romance languages can now be considered to depend on two things:

(5)   a   whether (clitic) movement of the reflexive results in A- or A′-binding (French, Italian vs. German, Dutch) (section 3).

   b   whether a restriction on length of the chain obtains. In English, Swedish, Spanish *be* and the foot of the chain may only be separated by one maximal projection, in Danish and French they may only be separated by two, whereas in German, Dutch, Italian they may be separated by any number of maximal projections (section 4).

The specifier of VP is taken to be an A-position, in the sense that a theta-role (the "external" one) is assigned to it, except in the cases where this theta-role is absorbed by the past participle morphology, *-en*. This absorption leaves the specifier of VP empty, and it is thus possible for, e.g., an ergative or passive D-structure object (on its way to the subject position) to move through this position.

As for the theta-role absorbed by *-en*, it may be reassigned by *have/be* to their own specifier (cf. "deblocking" in Haider 1985), unless this is prohibited by standard well-formedness conditions (i.e., unless the specifier already has a theta-role).

3. Movement of unstressed pronouns (or: Romance versus Germanic)

3.1. *Be*-selection

As mentioned above, one variation in *be*-selection distinguishes Germanic from Romance (at least French/Italian): Germanic reflexives select *have*, while Romance reflexives select *be*. This difference may be accounted for as a difference between the nature of pronoun movement in the two language groups, given the independently motivated assumption that *have/be* selection is insensitive to A′-bound traces discussed above.
Consider first the German example:

(6)   Ger.   ... daß meine Freunde$_i$ sich$_i$ [$_{I'}$ [$_{VP}$ t$_i$ [$_{V'}$ t$_i$ getroffen]] haben$_i$]
         ... that my   friends   REFL   met   have

The example is a subordinate clause to abstract away from verb-second effects. Though at first glance it may seem that *sich* in (6) has not moved at all, as direct objects in German always occur to the left of the verb, it is possible to see that *sich* has moved out of the VP if the sentence contains adverbials:

(7)   Ger.   ... daß meine Freunde [sich$_i$] *gestern im Park* t$_i$ t$_i$ getroffen
         haben
         ... that my friends REFL yesterday in the park met have

(8)   Ger.   a. ... daß meine Freunde *gestern im Park* [einen Mann]
            getroffen haben
            ... that my friends yesterday in the park a man met have
         b. ?*... daß meine Freunde [einen Mann] *gestern im Park*
            getroffen haben
            ... that my friends a man yesterday in the park met have

The examples in (8) show that when the direct object is not an unstressed pronoun (and in the absence of VP-internal topicalization and focus movement), it must occur adjacent to the verb. Thus (8a) is fine, and (8b) is ungrammatical. (8b) would be grammatical with a definite object like *den Mann* ('the man'), which may be seen as having undergone VP-internal topicalization. *Sich* however is an unlikely candidate for this kind of focalization.

As the position of *sich* in (6), i.e. adjoined to I′, is not one where arguments normally appear —cf. (8b)— we take it to be an A′-position, and its trace inside VP is thus A′-bound. This is further supported by the fact that an unstressed pronoun in this position may trigger a parasitic gap in German:

(9) Ger. ... daß meine Freunde sie [ohne PRO $t_{parasite}$ kennen gelernt
       zu haben] t_{real} einladen wollten
       ... that my friends them [without met to have] to invite wanted

which is completely impossible in French:

(10) Fr. *Mes amis *les* ont invités e_{real} [sans PRO avoir
        rencontré $e_{parasite}$]
        My friends them have invited [without to have met]

Sich is thus different from Romance reflexive clitics, which I take to A-bind their traces, cf. the following structure:

(11) Fr. Mes amis$_i$ [$_I^o$ se$_i$ sont$_i$] [$_{VP}$ t$_i$ [$_{V'}$ rencontrés t$_i$]]
        My friends   REFL are   met

Romance object clitics are genuine clitics, as can be seen, e.g., from the fact that they cannot topicalize ("You I have not seen"), nor can they occur as single-word utterances ("Who did he see? You"), in contrast to German unstressed pronouns.

The reason why the trace of the Romance reflexive may be seen as A-bound is that it is bound from I^o (but not by I^o, even though I^o as mentioned above is taken to be an A-position, but rather "through" I^o, as discussed in the following paragraph). Note that binding directly from the clitic position presumably is excluded as there is an X^o category that dominates the binder, i.e. the clitic, and not the bindee, i.e. the trace inside VP.

There is no conflict between different indices even when the clitic is not reflexive:

(12) Fr. Mes amis$_j$ [$_I^o$ l'$_i$ ont$_j$] [$_{VP}$ t$_i$ [$_{V'}$ rencontrée t$_i$]]
        My friends   her have   met

I here adopt a suggestion made by Chomsky (autumn lectures, M.I.T., 1987), based on Pollock (1988) and Baker (1988), to the effect that I^0 is "transparent" for the clitic, i.e. the clitic can govern as if it were in the position of I^0 but it cannot be governed as if this was the case. Then I^0 need not actually get the index of the clitic by percolation, and there is no conflict with I^0's own index.

Romance clitic reflexives are thus predicted to trigger *be*-selection (and past participle agreement), as the intermediate trace is A-bound, and therefore must be in an A-position.

That the clitic moves both into an XP-position and into an X^0 one is not a problem, as the first movement is an NP (the object) moving into an XP-position (specifier of VP), and the second movement is an N^0 (head of the object NP) moving into an X^0 position (from head of specifier of VP to adjoin to I^0).

3.2. Derived subjects

Another difference between Romance and Germanic unstressed reflexives that can be accounted for in terms of whether the reflexive A-binds or A'-binds its immediate trace is the fact that only in German(ic) can the reflexive cooccur with a derived subject.

As discussed by, among others, Burzio (1986) and Rizzi (1986), Romance reflexive clitics are impossible in sentences where the subject is derived, i.e., base-generated inside VP with an internal theta-role. An example of this is given in (13a), as opposed to (13b) where there is a non-clitic anaphor. The examples are from Rizzi (1986:70):

(13) Ital. a. *I nostri amici si   sono stati presentati
                 Our   friends to-each-other are   been   introduced
            b. I nostri amici   sono stati presentati l'uno all'altro
                 Our   friends are   been introduced one to the other

Rizzi (1986) accounts for the ungrammaticality of (13a) by assuming a chain well-formedness condition that crucially depends on each link of the chain locally binding the next and on each chain only containing one argument. In (13a) a chain between *i nostri amici* and its theta-assigned trace inside VP therefore cannot be generated, because the trace has a binder more local than the subject, namely *si*, and as *si* in this case is an argument, chain formation cannot include any other arguments, and thus *i nostri amici* does not get any theta-role. In other words, the theta-role assigned to the trace of the subject inside VP cannot reach the subject itself, because it cannot get any further than *si*.

In German, however, there are no restrictions on moved unstressed reflexives cooccurring with derived subjects:

(14) Ger.   ...daß deine und meine Freunde sich schon gestern
           vorgestellt wurden
           ... that your and my friends to-each-other already yesterday
           introduced were

This is compatible with the approach of Rizzi (1986) as outlined above, provided it is specified that each link of an A-chain must locally A-bind the next one (this follows from Rizzi [1987] if local binding [Rizzi 1986] is replaced by antecedent government). Then *sich*, which, as argued above, is in an A′-position, cannot interfere with the chain formation.

(13a) and (14) are analysed as follows:

(15) NP_i $[_{I^o}$ si_i sono] $[_{VP}$ t_i t_i $[_{V'}$ stati presentati t_i $t_i]]$

(16) NP_i $[_{I'}$ $sich_i$ $[_{I'}$ $[_{VP}$ t_i $[_{VP}$ t_i $[_{V'}$ t_i t_i vorgestellt]]]] wurden]]

In both cases the two theta-roles are assigned to the two traces (one of the subject, and one of the reflexive) inside V′. In (15)(=13a) the theta-role assigned to the trace of the reflexive is transferred to one of the traces in the specifier of VP, and from there to *si*. The theta-role assigned to the trace of the subject is also transferred to one of the traces in specifier of VP, and from there also to *si*, which is the local binder, and therefore this theta-role cannot reach the subject, which is left without a theta-role. Thus the sentence with the structure (15) is ungrammatical.

In (16)(=14) the theta-role assigned to the trace of the reflexive is transferred to the trace adjoined to VP, and from there to *sich*. As argued above, *sich* is in an A′-position, and therefore it is possible for it to move out of the VP via the adjoined position, an option which is not open to *si*, which we took to A-bind its immediate trace. The theta-role assigned to the trace of the subject is transferred to the trace in specifier of VP, and from there to its local (A-)binder, the subject. Thus the sentence with the structure (16) is grammatical.

Summing up section 3, I have argued that the differences between *se/si* in Romance and their corresponding elements in Germanic may be accounted for in terms of the basic difference between cliticization (Romance) and A'-movement without cliticization (Germanic). This basic difference shows up in (at least) two ways: *have* is selected over *be* in Germanic constructions of movement of unstressed reflexives, whereas *be* is selected in Romance[2] (section 3.1.). Derived subjects are allowed in these constructions in Germanic, but not in Romance (section 3.2.).

4. Other constructions (or Italian/German versus French/Danish versus Spanish/English)

Reflexives, as discussed in the previous section, do not necessitate any modifications of the basic idea from section 2. However, there are many other constructions that cannot be accounted for, unless the principle that *be* must be in an A-chain (i.e. govern a coindexed A-bound NP), and that *have* cannot be, is modified somewhat. What I will try to show in this section is that this principle applies to a different extent in the three following groups of languages: 1) German and Italian, 2) Danish and French, and 3) English and Spanish.

4.1. Framework: the AgrP analysis

In Pollock (1988), it is argued that an extra layer of structure exists between IP and VP: an Agreement Phrase (AgrP) which is the sister of I^o and the head of which, Agr, is the sister of VP.

A clause in the perfect tense is analysed in the following way:

(17) Fr. $[_{IP}$ Il a_i $[_{AgrP}$ t_i $[_{VP}$ t_i $[_{AgrP}$ Agr $[_{VP}$ vu   Marie$]]]]]$
He has   seen Marie

In other words, AgrP is selected by I (Pollock's "T") as well as by (some instances of) V. As for the arguments for the AgrP selected by I, cf. Pollock's paper.

Pollock (1988:51) gives the following argument in favour of the lower AgrP (i.e. the one selected by V): Certain adverbials exist which only occur VP-initially in French (cf. Pollock 1988:14), e.g. *à peine* ('hardly'), *presque* ('almost'). In certain circumstances, a verb may occur either after or before such an adverbial. This is taken to be a case of optional movement of the V to Agr^o (also in infinitives; cf. Pollock 1988:12), and is thus an argument in favour of this Agr^o. Consider

(18) Fr.   a   Pierre a *à peine vu* Marie
            b. Pierre a *vu à peine* Marie
                Pierre has (hardly) seen (hardly) Marie

Given that *à peine* must be VP-initial, *vu* in (18b) must have moved around it and into Agr^o (if there was no Agr^o, there would be no landing site for *vu*, as it must move out of the VP, but it can only move to the closest X^o which would then be the V^o where *a* is base-generated).

I now want to show that there are no indications of a similar kind that an AgrP also exists immediately above VPs that are embedded below the main verb. The following type of analysis will thus be assumed:

(19) Engl. $[_{IP}$ NP I $[_{AgrP}$ Agr $[_{VP}$ has $[_{AgrP}$ Agr $[_{VP}$ been $[_{VP}$ killed John]]]]]]

(19) is the structure of a passive construction at D-structure. The NP-movement involved in the derivation will be discussed below, in section 4.3. What is relevant here is the relative position of VP-initial adverbials and the participles. Consider now the following data:

(20) Fr.   a. Jean a presque été tué
            b. Jean a été presque tué
            c. *Jean a été tué presque
               Jean has (almost) been (almost) killed (almost)

which illustrate the difference between the two participles: The participle of the main verb, *été* in (one possible analysis of) (20b), may move around the adverbial and into an Agr^o, whereas the embedded participle, *tué* in

(20c), cannot do this. I will take (20c) to be an effect of the embedding of the VP of *tué* directly under the VP of *été* with no intervening AgrP. This means that AgrP is selected by I^o or by V^o if and only if this V^o is an auxiliary, i.e., either a modal or a *have/be* with temporal interpretation (perfect/past perfect).

Consistent with this analysis, and in spite of the simplified structures in previous sections, I will assume that any verb (with the possible exception of English modals) that may end up in I^o is in fact base- generated under a V^o, including *have/be* and modals.

As opposed to, e.g., Kayne (1987), I do not see the presence of an Agr^o as in any way necessary for a participle in V^o being able to show agreement. Participle agreement is a reflex of the relation between specifier and head, and thus does not involve anything outside the XP in question.

The idea that the A-chain membership requirement of *be* holds in one of three different degrees in the languages can now be expressed as a condition on the length of the chain: In English and Spanish (as well as Swedish, Rumanian and Portuguese) *be* and the foot of the chain may only be separated by one maximal projection, in Danish and French they may only be separated by two, whereas in German, Italian (and Dutch) they may be separated by any number of XPs. Below the separating XPs will be marked "XP♦".

4.2. Predicative adjectives

A predicative adjective is assumed to assign one theta-role, which is external, to its specifier position (I consider it to be the standard case that an external theta-role is assigned by X' to the specifier of XP, as opposed to an internal theta-role which is assigned by X^o to the complement of XP). The subject in (21) is thus base-generated in the specifier of AP and then it moves (via the intervening specifier positions) to the specifier of IP. The full structure is:

(21) [IP Mary *is* [AgrP t t [VP t t [AP♦ *t* ill]]]]

     be: Italian, German, French, Danish, Spanish, English

It is only the VP that is crucial here. V^o is realised as *be*, as it is coindexed with an a A-chain.

As only one XP intervenes between the base-generated position of *be* and the foot of the A-chain, viz. the AP marked ♦ , *be* is selected in all six languages.

Evidence for the trace in the specifier position of AP can be found in the agreement between the adjective and (the AP-specifier trace of) the subject in Danish, Spanish, French, and Italian. This agreement is thus assimilated to past participle agreement in that both are a kind of specifier-head agreement, following Kayne (1985).

4.3. Passives

As stated in section 2, I assume that a verb assigns its external theta-role to its specifier position (as was the case with adjectives in section 4.2.), and that this theta-role may then be absorbed by the past participle suffix *-en*, as discussed by for example, Jaeggli (1986), Roberts (1987), and Baker - Johnson - Roberts (1988). The internal theta-role is assigned to the complement NP.

(22) $[_{IP}$ Mary *is* $[_{AgrP}$ t t $[_{VP}$ t t $[_{VP}$ ♦ t photographed t $]]]]$

be: Italian, German, French, Danish, Spanish, English

The subject in (22) is base-generated as the object of *photographed*, and then it moves through the specifier position of VP (as well as a host of other specifier positions) on its way to the subject position. Movement is forced because the suffix, *-en*, prevents Case from reaching the object, as *-en* itself is assigned the Case in question (cf. Jaeggli [1986], Roberts [1987], and Baker, Johnson, & Roberts [1989]). If the object may be assigned partitive Case, i.e., if it is indefinite, it does not have to move (cf. Belletti [1988]).

V^o is realised as *be*, as it is coindexed with an A-chain. As only one XP intervenes between the base-generated position of *be* and the foot of the A-chain, viz. the VP marked ♦, *be* is selected in all six languages.

Evidence for the trace in object position is the fact that the subject has the theta-role of the object, and evidence for the trace in the specifier position of the lowest VP can be found in the participle agreement in Italian, French, and Spanish

4.4. Ergatives

In ergative constructions, *be* is only selected in two of the three language groups. I assume, with Burzio (1986), Perlmutter (1978), that ergative verbs assign only one theta-role, an internal one, to the object position. This distinguishes them from transitives, which assign more than one theta-role, and intransitives, which also assign only one theta-role, but an external one.

(23) $[_{IP}$ He *has* $[_{AgrP}$ t t $[_{VP}$ t t $[_{AgrP}$♦ t Agr $[_{VP}$♦ t come t]]]]]

be: Italian, German, French, Danish   *have*: Spanish, English

The subject of (23) is base-generated as the object of *come*, then it moves to subject position via the specifier of *come*. V^0 may be realised as *be*, as it is coindexed with an A-chain.

However, two XPs intervene between the base-generated position of *be* and the foot of the A-chain, viz. the AgrP and the VP marked ♦. Therefore *be* is only selected in those languages that allow more than one intervening XP between *be* and the foot of the A- chain, i.e. Italian and German, and French and Danish, whereas Spanish and English select *have*.

Evidence for the trace in object position may be found in a corresponding transitive construction: The subject of (24a) is taken to be base-generated as object because of the transitive construction in (24b)(examples from Burzio [1986:54]):

(24) Ital.   a   [Due navi nemiche]$_i$ sono$_i$ [t$_i$ [affondate t$_i$]]
                 Two enemy ships(fem) were   sunk(fem-pl)
           b. L'artiglieria   ha [affondato   [due navi nemiche]]
                 The army(fem-sg) has sunk(masc-sg) two enemy ships

Evidence for the trace in specifier of *come* is again tound in the agreement in Italian (cf. [24a], and French, (as in the passive construction).

4.5. *Be* itself

Be itself belongs in the third major type of construction, i.e. the type where only Italian and German have *be*, but French, Danish, Spanish, and English have *have*. As *be* does not assign any theta-role, I assume with Burzio (1986:148) and references therein that it is a raising verb. The analysis is as follows:

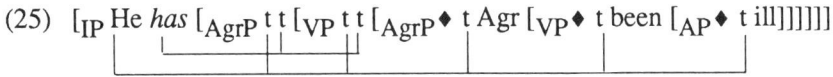

(25) $[_{IP}$ He *has* $[_{AgrP}$ t t $[_{VP}$ t t $[_{AgrP}$♦ t Agr $[_{VP}$♦ t been $[_{AP}$♦ t ill]]]]]]

be: Italian, German   *have*: French, Danish, Spanish, English

The trace in the specifier of AP in (25) and the selection of *been* has already been discussed in section 4.2. That there is a trace in the specifier of *been* can be seen from the fact that *been* shows agreement in Italian:

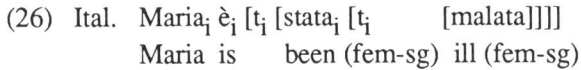

(26) Ital. Maria$_i$ è$_i$ [t$_i$ [stata$_i$ [t$_i$ [malata]]]]
             Maria is   been (fem-sg) ill (fem-sg)

V^o may be realised as *be*, as it is coindexed with an A-chain.

However, three XPs intervene between the base-generated position of *be* and the foot of the A-chain, viz. the AgrP, the VP, and the AP marked ♦. Therefore *be* is only selected in those languages that allow more than two intervening XPs between *be* and the foot of the A-chain, i.e. Italian and German, whereas French, Danish, Spanish, and English select *have*.

4.6. Other raising verbs

The rest of the raising verbs pattern like *be*, i.e., Italian has *be*, and French, Danish, Spanish, and English have *have*.

(27) $[_{IP}$ He *has* $[_{AgrP}$ t t $[_{VP}$ t t $[_{AgrP}$♦ t Agr $[_{VP}$♦ t seemed

$[_{IP}$♦ t to $[_{AgrP}$♦ t Agr $[_{VP}$♦ t be $[_{AP}$♦ t ill]]]]]]]]

be: Italian   *have:* French, Danish, Spanish, English

The traces in specifier positions of AP and of *be* were discussed in sections
4.2. (AP) and 4.5. (*be*). The evidence for the trace in specifier position of
the lower IP is that this is where the subject *Mary* appears if the clause is
finite:

(28) Engl.   It seems that [Mary has been ill]

The trace in specifier position of *seemed* is taken to exist because of the
agreement of Italian *sembrata* ('seemed'):

(29) Ital.   Maria è sembrata   essere malata
             Mary is seemed(fem-sg) to be   ill(fem-sg)

V^o may be realised as *be*, as it is coindexed with an A-chain.

However, no less than six XPs intervene between the base-generated
position of *be* and the foot of the A-chain, and therefore *be* is only selected
in those languages that allow more than two intervening XPs between *be*
and the foot of the A-chain, i.e., Italian, whereas French, Danish, Spanish,
and English select *have*.

4.7. Intransitives and transitives

I will finish the discussion of the various constructions in section 4 by briefly
mentioning the intransitive and transitive constructions, which take *have* in
all the six languages.

Intransitives and transitives both assign an external theta-role to the
specifier of VP. This is then absorbed by the past participle ending, and may
be reassigned by *have/be* to its specifier position. Intransitives only assign
this single theta-role, whereas transitives furthermore assign an internal
theta-role to their object position.

The analysis is as shown in (30) for intransitives and in (31) for transitives. In neither case could *be* possibly be selected, as there is no trace coindexed with and governed by *have/be*:

30) [$_{IP}$ He *has* [$_{AgrP}$ t t [$_{VP}$ t t [$_{AgrP}$ Agr [$_{VP}$ slept]]]]]

have: Italian, German, French, Danish, Spanish, English

(31) [$_{IP}$ He *has* [$_{AgrP}$ t t [$_{VP}$ t t [$_{AgrP}$ Agr [$_{VP}$ seen her]]]]]

have: Italian, German, French, Danish, Spanish, English

5. Conclusion

I have argued that *be* may be considered to be some kind of signal of identity, as it requires a certain type of coindexation, i.e., it requires membership of an A-chain (i.e., coindexation with an A-bound NP that it governs), and *have* does not allow such a membership.

The language specific variations are accounted for by analysing Romance unstressed reflexives as clitics and Germanic ones as non-clitics (section 3), and by assuming a parameter determining the maximum possible distance between *be* and the foot of the chain that triggers *be* (English, Spanish: one XP; Danish, French: two XPs; German, Italian: any number of XPs) (section 4).

Notes

1.   This paper builds on research carried out in collaboration with Rex Sprouse. For a more extensive treatment, see Vikner & Sprouse (1988).

Thanks are due to audiences at NELS 18, at the *2nd* "Focus on Grammar" Workshop, University of Lund, and at the *5th* Comparative Germanic Syntax Workshop. Thanks also go to Carl Vikner, Christer Platzack, Corinne Grange, Esther Torrego, Halldór Sigursson, Höskuldur Thráinsson, Ian Roberts, Itziar Laka, Jane Grimshaw, John Frampton, Joseph Emonds, Juan Uriagereka, Karen Zagona, Kjartan Ottóson, Liliane Haegeman, Luigi Burzio, Luigi Rizzi, Noam Chomsky, Pierre Pica, Richard Kayne, Tarald Taraldsen, and Tor Åfarli.

Part of the research involved was made possible by a grant from the "Fonds national suisse de la recherche scientifique", Berne, Switzerland.

2.   The fact that Spanish, Portuguese, and Rumanian select *have* in this construction is due to the interaction of the independent parameter discussed in section 4.1. below, as two XPs separate *have/be* from the foot of the chain, and these languages allow at most one XP to do this:

(i)   Span. Maria$_i$ se$_i$ ha$_i$ [$_{AgrP}$ e$_i$ [$_{VP}$ e$_i$ fotografiado   e$_i$]]
Maria REFL has photographed"

References

Baker, Mark
1988   *Incorporation* (Chicago: The University of Chicago Press).

Baker, Mark - Kyle Johnson - Ian Roberts
1989   "Passive arguments raised", *Linguistic Inquiry* 20: 219-252

Belletti, Adriana
1988   "The Case of unaccusatives", *Linguistic Inquiry* 19: 1-34

Burzio, Luigi
1986   *Italian syntax* (Dordrecht: Foris).

Chomsky, Noam
1986   *Barriers* (Cambridge, Mass.: MIT-Press).

Haider, Hubert
1985   "Von *sein* oder nicht *sein* : Zur Grammatik des Pronomens *sich*", *Erklärende Syntax des Deutschen*, edited by Werner Abraham (Tübingen: Gunter Narr).

Hoekstra, Teun
1984   *Transitivity* (Dordrecht: Foris).

Jaeggli, Osvaldo
1986   "Passive", *Linguistic Inquiry* 17: 587-622

Kayne, Richard
1985   "L'accord du participe passé en francais et en italien", *Modèles Linguistiques* 7: 73-89
in press "Facets of Romance past participle agreement", *Dialect variation and the theory of grammar*, edited by Paola Benincà (Dordrecht: Foris).

Perlmutter, David
1978   "Impersonal passives and the unaccusative hypothesis", *Berkeley Linguistics Society* 4: 157-189

Pollock, Jean-Yves
1989   "Verb movement, universal grammar and the structure of IP", *Linguistic Inquiry* 20: 365-424

Rizzi, Luigi
1986   "On chain formation", *The syntax of pronominal clitics*, edited by Hagit Borer (New York: Academic Press).
1987   "Relativized minimality" (Geneva: unpublished manuscript University of Geneva).

Roberts, Ian
1987   *The representation of implicit and dethematized subjects* (Dordrecht: Foris).

Vikner, Sten - Rex Sprouse
1988   "*Have/Be* selection as an A-chain membership requirement", *Working Papers in Scandinavian Syntax* 38

Index of Names

General Index

Jan Terje Faarlund

Syntactic Change
Toward a Theory of Historical Syntax

1990. 15.5 x 23 cm. X, 222 pages. Cloth.
ISBN 3 11 012651 6
(Trends in Linguistics. Studies and Monographs 50)

This research monograph presents a theoretical study of the causes and mechanisms of syntactic change in natural language.

Historical syntax has been the focus of growing interest in recent years, and this interest has raised important issues concerning the relationship between syntactic theory and explanations of syntactic change.

Based on a theoretical and metatheoretical discussion of the locus of linguistic change and the notion of explanation in historical syntax, this work provides an in-depth study of a variety of syntactic changes in Germanic languages. Those dealt with are mainly related to grammatical role and basic sentence structure such as the change from OV to VO order, the introduction of the verb-second constraint and the expletive topic in Germanic, as well as changes in the assignment of grammatical roles and semantic roles and the change from non-configurational to configurational sentence structure.

The conclusions are based on data from many, including older, Germanic languages.

mouton de gruyter
Berlin · New York

Dieter Stein

The Semantics of Syntactic Change

Aspects of the Evolution of <u>do</u> in English

1990. 15.5 x 23 cm. XIV, 444 pages. Cloth.
ISBN 3-11-011283-3
(Trends in Linguistics. Studies and Monographs 47)

This research monograph presents a foundation for the examination of the mechanism of language change.

As an example, a detailed analysis of the change in the semantics and syntax of English <u>do</u> is presented, showing that the Modern English syntactic pattern is the result of a complex interaction of language internal and external factors.

The study is based on an analysis of a wide range of texts. A series of interrelated changes in English was located in a period of beginning mass literacy and a written standard, with the demotion of dialectal uses to stigmatized forms. The micro-analysis of the internal evolution of the change shows a permanent dialectic between language internal forces and such external forces as style, prestige and other societal forces. The clustering of certain types of constructions in certain literary styles shows that the types of data obtained for a study depend critically on the choice of texts to be analyzed.

The results of the study suggest a complex and heterogeneous methodology for the explanation of syntactic change, results applicable to other questions and languages.

mouton de gruyter Berlin · New York